PART 1

Background

What Is Qigong?

Qigong is a Chinese system of holistic health practice, with roots dating back five thousand years. "Energy cultivation" is an excellent translation for Qigong, because it conveys the idea that, just as an agricultural field is cultivated with careful tending over time to produce food, your own field of life energy is cultivated so that your body and mind are nourished.

RIGHT: Chinese characters for Qigong, pronounced "cheegong".

Qigong brings body, breathing and mind together to perform movements and hold postures that exercise the whole person. While usually performed standing, it can also be performed seated. Although most Qigong is characterized by slow, flowing movements, it can also be still.

The art of Qigong is an effective method of reducing stress and promoting a relaxed body and calm mind. It increases flexibility, strength, balance and general wellbeing. Many people have found that Qigong practice brings youthful vitality and a positive outlook to their lives.

There is a Chinese saying that the "Yi leads the Qi". Yi is a calm, focused mind, full of intention. First, allow your body and mind to relax so that tension, unnecessary muscle action and superfluous mental activity do not

QI + GONG

The word Qigong is made up of two Chinese words:

Qi = air, energy, spirit, vigour, atmosphere, attitude

Gong = achievement, merit, result, effect, success, skill

get in the way. Next, bring your mind into a perfect state of attention in the present moment, which will allow you to develop the ability to move effortlessly and feel the flow of life energy through your body.

Qigong is suitable for any age, any ability and any type of personality. It can be adapted to fit any need. No one is excluded.

ABOVE: At one with nature.

The History of Qigong

The beginnings of Qigong emerged some five thousand years ago. Archaeologists have found ancient Chinese rock art in caves, depicting men in standing postures, similar to the standing Qigong we use today.

Chinese philosophers, alchemists and emperors have a long history of searching for the elixir of life. Some sought a potion or pill for immortality. Other seekers devoted their lives to finding an internal elixir, using special teachings and complex practices to transform a person's internal alchemy.

Qigong is a relatively modern word and was not in use until the 20th century. Many terms were used before that, for example Xingqi (promoting the circulation of Qi), Fuqi (taking Qi), Daoyin (guiding the energy flow), Tuna (exhaling and inhaling), Yangshen (nourishing the spirit) and Jingzuo (sitting still). In the 1970s the Chinese government began to use the term Qigong officially and it now refers to all self-healing exercise and meditation techniques from ancient times to the present.

From early times, there have been many written references to Qigong. In Chapter 10 of the Daoist classic *Daodejing* (The Way and Its Power) by Laozi (*c.* 6th century BCE), we find:

> *By harmonizing the Yang and Yin and embracing The One,*
> *you become unified.*
> *By concentrating the Qi (vitality) and inducing tenderness and purity,*
> *you become supple and free like a little child.*

This ideal of achieving the suppleness of a child, the bending ability of bamboo or a young sapling, in order to become resilient and in harmony with the flow of life, runs through all Daoist thinking.

In 1973 archaeologists excavating the tomb of King Ma (*c.* 168 BCE) near the city of Changsha, the capital of Hunan province, found a folded piece of silk in one of the coffins. This silk scroll, the Daoyin Tu, depicted the earliest drawings found to date of Daoyin postures, a traditional form of Chinese exercise. The scroll contained

LEFT: Daoyin Tu silk scroll, *c.* 168 BCE, discovered in a tomb in China in 1973.

44 figures painted on silk: men and women of different ages, wearing clothes from different walks of life, from peasant to government official. This suggests that therapeutic exercise was practised by all types of people.

It could be argued that Qigong, with both its documented research and its tradition of health and longevity, is the closest anyone has come to finding the "golden elixir of life".

CHINESE DYNASTIES

A dynasty means a succession of rulers from the same family. Each dynasty lasted until a contender removed the last ruler and began a new dynasty.

Note: Dates of early dynasties are approximate.

Neolithic cultures	10,000–2100 BCE
Xia dynasty	2100–1600 BCE
Shang dynasty	1600–1046 BCE
Zhou dynasty	1046–221 BCE
Qin dynasty	221–206 BCE
Han dynasty	206 BCE–220 CE
Six dynasties period	220–581 CE
Sui dynasty	581–618 CE
Tang dynasty	618–907 CE
Five dynasties period	907–960 CE
Song dynasty	960–1279 CE
Yuan (Mongul) dynasty	1279–1368 CE
Ming dynasty	1368–1644 CE
Qing (Manchu) dynasty	1644–1912 CE
Republic of China	1912–1949 CE
People's Republic of China	1949–present

Internal Alchemy

To the ancient Daoist sages, the human body had a symbolic inner landscape that related to the outer landscape of the world around them. The Chart of Internal Alchemy depicts a side view of a man seated in meditation, with an inner landscape of stars, mountains, rivers, forests, pathways and people. It represents important knowledge of how the inner landscape works to purify the body and spirit in order to cultivate health, longevity and one's inner nature, with the ultimate goals being immortality and spiritual transcendence. The earliest records of such symbology are estimated to date from around the 10th century.

Symbolism in the Chart of Internal Alchemy

Symbolism in the Lower Dantian: At the lower part of the spine, a girl and boy (Yin and Yang) are working on a treadmill. They are trying to invert the course of Jing and thereby preserve it. On their right, a fiery furnace creates heat to transform the watery Jing into steam and send it

ABOVE: The Neijing Tu, The Chart of Internal Alchemy. This illustration is based on a stone engraving from 1886 found at the White Clouds Monastery, Beijing.

upward. A little further up, a hard-working ox is ploughing the earth in preparation for the planting of the first seed for the cultivation of the golden elixir.

Symbolism in the Middle Dantian:
On the top of the round spiral shape, which represents the Middle Dantian, stands the Herd Boy. He holds the seven-star constellation of Ursa Major, which the Chinese refer to as The Seven Stars of the Northern Dipper. This is a constellation rich in Daoist mythologies and is a symbol of the centre of the cosmos. The Weaving Maiden sits below at her loom, near the kidneys. There is a famous Chinese story in which the Herd Boy (Yang) meets the Weaving Maiden (Yin) once each year to join the energies of Yin and Yang.

Symbolism in the Upper Dantian:
Nine mountain peaks are at the top of the head, representing Yang energy and the highest point we can climb toward heaven while bound to earth. The monk who brought Chan Buddhism to China in the 6th century, Bodhidharma (Da Mo), is shown standing, with both arms stretched toward heaven. Above him in black robes, seated in meditation, is the ancient sage Laozi, who is said to hold the secret of eternal truth. The two dots between Bodhidharma and

Laozi represent the sun and moon and also the eyes of the meditator.

There are many complex symbologies contained within the Chart of Internal Alchemy alluding to secret methods of transforming Jing into Qi into Shen and ultimately into divine energy, with the final goal being immortality.

To understand more of the meaning of the picture, we must look briefly at the Three Dantians and the Three Treasures.

The Three Dantians

The word Dantian is translated as Cinnabar Field. This implies the elixir of life, because cinnabar is mercuric sulphide and was an important ingredient in elixir of life potions and pills used in External Alchemy.

There are three major Dantians: Lower, Middle and Upper. However, if someone talks about "The Dantian", they are usually referring to the Lower Dantian.

The Lower Dantian: This is located approximately two fingers' width below and behind the navel at your physical centre of gravity. This Dantian is used as a focal point in Qigong practice and in martial arts. The Lower Dantian is your main energy reservoir and place of physical strength, stamina and stability. It is also the core of your "gut feelings", which cannot be explained by logic but which we learn to trust as we become more connected to this energy centre. As this Dantian is closest to the earth, it is the most

Upper Dantian

Middle Dantian

Lower Dantian

Yin of the three Dantians. In Qigong we complete our practice by symbolically gathering up the Qi energy with our hands and arms, moving them in a circular motion of collecting and bringing our hands, full of Qi, to rest at the Dantian.

The Middle Dantian: This is located behind the breast bone, at heart level. The Middle Dantian is your centre of emotion, empathy, compassion and love. Empathy allows you to communicate emotionally with others. If the heart area is relaxed and open, it is easier to relate to all living things. Balancing the Middle Dantian allows us to heal any emotional disorders that we might be carrying. When we practise Qigong, there are many exercises that open the chest area to allow the practitioner to feel emotionally free and at ease.

The Upper Dantian: This is located between the eyebrows, behind your forehead. The Upper Dantian is associated with intuition, higher intellect and spirituality, and it is often favoured in Qigong meditation because of its spiritual significance. This Dantian is looked upon as a gateway to divine transformation.

LEFT: The Three Dantians.

No individual Dantian has the capability of functioning on its own, in isolation from the others. For example, if you do not have the foundational strength and stability that the Lower Dantian provides, you will have no ability to energize and steady your heart and your head. If you do not have the compassion of the heart from the Middle Dantian, your Lower Dantian strength will become overbearing and lack the gentleness needed to deal with others and yourself. If you do not have the higher intellect of the Upper Dantian, your strength, courage and emotion will not be intelligently directed. The Three Dantians must work in harmony for us to be balanced.

In Qigong practice, we employ flowing movement, correct breathing, correct posture, efficient use of energy, relaxation, concentration, calmness, intention of purpose and understanding of our body, mind and emotions to achieve a balance of the Three Dantians for the purpose of engendering health, vitality and mental clarity.

The Three Treasures

The Three Treasures are Jing, Qi and Shen. Jing is life essence and vitality; Qi is breath and energy; Shen is mind and spirit. Jing, Qi and Shen are considered to be the Three Treasures of mankind, because their energies are essential to human life.

Jing: This belongs to the Lower Dantian. It is considered to be a Yin form of Qi, connected to earthly things and always moving downward, like water. Jing belongs to the material world. It is the germ of life, the reproductive energy of sperm and egg, the sexual secretions, the vigour of growth and vitality. Jing is influenced by our genes, nutrition and lifestyle choices.

Qi: This belongs to the Middle Dantian. When viewed in relationship to Jing and Shen, Qi is considered neutral, neither Yin nor Yang in itself, but capable of functioning in either

capacity. Qi moves in all directions. Qi is air, breath and life-force energy, and it affects all of our life processes.

Shen: This belongs to the Upper Dantian. Shen is considered to be a Yang form of Qi, connected to heavenly things and always moving upward, like fire. Shen is mind and spirit, and it affects our senses and nervous system. Our Shen is said to shine in the light of our eyes. When we reach a state of clarity in meditation, we nourish Shen.

Qigong exercises and meditation conserve, circulate and balance Jing, Qi and Shen.

Internal Alchemy in modern practice

The lasting impression of the Chart of Internal Alchemy for me is the fact that for over a thousand years, possibly much longer, Chinese culture has embraced ways of nurturing health, vitality, longevity and wisdom. They have journeyed inside themselves to use existing physical, mental and spiritual energies. Qigong can be part of this inner transformation for the better, which makes Internal Alchemy relevant to everyone today.

LEFT: If Jing is compared to the wax and wick of the candle and Qi to the candle flame, then Shen is the light and radiance given off by the flame.

Yin and Yang

To the ancient Chinese mind, we exist because earth has the perfect balance of Yin and Yang energies. Yin energy comes upward from the earth and is moist, cool and nurturing. Yang energy comes downward from the sky and is dry, warm and energizing. The "Qi" in Qigong means life energy. This life energy is a constantly alternating dance of Yin and Yang. When Yin and Yang interact, the physical world is created. When Yin and Yang are balanced in our bodies, health results and our Qi energy increases. Qigong exercises balance the energies of Yin and Yang within us through our meridian channels, throughout our body tissues and through our energy centres. Yin and Yang energies are always changing with the passage of time.

An understanding of Yin and Yang will add to your Qigong practice. In a healthy body, Yin Qi nurtures and Yang Qi energizes. When you breathe, your inhalation is Yin because you are bringing in Yin energy and nurturing the blood with oxygen. Your exhalation is Yang because you are exhaling heat and toxins and other waste products.

Whenever you move in Qigong, inward movements are Yin and outward movements are Yang. Downward movements are Yin and upward movements

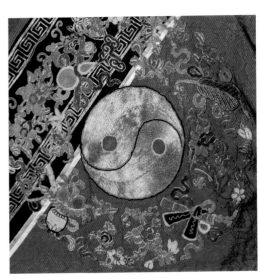

LEFT: Embroidery interpretation of the Yin Yang symbol.

are Yang. Qigong movements travel through a complete cycle of Yin and Yang, and to reflect this cycle the movements are continuous, fluid and rounded.

Your body is viewed as having Yin and Yang aspects. The front of your body is Yin and the back is Yang. Your lower body is Yin and your upper body is Yang. The inside of your body is Yin and the outer surface is Yang. Your Yin organs are the liver, kidneys, lungs, spleen and heart, while your Yang organs are the gall bladder, small intestine, stomach, large intestine and triple burner (see page 313). The Yin meridian channels are deeper, and the Yang meridians are nearer the surface.

Qigong cultivates a health-restoring balance of Yin and Yang energies.

The Yin Yang symbol

This well-known representation is also known as the Taijitu (supreme ultimate diagram). This image has an intrinsic elegance because it symbolizes a simple idea that can be endlessly complex. Though two-dimensional, the diagram could be thought of as three-dimensional. If you add the fourth dimension, to include time, then you could think

of it as a process of transformation, moving through time.

Every civilization attempts to provide a coherent view of the world. The Chinese have done this through the philosophical concept that all creation started from nothing, became unity and then divided into Yin and Yang, ultimately giving birth to all things.

The first recorded mention of Yin and Yang was in the *Classic of Changes*, the *Yijing*, thought to have originated in 2000–3000 BCE. Right up to the present day, the concept has been an intrinsic part of Chinese philosophy, affecting the way in which art, music, medicine, health, diet, cooking and indeed all things in life are viewed.

Yin Yang philosophy is not the same as Western dualism. A diagram of the latter would be a circle with a line down the middle with one side black and the other white. There would be no dots of white and black in each side to represent an interchange or mutual dependency. Also, there would be interminable argument over which side were best. There is no such argument about the Yin Yang theory because one side cannot exist without the other.

Everything is relative

Cold is Yin and hot is Yang. However, what is being compared is always

This table shows a few Yin and Yang opposites.

YIN	YANG	YIN	YANG
valley	mountain	old	young
dark	light	artistic	scientific
moon	sun	tiger	dragon
negative	positive	water	fire
cold	hot	passive	aggressive
body	mind	internal	external
contraction	expansion	nature	technology
earth	sky	feminine	masculine
relaxation	tension	vulnerable	impervious
inhalation	exhalation	saving	spending
below	above	quiet	loud
nourishing	energizing	rest	activity
weak	strong	black	white
intuition	logic	blue	red
yielding	resisting	slow	quick
synthesis	analysis	night	day

relative. If you were comparing hot to warm, then warm would be the more Yin of the two. A challenging Qigong move would be seen as Yang, and an easier, restorative move as Yin. However, this would all be a matter of degree. You might have two moves that are challenging, so both a Yang idea, but if one were less challenging, it would be Yin in relationship to the more challenging move.

Everything contains the seed of its opposite

In the middle of each half of the Yin Yang symbol is a dot. This symbolizes that within Yin is a measure of Yang, within Yang is a measure of Yin, and nothing is static. Yin and Yang are always influencing and changing each other. Night carries the seed of day. Day carries the seed of night. Spring carries the seed of Summer, which carries the seed of Autumn, which carries the seed of Winter, until the cycle begins again. The dot symbolizes the potential and ability to change and rebalance to create equilibrium. When we exhale, the ability to inhale is there waiting. When we expend energy, the ability to recharge our energy is there waiting. When we stretch out an arm or leg, we never extend any joint to its maximum; that little dot of Yin softness in every joint is what

allows our movement to be fluid and ever-changing without any stiffness.

Everything follows a cycle

Just as night follows day and day becomes night, our bodies also have natural cycles. For example, in Qigong we nourish and store our energy so that it can be expressed as activity. When we have used up our energy we need to replenish it once more, and in order to be healthy the cycle of storing and giving out energy must be perfectly balanced, so that we don't become depleted or over-energized.

When we practise Qigong we accumulate and store energy, a Yin process. Energy behaves like a clear, flowing stream. If the energy is blocked, it will stagnate. Free-flowing Qi can be used to repair our bodies, or to expend in the activities of daily life – a Yang process. If we use too much energy we will be depleted and our health will suffer. If we generate and hold on to too much, our health will suffer. Everything in Qigong is designed for a Yin Yang balance of Qi energy.

The moves in Qigong end the way they begin, so that a cycle is travelled and we feel complete.

PART 2

Essence

What Makes Qigong Different from Other Exercise?

Qigong is far more than just ordinary exercise. It is made up of many different aspects, and if any part is missing, it's not Qigong.

These essential qualities interconnect and affect one another. For example, attitude, breathing and relaxation affect your state of mind. Fluidity is not possible without relaxation or without correct posture and breathing. Balance is affected by posture, relaxation and state of mind. A calm state of mind and feeling connected increase confidence and sensitivity, which in turn allows you to be open to change and aware of your own sense of being.

These qualities develop with practice, over time. The hint

of a smile when practising works wonders! A smile releases your brain's feel-good chemicals, encouraging relaxation and other health benefits.

Movements should be as rooted as a tree, as balanced as a cat, as powerful as a surging wave and as free as a soaring eagle.

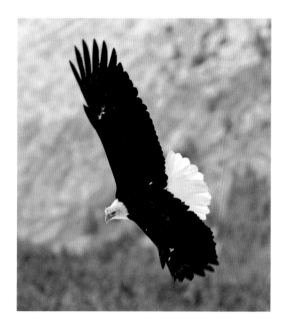

RIGHT: Total absorption in the present moment.

Mindset

*Without the correct mindset,
it's not Qigong.*

Your attitude in Qigong should
be receptive and open. Your mind
should be calm, composed and in the
present moment. Your concentration
should feel light and all-absorbing,
like a young child at play.

Breathing

*Without correct breathing,
it's not Qigong.*

Your breathing reveals your state
of mind. Soft, rhythmic, abdominal
breathing engenders a calm mind.
Breathing should be quiet, smooth,
even and free-flowing. When your
breathing is perfect, health benefits
and relaxation are enhanced.

Relaxation

Without relaxation, it's not Qigong.

Relaxation means there is no
unnecessary tension held anywhere
in your body or mind. Relaxation
allows you to be more sensitive and
improves awareness of everything
around you. Relaxation affects energy
flow, circulation and balance.

Posture

*Without correct posture,
it's not Qigong.*

Correct posture puts you in
complete harmony with gravity.
It means that everything is in the
optimum bio-mechanical alignment
to allow efficiency of movement with
no unnecessary effort. Good posture
requires that each vertebra in your
spine is perfectly spaced, with no
compression at any point.

Connection

*If you aren't connected,
it's not Qigong.*

Every part of your body should feel
connected, like an energetic network.
When you place your mental focus
at the Lower Dantian, just below
your navel, you will eventually feel
an integration radiating from this
central area to every other part of
your body. Connecting to this energy
centre cultivates a feeling of security,
confidence and power.

NOTE: See the Posture and
Movement Principles chapter, pages
70–3, for further clarification of some
of these points.

Qigong for Health, Martial Prowess and Spiritual Development

Qigong can be subdivided in many ways. A simple way is to look at the three main reasons that people practise Qigong.

ABOVE: Old Chinese illustration showing acupuncture points.

Health

Most people practise Qigong for its therapeutic benefits, and also because it is an enjoyable activity that brings general wellbeing. It helps a person become more relaxed and balanced, making the body stronger and more capable of healing itself. All of the Qigong movements in Part 4 of this book are therapeutic.

In Chinese thinking, physical health, emotional health and mental health are all part of the same continuum. In China, Qigong is used in hospitals and clinics alongside Western medicine. The country has conducted many research studies to verify the type of health benefits that Qigong can bring, and in China it is often prescribed as part of an overall health treatment for a multitude of conditions. Traditional Chinese Medicine is accepted worldwide as an alternative medicine choice. Interest has been so significant that in 2014 the US federal government created the National Center for

Complementary and Integrative Health (NCCIH). Its primary responsibility is to conduct research into alternative health approaches such as Qigong, which are presently being implemented within care settings such as hospitals, hospices and military health facilities across the United States.

According to Traditional Chinese Medicine theory, there are twelve Principal Meridians (energy pathways) plus eight Extraordinary Meridians in the human body, along with numerous minor ones, which form a network of invisible energy conduits throughout the body. These channels have over 400 acupuncture points situated at specific locations along them. If health is to be preserved, a balanced Qi flow must circulate throughout these channels.

There is a growing area of practice called medical Qigong which is popular among alternative medicine healers. Medical Qigong practitioners train in human anatomy and physiology, as well as in Qigong to cultivate their own energy and sensitivity. They prescribe specific exercises for particular conditions, often in combination with acupuncture and other energetic treatments which clear and energize the meridian channels in the body.

If you are interested in medical Qigong, it would be worth referencing the Bibliography and Further Reading section on page 308. There are numerous texts that fully explain meridian channels, acupoints and other Traditional Chinese Medicine theories. Many general medical practitioners are becoming increasingly interested in certain aspects of the efficacy of alternative therapies.

Martial prowess

Martial artists have always sought ways to improve their fighting skills, both to withstand blows and to condition their bodies against injury. Qigong practice can improve performance in any martial art and in any sport that requires stamina, balance, coordination, speed, flexibility and power.

Some types of martial Qigong are termed "hard" Qigong and can damage health if not accompanied by a calm mind trained in meditation, plus long and patient practice in skilled techniques. Hard Qigong methods are not covered in this book, but many of the Qigong moves that are included have a martial significance. In particular, see the Standing like a Post – Zhanzhuang chapter, pages 170–9, if you wish to increase your martial prowess. Zhanzhuang is considered essential training in martial arts to increase strength, power, resolve and stillness of mind.

Spiritual development

Qigong offers a path to greater self-awareness and inner peace. Our everyday thoughts are often circular, in that we recall the same thoughts over and over again and they won't let us rest. In the East these are referred to as "chattering monkeys" or "wild horses". Once our breathing and mind are calm, we are able to contemplate and meditate without the "chattering monkeys" obstructing mental clarity.

There is no one-way-fits-all concept to understand spiritual development, because we all have our own personal concepts, which may not fully agree with conventional thinking. A general viewpoint is that spiritual growth involves a process of inner awakening where we go beyond the limitations of the mind and begin to know who we really are. We begin to understand where truth resides in any situation, without our ego getting in the way. As we develop, our sense of inner strength increases, as does our ability to deal honestly and responsibly with everyday life without fear and anxiety. Life becomes more harmonious.

If this is a subject that appeals to you, have a look at the Qigong Meditation chapter. All Qigong exercises interconnect with spiritual development, if practised with a calm mind and attention in the present moment.

MERIDIAN CHANNELS

There are twelve Principal Meridians and eight Extraordinary Meridians. You could think of them as rivers of Qi energy that flow throughout the body. When you are healthy, the rivers flow smoothly, distributing life-force energy for optimum health. When the energy is blocked for any reason, the organs and tissues in the affected area suffer. Qigong helps to keep the energy flowing and to reduce and eliminate blockages.

Each of the twelve Principal Meridians is linked with an organ, which it affects. The Yin meridians are: Lung, Heart, Pericardium, Spleen, Kidney, Liver. The Yang meridians are Large Intestine, Small Intestine, Triple Burner, Stomach, Bladder, Gall Bladder.

The eight Extraordinary Meridians are: Conception Vessel, Governing Vessel, Penetrating Vessel, Belt Vessel, Yin Linking Vessel, Yang Linking Vessel, Yin Heel Vessel, Yang Heel Vessel.

Health, martial and spiritual categories interconnect

If you practise Qigong mainly for health, you will be enhancing your energy and stamina, which are qualities you need for martial ability. If you practise it in order to increase your martial ability or for spiritual development, your health will improve. And if you practise for martial ability or health in a mindful way, you will gradually become mentally calm and increase your ability to focus your mind. A calm mind is essential for spiritual development. There are no clear-cut defining lines between these categories, as they all overlap.

BELOW: Old Chinese illustration of men in martial combat.

Qigong Meditation

I have been practising meditation since I was 16 years old, but am I any good at it? Well, that's a little like asking whether you are any good at sleeping. If the surrounding conditions are right and the intention is there, it just happens, like falling asleep just happens. Meditation makes me feel more in tune with the symphony of life. It allows me to put things into perspective and to be more conscious of what is truly important.

What is meditation?

Meditation is quietening the mind while in a tranquil, open state of being. There are different levels of meditation: some are lighter levels where you are aware of everything around you, and some are deeper levels where your sense of time and ego disappear. All levels increase awareness of your inner nature and engender an appreciation of being in the present moment.

China's tradition of meditation is as rich as India's, and is mentioned in many ancient Chinese writings.

The word meditation is rooted in Sanskrit, Greek and Latin. The Latin verb *meditari* means to contemplate, think over, reflect. The Latin verb *mederi* means to heal, and it is comforting and enlightening to know that the idea of healing lies within the roots of the word "meditation".

LEFT: The author seated in meditation.

All Qigong practice has a meditative quality. At first you may not be aware that you are engaging in the initial stages of meditation, but whenever you focus all of your attention on what you are doing, you will begin to notice that your breathing becomes soft and rhythmic and your mind calm.

From a scientific point of view, meditation is a state where brain waves slow down. Brain waves are divided into four types: Beta, Alpha, Theta and Delta. Each type has a different wave pattern and can be measured on an electroencephalogram (EEG), which is a recording of brain activity.

- Beta, with 15–40 waves per second, is our everyday state when awake and active. This state is associated with fast, logical thinking and high levels of alertness.
- Alpha, with 8–15 waves per second, is our relaxed, peaceful, creative state of mind. It is associated with light meditation, concentration and enhanced learning capability.
- Theta, with 4–8 waves per second, is a state that occurs in deeper relaxation and meditation, and also in light sleep and dreaming. It is a very receptive, intuitive state where inspiration and insight occur.
- Delta, with 0.5–4 waves per second, is the state of deep, dreamless

sleep and deep meditation. Delta is associated with the unconscious mind, and usually only experienced meditators reach this state. Some say it is the gateway to the universal mind.

Our bodies heal and regenerate when the brain is in the Theta and Delta signal frequencies, and this is one reason that high-quality sleep is essential to our health. Meditation acts in a similar way to quality sleep, but while we are awake.

Why meditate?

It is possible for us to take responsibility for our own state of mind: to calm it, improve it and create a more positive reality. Meditation produces a state of deep inner relaxation, while at the same time stabilizing the mind and creating stronger Qi, or life force. In addition, meditation encourages personal and spiritual growth. It has a positive and balancing effect on a person's mental state and relieves conditions such as stress, anxiety, sleep disorders and depression, all of which contribute to a multitude of medical conditions. Meditation can also improve memory, confidence, insight, mental focus, mental clarity and possibly longevity.

If your mind is full of emotional turmoil, never-ending worries, problems and agitation, you will have little inclination, time or ability to extend energy and compassion toward others. Being constantly in a state of anxiety, stress and tension uses up a large proportion of a person's energy, and that means there isn't much energy left over to offer to others, to help with their needs and problems.

Benefits are cumulative, and even as little as 10 to 20 minutes' meditation a day, on a regular basis, can have a profound effect in your daily life. The Daoists have a saying that a true man walks in meditation, which means that it is possible for us to proceed throughout daily life with composure and a peaceful state of mind.

Meditation brings with it a sense of freedom as well as a sense of belonging to something greater than ourselves.

First steps to meditation

1 Breathing: Concentrate on soft abdominal breathing (see pages 67–8), like the perfect breathing of a young child. The way you breathe affects your body and mind.

2 Relaxation: Do a few relaxation, warm-up or stretching exercises (see the Warm-ups chapter, pages 74–85). Qigong exercises are an ideal preparation, as they gently lubricate and loosen all the joints and tissues of the body and calm the mind.

3 Posture: Whether you decide to stand or to sit on the floor or a chair, your spine should be extended, with no compression along any part of the spinal column. Imagine that your spine is lengthening so that the spaces between the vertebrae increase and you feel you are growing taller. From the waist up, feel that your body is so light and balanced, it almost seems as though it is floating. Your chin should be level to the ground, jaw relaxed, back of the throat feeling open. Your sitting should feel grounded through the seat bones and your standing should feel grounded through the feet. (See also the Posture and Movement Principles chapter, pages 70–3.)

4 Tip of tongue: With your lips lightly touching each other, place the tip of your tongue lightly on the upper palate (roof of your mouth), just behind your upper teeth. This encourages saliva flow, which lubricates the throat. If your throat is dry, your body won't be able to relax completely. The position also makes it easy for the jaw to relax – if your jaw is clenched, it tenses your face, neck and shoulder muscles. This tip-of-tongue position joins the Conception Vessel Meridian, which is Yin, and the

ABOVE: Eyes can be closed or open with eyelids lowered.

Governing Vessel Meridian, which is Yang, thereby joining Yin and Yang together energetically.

5 Eyes: Your eyes can be closed or open. Closed eyes filter out distractions more effectively, but if closing your eyes makes you feel dizzy or disoriented, keep them open. If open, look slightly downward, so that you are looking at the floor ahead of you. Sometimes when we look down there is a tendency to drop the head a little, so beware of this – drop the eyelids, not the head.

6 Attention: Focus your attention on your chosen object (see the Methods section, pages 40–4) for an extended length of time. If you are new to this, a minute might seem like a long time, but if you practise regularly, you will have no problem in eventually retaining your concentration for up to ten, even 20 minutes or longer. If you give all of your attention to one specific thing, all extraneous thoughts tend to slip into the background or temporarily disappear altogether.

WHAT IF MY MIND WON'T REST?

When you first begin, it is normal for the constant replay of your thoughts to continue their chattering within your head. Treat your mind like you would a very young child whose attention is wandering, and keep bringing him or her back to the task at hand. Eventually you will have built up a good habit, and with patience, love and direction, your much loved "child" will gain the ability to concentrate.

Methods

There are a great many meditation methods to choose from and they all have the same purpose: to create mental focus. Different schools promote their own favourites. No method is necessarily better than another, but some might suit you better than others. A selection is given here. Initially, following a method is important, so that you have a structure within which to focus your mind. Eventually, dependence on the method becomes less of a need, and fades into the background when deeper levels of meditation are reached.

You need only one method, but it is good to have an overview so that you have an appreciation of different approaches. The examples given here are for light forms of meditation, which consist of attention and concentration exercises to train your mind, but which also have a deep relaxation response.

Attention on the breath: There are multiple variations of meditation focussing on the breath, but one of the easiest and most popular techniques is to place your attention on your inhalation and exhalation and be aware of the movement that occurs in your body with the action of each breath.

Counting: This could be as simple as slowly counting from ten to one, or even from one hundred down to zero. A counting exercise that I use is to count from eleven to zero, and every time a thought appears between a count, return to eleven again. If you manage to reach zero, allow the mind to remain floating at the space around zero until a new thought arises, at which time you start again at eleven.

Sound: There are many ways to use sound. Some people use gongs, brass bowls, crystal bowls or various types of music to create a pleasing sound and vibration. Listening to the sounds of nature – for example, birdsong, trees in the wind, waves on the shore – can be forms of meditation if you give all of your attention to the sound.

Chanting: Repeating a mantra or chant over and over again is a time-honoured tradition in many cultures, including Qigong. The chant can be repeated out loud or silently to yourself. Chanting can be done either alone or in a group. The gentle, continuous vibration and repetition of the chant bring peace to the mind.

Prayer beads: Beads threaded together on a string are used in a number of different religions as a focal point for devotion. The number of beads is often symbolic, with different traditions using numbers symbolic to them, for example 18, 27, 54, 108. People who are not religious also use beads as a concentration tool. A set chant is repeated at each bead. This method offers the security of ritual and a steady framework within which to meditate.

Visualization: The variations of visualization are as endless as the imagination of the meditator or the tradition being drawn from. Visualization is often combined with breathing, for example creating a visualized route for the breath (see Microcosmic Orbit, pages 46–7).

Attention on an energy centre:

In Qigong we place our attention on energy centres called Dantians. The energy is called Qi. There are three main Dantians: Lower, Middle and Upper (see pages 20–3). In Yoga, we place our attention on energy centres called Chakras. The energy is called Prana, but it is the same as Qi. There are seven main Chakras: Root, Sacral, Navel/Solar Plexus, Heart, Throat, Brow and Crown.

Attention on an object or colour:

Any pleasing object can be used, but objects from nature such as a pebble from a beach or a leaf are usually easier to relate to. Different colours have different vibrations, and if no particular colour is specified, use a colour that resonates with you.

ABOVE: Each stone has its own character, texture, colour and balance.

Single-pointed attention: Place your attention at the Lower Dantian for longer and longer lengths of time, according to your concentration capacity. Meditation can be completely at this area during a dedicated time span. However, it is a common practice for martial artists to place half of their attention at the

Lower Dantian while going about their daily life. This practice has a de-focusing effect on random thoughts and disruptive emotions and creates stability and calm. When the mind is quiet, you become more aware of everything around you.

Mandala: This is a drawing or design that usually reflects or symbolizes the cosmos and is used as a focus for contemplation. In some cultures, sand is a favourite medium because it reflects the impermanence of existence in that it can be brushed away so easily. In other cultures a permanent and well-known mandala is used. You could use the Yin Yang symbol (see page 25) as a mandala.

Walking: People walk in a labyrinth, in a circle, in the forest or mountains or in any quiet place where there is the security of a known route. A labyrinth is a circular path that winds its way into a centre. The walker

LEFT: A mandala full of symbolism.

uses the same path to return, and so the entrance becomes the exit. Any circular path can be seen as a metaphor for the path we walk in life, and many people find it has a restorative and calming effect. The Qigong exercise Walking on Clouds (see pages 122–3) is performed in a circle and can be used as a walking meditation practice.

Candle gazing: The tradition of gazing at a flame probably began when man first lit a candle or fire. The image of the flame can be taken into the mind's eye to be held as an inner flame at the Upper Dantian spot between the eyebrows. Some people visualize a flame without need of a candle.

Stargazing: We have all looked up and gazed at the stars, but these days only a few of us spend any length of time stargazing as our ancestors once did before the advent of electricity, television and computers. The vastness of space brings us a sense of childlike awe and wonder, and to lose ourselves for a while in this deep space imbues us with a sense of eternity. To the ancient Chinese, stars had great symbolic attachments and much time was spent in stargazing.

Metaphor: This is a form of visualization where an image, usually taken from nature, is used as a symbol. A classic example is visualizing a lake and likening it to your mind. The visualization of a clear, deep, smooth lake is calming. When the surface of the lake is clear like a mirror, observing it reflects our true spiritual nature back to us.

Contemplation: A certain quality, ideal or philosophical statement is observed with an open, attentive mind. For example, what is loving kindness, what is its vibration, how is it best expressed? This type of meditation often leads to deeper understanding of life's most important questions.

Watching your thoughts: Watch your thoughts pass by at a distance, with no judgement or comment. When your thoughts appear at longer and longer intervals, move your attention to the spaces between the thoughts. The spaces are deeply calming and sometimes expand for long periods of time.

Create space: At the Middle or Upper Dantian, feel the energy expand, creating a sense of spaciousness. When things are going wrong in our lives, we can sometimes feel that we are contracting inward and closing down. The expansive, spacious feeling created with this meditation is very uplifting and helps us to expand outward, so that we no longer feel hemmed in by life events or narrow thinking patterns.

Moving meditation: Qigong meditation can be done while moving. Practise any easy Qigong move and perform it in a slow, flowing manner with complete attention so that no other thoughts enter your mind, and you will create a tranquil, meditative state which becomes "moving meditation". Other traditions use dance, either with form or freestyle, to instil a sense of complete absorption of the dancer into the dance.

Mindfulness: This is the daily practice of paying attention to what we are doing, while we are doing it, without any distraction from extraneous thoughts. Thoughts from the past or future disconnect us, preventing us from being in the present, and that means we could end up living a large part of our lives in our heads, rather than right now in the world, in the present moment.

Transparency: At the Middle or Upper Dantian, create a sense of spaciousness. Extend this feeling of space to every part of your body, or even to every cell if your imagination can extend to this. Feel that you are so spacious inside that you are almost transparent, and that every sound, emotion and thought can now pass through you without obstruction. Once you become accustomed to this practice, things such as unwanted sounds or negative energy in daily life will no longer trouble you.

Spiritual development

We all have our own personal interpretations of what spiritual development means. The following is merely my interpretation and, as for most people, it will probably change over time.

We all go through stages of development, and some of us want to stay at a certain stage, for our own reasons, and this should be respected. No stage should be rushed. In our youth, most of us are self-centred and might display manipulative, selfish behaviour and a lack of awareness of anything outside of our own needs and experience. If we grow beyond this stage we start to develop selflessness and compassion, and are able to discipline our personal desires so they do not harm or deprive others.

Further progression involves looking into our own minds and hearts for answers to the important questions of life, rather than accepting someone else's interpretation. This stage requires a lot of confidence about our own personal identity, as the certainties of life can seem to disappear. This is why many people find it easier to stay in a cosy, secure, but limited mental place with fixed ideas. Sometimes we may feel alone and deserted because no one understands our personal search for a wider worldview. Our childhood belief systems may start to seem inadequate as we mature and begin to look beyond our own background, culture or country. We might become cynical or feel superior, rejecting the things of our past, especially if conflict is involved.

If we are able to progress through this stage, we can look within ourselves for a deeper connection to all life, and start to view ourselves as connected to something greater, perhaps divine or beyond our current understanding. When we establish a true connection, we no longer feel alone or afraid, and begin to understand why people are the way they are, without the all too common inclination to judge, condemn or feel superior. We understand the need to realize that we all inhabit the world equally, together, and our sense of brotherhood with all life expands.

This stage leads us to want further development, fuelled by a curiosity to explore the limits of the human mind beyond what reason and logic can offer. We understand the cosmic joke of attempting to explore our current limits with a mind that is intrinsically limited, and enjoy nudging the boundaries, comfortable with the knowledge that there is no certainty, except perhaps change itself.

Once we open our minds to see the unity in all things, even divergent ideas, and start to understand the feeling and sensing of things, we realize the need to let go of our deeply embedded conceit and superficial identity. Once the ego lets go of its limpet hold, we realize that the ego is a separator, and things that once seemed essential no longer have value. Love and gratitude grow, forgiveness is natural and dealing with uncertainty is not such an issue.

As the feeling of connection with all things increases, so does trust in our own intuition and acceptance of the universal plan – whatever that may be. This freedom from ego bestows deep confidence and at the same time melts away self-importance. A feeling of spiritual oneness with something greater than ourselves continues to grow, bringing with it a true sense of inner peace that is serene, energizing and fascinating. And so the journey continues to the next level, wherever and whatever that may be.

Qigong meditation exercises

The following three well-known Qigong meditation practices instil a sense of calm and peace and have a cleansing quality. All three are performed in a state of light meditation, and awareness of what is around you is maintained.

The Microcosmic Orbit

The Microcosmic Orbit refers to a Qigong method for circulating energy around a circuit of two meridian channels. The Conception Vessel (Ren Mai) channel runs down the front of the body. The Governing Vessel (Du Mai) channel runs up the back of the body. The joining points for the two channels are at the perineum (the area between the anus and the genitals) and at the roof of the mouth.

The practice has a long history, and references appear in the *Yijing* c. 1000 BCE. The Daoists considered it to be a first step toward cultivating the golden elixir of immortality. They believed that if you circulated the energy along the Microcosmic Orbit as a daily practice, chronic physical ailments would disappear. They would practise even while walking and had a saying that a true man walks in meditation.

1 Take a sitting or standing position that is comfortable. See the three positions that follow for Clear Brow of the Sage, and choose your favourite. Close your eyes or lower your eyelids. Feel that your upper body is light, with the spine extended. Place the tip of your tongue on your upper palate, behind the teeth. Breathe with deep, soft abdominal breaths, through your nose, until your breathing has become naturally quiet, slow, fine and light, with a continuous, subtle, soothing rhythm. Continue to place attention on your breathing until your mind is calm.

2 Focus your attention at the Lower Dantian for a few minutes and feel that the Qi energy is merged with your breath. When you feel ready to begin, inhale softly and visualize the breath travelling from the meeting place of your tongue and upper palate, down the front of your body to the perineum. As you exhale, imagine Qi travelling up the back of your body along your spine, over the crown of your head and down to where your tongue touches the palate. This is one

breath cycle. The inhalation is Yin energy, the energy of earth. The exhalation is Yang energy, the energy of heaven. Begin with 10 breath cycles and gradually work up to 30 minutes or more.

Variations: There are different ways of circulating the Qi in the Microcosmic Orbit, but until you have a basic route established, as described above, variations can be counterproductive. One variation is to reverse the breathing direction. Another is to visualize significant acupoints along the Microcosmic Orbit. However, to practise variations prematurely can lead to energy blocks and disturbances – the exact opposite of the primary purpose of the exercise, which is to promote Qi energy flow. Once the Microcosmic Orbit has become natural to you, another variation is the Macrocosmic Orbit, which includes the arms and legs. Variations should not be attempted without the guidance of an experienced teacher.

LEFT: The Microcosmic Orbit

Clear Brow of the Sage

The name of this meditation implies that a person of wisdom does not have a furrowed brow or worry lines across the forehead because he or she has learned the art of calm and the attitude of open acceptance. Give this a try and become a sage for a moment in time. This is one of my favourite meditations, which I often teach at the end of classes while everyone stands in Holding a Tree position for about five minutes. Every one of us can achieve this clear brow for a few minutes, and I have seen some students extending the skill for longer periods of time, some even throughout a significant part of their day.

1 This exercise can be done sitting or standing. If standing, take a Shoulder-width Stance (see pages 54–5) and have your hands folded over the Lower Dantian. If you are feeling stronger, stand in a Horse Stance (see pages 58–9) in the Holding a Tree position (see page 176). If seated, sit with a straight back with feet apart and the soles of your feet in contact with the floor; resting your hands on your thighs allows your arms to relax.

2 Begin by placing your attention on your abdominal breathing (see pages 67–8), until it feels slow, calm and rhythmic. Now lead your inner vision to the Upper Dantian between your eyebrows. Expand the area between your eyebrows by releasing tense muscles, and extend this feeling to include the whole of the forehead, brow and temples. Look into the Upper Dantian with your inner vision and, as more and more tension releases, you will experience a feeling of expansion. To an observer you will appear peaceful and your brow area will appear clear of worry lines. Hold your focus at the Upper Dantian as though you are looking into a place of infinite space. This posture can be held for any length of time from one minute to half an hour or more.

Addition of an inner smile: Sometimes we add an inner smile. Imagine a gently curved smile positioned between your eyebrows and inside your head. On each exhalation imagine the corners of the smile pushing the eyebrows slightly further apart. Don't be surprised if a hint of a smile touches your mouth and you start to feel happy and at peace.

TRAINING THE BROW MUSCLES

Some people are unable to expand the forehead because there is a muscle memory of tension that does not initially respond to easing and smoothing requests from the brain. If this is the case with your forehead, place your fingers between your eyebrows and gently pull the flesh outward, tracing your brow line with your fingertips until they rest at your temples. Hold your fingertips at your temples for a few seconds.

Repeat the exercise several times. On your last repetition, lift your fingertips away from your temples and try to hold the open feeling of relaxed brow and forehead muscles. You may have to train your brow muscles repeatedly – they behave in the same manner as any other group of muscles that are used to being held repeatedly with tension, and will respond to gentle, consistent reminding.

Qi Washing

The idea of this meditation is that you can wash away physical and mental tensions and blockages, head to toe, using visualization or feeling, led by your intention. Recently, I met a student from many years ago

RIGHT: Qi Washing

and I asked him if he still practised Qigong. He said that the only thing he still practised almost every day was Qi Washing because it eased his emotional problems and made him feel mentally clean.

Qi Washing is best done standing, so that the feeling of gravity aids the washing process. Stand in a Shoulder-width Stance (see pages 54–5) with arms held loosely at your sides and your eyes closed.

Place your attention on slow, rhythmic, abdominal breathing until you feel calm and centred. Choose an appropriate image for the washing process: it could be an image of water or golden light or a colour that feels right. Whichever image you choose, feel that it is imbued with Qi energy. Move your attention to above the top of your head and feel the water, light or colour start to fall very, very slowly through your body, washing away any tension or blockage in your muscles, emotions or mind. Gradually the washing makes its way downward through your feet and into the ground beneath.

Visualizing the washing process is good, but feeling it is even better. Allow the cleansing to reach every small area of your being. Spend a minimum of two minutes and repeat several times if you wish. It is common to feel refreshed and relaxed at the end.

PART 3

How to Begin

Basic Stances

Your stance is the way you stand – how you place your feet and how you distribute your weight – and is the foundation for every Qigong move. It must be steady, balanced and rooted to the ground so that the upper body can be light and agile, just as the base of a tree must be rooted to the earth so that the upper trunk and branches are free to move with the wind. The seven fundamental stances required in order to perform all of the Qigong exercises in this book are shown in this chapter.

No. 1 Shoulder-width Stance

This is sometimes called a Parallel Stance, because the feet are parallel to each other. It is your most important stance because most movements begin and end with this stance. It can be used as a resting stance, as well as an opening and closing stance.

Place your feet so they are the width of your own shoulders apart, with your feet parallel and your knees relaxed.

Some people have much wider shoulders than others, and so their stance might look wider than yours. Always pay attention to your own body build, or you could end up with a stance suitable for your teacher, but not for you! An anatomically strong position is where the feet are directly in line with the hip joints so that there is a vertical line of force from the hip joints down through the knee and ankle joints. However, some people prefer a wider stance because a wider base provides more stability. Also, women often have larger hips than men, and many teachers advise using hip width or shoulder width, whichever is wider.

It is common for people to put more weight on their stronger leg, without being aware of it, so do your best to distribute your weight evenly – 50 per cent of your weight on each foot. Your knees should be in good alignment with your toes, which means they should be pointing in the same direction as your toes. When bending your knees, they must not project beyond your toes because this is a weak position that could damage your knee joints. You should be able to feel each toe in contact with the ground, and the inner and outer heel edges should also be in contact with the ground.

The Bubbling Spring point, Yongquan (see box, below), should be in contact with the ground to provide an energetic feeling of connection and rooting.

THE BUBBLING SPRING

The Yongquan or Bubbling Spring is the first acupoint on the Kidney Meridian channel. "Yong" means gush, well up, surge, and "quan" means a spring or fountain. The feet should not pronate (roll inward) or supinate (roll outward). The Bubbling Spring point should be in contact with the ground in all standing positions, and also when walking.

Starting posture

Shoulder-width Stance, with arms held loosely by your sides, is used as your starting posture for most Qigong moves. By beginning this way, you give yourself a chance to bring your attention to your posture and connection to the ground, and also to compose your mind.

Postural reminders

- Stand with feet shoulder-width apart and parallel to each other.
- Feel that your ankle, knee and hip joints are aligned.
- Your knees should feel soft, not locked. "Soft" means that there is a hint of a bend in the knees.
- Feel as though your spine is fluid like a string of pearls.
- Feel as though your upper body is light and floating from the waist up.
- Feel as though your lower body is heavy and rooted from the waist down.
- Relax your whole body, especially your shoulders, arms and hands.
- Imagine a weight on your tailbone, grounding you to the earth.
- Imagine your head suspended from above by a golden thread attached from the crown of your head up to a cloud in the sky, so that the back of your neck feels gently stretched upward without feeling fixed.

LEFT: Starting posture.

- Look forward with soft, relaxed eyes.
- Keep your chin level to the ground.
- Touch the tip of your tongue to the roof of your mouth and relax your jaw.
- Expand your forehead and brow, and relax your mind.
- Feel natural and in harmony with gravity.

Women place the right hand on first, with the left hand on top, just below the navel. Men place the left hand on first, with the right hand on top, just below the navel.

Closing posture

Shoulder-width Stance is used in the closing posture for each Qigong move or set of moves. By ending this way, you give yourself a feeling of completion and a feeling of having cultivated and stored energy.

Gather up Qi energy with a circular motion of your hands and bring it to the Lower Dantian, which is an energy field approximately 5cm (2in) below your navel, inside your body at your centre of gravity. Over time you will cultivate a store of vital energy.

RIGHT: Closing posture.

No. 2 Horse Stance

This is sometimes called Horse-riding Stance because it looks like the position you would take when riding a horse. This stance is known for strengthening all of the muscles in both legs equally and especially for strengthening the muscles around the knees. It is highly valued in all martial arts for training and conditioning purposes.

GOLDEN RULE FOR KNEES

Whichever stance you are practising, remember the golden rule for good knee safety and alignment: the knees should be in the same direction as your toes and should never project beyond your toes.

Bend both knees and step out to the side with your left foot to a position slightly wider than shoulder width. Your toes can be turned out by about 10 degrees. This slight turning out takes pressure off the knees and is recommended by osteopaths. Some people feel more comfortable with a larger turn-out, but no more than 30 degrees maximum or you lose the strength of the stance. Bend your knees out to the sides, not forward. Feel as though you are sitting on a horse. Keep your back vertical and feel your weight go down through your heels.

Horse Stances are performed at different widths: small, medium or large. A small Horse Stance is a tiny bit wider than a Shoulder-width Stance. A medium Horse Stance is noticeably wider than shoulder-width. A large Horse Stance has the feet as wide apart as half of your height, or even wider, and requires a considerable amount of muscle flexibility and strength to hold for any length of time.

Horse Stances are performed at different heights: high, medium-height or low. The lower you hold the stance, the more challenging it becomes. A high Horse Stance has the knees bent by only a small amount. The low, large Horse Stance is performed with thighs almost parallel to the ground. This requires strength, hip and muscle flexibility and a good understanding of alignment so as not to damage the lower back or knees.

If you have never practised a Horse Stance before, it is best to start in a small, high stance.

No. 3 Back Stance

This stance takes its name from the fact that most of your weight is on the back leg. Sometimes it is called an Empty Stance, because the front leg is empty of weight. A Back Stance is usually considered a defensive position.

Start in a Shoulder-width Stance, bend both knees, transfer 70–90 per cent of your weight onto your right leg, and then place your left leg forward. The back leg knee should remain bent and the front knee should be slightly bent. Keep your back erect. Repeat on the other side.

The stance can be performed with the front ankle flexed up, so that the toes on the front foot are lifted.

Alternatively, the front foot can be flat on the ground, dependent upon the move and the style.

If you are new to this stance, place only 70 per cent of your weight on the back leg and bend your back knee only as far as is comfortable.

No. 4 Cat Stance

This stance gets its name from the nature of the cat. When a cat is stalking, it often puts a front paw lightly forward to test the ground and ensure that all conditions are right, before either transferring its weight or leaping forward at its prey.

From a Shoulder-width Stance, transfer all of your weight to your right leg and bend your right knee. Place the toes of your left foot lightly on the floor. The front knee should be slightly bent and feel as though it is being lifted upward – this is called a "nimble" knee because it allows you to change quickly into either another stance or a kick. Keep almost all of your weight on the back leg. Repeat on the other side.

Cat Stances can be high or low. Low stances have the knees bent more and the front foot is placed further away.

If you have never done this stance before, keep your front step small so that the toes are close to your other foot, and keep your stance high.

No. 5 Nail Stance

The name of this stance comes from its resemblance to a nail being hammered into the floor. The nail is strong and straight, and when the toes of one foot are in this position, they add strength and balance to your stance. It is used as a transitional stance to keep your balance before proceeding to the next move.

Transfer almost all of your weight to the right leg. Bring your left toes to rest beside your right foot, but without your feet touching each other, and bend both knees. Lift your left heel as high as possible so that your foot becomes vertical, like a nail going into the ground. Repeat on the other side.

The Nail Stance can be performed with the balls of the toes on the ground, or with just the tips of the toes lightly touching the ground. It can be performed in a high stance or a low stance.

If this stance is new to you, start with the balls of the toes on the ground in a high stance. Whenever you are on one leg, you can use this stance to help keep your balance.

No. 6 Crane Stance

The crane is a symbol of longevity in China. It is also associated with swiftness, grace and elegance. The crane has great endurance to stand on one leg effortlessly over long periods of time. The Crane Stance is meant to look elegant and balanced.

Start in a Shoulder-width Stance. Transfer your weight to your right leg, and lift your left knee as high as possible, in front of you. Point the toes downward and allow the foot to naturally turn inward toward your centreline. In training for martial arts, the front leg is ready both to kick and to defend against kicks. In training for health, the stance teaches strength, elegance and balance. Repeat on the other side.

If this stance is new to you, lift the knee only as high as is comfortable, even if this means that your toes are close to the ground. As your balance and strength improve, try lifting the knee higher.

No. 7 Bow Stance

The front leg is an allusion to the curved front part of the bow and the back leg is straight like the drawstring of the bow. Occasionally it takes the name Mountain Climbing Stance because it resembles the action of lunging forward when climbing a steep hill or mountain. Some schools call it Front Stance or Forward Stance, because most of the weight is on the front leg.

Place your left foot one step ahead, bend your front knee and transfer 70–90 per cent of your weight forward.

Keep your knees in line with your toes. The soles of both feet should be firmly planted on the ground. Repeat on the other side.

Some schools have the back foot turned out at a 45-degree angle. Other schools have the back foot parallel to the front foot.

If you have never done this stance before, bring no more than 70 per cent of your weight forward.

Moving between stances

Moving from stance to stance is a good way to train your strength, balance and agility. Qigong exercises often move back and forth between Back Stance and Bow Stance. A traditional martial arts strengthening exercise is to move between Nail Stance and Horse Stance, side to side, for many repetitions. Vary the order of the stances when you practise. A good test of whether you know the stances is to have a friend call out the stance names in an unpredictable order, and see how smoothly you can move from one stance to another. Your stance is your foundation, and the more familiar you are with the basic stances, the more easily you will be able to learn any Qigong move.

Breathing

The breath of life

Breathing is essential to life. Correct breathing increases energy, reduces anxiety and rejuvenates your body. The most important breathing technique is abdominal breathing, which should be your everyday breathing method.

Breath of a child

This is also called abdominal breathing, belly breathing, natural breathing and Buddhist breathing.

As we get older, many of us restrict our breathing to the upper chest using short, shallow breaths. This is not nourishing to our bodies or minds.

When a young, healthy child breathes, the whole torso expands on each inhalation. It is effortless and perfect, and the child's energy seems inexhaustible. But as we age, the stresses and tensions of daily life take their toll. The diaphragm becomes sluggish, the intercostal muscles (the muscles between the ribs) become stiff and breathing efficiency starts to diminish.

Watch the breathing of a healthy child who is young enough that the

ABOVE: The sweet smell of Qi.

stresses of life have not yet taken their toll. Babies and young children breathe in and out through their noses. They breathe softly, smoothly and continuously, expanding and contracting the whole of the abdomen. The chest, belly, ribcage and back are mobile, expanding with each inhalation and contracting with each exhalation. When you watch them breathe, you feel you are watching the rhythm of life. Let them be your guides.

Many adults don't even realize that their breathing is shallow and restricted to the upper chest. During my time working in a mental-health unit teaching Qigong and yoga, I always included improving the way

THE VAGUS NERVE

This is the body's longest nerve, running through the brain, chest, diaphragm, intestines and organs. It is the main part of our parasympathetic nervous system and communicates with our brain through neurotransmitters. Abdominal breathing soothes the vagus nerve, which then sends messages to the brain to stimulate the relaxation response. This helps to relax and slow down our breathing rate, as well as improving our immune and nervous systems. It helps us to overcome depression and anxiety, and stimulates cell regeneration.

With advances in neuroscience, we now know that a large part of our feel-good hormones such as dopamine and serotonin are produced in the gut and that gut dysfunction is responsible for a much wider range of maladies than previously realized. Breathing abdominally helps to keep your "gut brain" happy.

clients breathed. It was one of the most transforming parts of their practice. They were often amazed to find they could lower their blood pressure, manage asthma, prevent anxiety attacks and feel more peaceful simply by improving their breathing. Abdominal breathing also improves the resonance of your voice and allows you to express yourself more fully in speaking or singing. Breathing abdominally massages the internal organs, improving digestion and circulation.

The main muscle used in inhalation, the diaphragm, is a dome-shaped sheet of muscle under your lungs. When you breathe in using your full lung capacity, this muscle contracts and the dome flattens out and pushes downward, expanding your abdomen.

It's much easier to start lying down, but eventually you will feel confident enough to try abdominal breathing while sitting and standing. Your breath rate will naturally start to slow down and you will become more peaceful.

How to breath abdominally

What if you are someone who has never thought about breathing abdominally? No problem! It's easy to learn.

Breathe to a count to regulate the breath

When you have become accustomed to abdominal breathing, try breathing to a count. Breathe in to a count

Abdominal Breathing

1 Lie down on the floor with your knees bent and your feet flat on the floor. This position will prevent your lower back from over-arching. Put a pillow under your head if this makes you feel more comfortable, and place your hands on your belly with fingertips touching. If you are unable to lie on the floor, lie on a bed. Breathe in deeply through your nose and then sigh aloud saying, "Ahhhh!" as you exhale.

2 Wait patiently for your body to breathe in, rather than initiating the inhalation yourself. Your first inhalation after the sigh will be a true abdominal breath and you will feel it expanding your abdomen; your hands will separate with the expansion. Your ribcage will also expand, and if you are lying on the floor, you might feel your back expanding. You may not feel a lot of expansion at first because unused breathing muscles may have gone to sleep for a decade or two, but if you practise they will wake up.

of four, pause for a second and then breathe out to a count of four.

Some teachers may advise breathing in through the nose and out through the mouth. The reason is that breathing out through a small space between your lips can make you more conscious of your breathing pattern, but as you progress you will no longer need to breathe out through your mouth.

Breathing to a count helps to shift your focus away from worries, concerns and even pain, and brings your focus to the smooth rhythm of your breathing. When your mind is still and your breathing is natural, you will no longer need to think about your breathing. However, it can take up to six months, and sometimes longer, to become instinctively proficient in abdominal breathing.

Other types of breathing

In addition to abdominal breathing, there are other methods of breathing, a few of which are briefly covered here. However, they are beyond the requirements of most people, but abdominal breathing is a prerequisite.

Dantian breathing

This is similar to abdominal breathing, but lower and more subtle. This breathing stimulates the kidneys and lower spine and increases the body's overall energy level. It increases the relaxation response, which helps you to react better to stress.

Locate the lowest place where your abdomen expansion originates. This is different for everyone because it is dependent upon body proportions. For some it will be as high as the navel, and for others as low as just above the pubic bone. Place your attention at the lowest point of expansion, including your lower back so that you become aware of expansion around your lower back and kidneys on the inhalation, and contraction on the exhalation.

Reverse breathing

This is sometimes referred to as Daoist breathing. Mastery of abdominal breathing is a prerequisite. Often used by martial arts experts, reverse breathing stimulates the Qi energy and allows the practitioner to lead Qi more efficiently to any part of the body.

When you inhale, pull the abdomen gently inward; when you exhale, push the abdomen gently outward. This is the reverse of abdominal breathing and should not be done for long periods of time. If done incorrectly, it can cause medical problems, including tension in the abdomen, pressure in the chest area and a rise in blood pressure. If you decide to train in this type of breathing, find a competent instructor.

Embryonic breathing

This is also known as internal, primordial or umbilical breathing. It refers to a state of breathing that is so subtle that to an observer it might appear as though the person has stopped breathing. In meditation, embryonic breathing often happens spontaneously as the meditator's mind becomes free of thoughts and enters a state of complete serenity.

Bring yourself to a state of calm with slow abdominal breathing. Feel that the breath is entering and leaving through your whole body with no effort from you. Imagine that the breath enters and leaves so effortlessly that it has almost disappeared. Once again, instruction from an experienced teacher is important.

Posture and Movement Principles

Understand a principle, and things fall into place.

All physical skills, whether Qigong, martial arts, sport, dance or any form of athletics, have posture and movement principles. Understanding these principles gives you a better understanding of how to get the most out of your activity, reduce injury risk, and learn and progress at a faster rate. All styles and variations of Qigong follow the same principles. Some of the guidelines relate to posture, while other points convey an idea that then translates into motion.

Suspended headtop: Feel as though you are suspended from the sky above. Imagine that there is a flexible silken thread attached to the topmost part of your head, lifting you upward and creating a light, supple feeling.

Imagine a weight on your tailbone: Imagine a weight gently pulling you downward, like a heavy tail. This creates more space in your lumbar spine and brings your pelvis into a neutral position.

Postural guidelines

Without the right posture, correct movement is impossible.

Be like a willow tree: Be relaxed and soft like a willow tree bending with the wind. There is an old Chinese proverb: a tree that is unbending is easily broken.

Be like water: When water meets an obstacle, it flows around it. When you come up against an obstacle, whether physical, emotional or mental, be like water.

KEEP JOINTS SOFT AND RELAXED

In Qigong, the joints are considered to be energy gateways and should be relaxed at all times. The main joints are the wrists, elbows, shoulders, ankles, knees, hips, pelvis, sacrum and all the spinal vertebrae. There are many minor joints in your fingers and toes. People argue over how many joints there are in the body because some are semi-movable, but let's say there are over 300 joints. There are too many to keep all of them consciously relaxed, but you could hold the concept of relaxation and imagine all of your joints as pearls threaded through elastic – all connected, so that when one joint moves it subtly affects all the others.

A locked joint is one that is at its end range of movement, with no feeling of space. Any joint can lock, but we will use the example of an arm or leg, as this is the easiest to see. When the arm or leg is straightened completely, to 180 degrees, for most people this would be end of range. In Qigong we never go all the way to the end of the range in any joint; we bend the elbow or knee slightly, so that there is softness in the joint.

Five to ten per cent of the population have joints that overextend. A hyperextended arm or leg goes past a straight line when fully extended and appears to bow backward. This can be related to loose ligaments and can lead to joint instability, increasing the risk of injury. If you have hypermobile joints, you will have to pay more attention to keeping your major joints in a soft position.

Feel light and heavy at the same time: The silken thread pulling upward from the top of your head and the weight on your tailbone pulling downward at the same time, will lengthen the spine. It will feel a little like an elastic band being pulled at both ends. Feel light from the waist up and heavy from the waist down.

LEFT: Water flowing around obstacles in a swirling dance.

Relax your shoulders: Many people carry tension in their shoulders, neck and back, without even realizing it. Consciously loosen your shoulder muscles and drop your shoulder blades so that they feel relaxed and heavy.

Heavy elbows: Allow your elbows to feel heavy as though they were dropping toward the floor. This helps to keep the shoulders relaxed.

Soften your chest: Many people carry tension in their chest muscles.

Some hold themselves in a tight military position and some, at the other end of the scale, cave their chest inward.

Consciously soften the chest muscles so that your chest feels soft and natural.

Be rooted: Feel rooted and connected to the earth, creating a feeling of stability and strength.

Align knees and toes: Knees are prone to injury if they are out of alignment. Your knees should be aligned in the same direction as your toes. Also, in any stance, the knees should never project beyond the toes, as this is a very weak position for your knee.

The spine operates as a unit: In most Qigong moves, your nose should be aligned with your navel. This means there should be no leading with your head.

Tip of tongue on roof of mouth: The tip of the tongue should be lightly positioned on the roof of the mouth, just behind the upper teeth. This is a safe, stable position that relaxes the jaw and promotes saliva flow. It also joins two meridian channels and increases energy flow.

Calm face: Your face should be calm and relaxed, with a smooth, unfurrowed brow. Often people pinch their eyebrows together when they over-concentrate or are worried. Keep the forehead smooth and trouble-free.

Alert, relaxed eyes: The eyes should display mental focus and attention in the present moment.

Use peripheral vision: When you expand your peripheral vision, you see more of what is around you. Stand with your arms held out to the sides at shoulder height, and look straight ahead but see both hands at the same time. Hey presto! You are now using and training your peripheral vision.

Movement guidelines

Your mental attitude can enhance the flow of movement.

Calm your mind: Keep a clear and calm mind so as not to inhibit your movement or energy flow.

No force is needed: Feel that you are allowing a move to happen. Moves should feel so natural that they are almost happening by themselves.

Move from your centre of gravity: All movement should feel as though it begins at your centre of mass, which is about two fingers' width below the navel when standing. The exact location varies a little from person to person depending on body proportions and weight distribution.

Roll your feet when walking: Imagine that you have rockers on your feet, like on a rocking horse. When walking forward, roll from your heel through to the end of your big toe. When walking backward, roll from your big toe down to your heel.

Step with lightness and agility: Make every step you take light and agile. When you first place a foot forward or back, it should touch the floor as lightly as a feather before you transfer your weight.

Move with power: Power comes from the ground and rises up through the legs, where it is directed by the hips and waist. It then flows up the spine and outward through the arms and hands.

Go with the flow: Movement should be continuous and flowing like a wave. The whole body should coordinate and move as one inter-connected unit. 'Going with the flow' also refers to an open mind able to allow change.

Move with agility: Your whole body should be agile and light and should move effortlessly.

Move gracefully: When moves are well balanced, relaxed, coordinated and rooted, they will become graceful.

Be connected: Each part of your body should feel connected to every other part. No part moves in isolation. There has been a wealth of new research about fascia, which helps us to understand this concept. Fascia is a specific type of soft tissue in your body that surrounds every organ, muscle, tendon, ligament, bone and nerve. It is full of neurons, which gather information, talk to other neurons and send impulses to the brain. Every part of you is literally connected to every other part through fascia and energy information. When one part moves, every other part listens and reacts.

The silk thread: There is a saying in Qigong and Taiji: never break your silk thread. This refers to the ancient method of drawing out silk filaments from the cocoon of the silkworm by hand, using dexterous arm movements that are continuous, graceful and circular to avoid breaking the thread. This saying reminds you to keep your moves graceful, continuous and flowing.

Be grounded: This relates to being rooted, but with the additional meaning of being fully present in the moment. Some people refer to this as being centred. When you give full attention to the present moment, your ego gets out of the way and you are able to move with more freedom.

Warm-ups

Warm-up exercises are a traditional way to prepare your body and mind for your Qigong practice. They wake up your body by gently increasing your circulation, activating the lymphatic system, priming your neural pathways, lubricating your joints and connective tissues and loosening up tight muscles, and they put you in a good frame of mind for practice.

Joint mobility exercises

Most people spend about 10 minutes doing warm-up exercises before starting their Qigong practice, but the length of time you spend is your decision. It would be easy to spend 20 minutes on warm-ups because they are so effortless and enjoyable. Choose from the ones that follow to develop a routine that suits you best.

Rotating the head

Rotate your head slowly and gently, within your normal comfort range and without hanging the head back.

Repetitions: Repeat three times each way.

Caution: if you have neck problems, leave this one out and do the Clock-face Circling instead.

Clock-face circling

Imagine a large clock face in front of you. Following the numbers with your nose, go around the clock face while mentally saying the time: 12, 1, 2, 3, 4, 5, 6, 7, 8, 9, 10, 11, 12. Saying the numbers smoothly to yourself helps to make the circling smoother. Circle clockwise, then anticlockwise.

Repetitions: Repeat the sequence 3 times.

Rotating the shoulders

Alternate rotating of the shoulders

Rotate your shoulders in large, slow, smooth circles.

Repetitions: Repeat 3 times backward and 3 times forward.

Rotate one shoulder then the other in slow circles. Rotate very smoothly in as large circles as possible. Try to make the circles so large that you can feel the muscles in your back and chest loosening. Alternate the right then the left shoulder.

Repetitions: Repeat the movement 3 times backward and 3 times forward.

Shrugging the shoulders

Lift your shoulders up to your ears, then let them drop gently with gravity.

Repetitions: Repeat 3 times.

Rotating the shoulders using elbows

Touch your right-hand fingers to your right shoulder and rotate your elbow in the largest circles you can manage, then do the same with your left elbow.

Repetitions: Rotate each elbow 3 times backward and 3 times forward.

Note: Some people have difficulty touching their fingers to their shoulder. This is not a problem – simply place your fingers as near to your shoulder as possible.

Rotating the arms

Opening the collarbone

Rotate one arm at a time, slowly, in the largest circle you can comfortably manage.

Repetitions: Repeat 3 times backward and 3 times forward with each arm.

1 Start with feet shoulder-width apart with your arms by your sides, hands touching your thighs.

2 Turn both shoulders and hands backward, pinching your shoulder blades together, palms facing forward. Press your shoulder muscles down and keep your little fingers in contact with your thighs. Hold for 10 seconds.

Repetitions: Repeat 3 times.

Circling the wrists

Circling the fists

Rotating the hips

Hold both arms in front of you and rotate the wrists in the largest circles you can manage.

Repetitions: Rotate 3 times clockwise and 3 times anticlockwise.

Hold both arms in front of you and make fists. Rotate the wrists in the largest circles you can manage.

Repetitions: Rotate 3 times clockwise and 3 times anticlockwise.

Place your hands on your hips and circle your hips in large circles.

Repetitions: Rotate 3 times clockwise and 3 times anticlockwise.

Rotating the knees

Rotating the ankles

Place your hands on your hips and circle your knees in small circles.

Repetitions: Rotate 3 times clockwise and 3 times anticlockwise.

Caution: If you have knee problems, I would advise leaving this exercise out.

Place the toes of one foot slightly behind you, and circle the foot, keeping the toes on the floor.

Repetitions: Rotate 3 times clockwise and 3 times anticlockwise.

Foot rocking

Rock both feet gently from heel to toe, 3 times.

Rock both feet gently from side to side, 3 times.

Heel dropping

Rise up onto your toes and gently drop your heels to the floor using gravity so that you feel a slight vibration or shudder through the rest of your body.

Repetitions: Repeat 3 times.

Caution: If you have foot problems, I would advise leaving this exercise out.

Rock both feet to the outer edges and the inner edges, 3 times.

Shaking the arms and legs like jelly

Start by loosely shaking your right arm from the shoulder joint, then do the same for the left arm. Loosely shake your right leg from the hip joint, then the left leg. Feel that the joints you are shaking feel like jelly wobbling. When you shake your arm, feel the shoulder, elbow, wrist and finger joints loosen. When you shake your leg, feel the hip, knee, ankle and foot joints loosen. Feel that you are shaking all the tension away. You can have fun with this one and shake both arms and a leg together.

Spend about 10 seconds on each arm and leg.

Swinging the arms

Arm swinging is very popular in China because it opens up the chest and heart area, as well as relaxing the shoulders and offering all of the benefits mentioned previously. For many people, it is difficult to release muscular control of the arms, but try your best not to let muscle action interfere with the arm swinging. Let the arms completely relax and feel as though they are moving naturally with the momentum of the move. There are many ways to swing your arms, and some ways have their own special Qigong name, as do the three shown here.

LEFT: Swinging the pendulum.

MINGMEN

The Mingmen is an acupuncture point on the lower back of the body between the kidneys, just below the second lumbar vertebra. It is the fourth point along the Governing Vessel meridian. *Ming* means life and *men* means door or gate. The Mingmen is commonly referred to as the Door of Life.

Knocking on the Door of Life

The Door of Life refers to the Mingmen acupoint, which is said to provide you with extra energy when stimulated. It is a point on the Governing Vessel meridian, which is located on your back opposite your navel (see box, opposite). When your arms wrap around your waist with the momentum of this Qigong exercise, the back of your forearm or wrist will contact this point.

Start with feet shoulder-width apart, knees bent, and twist your spinal column from right to left. Allow your arms to swing loosely with the momentum of your waist turning and let them wrap around your body naturally. It is best to start gently with this swing and then increase the momentum gradually, if appropriate. If it makes you feel dizzy, perform it very slowly and gently.

Repetitions: Repeat the sequence 7 times or more.

Sparrow Shaking the Earth

A bird cannot fly without first putting weight down into the earth to provide a rebound effect for its liftoff. Imagine a tiny sparrow pushing all of its weight into the earth so that it has enough rebound energy to launch itself into flight. There are many stories of Chinese martial artists who hold a bird in their palm and each time the little bird pushes down to take off, the martial artist drops his hand at the right moment to prevent liftoff. They did not do this to be cruel to the little bird, but to demonstrate their sensitivity.

1 Start with feet shoulder-width apart. Swing your arms forward.

2 Shake your arms downward as you bend your knees and create a bouncing action.

3 Allow the rebound of the bounce to swing your arms behind you.

4 Shake your arms downward as you bend your knees and create a bouncing action. When swinging the arms, bend the elbows a little to keep the arms soft.

Repetitions: Repeat the sequence 7 times or more.

Swinging the Pendulum

A pendulum swings back and forth effortlessly through momentum. In this exercise, imagine that your arms are like pendulums and one swings in front of you to the left as the other swings behind you to the right, then vice versa. The momentum created with this swing is coordinated with bouncing your weight into the floor and feeling the rebound as part of the swing.

1 Start with feet shoulder-width apart with arms held loosely by your sides. Bend your knees to initiate the swing as you turn your waist to the left, at the same time swinging your right arm across the front of your body to the left and your left arm behind your body to the right. Allow your elbows to bend naturally with the swing.

2 Bend your knees as your arms come out to your sides mid-swing.

3 Bend your knees to initiate the swing and bounce weight into the ground as you turn your waist to the right, at the same time swinging your left arm across the front of your body to the right and your right arm behind your body to the left. Allow your elbows to bend naturally with the swing.

4 Bend your knees as your arms come out to your sides mid-swing.

Repetitions:
Repeat the sequence 7 times or more.

PART 4

Qigong Movements

Styles of Qigong

No one is quite certain how many styles of Qigong there are, because it's a bit like asking how many recipes for cookies there are. Most people are content with the idea that there are thousands of styles, but others like to give an exact estimate – which usually lies somewhere between three thousand and a hundred thousand.

Qigong knowledge was traditionally passed down from master to student with little or no documentation, but today there is a multitude of written and visual documentation covering many different styles. In fact, we now suffer from a surfeit of knowledge, with so many different styles and variations and opinions that it can sometimes seem like a confusing maze of information and opposing viewpoints.

Learning online or from a DVD or book is a possible alternative, but the assistance of a knowledgeable teacher is invaluable. Without the feedback from a qualified, experienced teacher, it can be difficult to know if we are doing movements correctly and to best effect. Certain aspects, for example misalignment, or attempting moves beyond your current physical ability, could result in injury.

All styles of Qigong are based on the same principles and have the characteristics of fluid movement without strain or effort. They all embody relaxation, natural breathing and tranquil awareness. All styles work to rebalance internal Qi energy, and to remove energy blockages in the body.

There is no particular value in learning numerous styles of Qigong. You will usually attain greater benefits in learning just one or two styles and spending time gaining a deeper understanding of them. Quality is far more important than quantity.

Styles are many and varied. Their origins are deeply rooted in Daoism, Buddhism, Confucianism, Traditional Chinese Medicine and martial arts. Over centuries the styles have blended and altered, and new styles are constantly being constructed. Sometimes this is at the request of an official institution, and sometimes because a Qigong master or doctor who has used Qigong to help his students, his patients or himself to recover from an illness, wishes to present moves in a new way that is more effective or simpler.

Selection of well-known Qigong forms

The following is a selection of different styles of Qigong, just to give you an idea of the variety available. Some have ancient roots and have changed very little over the centuries, while others are more modern.

Muscle-Tendon Change Classic – Yijinjing: This Qigong is based on exercises developed by Bodhidharma, a Buddhist monk, during his stay at the Shaolin temple in the 6th century. The best-known set practised today is based on a 12-movement set compiled by Pan Wei in the Qing Dynasty.

Five Animals – Wuqinxi: Also called The Five Animal Play, this is a form of Daoyin Qigong. It is based on the movements of the tiger, deer, bear, ape or monkey, and crane or bird, and is often credited to the physician Hua Tuo in the late Han dynasty. Many different versions developed in later centuries. See the Five Animal Qigong chapter.

Primordial Qigong – Wujigong: Tradition tells us that this was developed by the semi-legendary Daoist sage Zhang Sanfeng, who lived in the Wudang mountains during the Ming dynasty. Wujigong is said to predate his later creation of Taijiquan. It contains Daoist philosophy including the idea of wuji as original emptiness.

Six Healing Sounds – Liuzijue: In this Qigong, six different sounds are voiced on an exhalation. They can also be repeated silently to yourself. Each syllable resonates with different parts of the body.

RIGHT: Monkey plucking fruit – from Five Animal Qigong.

**Eight Pieces of Brocade –
Baduanjin:** This Qigong developed
from the ancient Daoyin techniques.
There is a standing style and a seated
style. There are several well-known
variations from the Qing dynasty. See
the Eight Pieces of Brocade chapter.

**Seated Twelve Pieces of Brocade
– Shierduanjin:** This Qigong was
a development of the Eight Pieces
of Brocade in the Qing dynasty. It
concentrates mainly on the upper
body. See the Seated Twelve Pieces
of Brocade chapter.

Standing like a Post – Zhanzhuang:
These are stationary positions and
the word "post" suggests a deeply
rooted tree. Zhanzhuang is viewed as
fundamental training in martial arts.
See the Standing like a Post chapter.

Health Preservation – Baojian:
This Qigong consists of self-massage
as well as slow, gentle movements.
It is a Daoyin technique combined
with massage and is practised in a
seated position.

Relaxation – Fangsong: This is
a modern Qigong. There is no
physical movement required and
it can be done while lying down or
while sitting. It involves conscious
relaxation from head to toe, with
visualizations.

**Eighteen Movements Taiji Qigong
– Shibashi:** Developed in 1979 by
Lin Housheng, this set of eighteen
movements is one of the most
popular Qigong sets in the world
today. See the Eighteen Movements
Qigong chapter.

Rejuvenation – Daojia Yangsheng:
Also called the Daoist Art of Nurturing
Life and Attaining Longevity, this was
created by Daoists in the Han dynasty.
It is a Daoyin technique aimed at
preserving health and restoring youth.

LEFT: Posture No.5
(Water) from Five
Element style Standing
Post Qigong.

Wild Goose – Dayan: This style originated over 1,800 years ago in the Jin dynasty from Daoist monks in the Kunlun mountains. There are many Wild Goose routines. Some are short while some are very long involving over 60 movements linked together. All of the moves are redolent of the grace and freedom of a wild goose.

Spontaneous – Zifagong: This technique of letting the body move by itself, without interference from the mind of the practitioner, requires a large, safe space. Spontaneous movements could involve bending, walking, twisting, shaking, lying or sitting on the floor, jumping, crying or laughing. As there is a risk of falling or being bumped by another participant, people with fragile joints or bones or with poor balance could be at risk. In addition, people with mental health illness or nervous disorders could be triggered into an unstable state of mind. At its best it can be a way of using the body's own intelligence to clear Qi blockages – moves that no one else would think of recommending because they are so individual. An experienced instructor is essential to prevent accidents or overreactions and bring everyone back to a relaxed and normal state of mind before leaving the class.

Emei Qigong: This is named after Mount Emei, a sacred mountain in Sichuan Province, China. Buddhists have built temples on Mount Emei since the 1st century CE, and 800 years ago a Buddhist monk developed Emei Qigong. In the 1970s it came to public notice when it was first taught openly to doctors and the general public by the 13th lineage holder, Wei Zhong Fu. This Qigong uses movement and sound vibration and is best known for its healing techniques.

Sleeping – Shuigong: This is different from normal sleeping. It involves techniques to bring the practitioner to a state that is just on the edge of sleep, where the body is completely relaxed and aware but appears to be sleeping. Reputed to develop abilities of healing and mysticism, and to provide insight into the future, it is linked with Daoist beliefs from a thousand years ago, having re-emerged in China in the late 1980s.

Fragrant – Xiangong: The fragrance refers mainly to the sweet smell of health. This unusual Qigong is reputed to have been kept secret for two thousand years. It came to be taught openly in China in the late 1980s by Master Tian Ruisheng, when he was lauded as the last living master of the style and a master of healing. There are different levels, and the first level consists of 15 simple movements.

Wisdom Healing – Zhineng: This is a set developed by Dr Ming Pang, who founded the Beijing Qigong Research

Society in 1979. With the focus on health and healing, the set has been used in hospitals and clinics. It is a combination of various ancient healing practices including sound vibration, movement and meditation.

Dragon and Tiger – Longhu: This set was first openly taught by Dr Zhang Jia Hua, who was Vice-President of the All China Qigong Association. She taught this form mainly during the 1970s and certified over 20,000 instructors. The inspiration is to develop the agility of a flying dragon and the relaxed power of a tiger.

Shaolin Qigong: In the 6th century, a Buddhist monk called Bodhidharma came to the Shaolin Monastery and taught the monks exercises to preserve their strength and health. These Qigong exercises have been handed down through the centuries and are still taught at the Shaolin Monastery today. Although the Shaolin monks are famous for their athletic feats requiring hard Qigong, the Shaolin health Qigong is internal, soft Qigong.

Neigong: The roots for Neigong and Qigong are the same. Many people debate whether Neigong is a form of Qigong. Neigong means internal cultivation or skill and is usually associated with internal Chinese martial arts such as Taijiquan, Baguazhang and Xingyiquan. Qigong concentrates more on the breath and circulation, and Neigong concentrates more on the internal organs and nervous system. The purpose of Neigong is to train a high level of coordination, stamina and internal strength while relaxing muscles, sinews, nerves and joints. The set that I learned is comprised of Twelve Yin and Twelve Yang exercises, which require a great deal of time and commitment to practise.

Individual Qigong moves

In addition to countless sets of Qigong, there are also thousands of well-known individual Qigong moves. Some are moves that have been taken from an existing set to be practised individually. Others have been developed over centuries as individual Qigong exercises. See the A Collection of Favourites chapter.

Modern sets

New sets are regularly being compiled. There was an explosion of new styles in China in the 1980s and 1990s. Many of these were styles that had been kept secret for centuries and passed down orally through generations, but were made public because of the new spirit of the age.

Ancient sources are constantly employed for new inspiration.

Master teachers select from existing sets of Qigong and include them in modern sets, sometimes with new modifications. Sometimes they include moves taken from Taiji forms and repeat them with slight variations as Qigong moves. Sometimes masters base new forms on principles underlying techniques from the past and repackage them to be more attractive and relevant to modern-day society – names might include Weight Loss Qigong, Beauty Qigong, Qigong of Unconditional Love, Healthy Living Qigong, Infinite Qigong or Core Energy Qigong. Some of these new sets are excellent, and there is no doubt that hundreds more new forms of Qigong will appear in the future.

Over the years, I have become familiar with many of the styles mentioned in this chapter. The styles of Qigong that I currently practise and teach are Standing like a Post, Twelve Yin and Twelve Yang Neigong, Eight Pieces of Brocade, Eighteen Movements, Seated Twelve Pieces of Brocade, Five Animals, Shaolin Qigong and all of the individual Qigong movements in the chapter A Collection of Favourites.

RIGHT: Initial position for Bending and Twisting like Bamboo, see page 139.

A Collection of Favourites

There are thousands of Qigong exercises that do not belong to a particular set and are great fun to practise on their own. I would encourage you to try some of the exercises in this chapter. If you find certain ones that you especially like and that you feel work well together, then do compose a set of your own choosing. For a balanced practice you will need to mix stances.

For example, choose one in a Shoulder-width Stance (see pages 54–5), one in a Horse Stance (see pages 58–9), one that involves balancing or putting weight on one leg, and one where you shift your weight forward into a Bow stance (see page 64).

I have suggested a number of repetitions and timings, but as you become more experienced, use the number of repetitions and timings that are right for your current needs. Create adaptations to any move, making it more accessible. For example, hold on to a solid chair or table if you need to steady yourself, before trying out a challenging move requiring balance skills.

There are different opinions as to which foot should be put forward first. Some people say it should be the left foot, others prefer the right, and they all have their reasons. With the exercises that follow, it doesn't really matter which foot you decide to use first. Having said that, with any exercise involving balance it is helpful to use your strongest leg first, in order to build confidence.

You may wish to browse through the Basic Stances chapter, if an unfamiliar stance is mentioned.

LEFT: Bouncing a Ball, see pages 120–1.

Soaring Dragonfly

To be a dragonfly soaring over a pond is a magical image. Its colours are iridescent in the sunshine, and its beauty and speed symbolize living life to the full. In China, people associate the dragonfly with harmony, prosperity and good luck.

Repetitions: Repeat the sequence 1 to 3 times.

HEALTH BENEFITS

Soaring Dragonfly increases balance, energy and overall strength. It also builds confidence.

Start with feet shoulder-width apart. Transfer your weight to your left leg and lift your right leg so it is parallel to the ground, or as high as your balance will allow. Keep your pelvis level and avoid the tendency to lift the hip higher on the side that has the raised leg. Reach forward with your arms and soar. Repeat on the other side. Hold the posture for 30 seconds or more on each side.

Breathing: Breathe smoothly and abdominally throughout (see pages 67–8).

Modified: To begin, you might like to keep your back toes in contact with the floor, or hold onto a table or chair. When you gain confidence, lift your foot slightly off the floor.

Little Buddha Praying

This charming and very popular sequence conjures up the image of a young Buddhist child praying, within a movement that contains poise, balance and devotion.

1 Start with feet shoulder-width apart with your feet parallel and arms relaxed by your sides.

2 Bring your feet together and bring your palms together into a prayer position.

3 Raise your palms over your head. Keep your shoulders relaxed and down.

Repetitions: Repeat the sequence 7 times.
Once to the left and right = 1 repetition.

4 Step out lightly to the left into a Horse Stance (see pages 58–9) as you lower your hands to shoulder height with fingers up.

HEALTH BENEFITS

This beautiful sequence trains your balance and coordination. It exercises and strengthens the whole body while improving your ability to move gracefully and smoothly.

---

5 Continue to circle your arms downward. At hip height bring your palms together and lift them upward along your centreline to chest height as you shift your weight smoothly to your left leg and place your right foot behind your knee.

continued next page →

6 Bend your left knee and sink your weight.

7 Keeping your palms together, raise them over your head as you straighten your supporting leg.

8 Step out lightly to the right into a Horse Stance as you lower your hands to shoulder height with fingers up.

Modified: If you have ankle, knee or hip problems, use a smaller, higher stance. Also, rather than tucking your foot behind your knee, place your toes on the ground, beside the other foot in a Nail Stance (see page 62).

9 Continue to circle your arms downward. At hip height bring your palms together and lift them upward along your centreline to chest height as you shift your weight smoothly to your right leg and place your left foot behind your knee.

10 Bend your right knee and sink your weight.

Ending the sequence: To finish, lower the foot tucked behind your knee and bring it into a Shoulder-width Stance (see pages 54–5). Bring your palms to rest at the Lower Dantian (see pages 20–1).

Breathing: Breathe in when you lift your arms. Breathe out when you lower your arms. Breathe in when you tuck your foot behind your knee. Breathe out when you bend your knee.

Retrieving Moon from Sea

This move contains an allusion to an ancient Chinese poet who became so drunk, with both wine and the beauty of the moon, that he tried to scoop up the moon from the water.

Repetitions: Repeat 7 or more times, taking note of how your body responds before doing more repetitions. Martial artists do as many as 360 repetitions.

> **HEALTH BENEFITS**
> There is a saying that you are as youthful as your spine. This exercise encourages a flexible spine and hips, strong legs and good balance – all qualities essential for a youthful body.

1 Stand with your feet wider than hip width apart, and squat with your spine parallel to the ground, eyes looking at the floor, and arms straight between your legs, with palms facing each other behind your legs.

2 Reach forward and up, lengthening your spine.

Breathing: There are two choices; choose the method that is most natural for you.

- The first choice is easier and more suitable for beginners. Breathe out as you squat, breathe in as you stretch up, breathe out as you lean back, and breathe in as you return to vertical.
- The second choice is more suitable if you are experienced and your breathing is slow and smooth. Breathe in as you bend forward and squat, and breathe out as you stretch up and lean back.

Whichever pattern you choose, It is important to breathe out when you lean back, because your spine naturally extends on the exhalation.

Modified: If you have high or low blood pressure or feel like taking it easy, make your squat higher and lean forward only to 45 degrees. If you have back or neck problems, there is no need to lean back. Simply reach up and look up.

3 Bend backward by bending your knees and pushing your hips forward so that you can feel the backward curve from your heels to your fingertips. It is important not to bend only from your waist, as this could place undue compression on your lumbar vertebrae.

4 Return to your starting squatting position.

Tiger Embraces Head

Imagine that you are a fierce tiger wanting to hug another tiger by wrapping your arm around its neck or head. This image reminds you that it is a hook punch, which means that you will have a 90-degree bend at the elbow.

Repetitions: Repeat the sequence 7 times, and work up to a number that suits your needs.

Feel the connection between your waist, hips and legs as you turn. Your hips and legs will move slightly when you twist your waist, and it's important to allow the whole body to flow with the move while feeling rooted to the floor through your feet.

1 Stand in a Horse Stance (see pages 58–9) with your fists turned upward at your hips.

2 Twist your waist to the left as you curve your right forearm to deliver a hook punch. As you twist, bend your elbow to 90 degrees with the fist palm down.

3 Twist your waist to the right as you deliver a hook punch with your left fist, palm down, elbow bent at 90 degrees. At the same time, retract your right arm, twisting the forearm so that the fist is palm up by the time it reaches your hip.

HEALTH BENEFITS

This builds strong legs and a firm, rooted base, which means more power and better balance. The twisting of the waist makes you agile and supple and massages internal organs. The twisting of the forearms is good for joint and tendon mobility in the arms.

Breathing: Breathe out as you twist to deliver the punch and breathe in during the transition. This exercise can also be done more quickly to train the waist, in which case there is no need to match the breath to the move, simply breathe smoothly and abdominally.

Pushing Mountains

To move the immovable is quite a task to set yourself. The hidden meaning implies that you are like a mountain yourself and by attempting the impossible, you become strong and grounded, just like the mountain you are pushing. You will become able to achieve things that are extremely difficult.

1 Stand in a medium-height Horse Stance (see pages 58–9) with fists at your hips.

2 Sink down into a low Horse Stance as you push your right hand forward to finish with your palm facing away and fingers pointing up.

Repetitions: Repeat the sequence 7 times.

HEALTH BENEFITS

This mobilizes all the joints in the body and strengthens the arms, shoulders and legs. If you imagine you are pushing a mountain, this creates such a strong mental image that you feel more rooted and stable, much like the mountain you are pushing.

Modified: If you have knee problems, stay in a high Horse Stance.

3 Retract your right hand and make a fist at your hips as you return to a medium-height Horse Stance.

4 Repeat with the left hand.

Breathing: Breathe out as you push your palm forward. Breathe in as you retract your hand and make a fist.

Heavy Elbows

With this exercise, gravity is your helper. Imagine that heavy weights are attached to your elbows, pulling you lower and lower effortlessly.

1 Fold your forearms across one another and bend forward from your hips with your knees slightly bent. Imagine that there is a weight pulling your elbows to the floor. Stay there for a minute or more, and on each exhalation imagine that the weight on your elbows is increasing, encouraging you to stretch your back further.

2 Twist to the left as far as you feel is comfortable. Remain there for up to 30 seconds.

Repetitions: Repeat the sequence 1 to 3 times.

Breathing: Use slow, smooth, abdominal breathing throughout the exercise.

Modified: If you have high or low blood pressure or any condition that makes you feel dizzy, try bending forward only a little at first, and if you find that the exercise isn't right for you, put it to one side for the time being.

3 Twist to the right as far as you feel is comfortable. Remain there for up to 30 seconds.

4 Twist back to the front for up to a minute and feel your back and legs continue to stretch.

Ending the sequence:
To end, slowly roll up, bringing your head up last.

HEALTH BENEFITS

This exercise stretches your hamstrings, hips, shoulders and neck. It decompresses the spine and neck. When you twist, you add a stretch to the sides of your body. It also calms the mind.

Rising Star

This Qigong definitely makes you feel like a child again, pretending to be a star with your two arms, two legs and head forming the five points of the star. Our model makes it look easy, but it requires a lot of core strength and you may need to modify it at the beginning.

1 Lie on your back with arms and legs apart.

2 Raise your head, arms and legs up from the floor. Imagine that energy is radiating out from your body's centre through your legs and arms.

Repetitions: Repeat 3 times and hold for up to 30 seconds each time.

Breathing: Breathe smoothly and abdominally throughout. In this posture there is a tendency to hold your breath, so keep your attention on continuous, smooth breathing to prevent this.

HEALTH BENEFITS

Rising Star strengthens all core muscles of the body.

Modified: If you have any back or neck problems or high blood pressure, keep your legs on the floor and lift your upper body only. Hold only for 3 seconds to start, and build up the length of time holding the position as is appropriate for you.

Swimming Dragon

In Chinese mythology, a dragon swims in the sky as well as in the water and makes intricate circles and loops along its flight path. This popular exercise involves making three horizontal figure-of-eight patterns: one at head height, one at chest height and one as low as you feel comfortable with. When you trace your figure-of-eight patterns, use your wrists as much as possible, bending the underneath wrist back with light pressure from the top hand on every downward swoop of the figure of eight.

1 Start with feet shoulder-width apart with the palms of your hands pressed together and retain this hand position throughout.

2 Start your horizontal figure of eight to the left and push out your right hip. Make your first figure of eight at head height.

3 When your arms swoop to the right, move your hips in the opposite direction, to mimic the dramatic swirling of a coiling dragon.

Repetitions: Repeat the sequence 7 times.

continued next page →

4 Make your second figure of eight shape at chest height.

Breathing: Breathe in when your hands move to the left. Breathe out when your hands move to the right. Breathe in when you rise up onto your toes. Breathe out when you lower your heels.

6 After completing your lowest figure of eight, bring your hands to your centreline.

HEALTH BENEFITS

This exercise mobilizes every part of your body and is great fun to perform. It improves balance and mobility.

5 Make your third figure of eight as low as you feel comfortable with.

7 Straighten your legs as you lift your arms above your head and rise up onto your toes.

8 Lower your heels as you bring your palms back to your starting position.

Exchanging Heaven and Earth

Heaven is Yang and earth is Yin. In this exercise one arm is rising, palm up, toward heaven. The other arm is lowering, palm down, toward earth. As you change your arm position, you are symbolically exchanging Yin and Yang. The idea is to balance the spiritual qualities of heaven with the material qualities of nature into a healthy vibrant person who lives in harmony with all things.

Modified: Many people have stiff shoulders and need to modify moves. If your shoulders are stiff, bend your elbows more and push up and down to either side of your centreline. If shoulder stiffness prevents your hand from pushing straight upward, alter the angle to push more forward.

1 Before you begin, imagine that your shoulder joints are young and springy. Stand with feet shoulder-width apart and stretch your right arm upward with your palm toward the sky, and stretch your left arm hand downward with your palm toward the earth. Line your hands up along your centreline.

HEALTH BENEFITS

This improves shoulder and arm flexibility and also breath coordination.

2 Bring both palms toward each other until they are at chest height, both palms turned down.

3 Stretch your left arm upward, palm toward the sky, and your right hand downward, palm toward the earth.

Breathing: Breathe out as your arms stretch upward and downward. Breathe in as your hands come toward each other at chest height.

Repetitions: Repeat the sequence 7 times.

Rolling the Qi Ball

We hold an imaginary ball of Qi energy between our hands throughout this exercise. (See How to Feel Your Qi Ball, page 169).

1 Begin in a Back Stance (see page 60) with most of your weight on your back foot, and your left foot forward on the heel.

2 As you lift the Qi ball forward in a gentle arc, transfer your weight forward into a Bow Stance (see page 64).

3 As you roll the Qi ball backward, transfer your weight into a Back Stance with your front toes lifted.

HEALTH BENEFITS

Rocking from a Back Stance to a Bow Stance builds strength and balance and improves circulation through the legs. Lifting the front toes aids ankle mobility. Feeling the Qi Ball makes you more sensitive to your own electromagnetic field.

Repetitions: Repeat 7 times with the left leg forward, and 7 times with the right leg forward.

Breathing: Breathe out as you transfer your weight forward. Breathe in as you transfer your weight back.

Punching to the Sides with a Fierce Glare

This brave warrior has a fierce glare and displays martial spirit. Look straight ahead with intensity, but without pinching your eyebrows together.

Take a large Horse Stance (see pages 58–9) and punch out to the sides of your body with your fists turned so the palms are down. Use your peripheral vision to include your fists within your field of vision. Imagine that Qi energy is directed outward through your eyes and arms, and stay mentally connected to your Lower Dantian (see pages 20–1). Keep your shoulders relaxed and down. Hold for 30 seconds to 2 minutes.

Repetitions: Repeat 1 to 3 times.

Breathing: Breathe smoothly and abdominally throughout (see pages 67–8).

HEALTH BENEFITS

This exercise increases your overall strength and energy. The use of your eyes and intention increases mental focus.

Modified: Use a small, high Horse Stance (see page 58). Hold for 10 seconds.

Opening a Fan

Folding fans first became fashionable in China in the Song Dynasty (960–1279 CE) and were often made of beautifully painted precious materials. They were opened just far enough to show the poetry or design to advantage without causing stress to the fan's ribs and folds. Imagine that your whole body is a folding fan. When you reach up, your fan is folded. When you twist and open your arms out, your fan opens. When your arms open, be gentle so that your fan is shown to best advantage.

PERIPHERAL VISION

This is the part of our vision that occurs outside the centre of our gaze. As we age, our field of vision can narrow, but it is possible to train it back again, as long as there are no medical conditions preventing this. Look straight ahead and stretch your arms out to the sides and try to see both hands. If you can't see them, move them forward and closer together until you can just see both hands. Keep looking straight ahead and move your hands outward again by just a tiny amount, and eventually you will be able to retrain your eyes to see a wider field. Scientists have found that this type of training stimulates brain activity relating to memory and focus.

1 Stand with feet shoulder-width apart and bring your palms up to face each other, without touching, at chest height.

2 Lift your arms straight above your head.

Repetitions: Repeat 7 times. Once twisting left and once twisting right = 1 repetition.

Breathing: Breathe in as you lift your arms. Breathe out as you lower your arms.

3 Turn your waist to the right and bend your knees as you open your arms out to your sides at shoulder height, palms outward, with the fingers pointing up and the elbows bent down just a little. Turn your head as a unit with your spine so that you can see both hands – this trains your peripheral vision.

4 Turn your waist back to the front as you straighten your knees and lift your arms over your head with palms facing each other but not touching.

continued next page →

HEALTH BENEFITS

Twisting the waist massages the internal organs. This exercise strengthens and tones the whole body. It also trains peripheral vision.

5 Lower your hands to chest height to your starting position.

6 Lift your arms straight above your head.

7 Turn your waist to the left and bend your knees as you open your arms out to the sides at shoulder height, palms outward, with the fingers pointing up and the elbows bent down just a little. Turn your head as a unit with your spine so that you can see both hands.

Holding a Golden Plate of Fruit

Different kinds of fruits confer different types of blessings in Chinese culture. For example, fresh fruit symbolizes life and new beginnings and is popular as an offering to friends and relatives. Make sure that you have a few peaches on your plate, as this is a symbol of longevity. With this Qigong you are truly bending over backward to please your guests!

Repetitions: Repeat 1 to 3 times.

Breathing: Breathe out as you lean back and continue to breathe abdominally (see pages 67–8) throughout the hold. If you lean back quite far, your abdomen will be stretched to maximum, in which case it is better to breathe into the sides of your body, expanding your ribcage on each inhalation.

HEALTH BENEFITS

Increases flexibility of the hips and spine as well as developing core strength.

Stand in a Horse Stance (see pages 58–9) with palms facing up at either side of your head, elbows bent. Lift your chest and arch your upper back as you push your hips forward and lean back. Keep your palms facing the ceiling so that you don't drop any fruit, as you bend further back. Keep your chest and ribcage lifted during the hold so that you don't compress the lumbar spine. Hold for between 30 seconds and 1 minute. Return to an upright position without dropping your fruit.

Modified: If you have any back or neck problems, don't lean back. Just look up.

Bouncing a Ball

This exercise is often utilized as a preparation for Walking on Clouds (see pages 122–3), but you can also use it on its own. Use Fair Lady's Hand (see box, opposite) throughout the sequence.

1 Place your left foot forward in a Cat Stance (see page 61). Keep your supporting leg slightly bent throughout the sequence. Imagine that there is an invisible string from the middle of your palm attached to the top of your knee.

2 Lift your left wrist as though you are lifting the knee with the imaginary string.

3 Lower your wrist as though you are lowering the knee with the imaginary string.

Variation: Sometimes the exercise is performed by lifting the foot with the opposite hand, which is slightly more difficult for the coordination, but fun to try.

FAIR LADY'S HAND

This is used in Qigong and in Chinese martial arts. Imagine that you are moving your hand through water. Raise your hand as though it is being lifted by the wrist bone, with fingers relaxed downward. Now sink your hand down, led by the heel of the palm which creates a lift through the fingers so that they float upward.

Modified: Place one foot forward, and when you lift your knee with the invisible string, lift only your heel – keep your toes on the ground.

Repetitions: Repeat 7 times on the left and 7 times on the right.

Breathing: Breathe in as you lift your leg. Breathe out as you lower your leg.

HEALTH BENEFITS

Bouncing a Ball strengthens the stabilizing muscles of the legs and improves balance, stability and grace of movement.

Walking on Clouds

This is a well-known Qigong circle-walking exercise (see pages 42–3). It is popular throughout the world and is also used in Chinese hospitals and clinics, often alongside Western medicine, to strengthen and energize patients with many different conditions, including cancer. The only criterion is that the patient is strong enough to walk.

Your steps should be light and agile, as though you are walking on clouds. No one should be able to hear your footfalls. Roll your foot as much as possible into the next step. When the heel of your front foot sets down, roll through to the tip of the big toe. When your back heel starts to lift, roll through to the tip of the big toe before lifting your foot.

1 Start with feet shoulder-width apart and spend a few moments to calm your mind with slow abdominal breathing (see pages 67–8).

2 Lift up your right hand and imagine a piece of string attached across your body to lift up your left knee. Keep your supporting leg slightly bent at the knee.

3 Lower your right hand as you lightly touch your left heel to the ground.

HEALTH BENEFITS

The longer you practise and the slower you walk, the stronger and better balanced you will become. After a few minutes of quiet practice, circle walking becomes lightly meditative, which is soothing to the mind and nervous system.

Breathing: Breathe in as you slowly lift your leg. Breathe out as you slowly lower your leg and transfer your weight.

4 Roll your left foot down and transfer all of your weight to your left leg, as your back foot rolls up and your right hand comes to rest at your side.

5 Raise your left hand and your right leg.

6 Lower your left hand as you lightly set down your right heel.

7 Roll your right foot down and transfer all of your weight to your right leg, as your left hand comes to rest at your side.

Continue walking your circle. Start with one complete circle, which should take you 2 to 5 minutes to complete, depending on the size of your circle, and increase repetitions as you progress.

Ending the sequence:
End as you began in a Shoulder-width Stance (see pages 54–5) and spend a few moments to feel grounded and connected to the earth, before moving away.

Embracing the Moon

The moon has always been of great significance in Chinese culture. The full moon is seen as a sign of good fortune, abundance and harmony. On the 15th day of the 8th month of the lunar calendar, as the Autumn moon waxes into its full glory, the Chinese celebrate the Moon Festival. By embracing the moon, the implication is that you are embracing good fortune and harmony.

Repetitions: Repeat the exercise 7 times to the left and 7 times to the right.

Breathing: Breathe in as you lift your arms up. Breathe out as you bring your arms down.

1 Stand in a Horse Stance (see pages 58–9) with your arms slightly curved and the palms up, as though holding a two-dimensional moon or disc. Hold this imaginary disc throughout the exercise.

4 Shift your weight to your right leg until your left leg is almost straight. At the same time circle your arms over to the right and downward to shoulder height.

HEALTH BENEFITS

Creates flexibility in the hips and shoulders and develops leg strength and balance.

2 Shift your weight to your left leg until your right leg is almost straight. At the same time circle your arms over to the left and upward to shoulder height.

3 Shift your weight back into a horse stance as you circle your disc to above your head.

5 Shift your weight into a Horse Stance as you circle the disc back to your starting position, lowering your Horse Stance if possible, so that your hips feel springy at the lowest part of the circle.

Modified: Take a high, small Horse Stance and make smaller circles with your arms.

Yin Yang Circles

Yin and Yang are the complementary forces in nature that interact in an eternal dance of life. The Yin Yang symbol depicts a dynamic balance between the two opposites, divided by an S-shaped curve. In this Qigong you trace this "S" curve with the little finger side of your hand, symbolically tracing and becoming part of the delicate balance of harmony. Your hand will trace only the inner spiral shape of the Yin Yang circle, which changes over at halfway, so thinking of it as a very curvy figure of eight will make this Qigong much easier.

1 Stand in a Back Stance (see page 60) with your weight on your right leg. Bring your right arm to rest behind your waist, where it will remain throughout the sequence. Lift your left hand to just above head height, palm down.

2 As you transfer your weight forward into a Bow Stance (see page 64), trace the downward spiral as though drawing with the little finger side of the left hand, turning your waist to move your arm.

HEALTH BENEFITS

Yin Yang Circles increase flexibility through the shoulders, arms, hips and waist and improve balance. The additional twisting and the challenge of coordination improve proprioception, see box, page 128.

Repetitions: Repeat 7 times on the left and 7 times on the right.

Breathing: Breathe out as you transfer your weight forward, and breathe in as you transfer your weight back.

3 Remain in a Bow stance as you bring your hand to the bottom of the downward spiral.

4 Remain in a Bow Stance as you turn your waist to move your left hand across to the side of your left knee.

continued next page ➡

5 As you transfer your weight back, turn your wrist up to enable you to trace the upward spiral as though drawing with the little finger side of your left hand.

6 Bring your left hand to just above head height, palm down, ready to start your next Yin Yang Circle.

PROPRIOCEPTION

Our body's ability to sense where our arms and legs and other parts of our body are in space and in relationship to each other, without having to look, is called proprioception. If a joint has been damaged in any way, or if there has been damage to the nervous system, proprioceptive ability usually needs to be retrained. By using exercises like Yin Yang Circles, which challenge your coordination and spatial awareness, proprioception can be retrained. To start with, simply trace a figure of eight with your hand, which you can do sitting down or standing. Later, add in the challenge of transferring your weight from a Back Stance to a Bow Stance.

Seven Stars Stance

The star constellation known as Ursa Major, popularly known as The Great Bear, The Big Dipper or The Plough, contains seven bright stars. These seven stars had great significance to the Chinese, and many stories were formed around them. Chinese astronomers called this constellation the Jade Balance of Fate, and Chinese peasants called it the Grain Measure. References are made to the seven stars in Qigong, Taiji and other Chinese martial arts.

Repetitions: Repeat the sequence 1 to 3 times.

Breathing: Breathe smoothly and abdominally (see pages 67–8) while holding the stance.

HEALTH BENEFITS

This posture is used for stance training, which helps build strength throughout the body. It also develops will and fortitude.

Stand in a Back Stance (see page 60) with your left foot forward on the heel. Place your left hand on your centreline, with the fingertips at nose height. Place your right hand with the fingertips pointing toward your left wrist. Relax your elbows and shoulders. Repeat on the right. Hold for between 30 seconds and 5 minutes each side.

Modified: Hold in a high stance for a short length of time. Start with 10 seconds and build up from there.

Drawing a Circle

The circle is a powerful symbol in all cultures. In China it means fulfilment and completeness. It has no beginning and no end and therefore is a symbol of eternity. By drawing the shape of a circle with your hands, you are participating in the ultimate perfection of oneness.

1 Stand in a Horse Stance (see pages 58–9), hands at chest height with palms facing each other. Try to keep the fingers turned upward throughout the move.

2 Lift your hands straight up above your head.

Breathing: Breathe in when you lift the hands. Breathe out when you push your hands out to the sides and downward.

Repetitions: Repeat 7 times.

HEALTH BENEFITS

Exercises and strengthens the wrists, forearms and shoulders.

3 Bring your arms downward, keeping the fingers up. Separate your hands out to the sides with fingers up and palms pushing away.

4 At hip height, turn your fingers inward toward each other, still attempting to keep the fingers turned up. Keep your hands moving up your centreline to your starting position for your next repetition.

Standing on One Leg with Hands on Balloons

Imagine how placing your hands on huge balloons would improve your balance. With this exercise you have the opportunity to try it, but with imaginary balloons. You might be surprised how well they work!

Repetitions: Repeat the sequence 1 to 3 times.

Breathing: Use slow, smooth, abdominal breathing (see pages 67–8) throughout the exercise.

Modified: Stand on your left leg with your knee slightly bent, with the heel of your right leg lifted. Hold this position from 30 seconds to 2 minutes. Repeat with the other leg.

Place your hands at hip height as though they are resting on imaginary balloons. Stand on your left leg with your knee slightly bent and lift your right knee into a Crane Stance (see page 63). Hold this position for between 30 seconds and 2 minutes. Repeat with the other leg.

HEALTH BENEFITS

This exercise trains the balance. As we age, our balance deteriorates, but we can train it back again with simple Qigong exercises like this one. Good balance reduces the risk of falling and builds confidence.

Holding a Ball in a Cat Stance

A cat can stay poised for long lengths of time if it is patiently waiting and watching. It is fun to pretend you can be as poised as a cat.

HEALTH BENEFITS

Standing Qigong builds strength and balance throughout the body. It also builds the mental qualities of determination, patience and calm.

Modified: Use a Shoulder-width Stance (see pages 54–5). After practising for some weeks, you may feel strong enough to try a Cat Stance for 30 seconds or longer. Or try 3 repetitions of the sequence, holding for only 10 seconds at a time with each leg.

Hold an imaginary ball. Transfer your weight onto your strongest leg first, slightly bending your knee. Lift your other knee into a Cat Stance (see page 61). Hold for 2–5 minutes. Repeat with your other leg forward. This is a Standing Like a Post exercise (see pages 170–9) which is very popular and often used on its own to build strength, energy and equanimity.

Breathing: Use slow, smooth, abdominal breathing (see pages 67–8) throughout the exercise.

Embracing Arms

What is it that you are embracing? You are embracing "The One" but in this exercise you must be prepared to let it go. It will always be there waiting for your gentle embrace, as long as you are willing to let it go. Embracing The One is a common theme in Daoism. It means that you are embracing the source of creation, but if you grasp too fiercely in an attempt to control it, you will lose all it represents.

1 Stand in a Back Stance (see page 60) with your left foot forward, toes up and your arms by your sides with palms up at hip height.

2 As you begin to transfer your weight forward, move your arms out to the sides and upward, palms down.

Repetitions: Repeat 7 times with your left foot forward and 7 times with your right foot forward.

Breathing: Breathe out as you transfer your weight forward. Breathe in as you transfer your weight back.

HEALTH BENEFITS

This enhances circulation and the feeling of flow. When performed like the ebbing and flowing of the tide, the movement is very soothing to the nervous system.

3 Continue to transfer your weight forward into a Bow Stance (see page 64) with your palms down at chest height in front of you.

4 As you transfer your weight back, bring your arms down toward your hips with palms up, ready for your next repetition.

Bear Pushing a Wall

In the Han Dynasty (206 BCE to 220 CE), the bear was honoured and used as a totem. The art of the period – such as jade objects, lacquerwork, pottery and bronze mirrors – was decorated with images of bears. In Feng Shui, placing a representation of a bear inside the entrance of your house is thought to protect the house and its inhabitants. Bears are calm, courageous creatures with mighty paws that can push over any obstacle. With this Qigong, your palms are emulating the strong paws of a bear in your endeavour to push over a wall.

1 Stand in a Horse Stance (see pages 58–9) and bring your hands to chest height, palms up, with the fingers of each hand pointing toward each other.

2 Twist your waist to the left as you sink your weight, and push out at shoulder height. The bear is pushing a wall, which means you will need to extend your right arm more in order to give a level push against the imaginary wall.

Modified: If you have any knee problems, stay in a high Horse Stance throughout the sequence. Twist your upper body only 45 degrees and push to the corner.

HEALTH BENEFITS

Twisting in a Horse Stance stimulates the internal organs, especially the kidneys and intestines. The mental image of a strong bear pushing against a wall strengthens the body and the mind.

Repetitions: Repeat the sequence 7 times. Pushing to the left and right = 1 repetition.

Breathing: Breathe out as you twist and lower your stance. Breathe in as you lift into a higher stance and return to the front.

3 As you twist back to the front, bring your palms back to your starting position.

4 Twist your waist to the right as you sink your weight, and push out at shoulder height. Extend your left arm more in order to give a level push against the imaginary wall.

5 As you twist back to the front, bring your palms back to your starting position.

Weight Shifting

Who would have thought that such a simple exercise could be so useful? When standing, our venous system must move our blood against the force of gravity. When we stand still for long lengths of time, the blood pools in our leg veins, and our legs, ankles and feet can ache and swell.

1 Stand with feet shoulder-width apart with your arms relaxed at the sides of your body.

2 Bend both knees, press into the floor with your right foot and slowly transfer all of your weight to your left leg.

3 Keep both knees bent, press into the floor with your left foot and slowly transfer all of your weight to your right leg.

HEALTH BENEFITS

This pumps blood through the lower legs and improves circulation. The action of weight shifting squeezes the leg muscles, which encourages the venous pump and helps prevent blood from pooling in the feet and ankles. It also massages the feet.

Repetitions: Repeat the sequence 7 times or more.

Breathing: Breathe in as you transfer weight to the left. Breathe out as you transfer weight to the right.

Bending and Twisting like Bamboo

Bamboo is a Chinese symbol of longevity because of its natural resilience.
It has deep roots and an innate pliancy that allows it to bend in the wind and
go with the natural flow of nature. Its smooth exterior and straight, graceful
lines symbolize virtue and simplicity. When you bend and twist like bamboo,
you will become flexible and strong like this revered plant.

1 Stand with feet shoulder-width apart with your fingers interlocked above your head, palms up. Stretch upward through the heels of your palms. Keep the palms up and fingers interlocked throughout the sequence.

2 Bend from your hips over to the left, far enough for you to feel a stretch through your right side.

3 Return to your starting position.

Repetitions: Repeat the sequence 7 times.

continued next page →

5 Return to your starting position.

6 Twist to the left as far as is comfortable.

4 Bend from your hips over to the right, far enough for you to feel a stretch through your left side.

Breathing: Breathe out as you bend to the side. Breathe in as you return to upright. Breathe out as you twist. Breathe in as you return to the front.

HEALTH BENEFITS
Builds strength and flexibility through the arms and shoulders. Stretches the sides of the body. Stimulates the internal organs.

7 Return to your starting position.

8 Twist to the right as far as is comfortable.

9 Return to your starting position.

Modified: If you are not used to keeping your arms up for long periods of time, or if you have any back, neck or shoulder problems, start with 1 repetition and increase the number of repetitions when you feel ready.

Rotating the Waist to Strengthen the Kidneys

In Traditional Chinese Medicine, the kidneys are believed to be your most important organs. They are located just below the ribcage, one on each side of the spine. Every day the network of filters within the kidneys purifies your blood of waste products, allowing your body to function well. Good health relies on balanced and abundant kidney Qi, which is thought to nourish and strengthen all of the other internal organs. This exercise massages and warms the kidneys and strengthens your kidney Qi.

Repetitions: Repeat 7 times to the left and 7 times to the right.

1 Start with feet shoulder-width apart with your palms on your kidneys and your thumbs pointing forward around your waist.

2 Bend forward from your hips as far as is comfortable.

3 Bend to the left, moving your hips to the right.

HEALTH BENEFITS

This strengthens and limbers the waist, and massages the kidneys, which "tones" them and increases blood circulation.

Modified: If you have any back or neck problems, or any blood pressure issues, don't lean forward or back more than a few degrees. If you have any wrist or hand problems, place the backs of your hands on the kidneys.

Note: Circle your upper body smoothly throughout the complete circle, with no stopping points.

Breathing: Breathe in as you circle to the left. Breathe out as you circle to the right.

4 Lean back and push your hips forward.

5 Bend to the right, moving your hips to the left.

6 Circle back to your bending-forward position, ready for your next repetition.

Bird's Beak to Palm Strike

The martial meaning of forming a "bird's beak" is to hold the fingers together to enable them to strike with force and yet be protected from damage. A bird's beak is incredibly strong and so is a good image for martial use. From a health point of view, this is an excellent exercise to bring strength and flexibility to the shoulders, forearms and wrists.

Repetitions: Repeat the sequence 7 times.

BIRD'S BEAK HAND

Used in Chinese martial arts, the Bird's Beak hand is sometimes called a Hook hand, referring to one of the martial applications. Drop your fingers down from the wrist and bring your thumb to touch the other fingers. Hold your wrist bone up as the highest point of the hand.

1 Stand in a Horse Stance (see pages 58–9) with your arms lifted out at about 45 degrees to your sides. Make your hands into Birds' Beaks just above head height.

Breathing: Breathe out as you Palm Strike. Breathe in as you lift your wrists to form Birds' Beaks.

Modified: If you have any knee problems, stay in a Shoulder-width or small, high Horse Stance throughout the movement. If you have any shoulder, neck, spine or heart problems, hold your arms lower.

2 Drop your elbows a little and let your hands relax as a transition movement to prepare for the Palm Strike. Push out through the palms as though you are pushing something away from you. Slowly lift up the wrists into Birds' Beaks to repeat the sequence.

HEALTH BENEFITS

This strengthens the arms and makes the wrists flexible. The arm position encourages upper-body lymph drainage assisted by gravity. Also, as the muscles work, they push lymph fluid through the lymph vessels.

hing a Wave in Different Directions

The fluidity of water is a quality emphasized in Qigong. A wave is a perfect image of strength created through the energy of ebb and flow. In this Qigong you push forward with the strength of a flowing wave, and then gather your energy as you ebb, ready to flow again in different directions.

1 Stand in a Back Stance (see page 60) with your left foot forward, your hands in front of your chest, relaxed from the wrist bones. Keep both soles of the feet down throughout the sequence.

2 As you transfer your weight forward, push down and up as though you are following the downward arc of a wave before it crests. When your weight has fully transferred into the Bow Stance (see page 64), your hands will be at the crest of your wave at shoulder height.

Repetitions: Repeat the sequence 7 times or more with the left leg forward and again with the right leg forward.

Note: When pushing out at angles, alter the direction of your front toes slightly to follow the line of the push.

Breathing: Breathe out as you push forward. Breathe in as you transfer your weight back.

3 Transfer your weight back as you lift your wrists and bring your arms back to your starting position with your hands relaxed from the wrist bones, in front of your chest.

4 Push again, with your waist and shoulders directed 30–45 degrees to the left.

continued next page →

5 Transfer your weight back as you lift your wrists and bring your arms back to your starting position with your hands relaxed from the wrist bones, in front of your chest.

6 Push again, with your waist and shoulders directed 30–45 degrees to the right. When pushing out at angles, alter the direction of your front toes slightly to follow the line of the push.

HEALTH BENEFITS

Slow wave-like movements calm the nervous system. Pushing in different directions trains the balance.

REMINDER

Keep your knees in line with your toes. It is easy to forget this important alignment principle when pushing at different angles.

Twisting the Arms

Many people, over time, build up such tight muscles and tendons in their arms that they reduce their ability to straighten them. This exercise improves both strength and flexibility and also activates the six upper-body meridian channels. Soon you will be able to twist your arms further and further and keep the arms straighter as the tissues loosen. This will contribute to greater strength, grace and freedom in all of your movements.

1 Stand with feet shoulder-width apart with your arms held straight out in front of you at shoulder height, with the left palm up and the right palm down.

2 Slowly twist both arms until the left palm is down and the right palm is up.

Modified: If it is difficult to keep your shoulders relaxed, lower your arms to chest height, bend your elbows slightly and do fewer repetitions. If your shoulders are stiff, there will be a tendency to lean back to compensate. Be aware of this and lower your arms to a level where you can remain upright.

HEALTH BENEFITS

Strengthens the muscles and tendons in the arms and shoulders and also makes them more supple.

Repetitions: Repeat the sequence 30 times.

Breathing: Breathe in as you twist your left palm up. Breathe out as you twist your left palm down.

Swirling a Plate

The idea in this Qigong exercise is to use your body as much as possible to swirl your plate, which is full of water, and not lose one drop. The instructions can sound confusing, but if you simply begin with the intention of keeping your plate flat so that no water spills, you will circle the hips naturally to balance the swirling of the plate. When practising outside in warm weather, I sometimes provide students with real plates full of water, and there is always lots of laughter as some of us accidentally tip our plates and get wet.

Repetitions:
Repeat 7 times with the right hand and 7 times with the left hand.

1 Stand with feet shoulder-width apart with your left hand resting behind your waist. Hold an imaginary plate on your right palm at hip height. Your imaginary plate is brimming with water and your objective is to not let one drop spill. Follow the plate with your eyes throughout the sequence.

2 As you turn your right hand inward move your hips over to the left.

Breathing: Breathe naturally and abdominally (see pages 67–8) throughout the sequence.

HEALTH BENEFITS

Swirling a Plate brings flexibility to the spine, hips and shoulders. It also improves circulation and the feeling of flow, with the whole body being in a continuous soft spiral motion.

3 As you curve your right hand away by rotating your wrist so that your fingers point away from you, move your hips to the right.

4 Bring your plate across a high diagonal in front of your body over to the left above head height.

5 Lean back to take your plate behind your head and bend back as far as is comfortable, moving your hips forward.

continued next page ➞

6 Circle your plate over to the right as your move your hips to the left.

7 Bring your plate down in front of you on a diagonal to your left hip as your hips move to the right. Circle your plate inward and move your hips a little further to the left to begin again to repeat the swirling cycle.

Modified: If you have any back or neck problems, don't lean back, just look up.

Elastic Qi Ball

In this Qigong you stretch and then condense Qi. Although the exercise is fun when you imagine the feeling, it is even more fun when you can actually feel something. The feeling of Qi energy is tangible for many people. See the How to feel your Qi Ball box on page 169 to find out about having the Qi feeling. The more relaxed you are, the more sensitive you become and the more you will feel the Qi.

1 Stand with feet shoulder-width apart with your hands placed at chest height holding a Qi ball.

2 Imagine that your Qi ball is elastic, and slowly pull your palms apart.

3 Push your palms toward each other and feel as though you are condensing the Qi energy to make your ball smaller.

HEALTH BENEFITS

The Elastic Qi Ball trains the hands' sensitivity, and it focuses and calms the mind.

Repetitions: Repeat the sequence 7 times or more.

Breathing: Breathe in as you draw your hands apart. Breathe out as you condense your Qi ball.

Yin Opens, Yang Closes

Yin energies are associated with closing inward for rest, nourishment and regeneration. Yang energies are associated with opening and expanding outward, releasing and directing energy. However, in this exercise the Yin Yang ideas are reversed. Perhaps this is a reference to one of the theories of the influential philosopher Dong Zhongshu (195–115 BCE) in his *Luxuriant Dew of the Spring and Autumn Annals*, when he advised that a spring drought indicated too much Yang and not enough Yin, and so one should "open Yin and close Yang".

1 Stand in a Horse Stance (see pages 58–9) and open your arms to about 45 degrees, with your palms down, at or above head height. Open your chest and keep your shoulders relaxed and down.

2 Turn your palms up and, keeping your arms almost straight, bring your wrists inward to cross over each other, with the right wrist underneath, as Yang closes. Allow your back and shoulders to stretch and your chest to sink down.

Modified: If you have any shoulder, neck or back restrictions, lowe[r] arms to chest height and do fewer repetitions. When a person ha[s] shoulders, there is a tendency to compensate by leaning back from the lower waist, which could be damaging to the lumbar spine. To avoid this, keep your hands lower, at around chest height.

Repetitions: Repeat the sequence 7 times.

Breathing: Breathe in as your arms open, and breathe out as your arms close. Imagine that they are acting like the long arms of a bellows – when you close the arms of a bellows, the air is squeezed out; when you open the arms of a bellows, the air is sucked in.

3 Turn your palms down and open your arms to about 45 degrees, palms down, as Yin Opens. On your next repetition, when you cross your wrists, as Yang Closes, bring the left wrist underneath.

HEALTH BENEFITS

Strengthens the arms and shoulders. Works the whole of the upper body, including the respiratory system.

Flying Roc

A Roc is a mythical bird of prey that has great strength and an enormous wingspan. In Chinese mythology it is also referred to as a Peng. It looks similar to a gigantic eagle and has such a large wingspan that in flight its wings are like clouds covering the sky. When you open your arms, also open your heart to feel the majesty of this great bird taking flight.

1 Stand in a Horse Stance (see pages 58–9) and hold an imaginary ball, with your right hand on top and your left hand underneath.

Repetitions: Repeat the sequence to left and right 7 times.

2 Shift your weight to your left leg, keeping your left knee bent and allowing the toes of your right foot to pivot as needed. At the same time open your arms, as though you are a great flying bird. Bring your left hand to head height or above, palm up, and at the same time bring your right hand out at chest height, palm down.

Breathing: Breathe in as you hold the ball. Breathe out as you spread your wings.

HOLDING A BALL

This is a symbol of harmony. Hold your top hand at chest height and your lower hand just below navel height. This symbolizes joining the Middle Dantian with the Lower Dantian, so that both work in harmony.

HEALTH BENEFITS

This exercise gently stretches the arms and chest, strengthens the legs and produces a feeling of exhilaration through emulating the flying actions of a huge bird.

3 Shift your weight back to a Horse Stance and hold an imaginary ball, with your left hand on top and your right hand underneath.

4 Shift your weight to the right leg, keeping your right knee bent and allowing the toes of your left foot to pivot as needed. At the same time open your arms, as though you are a great flying bird. Bring your right hand to head height or above, palm up, and at the same time bring your left hand out at chest height, palm down.

5 Shift your weight back to a Horse Stance and hold an imaginary ball, with your right hand on top and your left hand underneath, to continue the sequence.

Lifting the Heels

Improving your balance improves your self-confidence and reduces the risk of falling. If you have strong, flexible feet, ankles and calves, you will have better balance. Many people allow the muscles in their feet to weaken from disuse, so this is an excellent exercise to keep these muscles strong and supple. It is best done with bare feet, but you may wish to start in shoes. If your balance isn't what it once was, hold on to a chair or other solid object.

Repetitions:
Repeat 7 times.

1 Start with feet shoulder-width apart with your hands at hip height in front of you, with the palms facing upward and the fingertips angled toward each other.

2 Slowly raise your heels and at the same time lift your hands upward along your centreline to chest height, keeping your shoulders and elbows relaxed downward.

HEALTH BENEFITS

Lifting the Heels improves balance and coordination.

Modified: Place your hand on a wall, table or chair back for balance.

3 Turn your palms down.

4 Slowly lower your heels as you press your palms downward to hip height.

Breathing: Breathe in as your raise your heels. Breathe out as you lower your heels.

Twist to Look at the Moon

The moon, especially the full moon, has always been an inspiration in Chinese poetry. It connects people because loved ones, who might be far away, will be looking at the same moon, and so the moon is full of emotion. One of the best-known Chinese poems is by the celebrated Tang dynasty poet, Li Bai (701–762 CE), whose poetry is still popular today.

QUIET NIGHT THOUGHTS

Moonlight by my bedside beaming
First mistook for white frost gleaming
Turned to look up at the full moon
Thought of home and fell back sighing

(tr. Anon)

1 Stand in a Horse Stance (see pages 58–9) and bring your hands to just above head height, palms facing away, with the fingertips of each hand angled toward each other.

2 Twist your upper body to the left as far as is comfortable.

3 Keep your arms in position and turn your upper body back to the front.

Repetitions: Repeat the sequence 7 times.

Breathing: Breathe out as you twist. Breathe in as you turn back to the front.

Modified: Stand with feet shoulder-width apart or small Horse Stance to make twisting easier. If it is difficult to keep your shoulders relaxed, then lower your hands to face height.

4 Twist your upper body to the right as far as is comfortable.

5 Keep your arms in position and turn your upper body back to the front to repeat the sequence.

HEALTH BENEFITS

This strengthens the arms and shoulders. The twisting action makes the waist and hips more supple and massages internal organs.

Coiling Python

Pythons are among the largest and most powerful snakes in the world. They are constrictors, which means that they coil themselves around their prey and crush it. Female pythons also coil around their eggs to protect them. One thing is certain – a python is an expert at coiling, and in this Qigong you will be using this image to coil further and further.

1 Start in a Horse Stance (see page 58–9) with your hands on your thighs, and lean forward at up to 45 degrees.

2 Twist your upper body to the left and look left as you rotate your right shoulder inward.

Repetitions: Repeat the sequence 7 times.

Breathing: Breathe out as you twist. Breathe in as you return to the front.

HEALTH BENEFITS

Strengthens the legs and encourages flexibility in the shoulders, waist, spine and hips. Twisting massages the internal organs.

4 Twist your upper body to the right and look right as you rotate your left shoulder inward.

3 Twist back to the front.

Modified: Stand in a small, high Horse Stance (see page 58) and twist only as far as is comfortable.

5 Twist back to the front.

Seated Pushing the Sky and Twisting

Qigong is often performed in a seated position, either on the floor or in a chair. I have taught classes to people who are confined to wheelchairs, and they enjoy the class as much as people who can stand.

HEALTH BENEFITS

This exercise brings flexibility to the shoulders, spine, waist and hips, and strengthens the upper body.

1 Sit in a cross-legged position, interlock your fingers and push upward through the heels of your palms toward the sky. Hold this position for 1 minute or more.

Breathing: Breathe out as you push upward and then continue to breathe softly and naturally during your holding time. Breathe out as you twist and then continue to breathe softly and naturally during your holding time. Breathe in as you return to the front.

Modified: Use a high cushion or chair to sit on. If pushing your arms straight upward is uncomfortable, hold them forward of your head with the elbows more bent. Reduce the length of each hold to what you can easily manage.

2 Twist to the left as far as is comfortable. Hold this position for 1 minute or more.

3 Twist to the right as far as is comfortable. Hold this position for 1 minute or more.

Ending the sequence: To end, bring your hands down to rest in your lap. You may need to circle your shoulders a few times each way to ease any muscle strain.

Twisting and Coiling Qi

Many Qigong moves emphasize twisting and coiling to strengthen the Qi.
In martial arts the ability to coil and store up energy, then uncoil like a spring
to release energy, is a valuable skill. In terms of health, twisting gives your
internal organs a deep massage, increases circulation, removes stagnant Qi and
stimulates meridian channels. When you gently twist and untwist muscles and
tissues, they are stretched and then released, creating a soft, flexible, nimble
body full of energy.

1 Stand with feet
shoulder-width
apart with your hands
above your head,
palms facing away.

Repetitions: Repeat
the sequence 7 times.

2 Pivot on left heel and right
toes and twist 180 degrees to
face behind you as you bend your
knees and twist into a stance with
your right heel lifted. As you twist,
rotate your forearms so that your
palms face inward and drop your
elbows downward.

3 Twist back to
the front as you
straighten your knees
and bring your arms
back to the starting
position.

HEALTH BENEFITS

This improves balance, leg strength and coordination. Twisting massages the internal organs.

Modified: If you have any knee problems or if your legs are weak, make no attempt to twist 180 degrees. Twist only 45 degrees and bend your knees only slightly.

4 Pivot on your right heel and left toes and twist 180 degrees to face behind you, as you bend your knees and twist into a stance with your left heel lifted. As you twist, rotate your forearms so that your palms face inward and drop your elbows downward.

5 Twist back to the front as you straighten your knees and bring your arms back to the starting position.

Breathing: Breathe out as you twist and turn to the back. Breathe in as you twist to your starting position.

Playing with a Qi Ball

Now is the time to use your imagination and become playful. Qigong is enjoyable and fun, but sometimes people approach it too seriously. Anxiety and muscle tension disappear when you are having fun. If you are suffering from play deprivation, give this Qigong a try.

Breathing: Breathe naturally and abdominally (see pages 67–8) throughout the sequence.

Stand with feet shoulder-width apart, holding an imaginary ball of Qi between your hands. Imagine that this ball floats off on its own volition, in different directions, at different heights, twisting and rolling as your body follows. Keep a light hold on the ball and follow its slow meanderings, wherever it might lead you. Play with the Qi Ball for 2 minutes or longer.

HOW TO FEEL YOUR QI BALL

Rub your palms together for 30 seconds, shake your wrists and arms for 30 seconds, then rub your palms together again for 30 seconds. Bring your palms toward each other as though holding a small ball. Many people are now able to "feel" the ball. This is your own electromagnetic field which you have just stimulated. It takes a while to get used to the feel, but once you become accustomed to it, you can use this feeling with any Qigong exercise.

HEALTH BENEFITS

Playing with a Qi Ball increases mobility and flow throughout the body and brightens mood because it makes you feel like a child playing.

Standing like a Post – Zhanzhuang

Zhanzhuang Qigong is known by various names: Standing like a Post, Standing Post, Standing Pole, Standing Meditation and Standing Like A Tree. *Zhan* means to stand or to halt, and *zhuang* means post, stile or stake. Standing postures have an ancient history and are seen in prehistoric Chinese rock art. One theory is that Stone Age hunters had to stand perfectly still for long periods of time with perfect awareness and heightened senses while patiently waiting for prey.

Although the postures are still, the breath and Qi energy are moving. This is a good example of movement within stillness, Yang within Yin. The Chinese word for movement is *dongjing*: *dong* means movement and *jing* means stillness and calm. It is interesting that even the word for movement contains the underlying perception of stillness to create a Yin-Yang balance.

Zhanzhuang builds internal energy, tenacity and strength while at the same time bringing stillness and peace to the mind. Standing still while holding a stance is fundamental to all Chinese martial arts. The time-honoured thinking behind this is that you cannot begin to move if you do not know how to stand.

ABOVE: Standing Like a Tree.

Wang Xiang Zhai (1885–1963) is often referred to as the greatest known Zhangzhuang teacher. He was a renowned martial artist and healer, who believed that the ordinary is the extraordinary. Famous for treating everyone as an individual, he taught different techniques to different students. He was against the idea of making a catalogue of techniques "written in stone" that everyone would slavishly follow, as this went against the spirit of freedom and individual creativity.

Three stages of standing

Master Wang said that there are three stages of standing.

First stage – the Test of Discomfort

When you first stand for longer than a couple of minutes, your muscles will talk back to you. If you are not used to holding a Horse Stance (see pages 58–9), or holding your arms in a certain position, you will begin to feel discomfort. Whenever you notice muscles that are tense, bring your attention to the area of tension and consciously relax the muscles and surrounding tissue as much as you are able. Even the smallest muscle contraction that is not absolutely essential in holding the posture should be released.

Constantly check and recheck your posture from head to foot and release any knots of tension. If the idea of searching out places where tension is held is new to you, be assured that this skill will develop with practice. Be open to the possibility of tension being held in your mind or in your emotions or attitude, as this too must be released.

Shaking and trembling as a result of muscle fatigue can accompany this stage. Should this occur, alter the posture slightly to make it easier, and if the trembling does not stop after about 30 seconds, take a complete rest. There is no point in forcing yourself into a position that exceeds your current ability.

Once you are able to identify areas of tension, relaxing them will become easier and easier. This skill takes time, but if you persevere there are many reward: increased health, energy, strength, stability, balance and ability to concentrate. As you gain more awareness of your body, you will sense how it works as a unit, and how every part connects with and affects every other part. This sense of connection will inform all of your Qigong practice.

Second stage – the Test of Fire

When you are able to relax every muscle that isn't essential in maintaining the posture, the initial discomfort diminishes or disappears. As a result of increased relaxation through your muscles, joints and connective tissue, your circulation will be boosted and your body might suddenly heat up. In Chinese terms, your blood and Qi are freely flowing. Your hands and feet and other areas of your body might become uncomfortably hot, and you might break out into beads of sweat. When your body gets used to the increased circulation, the heat will diminish to a comfortable level.

Third stage – the Test of Patient Growth

This is the hardest stage of all to achieve, when standing feels comfortable and easy, and your body is so used to the postures that there is little effort involved. This gives you the opportunity to place all of your attention on Qi flow, your breath or one of the Dantians (see pages 20–2). At this stage, impatient and irrelevant thoughts may interfere, as there is no longer a physical challenge to occupy your mind. This is where there needs to be a mental shift away from the purely physical to an overall observation of your inner feeling, and an awareness of internal energy. The stiller and more relaxed you can be, the more your energy will connect and flow throughout your body and nervous system.

The Five Elements

One of the best-known Zhanzhuang sets uses the Five Elements as inspiration for its five postures, and so before we begin the set, it will be useful to take a brief look at the Five Elements.

RIGHT: The Five Elements: Wood, Fire, Earth, Metal and Water.

Wood, Fire, Earth, Metal and Water are the Five Elements, known as Wuxing. In Chinese philosophy these are viewed more as processes or phases in nature, rather than true elements. Each has the ability to generate or subdue the other elements. The Five Elements are used to explain a multitude of phenomena found in nature as well as in the workings of our own bodies. Complex charts are available showing relationships and interactions with all aspects of our world, should you wish to explore further. The Five Element theory is extremely important in Traditional Chinese Medicine.

木 **Wood:** This element is Yang in nature, and is associated with renewal, growth and flexibility. Wood is associated with the beginning of new life and expansion, but also with aggression and anger if not balanced. It corresponds to the Liver and Gall Bladder Meridians

火 **Fire:** This element is Yang and is associated with strength, dynamism and creativity. Its heat can bring warmth and enthusiasm, but also restlessness and overexcitement if not balanced. It corresponds to the Heart, Small Intestine, Pericardium and Triple Burner Meridians.

土 **Earth:** This element is a balance of Yin and Yang. It is associated with balance, stability and nurturing. It has the quality of patience and thoughtfulness, but also stubbornness and self-centredness if not balanced. It corresponds to the Spleen and Stomach Meridians.

金 **Metal:** This element is Yin and is associated with contraction and consolidation. It is connected to inspiration and determination, but also an over-controlling tendency and rigidity if not balanced. It corresponds to the Lung and Large Intestine Meridians.

水 **Water:** This element is Yin and is associated with fluidity and softness. It brings harmony, calmness and adaptability, but also can harbour fear and a lack of conviction if not balanced. It corresponds to the Kidney and Bladder Meridians.

Five Element Standing Post Qigong

When performing the five postures, the Five Elements interact to create a state of Yin-Yang balance and harmonious Qi flow. Different meridian channels are stimulated by each posture, and by performing all five postures you will be activating all of the main meridians. There are differing opinions concerning which channels are involved because some of the postures stimulate several meridian channels simultaneously. I have practised this set of Five Element Postures for many years and hope that you enjoy and benefit from it.

Warm-ups

Begin with some gentle loosening exercises to gently warm up the body and mobilize your joints. Choose a few moves from the Warm-ups chapter, or use your own warm-ups if you prefer.

Breathing

Use soft abdominal breathing throughout. See the Breathing chapter for more information.

Stance and posture

All of the positions in Five Element Standing Post use a Horse Stance. Choose a small, medium or large Horse Stance, according to your preference. See pages 58–9 for more information about the Horse Stance, and see the Posture and Movement Principles chapter for more advice on posture.

Eyes

Eyes can be closed or open. If open, the gaze should be soft with the eyes relaxed. Another alternative is to lower the eyes by 45 degrees so that you are looking toward the floor in front of you.

Hands

In all of the postures the hands should be soft and relaxed, with the fingers held slightly apart.

木 Posture no. 1 – Wood

Take a Horse Stance and stretch your palms out to the sides, slightly forward of the body at hip height. Flex your wrists so that your palms face downward to the earth. Hold for 2 to 5 minutes.

Each posture can be modified for different abilities. This is the modified Wood Posture.

火 Posture no. 2 – Fire

Retain your stance and smoothly move the arms to a position above your head with palms facing away. Angle the fingers of each hand toward each other. Hold for 2 to 5 minutes.

Modified Fire Posture

土 Posture No. 3 – Earth

Retain your stance and smoothly move the arms down to chest height with palms facing inward as though holding a tree. This is the best-known of the five postures and is widely known as Holding a Tree, which gives a wonderful image of your rooted connection to the earth. Often this posture is used on its own and held for 5 to 30 minutes or longer. Hold for 2 to 5 minutes if part of the set.

Modified
Earth
Posture

金 Posture No. 4 – Metal

Retain your stance and smoothly bring the arms together at chest height, with your elbows, forearms and little fingers touching, palms up. Allow your back to stretch as you twist the forearms slightly, bringing the thumb side of your hands slightly lower than the little-finger side. Hold for 2 to 5 minutes.

Modified
Metal
Posture

水 Posture No. 5 – Water

Retain your stance and smoothly lower your arms in front of your body as though holding a circle at hip height, palms up, with the fingertips of each hand lined up toward each other. Hold for 2 to 5 minutes.

Modified Water Posture

How long to practise

An average length of practice for all five postures would be approximately 25 minutes – 5 minutes for each posture – but at the beginning, 2 minutes per posture might be sufficient. Your needs will change as you progress, so when you feel confident make your own decisions about timings.

After standing

After standing for a long time, it is important to restore good circulation to the legs and to move the feet gently so that they become soft and flexible. There are 33 joints in the foot and you want them all to be pliable.

Rocking and circling the feet: Stand with feet shoulder-width apart with the backs of your hands resting on the kidneys. Rock forward and back on your feet about 7 times. Now make circular movements on the feet by shifting your weight in circles, clockwise then anticlockwise about 7 times each way. This massages the feet, makes your ankles more supple and restores good circulation to your legs.

Dropping the heels: Stand with feet shoulder-width apart with the backs of your hands resting on the kidneys. Lift the heels a little and let them drop suddenly so that a soft, shuddering vibration travels up through your body. This gently stimulates the entire nervous system.

Walking with hands on still water

Walking "through water" complements your Five Element Zhanzhuang practice, and it is a soothing and energizing way to end your practice session. This exercise can also be used on its own as a walking meditation.

Walk slowly, as though walking through water, rolling your feet with every step. Let one leg completely empty of all tension as you transfer weight to the other leg. When you place weight on one leg completely, before transferring weight, you are participating in a strong interplay of Yin and Yang. Keep your attention on maintaining a level height in your walking so that you don't bob up and down or lose contact with the imaginary water under your palms. Feel the resistance of the water against your legs.

1 Start with feet shoulder-width apart with your arms hanging loosely at your sides.

2 Flex your wrists so that the palms of your hands are facing toward the ground, and imagine that they are floating on smooth, level water. Keep this feeling of the hands floating on water throughout the sequence. Bend both knees and step forward with your left foot. Touch the heel to the floor noiselessly and with no weight, then slowly roll the sole of the left foot down.

3 Keeping all the weight on your left foot, roll the right foot up onto the toes.

4 Bring the right foot through slowly, and keep your left knee bent.

5 Place the right heel on the floor, light as a feather, before you begin to roll the sole of the foot downward to the floor.

Walk forward in a straight line, keeping your attention on the smoothness of your walking against the resistance of the water and the feeling of buoyancy in your hands resting on the water.

Walking backward is more difficult, but if you feel confident, give this a try.

All the principles are exactly the same, but in reverse, so that your toes touch down first as you step back.

Spend a minimum of 5 minutes slowly walking with full attention.

Eight Pieces of Brocade – Baduanjin

The Eight Pieces of Brocade is one of the best-known Qigong sets. It has a long history and is mentioned in ancient texts such as *The Ten Compilations on Cultivating Perfection* (*Xiuzhen Shishu*), c. 1300. Various people have been credited with its invention, including two of the legendary Eight Immortals, Zhongli Quan and Lü Dongbin. The set has also been attributed to the semi-legendary General Yue Fei, c. 1100, who is said to have taught the exercises to his troops to keep them strong and ready for battle. As a result of being handed down over the centuries, the set has gained many variations.

Silk brocade is a fabric of excellence, and we can therefore infer that these exercises were considered to be of the highest quality. The set strengthens the body, improves flexibility of the sinews, nourishes the Qi and balances the Yin-Yang energy in the body, thus promoting longevity. The translation of *ba* (eight), *duan* (pieces) and *jin* (brocade) could also be a Chinese pun because of the additional meanings of the syllables: *ba* (to pull up, promote, capture), *duan* (broken, weakened) and *jin*

(tendon, muscle, sinew). It would be typical of the Chinese poetic tradition to offer a beautiful image of the silken brocade and at the same time imply a practical health allusion.

This style, which I learned many years ago, is the Immortal Family Style of Baduanjin, Xian Jia Baduanjin, taught to me by Dan Docherty, an international teacher of great renown. He learned from his teacher Cheng Tin Hung, who learned from his uncle Cheng Wing Kwong, who was a student of Wu Jianquan. The style is not as well known as some but is totally accessible to all. It will be of particular interest to those who are familiar with the better-known styles.

This set consists of eight sections, some of which have two parts. Although it is intended to be practised as a set, you can take any part of the set and practise it individually, according to your preference. The set as a whole regulates Qi energy. It is suitable for beginners and the experienced alike and can be modified where required. Although most of the exercises are shown standing, they can easily be adapted to a seated position.

No. 1 Gnash Teeth, Swallow Saliva

Part one – Gnash Teeth

Part two – Swallow Saliva

Tap your teeth lightly and slowly together 36 times. You may keep the lips touching if you prefer.

Breathing: Breathe naturally, gently and abdominally (see pages 67–8).

Fill your mouth with saliva and swallow 3 times.

Breathing: Breathe naturally, gently and abdominally (see pages 67–8).

HEALTH BENEFITS

Saliva has antiseptic qualities and swallowing it aids the digestive process and is said to prevent stomach ulcers.

HEALTH BENEFITS

Stimulates the nervous system and relaxes the jaw.

No. 2 Wash Face, Beat Drum

Part one – Wash Face

Use the heels of your hands or fingertips if you prefer a lighter touch. Stroke downward, as if washing your face, one hand after the other, 36 times.

HEALTH BENEFITS

Relaxes the muscles of the face, increases circulation and has a soothing effect on the nervous system. Any gentle stimulation of the facial tissues lubricates the underlying fascia and helps to prevent wrinkles.

Part two – Beat Drum

HEALTH BENEFITS

This stimulates the nervous system and is also very soothing.

1 Gently place your palms over your ears with your fingers cupping the curved projections at the base of your skull.

2 Flick your index fingers off the middle fingers onto your skull to create an echoing, drum-like sound, 24 times.

Breathing: Breathe naturally, gently and abdominally (see pages 67–8).

No. 3 Shove Shoulders, Support Sky

Part one – Shove Shoulders

Circle shoulders forward, up and back, and then drop them downward as though gravity is pulling them down at the end of each circle.

Repetitions: Repeat 7 times each way.

Breathing: Breathe naturally, gently and abdominally (see pages 67–8).

HEALTH BENEFITS

This relaxes the shoulders, reduces tension and facilitates mobility.

Part Two – Support Sky

1 Start with feet shoulder-width apart and link fingers together.

2 Lift hands upward, and at chest height begin to turn palms upward.

3 Push palms up toward the sky and rise up onto your toes.

4 Let fingers flick apart at the uppermost part of the stretch.

Repetitions: Repeat 7 times.

Breathing: Breathe in as you lift your hands. Breathe out as you lower your hands.

HEALTH BENEFITS

Creates mobility in the shoulders and arms, stretches the whole body and improves balance.

5 Circle arms downward out to sides of body, lowering heels. Time this carefully so that by the time your arms arrive at shoulder height, your heels are on the floor.

6 Bend your knees as you continue to circle your arms downward.

No. 4 Draw Bow to Left and Right

Repetitions: Drawing the Bow to the left and to the right = 1 repetition. Repeat 7 times.

1 Begin in a Horse Stance (see pages 58–9), hands at the front of your body with palms up and fingertips toward each other, ready to lift your hands up to your centreline.

2 Lift your palms up to chest height, keeping the fingertips toward each other.

3 Draw the bow to the left by stretching out your left arm. Point your left index finger to the sky. Your index finger is used to site your target. At the same time draw the bow string with your right hand, keeping your right forearm parallel to the ground. Focus your eyes, nose and left index finger in the same direction and see your target far in the distance.

Breathing: Breathe in as you bring your hands up to chest height. Breathe out as you draw the bow, let the arrow fly and bring both arms to shoulder height palm down. Breathe in as you circle the arms down and up to chest height. You are breathing in to collect the Qi energy so that you have the energy to shoot your arrow far into the distance. Breathe out directing the Qi energy as you release your arrow.

continued next page ⟶

4 Open your chest to let your arrow fly as you release the bow string and bring both arms out to the sides, shoulder height, palms down.

5 Lower both arms smoothly and bring your hands to the front of your body with palms up and fingertips toward each other, ready to draw the bow to the right.

Modified:
All moves can be modified to sit in a chair.

HEALTH BENEFITS

Improves posture, expands the chest and the lungs, strengthens the arms, legs and hips, and improves coordination. The move lends a feeling of martial power.

No. 5 Massage the Dantian Point

HEALTH BENEFITS

Stimulates the Lower Dantian. Said to cure impotence and increase sexual wellbeing.

1 Start with feet shoulder-width apart. Place both palms below the navel and massage around the Dantian in small circles 36 times with your right hand nearest to your flesh, in the direction in which the right hand fingers are pointing.

2 Repeat 36 times with the left hand nearest to your flesh, in the direction that the left hand fingers are pointing. (Traditionally one hand cups the genitals, with the middle finger on the perineum, while the other hand rubs in small circles around the Dantian in the direction in which the fingers point, 36 times for each hand.)

Breathing: Breathe naturally, gently and abdominally (see pages 67–8).

No. 6 Rub Internal Kidneys Point

Repetitions: Do this exercise 36 times.

Breathing: Breathe naturally, gently and abdominally (see pages 67–8).

Modified: Making fists is easier on the wrists.

Stand in a Horse Stance (see pages 58–9) and warm your hands by rubbing them together. Ideally this massage is done on bare flesh and it is always good to warm your hands first. Place your palms on your kidneys. If this hurts your wrists, make fists and use the thumb side of each fist to rub. Rub in circles around the kidney area.

HEALTH BENEFITS

Stimulates the kidneys, soothes backache and stimulates kidney Qi. Said to cure impotence and increase sexual wellbeing.

No. 7 Rub under Spine Point

1 Begin in a Horse Stance (see pages 58–9) and warm your hands by rubbing them together. Ideally this massage is done on bare flesh, and it is always good to warm your hands first.

2 Place two fingers on the area just underneath your coccyx. Massage the area using small circles.

Repetitions: Repeat this 36 times.

Breathing: Breathe naturally, gently, and abdominally (see pages 67–8).

HEALTH BENEFITS

Stimulates the nervous system and increases sexual wellbeing. This also improves circulation in veins and arteries in the legs and is beneficial for those with varicose veins.

No. 8 Gushing Spring, Washing Legs

Part one – Gushing Spring

Modified: Use a chair if sitting on the floor is difficult.

Sit cross-legged on the floor, or on a chair if this is easier. Remove your shoes and socks. Hold your left foot with your left hand and, with the heel of your right palm, rub in circles around the Bubbling Spring point (see page 55) or over the complete sole of the foot, 36 times. Repeat with the right foot held by the right hand, rubbing in circles 36 times.

Breathing: Breathe naturally, gently and abdominally (see pages 67–8).

HEALTH BENEFITS

Good for foot circulation and for nerve and acupoint stimulation.

Part two – Washing Legs

1 Stand on your left leg and rotate the right leg 7 times one way then 7 times the other way, as though you were washing your foot and lower leg under a small spring or waterfall. Look at your moving leg if you wish to add a challenging element to your balance.

2 Repeat with the other leg.

Repetitions: Repeat 7 times for each leg.

Breathing: Breathe naturally, gently and abdominally (see pages 67–8).

HEALTH BENEFITS

Good for ankle, knee and hip joint mobility. Trains balance.

Seated Twelve Pieces of Brocade – Shierduanjin

The famous Eight Pieces of Brocade (see chapter), with over a thousand years of history, was expanded in the 19th century to include twelve pieces. The seated set focuses on flexibility and strengthening the upper part of the body, clearing blockages in the upper body meridian channels, and energizing the internal organs. These moves can be practised in any sitting position, either on the floor or on a chair, and can be adapted for all levels of mobility.

Although the set has an ancient tradition with many variations, the moves used in this book were compiled and tested by The Chinese Health Qigong Association to form a modern set to the highest standard.

I am grateful to Master Faye Li Yip for teaching me this set of Seated Twelve Pieces of Brocade. Faye Yip was born in Beijing and began her study of martial arts in childhood. She has studied with different masters, including her distinguished father, Professor Li Deyin, and has been awarded many medals and honours in recognition of her excellence in a wide variety of martial arts. Faye Yip has lived and taught in the United Kingdom since the 1990s and also teaches internationally. She is a co-founder of the Deyin Taijiquan Institute (GB), President of the British Health Qigong Association and Executive Committee member of the International Health Qigong Federation.

To begin

This set consists of eight sections, some of which have two parts. Although it is intended to be practised as a set, you can take any part of the set and practise it individually, according to your preference.

Warm-ups

Begin with some gentle loosening exercises to gradually warm up your body and mobilize your joints. Choose a few moves from the Warm-ups chapter or use your own method of warming up if you prefer.

Sitting position

You can sit on either the floor or a chair. If you choose to sit on the floor, use a cushion that is a little higher toward the back. It is not necessary to buy a special wedge-shaped cushion – simply fold a blanket that creates a lift of about 3cm (1¼in) higher under your seat bones so that you can sit effortlessly with a straight back and feel that your upper body is light, as if suspended from above. As with all Qigong, the shoulders and chest should be relaxed.

Calm the breath and the mind

Sit with your hands on your knees. Take a few moments to bring your mind to rest with slow abdominal breathing (see pages 67–8).

There is no need to match the breath with the moves. Simply breathe naturally throughout the set.

No. 1 Calming the Heart and Positioning the Hands

HEALTH BENEFITS

Expanding the chest relaxes the heart area and stimulates the flow of Qi.

1 Slowly lift your arms out to the sides to head height or above, with palms up, and expand your chest.

2 Bring your arms forward, with palms down, to shoulder height, shoulder-width apart.

3 Bring the hands to rest on your knees, and make fists. Close your eyes for 30 seconds.

STIMULATING THE UPPER BODY MERIDIANS

There are six meridian channels that begin or end in the fingers. The six upper body meridians are the Heart, Small Intestine, Large Intestine, Lung, Pericardium and San Jiao. The Healing Fist stimulates some of these meridians, but if the folding of your thumb hurts your hand for any reason, use the Basic Fist.

Healing Fist: Fold your thumb inside your fist, lightly press the thumb against the base of the ring finger, and relax the centre of your palm. Fold your fingers around the thumb.

Basic Fist: Fold your thumb around the outside of the fingers as shown.

No. 2 Tapping the Teeth and Sounding the Drums

HEALTH BENEFITS

Tapping the Teeth strengthens the gums and roots of the teeth, stimulates the flow of saliva and helps to keep the mouth healthy. Nerves in your teeth connect to nerves that branch out into your organs, muscles and glands.

Sounding the Drums creates a vibration through your skull, which stimulates the brain and nervous system but is at the same time very soothing.

1 Rest your hands at the front of your hips, looking straight ahead.

2 Bring your arms out to the sides to shoulder height.

continued next page →

3 Bend your elbows, keeping them back so that your chest remains open, and place the tips of your middle fingers lightly into your ears.

4 Gently tap your teeth together 36 times, as though you have something chewy between your teeth. Keep your lips lightly touching.

SOUNDING THE DRUMS

Place your palms over your ears so that your fingers touch the lower part of the cranium. Cross your index fingers over your middle fingers, then let them flip downward off the middle fingers to strike the lower skull 24 times, to create a resonating sound inside your head.

No. 3 Shaking the Heavenly Column

The Heavenly Column refers to your spinal column.

HEALTH BENEFITS

The different positions shown here stimulate the meridians and bring increased flexibility to spine, neck, shoulders and waist.

1 Rest your hands at the front of your hips, looking straight ahead.

2 Slowly lift your arms out to the sides to shoulder height, palms facing back, while twisting and looking to the left.

3 Turn back to the front and bring both arms straight ahead at shoulder height, palms down.

4 Hold a ball shape with the left arm on top at chest height and the lower hand just below navel height.

5 Lower the left palm to meet the palm of your right hand.

continued next page →

6 Keeping the hands palm to palm, move both hands over to the right thigh and turn your head to the left.

7 Push your top hand downward as you look up and hold this position for about 10 seconds.

8 Bring your hands to rest at the front of your hips.

10 Turn back to the front, bring both arms straight ahead at shoulder height, palms down.

11 Hold a ball shape with the right arm on top at chest height and the lower hand just below navel height.

12 Lower the right palm to meet the palm of your left hand.

9 Slowly lift your arms out to the sides to shoulder height, palms facing back, while twisting and looking to the right.

13 Keeping the hands palm to palm, move both your hands over to the left thigh and turn your head to the right.

14 Push your top hand downward as you look up and hold this position for about 10 seconds.

Repetitions: Repeat the sequence 3 times. End by bringing your hands to rest at the front of your hips.

No. 4
Hugging
Kunlun

Kunlun is the name of a long mountain range in western China. In Chinese mythology the Kunlun mountains were a high sacred place, and if you could reach the peaks you would be able to attain wisdom and reside in a place of everlasting love.

Part one

1 Raise your arms straight up beside your ears.

2 Bring your hands to the back of your head and link your fingers together, keeping your elbows out to the sides.

6 Twist forward.

7 Turn your upper body to the right.

8 Tilt your body to the left to stretch muscles along the right side, as you look up to the right.

3 Turn your upper body to the left.

4 Tilt your body to the right to stretch muscles along the left side, as you look up to the left.

5 Return to an upright position.

9 Return to an upright position.

10 Twist forward.

Part two

1 With hands still behind your head, lift up your chin, look up, and expand your chest as much as possible.

2 As you lower your chin and look down, lower your elbows to hug the sides of your head.

3 Separate your hands and slide them along your cheeks until your chin is cupped in your palms.

Repetitions:
Repeat the entire part one and part two sequence 3 times. At the end of the third repetition, draw your hands into clenched fists.

4 Still cupping your chin in your palms, raise your head up and back as far as is comfortable and look up.

5 Return to an upright position and lower your palms to rest at the front of your hips, looking straight ahead.

No. 5 Rotating Winches

Part one

Repetitions:
Repeat these first
four steps 6 times.

1 Place both fists behind you with the backs of your fists on the kidneys.

2 Turn your upper body to the left, bend your left elbow, and bring your fist to shoulder height, as though you have pulled the imaginary winch back.

5 Place both fists behind you with the backs of your fists on the kidneys.

6 Turn your upper body to the right, bend your right elbow, and bring your fist to shoulder height, as though you have pulled the imaginary winch back.

7 Lean to the right and stretch your right arm out past your right knee while keeping your eyes on your fist.

3 Lean to the left and stretch your left arm out past your left knee while keeping your eyes on your fist.

4 Straighten your upper body and draw your left fist back to the side of your waist. The complete movement of drawing your arm back and then sending it forward in steps 2–4 will trace an oval shape, so that you feel you are turning a winch or hand-operated crank.

Repetitions: Rotate your winch 6 times on each side.

8 Straighten your upper body and draw your right fist back to the side of your waist.

Ending the sequence: Return to your starting position with the backs of your fists on the kidneys.

Part two

Shoulder Rotations

With your fists at your kidneys, rotate your shoulders back, up, forward and down 6 times. Now rotate your shoulders in the other direction 6 times.

Elbow Rotations

Repetitions: Repeat 6 times twisting left to begin, then 6 times twisting right to begin.

1 Slide your hands up alongside your ribs and rest your fingertips on your shoulders.

2 Bring your elbows down.

3 Rotate your upper body to the left as you bring your front elbow forward and up and your back elbow backward and up.

HEALTH BENEFITS

This routine stimulates meridian channels and tones the internal organs. It is a wonderful exercise to increase flexibility throughout the shoulders, back and spine.

4 As the elbows continue circling, turn back to the front when you will be at the top of your circles with both elbows up by the sides of your head.

5 Rotate your upper body to the right as you bring your front elbow forward and down and your back elbow backward and down.

6 As the elbows continue circling, turn back to the front when you will be at the bottom of your circles with both elbows down, ready to start your next rotation sequence.

No. 6 Propping up the Sky and Pressing the Skull

1 From the previous exercise, slide your palms down to your lower back.

2 Slide your hands along your thighs to your knees, and pull the knees up.

3 Slide your right leg forward, toes facing up.

HEALTH BENEFITS

This exercise stretches the spine, ribcage, shoulders, arms and neck and stimulates meridian channels.

USING A CHAIR

If you are sitting in a chair, do not attempt to completely straighten your knees – there is no floor underneath to support them, as there would be if you were sitting on the floor.

6 Raise your hands up in front of you until they are above your head, palms up, and point your toes.

Repetitions: Push up and down (steps 6–7) 9 times in all, ending with your hands on top of your head and your toes up.

STARTING GENTLY

If you find it difficult to straighten your knees, keep them a little bent. Many people find it difficult to maintain a straight back throughout, so if 9 repetitions are too strenuous, start with 3 and work up.

4 Slide your left leg forward, toes facing up.

5 Interlock your fingers in front of your waist, palms up.

7 Keeping your fingers interlocked, turn your hands palms down and place them on top of your head. Press up with your head against your palms, stretching your neck upward. At the same time flex your ankles so that your toes come back toward you.

8 Press your hands upward again as you turn your palms up and point your toes to begin your second repetition.

No. 7 Bending to Touch the Feet

Part one

1 Start from the previous move with legs stretched out in front of you, toes up, and bring your arms straight up by your ears, with your palms facing each other.

2 Fold forward at the hips, keeping the back flat until you are leaning forward about 45 degrees. Hold your toes and look forward. Flex your toes back toward you and gently push your waist forward so that you are not rounding your lower back.

4 Let go of your toes and slide your hands back along your legs as you sit up, and place your palms at the front of your hips.

MODIFYING THE FORWARD BEND

Not everyone is able to hold the toes in a forward bend easily. To modify, walk your hands down your legs toward your toes and stop wherever is right for you.

3 Bring your chin down and look at your knees, stretching the back of your neck.

5 Push your arms back behind you with the palms facing away.

Repetitions: Repeat the sequence 6 times.

Part two

1 Bring your hands to rest at the front of your hips.

2 Very carefully bend one knee at a time, leaning forward and taking hold of the opposite foot to bring it back to a cross-legged position.

3 End by bringing your palms to rest on the front of your hips.

HEALTH BENEFITS

This routine stretches the back, neck, legs and waist and stimulates many meridian channels. It also stretches the nerves around the lumbar vertebrae, which extend into the pelvic organs and legs and which can become compressed.

No. 8 Massaging Jingmen on the Back

1 Sit cross-legged with your palms resting at the front of your hips.

2 Bend forward and stretch your arms backward with the palms up. Look down and ahead.

HEALTH BENEFITS

The massage in this sequence tones the kidneys, energizes meridians and strengthens the lumbar region. It also stimulates the Jingmen point (see box, page 214), which gives this exercise its name.

3 Move your arms out to the sides, and turn the palms down.

continued next page →

4 Straighten your body as you bring your arms forward and bring your palms together.

5 Bring your palms down below your navel, press them together, and twist them around to bring your left hand on top with the fingers pointing to the right and your right hand underneath with the fingers pointing to the left.

THE JINGMEN POINT

The Jingmen is an acupuncture point above the kidneys toward the sides of the body. It is the 25th point along the Gall Bladder meridian. *Jing* means capital of a country and *men* means door or gate.

8 Bring your palms to rest at the front of your hips.

6 Bring your palms together in front of your chest.

7 Bring your palms down below your navel, press them together, and twist them around to bring your right hand on top with the fingers pointing to the left and your left hand underneath with the fingers pointing to the right. Repeat the sequence 7 times, alternating your hands, ending with the left palm on top.

9 Slide your hands along your sides to your lower back and place your palms over your kidneys. If this is difficult, use the backs of your hands.

10 Rub your hands up and down to massage the lower back 24 times.

No. 9 Massaging the Belly and Abdomen

Repetitions: Repeat this circular abdominal massage 6 times. On the final repetition, rest your palms on your lower ribs at your waist.

1 Bring your palms to either side of your ribcage just under chest height.

2 Turn your fingertips downward and massage inward.

3 Keeping your fingertips facing downward, massage downward along your abdomen.

4 Move your hands outward along your lower abdomen.

No. 10 Burning the Navel Ring

1 Overlap your palms at your navel, with the left hand touching the navel. Close your eyes and place your attention at the navel for 2–5 minutes, imagining that the navel area is growing warmer.

2 Open your eyes and massage around your navel clockwise 3 times and anticlockwise 3 times in small circles, with the Laogong acupoint (see box, below left) at the centre of your palms over the navel area.

LAOGONG

The Laogong point is often mentioned in Qigong because it is a very powerful acupuncture point. It is the eighth point on the Pericardium meridian. Lao means labour and gong means palace, so literally it means the palace of work.

HEALTH BENEFITS

In Traditional Chinese Medicine the navel is our connection point to our mother in the womb and at birth, and an important acupoint. Concentrating on the area and then massaging it enhances circulation and vitality and also soothes the nervous system.

No. 11 Rotating the Upper Body

1 Place your hands on top of your knees and close your eyes.

2 Tilt your body forward to begin the circling to the left.

3 Rotate your upper body to the left, anticlockwise 6 times.

HEALTH BENEFITS

Rotating the waist strengthens the spine and stimulates the abdominal organs.

STRAIGHT AND STABLE

When rotating the body, keep your spine straight so that you don't slouch or drop your head, and keep your seat bones firmly on the mat so that you maintain a stable base.

4 Repeat the sequence, rotating the body to the right, clockwise 6 times.

Ending the sequence: Sit erect and open your eyes.

No. 12 Rinsing the Mouth and Swallowing Saliva

Repetitions: Repeat this section 2 more times so that all of your saliva is swallowed.

1 Start with your palms resting at the front of your hips.

2 Move your hands away from your body, out to the sides, and push backward, palms away.

HEALTH BENEFITS

Massaging your gums with your tongue helps to keep the gums firm and healthy. Saliva is considered to be an elixir in Chinese medical tradition and was sometimes referred to as Heavenly Dew. Saliva contains enzymes and hormones that aid digestion and nourish the body.

continued next page →

3 Bring your arms around in a circle in front of your abdomen, palms facing your navel, fingertips pointing toward each other.

4 Bring your hands to the top of your hips, thumbs up, as you make fists, and rest them while you rinse the mouth with saliva (see box, opposite).

6 Straighten your arms upward with palms facing out.

7 Turn your palms inward and make fists.

5 Let go of your fists and bring your hands upward to chest height.

HOW TO RINSE THE MOUTH WITH SALIVA

Keep your lips lightly touching and use your tongue in a circle to clean your mouth, right to left along the top gums then left to right along the bottom gums, then the same but inside the gums. Make 6 repetitions, cleaning the gums outside and then inside the teeth, without swallowing, so that you can use the saliva you are creating for the next step.

Using the saliva collected, rinse your left cheek and then your right cheek 36 times, but don't swallow your saliva.

Repeat this sequence 3 times and you will gather a lot of saliva.

8 Bend your elbows downward.

9 Move your fists down and place them at the top of your hips with thumbs up, and swallow about one-third of your saliva, imagining that it is going down to the Lower Dantian.

To close

1 Start with your fists at the top of your hips with thumbs up. As you inhale, roll the shoulders back, expand your chest and hold the inhalation for 2 seconds.

2 Bring your hands to shoulder height and cross your wrists at chest height with the left hand nearest to your chest and both palms of the fists turned toward you. Press your chest gently with your wrists and relax your chest.

3 Release your fists and lower your palms to the tops of your knees, palms up.

Relax

1 A good way to end the sequence is to lie on your back, and hug one knee into your chest, then the other.

4 Raise your hands to head height and out to the sides at about 45 degrees as you look up.

5 Bring your arms inward, palms down, to shoulder-width apart at chest height.

6 Place your palms on top of your knees, palms down, and rest in this position for 30 seconds or more.

2 Now hug both knees and rock side to side a few times, massaging your back.

3 Slowly straighten your legs back to the floor, relax your arms either on the floor or across your belly with one hand over the other. Close your eyes and completely relax for a few minutes.

Eighteen Movements Qigong – Shibashi

This is one of the most popular and most practised Qigong sets in the world today. It was created in 1979 by Professor Lin Housheng, who was inspired by Yang-style Taijiquan. For this reason it is often referred to as Taiji Qigong in Eighteen Movements. Lin Housheng was born in 1939 in Fujian province, southeast China. By the 1980s he had become a Qigong superstar and it was estimated that around one-fifth of the Chinese population practised Lin's Qigong. In 1989 he visited the United States for the first time and became an American citizen in 2010. Further sets of Eighteen Movements Qigong followed, and by the 1990s Professor Lin had compiled six sets in all, adding up to a total of 108 moves.

To begin

The exercises that follow are the first and most popular set of Eighteen Movements Qigong. They are simple and easy to learn, but are nonetheless very effective in creating a feeling of relaxation, calmness and increased energy. Professor Lin recommended that each move should be repeated six times. If you perform the complete set in one session, each move should flow seamlessly into the next move. However, any of the moves can be performed singly if you prefer.

Warm-ups

Begin with some gentle loosening exercises to gently warm up the body and mobilize your joints. Choose a few moves from the Warm-ups chapter, or use your own warm-ups if you prefer.

Breathing

Use soft abdominal breathing throughout (see page 67–8).

Modifying the moves

Each move can be easily modified to suit persons of all ages and abilities, including those who require a chair.

Transitions

Ideally, each move should flow into the next. I have set out the transitions so that they are easy to follow, but the more flowingly you can connect into the next move, the better.

> **MOVE THROUGH WATER**
>
> To encourage a smooth, flowing look and feeling, imagine that you are performing the moves in water.

No. 1 Regulate the Breath

1 Start with feet shoulder-width apart with arms by your sides.

2 Lift the arms straight ahead of you to shoulder height, palms down but leading with the wrists.

3 Lower your arms to hip height, palms down, while bending the knees.

Transition: Return to Shoulder-width Stance (see pages 54–5), arms at your sides, ready to lift your arms upward in front of you for the next move.

Repetitions: Repeat the sequence 6 times.

Breathing: Breathe in as you lift your arms. Breathe out as you lower your arms and bend your knees.

No. 2 Open the Chest and Heart

This move starts and ends like the first move, but with arms opening at chest height in the middle of the move.

Repetitions: Repeat the sequence 6 times.

1 Start with feet shoulder-width apart with arms lifted forward at shoulder height, palms down.

2 Turn your palms to face each other and separate your arms out to the sides.

Breathing: Breathe in as you lift and separate your arms. Breathe out as you close and lower your arms.

4 Turn your wrists in a gentle circle so that your hands are palm down.

5 Lower your arms as you bend your knees.

Transition: End with a Shoulder-width Stance (see pages 54–5), arms by your sides, ready for the next move.

3 Bring your arms back to shoulder width, palms still facing each other.

No. 3 Paint a Rainbow

Repetitions: Repeat the sequence 6 times.

1 Start with feet shoulder-width apart and lift both arms in front of your body at least to shoulder height.

2 Bend your knees and shift your weight to your right leg as you lower your left arm, outstretched at shoulder height with the palm up, and position your right hand, palm down, above the crown of your head. Bend your upper body slightly toward your outstretched arm. Keep in a Shoulder-width Stance (see pages 54–5), or pivot on your left toes, as our model, if this is better for your knees.

Breathing: Breathe in as you lift your arms. Breathe out as you bring your arms into position with one arm out and one palm over your head. If you have a long breath, inhale as you turn to the left and exhale as you turn to the right.

Transition: Return to a Shoulder-width Stance (see pages 54–5) or a small Horse Stance (see page 58), arms at your sides, ready for the next move.

3 Lift your arms over your head as you face forward in preparation for turning right. Shift your weight to the left leg as you bend both knees and lower your right arm, outstretched at shoulder height with the palm up, and position your left hand, palm down, above the crown of your head. Bend your upper body slightly toward your outstretched arm. Keep in a Shoulder-width Stance (see pages 54–5), or pivot on your toes, as our model, if this is better for your knees.

No. 4 Circle Arms and Separate Clouds

Repetitions: Repeat the sequence 6 times.

Breathing: Breathe in as you lift your arms. Breathe out as you lower your arms.

1 Start with feet shoulder-width apart or small Horse Stance (see page 58) with arms lifted out to your sides at head height.

2 Bend your knees as much as is comfortable as you lower your arms until the wrists cross in front of you, with the right arm on the inside, palms facing inward.

3 Keep your wrists crossed as you raise your arms upward above your head while straightening your knees.

4 Separate both arms and circle them out to the sides with the palms facing away, ready to repeat the move.

Transition: Return to a Shoulder-width Stance or small Horse Stance, arms at your sides, ready for the next move.

No. 5 Roll Arms Backward

1 Start with feet shoulder-width apart or small Horse Stance (see page 58) with your arms at chest height straight ahead, palms down, and with your knees bent.

2 Turn your waist to the right as you drop you right hand to your hip, palm up, and let your eyes follow the hand.

3 Circle your right hand up and around to ear height, palm down.

Repetitions: Repeat the sequence 6 times.

Breathing: Breathe in as you look down and twist. Breathe out as you look to the front and move your hand forward.

4 As you turn your waist back to the front, turn your left palm up so that when your palms pass each other on your centreline, they are facing each other.

continued next page →

5 Extend your right palm to the front and drop your left hand to your hip, palm up, and let your eyes follow the hand.

6 Circle your left hand up and around to ear height, palm down.

7 As you turn your waist back to the front, turn your right palm up so that when your palms pass each other on your centreline, they are facing each other.

8 Extend your left palm to the front and drop your right hand to your hip, palm up, and let your eyes follow the hand, to continue the sequence.

Transition: Bring both arms to chest height straight ahead, palms down, remaining in your Shoulder-width Stance or small Horse Stance, ready for the next move.

No. 6 Row the Boat in the Middle of the Lake

Repetitions: Repeat the sequence 6 times.

1 Start with feet shoulder-width apart or small Horse Stance (see page 58) with both arms out in front of your body at chest height, palms down. Bend your knees as much as is comfortable and lean the upper body forward to about 45 degrees.

2 Bring both arms down to the sides and roll your shoulders back as you turn your palms up and straighten your legs a little.

3 Bend your knees as much as is comfortable and circle your arms outward and forward to repeat the sequence.

Breathing: Breathe in as you lift your arms back and up. Breathe out as you bring your arms forward.

Transition: Return to a Shoulder-width Stance, arms at your sides, ready for the next move.

No. 7 Lift a Ball Across your Body

Repetitions: Repeat the sequence 6 times.

1 Start with feet shoulder-width apart with arms at your sides.

2 Lift an imaginary ball to head height with your right hand across a diagonal in front of your body, lifting both heels as you lift the ball. (If lifting both heels is too difficult, lift only your right heel.)

3 Bring your right arm downward, palm down, bending your knees and lowering your heels.

Breathing: Breathe in as you lift the ball upward. Breathe out as you lower your arm.

4 Lift an imaginary ball to head height with your left hand across a diagonal in front of your body, lifting both heels as you lift the ball. (If lifting both heels is too difficult, lift only your left heel.)

5 Bring your left arm downward, palm down, bending your knees and lowering your heels.

Transition: End with a Shoulder-width Stance, arms by your sides, ready for the next move.

No. 8 Turn to Look at the Moon

Repetitions: Repeat the
sequence 6 times.

1 Start with feet shoulder-
width apart with your
arms by your sides.

2 Slowly swing both arms up to the left, twisting left
and following the hands with your eyes, allowing the
hands to flow naturally. Imagine that you are looking at
the moon slightly behind you.

Breathing: Breathe out as you twist and look behind at the moon. Breathe in as you return to the front.

3 As you twist back to the front and lower your arms, bend your knees as much as is comfortable.

4 Follow the swing through to the right, letting your eyes follow the move.

5 Slowly swing both arms up to the right, twisting right and following your hands with your eyes.

Transition: Step out to the left into a small Horse Stance (see page 58), arms by your sides, ready for the next move.

No. 9 Twist Waist and Push Palms

1 Start in a small Horse Stance (see page 58) with palms up at your waist.

2 Twist your waist to the left as you push out with your right palm at shoulder height toward the left corner.

3 Draw your hand back, palm up, as you twist back to the front.

Repetitions: Repeat the sequence 6 times.

Breathing: Breathe out as you twist and push. Breathe in as you withdraw your hand to your waist.

4 Without stopping, twist your waist to the right as you push out with your left palm at shoulder height toward the right corner.

5 Draw your hand back, palm up, as you twist back to the front to begin the sequence again.

Transition: End in a small Horse Stance, arms by your sides, ready for the next move.

No. 10 Cloud Hands

Repetitions: Repeat the sequence 6 times.

1 Start in a small Horse Stance (see page 58) with your left arm across your chest, the palm turned toward your face and your waist turned to the right.

2 Turn your waist to the left, allowing the waist to move both arms. Let your eyes follow the left hand. As you twist, feel that the left hand is floating in the clouds and that the right hand is pushing against water.

3 Twist as far as is comfortable and exchange hands so that the right hand lifts to face height and the left hand lowers.

Breathing: Breathe in when turning left. Breathe out when turning right.

4 Turn your waist to the right, allowing the waist to move both arms. Let your eyes follow the right hand.

5 Twist as far as is comfortable and exchange hands so that the left hand lifts to face height and the right hand lowers. Keep the waist twisting smoothly throughout, with no stopping points.

Transition: End with feet shoulder-width apart, arms by your sides, ready for the next move.

No. 11 Scoop the Sea and Look at the Sky

1 Start with feet shoulder-width apart with your arms by your sides, and step forward with your left foot, keeping your weight on your back foot.

2 Transfer your weight forward into a Bow Stance (see page 64) and lean forward to scoop up water from the sea, crossing your wrists with the right hand underneath.

3 Transfer your weight into a Back Stance (see page 60), keeping the sole of your front foot down, as you lift your body and hands above your head and look up, leaning backward slightly as though looking at the sky.

Repetitions: After 6 repetitions, change legs and repeat 6 times with the right leg forward.

4 Separate your hands and bring them out to the sides in arcs, as though you are scattering the water you have scooped up.

5 Bring your arms down in a circular action as you shift your weight forward to a Bow Stance to repeat the sequence.

Breathing: Breathe out when you transfer your weight forward. Breathe in when you transfer your weight back.

Transition: Step into a Shoulder-width Stance and move into a Back Stance with the left foot forward, arms by your sides, ready for the next move.

No. 12 Undulating Waves

This move has a rocking motion, lifting the front toes up as you rock back and lifting the back heel up as you rock forward. Imagine that you have rockers on the bottoms of your feet. Keep your knees slightly bent throughout.

1 Start in a Back Stance (see page 60), left foot forward with toes up, arms at waist height, palms down.

2 Shift your weight forward, lifting your back heel, and lift your wrists up with palms facing down.

Repetitions: Repeat the sequence 6 times. Change legs and repeat 6 times.

Breathing: Breathe out when you rock forward. Breathe in when you rock back.

3 As you transfer your weight into a Back Stance, lift your wrists up.

4 Remaining in your Back Stance, smoothly bring your arms down to waist height, palms down.

Transition: Step back into a Shoulder-width Stance (see pages 54–5) and move into a Back Stance with the left foot forward, arms by your sides ready for the next move.

No. 13 Flying Dove Spreads its Wings

Like the previous movement, this has a rocking motion – you lift the front toes up as you rock back, and lift the back heel up as you rock forward. Keep your knees slightly bent throughout.

Repetitions: Repeat the sequence 6 times. Change legs and repeat 6 times.

Breathing: Inhale as your arms open, exhale as your arms close.

1 Start in a Back Stance (see page 60), your left foot forward with the toes up, and your arms out to the sides at shoulder height with the palms facing forward. Imagine that your arms are like the wings of a dove.

2 Shift your weight forward and lift your back heel as you close your wings so that the palms come toward each other.

3 Transfer your weight into a Back Stance, opening your wings, to repeat the move.

Transition: To end, step into a small Horse Stance.

No. 14 Forward Punch

Repetitions: Repeat the sequence 6 times.

Breathing: Breathe out as you punch. Breathe in as you bring your fist back to your waist.

1 Start in a small Horse Stance (see page 58) with your fists at your waist, palms up.

2 Punch forward with your right fist, twisting the fist to a palm-down position. Focus your eyes on the punch.

continued next page →

3 Withdraw your right fist, twisting the fist to a palm-up position.

 4 Punch forward with your left fist, twisting the fist to a palm-down position. Focus your eyes on the punch.

5 Withdraw your left fist, twisting the fist to a palm-up position, to begin the next repetition.

Transition: Step into a Shoulder-width Stance (see pages 54–5), arms by your sides, ready for the next move.

No. 15 Wild Goose Flying

Imagine that your arms are as graceful as the wings of a wild goose, and feel the air resistance as you slowly move them up and down.

Repetitions: Repeat the sequence 6 times.

1 Start with feet shoulder-width apart and bring your arms to your sides in a slightly curved position.

2 Lift both heels as you lift your arms out to the sides to head height or higher, in graceful arcs, leading the move with your wrists.

3 Slowly bring your arms downward to your sides as you drop your heels, bending your knees as much as is comfortable, ready for the next repetition. Some people like to lean forward slightly as they bend their knees.

Breathing: Breathe in as you lift your arms. Breathe out as you lower your arms.

Transition: End with a Shoulder-width Stance, arms by your sides, ready for the next move.

No. 16 The Great Wheel Turns

With this move, feel that your waist is leading the turning of the great wheel, and let your arms follow naturally.

1 Start with feet shoulder-width apart with your arms as though holding a large wheel.

2 Bend your knees as much as is comfortable and turn your waist to the left.

3 Lift both arms in an arc over to the left above your head as you straighten your legs.

Repetitions: Repeat the sequence 3 times to the left and 3 times to the right.

Breathing: Breathe in as you lift your arms. Breathe out as you lower your arms.

4 Turn your waist to the right, arms above your head.

5 Lower your arms in an arc as you bend your knees as much as is comfortable.

6 Return to your starting position to repeat the sequence.

Transition: End with a Shoulder-width Stance, arms by your sides, ready for the next move.

No. 17 Bouncing a Ball with Steps

Imagine that your right hand is connected to your left knee and creates an action a little like bouncing a ball. Feel like you are slowly marching in position.

1 Start with feet shoulder-width apart with your arms by your sides.

2 With the wrist leading, lift your right hand to shoulder height, as you lift your left knee.

3 Drop your right hand downward as you lower your left foot to the floor.

Repetitions: Repeat the sequence 6 times.

Breathing: Breathe in as you lift your hand and foot. Breathe out as you lower your hand and foot.

4 Lift your left hand, wrist leading, to shoulder height, as you lift your right knee.

5 Drop your left hand downward as you lower your right foot to the floor.

Transition: End in a Shoulder-width Stance with arms by your sides, ready for the next move.

No. 18 Balance the Qi

Repetitions: Repeat the sequence 6 times.

1 Start with feet shoulder-width apart with your knees bent and your arms out to the sides a little, as though you are about to scoop up the Qi energy.

2 Bring your hands in front of you with the palms up and the fingertips of both hands toward each other.

3 Lift your palms up your centreline to chest height or higher, as you straighten your knees.

4 Turn your palms down gently, as though your hands are floating.

Breathing: Breathe in as you lift your hands. Breathe out as you lower your hands.

To close

5 Lower your hands down your centreline as you bend your knees as much as is comfortable.

1 Rub your hands together a few times.

2 Bring your hands to rest just below your navel with the palms facing inward, with the right hand closest to the body for women, and the left hand closest to the body for men.

Rest in this position for a few moments.

Transition: Bring your arms to your sides, ready to close the sequence.

Shaolin Qigong

The tradition of Shaolin Qigong began with Bodhidharma, a Buddhist monk who lived during the 5th and 6th centuries, and who came to the Shaolin Monastery in Henan province. He taught the monks Qigong and left behind a manual called *The Muscle and Tendon Transforming Classic* (*Yijinjing*) which contained hundreds of exercises aimed at promoting health, strength, flexibility, balance, coordination, speed and endurance. Much of this famous book has been lost over time, and a multitude of popular Qigong sets are claimed to have been sourced from the book. The oral tradition, teaching and practice based on the *Yijinjing* continue at the Shaolin Monastery to this day.

The exercises that follow were taught to me by Shifu Yang Rui, who lived and trained at the Shaolin Monastery for ten consecutive years as a Shaolin disciple. Fifteen years ago he moved to the UK and now lives and teaches in London. He is the Head and Chief Instructor of Shaolin Culture and teaches Shaolin Qigong and Gongfu. He also teaches Chen-style Taijiquan, which he learned from Grandmaster Chen Zheng Lei. He returns to the Shaolin Monastery each year to keep in touch with his roots.

Shaolin Qigong is a relatively new experience for me, and I am grateful for Shifu Yang Rui's patient guidance. The slowness and meditative quality of these exercises are restorative and strengthening. With Shaolin Qigong, the most important aspect is to be aware of your internal connections and to feel and maintain the energy and connection to the Lower Dantian.

The following exercises are a small selection of moves of Shaolin Health Qigong taught to me by Shifu Yang Rui from the *Yijinjing* through the Shaolin tradition.

It is up to each individual to decide how long to hold positions and how many repetitions to do. Also, the moves are performed with a slight amount of tension held throughout the body, which elicits a feeling of connection. Tension is a Yang quality, while relaxation is a Yin quality. The art is to know the exact amount of tension and relaxation to use, and this skill is difficult to learn without personal feedback from an experienced teacher.

To begin

After Warm-ups and calming the breath and mind, begin the Shaolin exercises with Balance the Qi (see page 258) and Collect the Qi Energy (see pages 270–1), no matter how few or how many exercises you choose to do. This ritualistic sequence primes the body and mind for what is to follow and allows time for you to move into a receptive state. The feeling of full body connection is elusive and so it is important to prime your mind, nervous system and neural pathways before you begin.

Breathing

Use smooth, quiet abdominal breathing throughout. The movements that follow can be performed so slowly that attempting to link your breath with the move would be impossible without holding your breath – and you should never hold your breath. It is a vehicle for Qi and must always be flowing.

Warm-ups

Prepare with 10 minutes of loosening exercises. Choose from the Warm-ups chapter or from your own favourites.

Eyes

With all of the stationary moves, your eyes can be open or closed. When you close your eyes, external distractions are diminished, and this aids your ability to feel your internal connections more easily.

Calm breathing and mind

Spend a few moments to calm your breathing and mind. It is important to feel relaxed and at ease before you begin.

Balance the Qi

Repetitions: Repeat slowly 3 times.

Breathing: Use slow abdominal breathing. Breathe in as you lift your hands, and breathe out as you lower your hands. If you choose to perform the move more slowly, there is no need to link your breath with the move.

1 Stand with feet shoulder-width apart or a small Horse Stance (see pages 58–9), knees bent, with your hands in front of your body, palms facing upward and fingertips angled toward each other.

2 Lift your hands upward, along your centreline, to shoulder height or higher, as you slowly straighten your knees. Keep your shoulders and elbows relaxed downward.

3 Turn your palms to face downward.

4 As you slowly bend your knees, press your palms downward along your centreline with your fingers toward each other.

Note: If your shoulders are stiff or rise up accidentally when you lift your hands, then lift your hands to a lower height. Shoulder relaxation is far more important than the height of your hands in any Qigong.

Holding the Sky

This is a fascinating exercise. On the face of it you could say that it is similar to Collect the Qi Energy (see pages 270–1), but it feels completely different because of the long holds, feeling the weight of the sky and the different timing for straightening the legs.

1 Start with feet shoulder-width apart or small Horse Stance (see page 58), knees bent, hands palms down in front of your body with the fingers pointed inward toward each other.

2 Keep your knees bent as you slowly lift your arms, with palms up, to shoulder height. Push out through the middle fingers just enough to feel an elastic quality through the chest, arms, hands and fingers. Also feel a whole body connection from the Lower Dantian. Hold this posture for between 30 seconds and 2 minutes or longer.

Repetitions: Repeat 3 times.

continued next page →

Sitting: Holding the Sky can also be done sitting. It is important to sit on a cushion to enable the posture to be effortless so that it can be held for long lengths of time if you wish. There may be times when you want to hold this position for 10 minutes or more.

3 Straighten your knees slowly while keeping your arms held out, feeling the weight of the sky as your legs push up, as though against heavy resistance. When your legs are straight, lift your arms above your head slowly.

4 Press your hands downward in front of your body with the fingers pointed inward toward each other as you very slowly bend your knees. Hold the end posture for between 30 seconds and 2 minutes or longer.

Breathing: Use slow abdominal breathing (see pages 67–8). The moves are done so slowly that it is neither possible nor desirable to match the breath to any particular part of the move.

Pushing with Slow Stepping

Repetitions: Take as many steps as feels right for you, but do a minimum of 5 steps.

1 Start with feet shoulder-width apart, palms facing downward in front of you.

2 Bring your arms to your sides, with palms forward, as you transfer your weight to your left leg and lift up your right foot, ready to step. Hold this position for 30 seconds or longer.

3 Step out diagonally to the right. Touch your heel lightly to the floor.

continued next page ➔

4 Roll your foot down as you transfer your weight forward into a Bow Stance (see page 64). At the same time, move your arms out to the sides in an arc forward to chest height in front of you, palms facing away as though gently pushing.

5 Slowly shift your weight onto your back leg, keeping both feet flat on the floor as you bring both hands in toward your chest, with palms facing inward, and then turn the palms outward ready to push.

6 Shift your weight forward into a Bow Stance as you gently push with both palms. Hold this position for 30 seconds or longer.

Breathing: Use slow abdominal breathing (see pages 67–8). The moves are done so slowly that it is neither possible nor desirable to try to match the breath to any particular part of the move.

7 Slowly shift your weight onto your back leg, keeping both feet flat on the floor as your arms travel back in gentle outward arcs, as though opening curtains, to come to rest at your sides with palms forward.

8 Slowly shift your weight forward onto your right leg as you lift your left foot off the ground, ready to step. Hold this ready to step position for 30 seconds or more.

9 Step out diagonally to the left, to repeat the sequence to the left.

Pushing to the Front, Sides and Sky

1 Start with feet shoulder-width apart or small Horse Stance (see page 58), palms facing downward in front of you. Keep your knees bent and hold your internal connection to the Lower Dantian throughout the sequence.

2 Bring your hands up to chest height, palms up.

3 Push forward slowly and hold the end position for 30 seconds or more.

Repetitions:
Repeat 3 times.

Breathing: Use slow abdominal breathing (see pages 67–8). If you decide to do the moves more quickly, then breathe out as you push away from your body and breathe in as the arms come back toward your body. If you decide to do the moves very slowly with longer holds, it is neither possible nor desirable to match the breath to any particular part of the move.

4 Bring your hands in toward your chest, palms up.

5 Push out to the sides of your body with your palms facing outward, and hold the end position for 30 seconds or more.

6 Bring your hands in toward your chest, palms up.

7 Push to the sky and hold the end position for 30 seconds or more.

Punching with Twisting Punch

Repetitions: Repeat right and left punches 3 times.

1 Start with feet shoulder-width apart or small Horse Stance (see page 58), with your fists facing upward at your hips. Keep your knees bent throughout the sequence.

2 Slowly punch forward with your favourite hand, keeping your fist facing up.

3 When your arm has almost reached its target, rotate your forearm, coordinating the spiralling action of turning the fist palm down by the time it reaches the imaginary target. Hold this position for 30 seconds or more and see if you can maintain the Qi connection with your whole body. Repeat the sequence with the other hand.

Breathing: Use slow abdominal breathing (see pages 67–8). If you decide to do the moves more quickly, then breathe out as you punch and breathe in as you retract your fist. If you decide to do the moves very slowly with longer holds, it is neither possible nor desirable to match the breath to any particular part of the move.

Holding the Qi Ball

1 Start with feet shoulder-width apart or in small Horse Stance (see page 58), holding an imaginary ball of Qi energy. Stand for 2 minutes or longer, paying attention to the energy connection between your hands and to the rest of the body.

2 Slowly pull your hands apart and see whether the connected feeling remains. If it does, pull your hands away further.

3 Play with different distances, noticing any subtle alterations in feeling, and find out whether there is a point where you feel either less or more connection. The key to this exercise is paying attention to a total connection between the Qi ball, the Lower Dantian and the whole of your body.

4 End by bringing your hands back to the starting position.

Breathing: Use slow soft, abdominal breathing (see pages 67–8) throughout.

To end

End with Collect the Qi Energy (see pages 270–1) to bring your practice to a close, regardless of how few or how many exercises you have chosen to perform.

Five Animal Qigong – Wuqinxi

Scholars often accredit Hua Tuo (140–208 CE), a famous physician of the late Han Dynasty, with formulating The Exercise of the Five Animals. His intention was to expel illness and slow down the ageing process to encourage longevity.

Over the centuries, many different versions of Five Animal Qigong were developed. It is sometimes called Five Animal Frolics, which conveys the playfulness that is intended in the actions of the animals.

I was first introduced to this delightful set of exercises in 1997 during the eight-day 2nd European Tai Chi and Qi Gong Congress Forum in Hungary. I attended Michael Singer's workshops throughout the Forum. At that time Michael was a noted teacher of Taiji and Qigong who taught mainly in Vienna and Budapest. I'll never forget the fun we had pretending to be an animal, outside under the trees on warm July mornings.

The Wuqinxi version, shown here, is one that I particularly like. Alina Kisina, who is my student in Qigong, learned this version in Armenia several years ago from Professor Liu Hong, who has since returned to China to teach at Shanxi University. I feel that Alina has consummately captured the spirit of the five animals.

LEFT: Deer Twists with Antlers.

The five animals and Qigong

Animal	Element	Season	Organs affected	Emphasis
TIGER Courageous and fierce	Wood	Spring	Liver and gall bladder	Grasping and stretching, in much the same way as the tiger stalks and catches its prey.
DEER Light and graceful	Water	Winter	Kidneys and bladder	The graceful, playful movements of the deer as it twists and runs.
BEAR Heavy and rooted	Earth	Late Summer	Spleen and stomach	The strength and determination displayed by the bear as it moves heavily forward, rooted to the earth.
MONKEY Clever and agile	Fire	Summer	Heart and small intestine	Quick, cheeky movements and agility, like those of the monkey in search of food.
CRANE Balanced and free	Metal	Autumn	Lungs and large intestine	Balance and sensitivity to the air currents, allowing the freedom of flight.

Each animal exercise has two parts. The first part shows the animal stretching and warming up for the second part, where the animal achieves its goal. The tiger stretches its claws in the first part, before attacking its prey. The deer gracefully limbers up in part one, before running. The bear rotates his heavy upper body in the first part, before heavily ambling forward. The cheeky monkey has a good look around in part one, before risking going forward to steal and eat its fruit. The crane stretches its wings in the first part, before taking flight. Although these animals are traditionally performed as a set, if you wish you can choose your favourite animal and give just that one a try.

To begin

Spend a few moments calming your breathing and mind.

Collect the Qi Energy

After each animal, perform this sequence before going on to the next animal.

Repetitions: Repeat 3 times.

1 Start with feet shoulder-width apart with hands in front of your body at hip height, palms up, fingertips of both hands toward each other.

Breathing: Breathe in as you lift your hands.
Breathe out as you lower your hands.

2 Bring your hands out to your sides, palms up, and lift your arms upward in gentle arcs to shoulder height.

3 Continue to lift your hands in upward arcs until they are above head height.

4 Press your palms downward along your centreline with the fingertips toward each other.

Tiger

Part one – Tiger Stretches its Paws

1 Start with the final posture of Collect the Qi Energy as shown on pages 270–1.

2 Make fists by first stretching your fingers one at a time, starting with the little fingers.

3 Now close the fists with the thumbs on the outside.

4 Lift your fists up to chest height.

Repetitions: Repeat the sequence 3 times.

Breathing: Breathe in as you lift your hands. Breathe out as you lower your hands.

5 Release your fists as you open your palms at just above chest height and push up to the sky with palms up and fingers toward each other. Look up as your eyes follow your hands.

6 Make fists by first stretching your fingers one at a time, starting with the little fingers.

7 Now close the fists with your thumbs on the outside.

continued next page →

8 Bring your fists down to just above chest height.

9 Open your fists, palms down, with the fingertips toward each other.

10 Lower your hands to hip height to your starting position.

TIGER CLAW HAND

Bend the joints in your fingers and thumbs to make fierce tiger claws.

Part two – Tiger Seizes its Prey

Repetitions: Repeat the sequence 3 times.
One repetition = to the front, to the left, to the front, to the right.

1 Start with feet shoulder-width apart and make loose fists.

2 Bring your loose fists up to shoulder height in front of you, look up and arch your back, slightly bending your knees.

3 Lean forward from your hips, keeping your legs and back straight, and stretch out your arms to catch your prey with fierce tiger claws and fierce eyes.

4 Bend your knees, release your claws and slowly bring your hands down toward your thighs, palms down toward the ground.

continued next page →

Breathing: Breathe in as you lift your hands and catch your prey with tiger claws. Breathe out as you release your claws and move back to an upright position in Shoulder-width Stance.

5 Stand with feet shoulder-width apart and make loose fists.

6 Bring your loose fists up to shoulder height in front of you, look up and arch your back, slightly bending your knees.

7 Step out at 45 degrees with your left foot, lean forward from your hips, keeping your weight on the back leg, and catch your prey with tiger claws and fierce eyes.

8 Bend your knees, release your claws, and slowly bring your hands down toward your thighs, palms down toward the ground.

9 Stand with feet shoulder-width apart and make loose fists.

10 Bring your loose fists up to shoulder height in front of you, look up and arch your back, slightly bending your knees.

continued next page →

11 Lean forward from your hips, keeping your legs and back straight, and stretch out your arms to catch your prey with fierce tiger claws and fierce eyes.

12 Bend your knees, release your claws and slowly bring your hands down toward your thighs, palms down toward the ground.

13 Stand with feet shoulder-width apart and make loose fists.

14 Bring your loose fists up to shoulder height in front of you, look up and arch your back, slightly bending your knees.

15 Step out at 45 degrees with your right foot, lean forward from your hips, keeping your weight in the back leg, and catch your prey with tiger claws and fierce eyes.

16 Bend your knees, release your claws and slowly bring your hands down toward your thighs, palms down toward the ground.

Ending the sequence: After 3 repetitions, return to Shoulder-width Stance.

Collect the Qi Energy: Perform this once as shown on pages 270–1, before going on to the next animal.

Deer

Part one – Deer Twists with Antlers

Repetitions: Repeat the sequence 3 times.
One repetition = twist with antlers to the left and the right.

1 Start with your feet shoulder-width apart, arms at your sides with loose fists.

2 Bring your loose fists to shoulder height on the left.

3 Change your loose fists to deer antler hands (see box, opposite).

DEER ANTLERS

Make deer antler hands by folding your two middle fingers in toward the palm of your hand. Keep your thumb, forefinger and little finger straight.

4 Lift your deer antlers up in an arc over to the right as you step out with your right foot angled outward. Keep the weight on your back leg as you twist and look behind and down. Keep your lower elbow tucked in close to your ribs and the upper elbow over your head.

5 Lift your deer antlers up in an arc over to shoulder height on the left as you bring your right foot back to Shoulder-width Stance.

6 Release your deer antler hands and make loose fists.

7 Drop your loose fists down in an arc in front of you and bring them up to shoulder height on the right.

8 Change your loose fists to deer antler hands.

Breathing: Breathe in as you lift loose fists up to shoulder height, make deer antlers and twist. Breathe out as you return to the front.

9 Lift your deer antlers up in an arc over to the left as you step out with the left foot angled outward. Keep the weight on your back leg as you twist and look behind and down. Keep your lower elbow tucked in close to your ribs and the upper elbow over your head.

10 Lift your deer antlers up in an arc over to shoulder height on the right as you bring your left foot back to Shoulder-width Stance.

11 Release your deer antler hands and make loose fists.

Ending the sequence:
After 3 repetitions, bring your loose fists to your sides in Shoulder-width Stance, ready for part two.

Part two – Deer Runs

1 Stand with feet shoulder-width apart with loose fists.

Repetitions: Repeat the sequence 3 times. One repetition = sequence with left leg forward and sequence with right leg forward.

2 Bring your loose fists up to shoulder height, in front of and close to your body, with your elbows bent. Step forward with your left foot into a Bow Stance (see page 64) as your arms straighten, still with loose fists in front of you.

3 Transfer your weight to your back leg as you make deer antler hands, with elbows turned slightly out and the backs of your hands facing each other. Look down to your front foot and keep it flat on the ground.

Breathing: Breathe in as you transfer weight forward. Breathe out as you transfer weight back.

4 Shift your weight forward into a Bow Stance as you straighten your arms in front of you and make loose fists.

5 Transfer your weight to your back leg and step in, bringing your left toes close to your right foot, as you bring your arms in and down. Hop gently to the left foot ready to step forward with the right leg to repeat.

Ending the sequence:
After your third repetition step back to Shoulder-width Stance, smoothly, without a hop, and release your fists.

Collect the Qi Energy: Perform this once as shown on pages 270–1, before going on to the next animal.

Bear

Part one – Bear Rotates its Waist

All of part one is in Shoulder-width Stance and your upper body makes circles, first in one direction, then in the other direction.

Repetitions: Repeat the sequence 3 times. One repetition = rotating the upper body one complete circle to the right and one complete circle to the left.

Breathing: Breathe in as you circle from the front to the side and back. Breathe out as you circle from the back to the side and front.

1 Start with the final posture of Collect the Qi Energy (see page 271).

2 Lift your hands up to your breast bone and look down as you make bear paws, touching your hands together at the index fingers.

BEAR PAWS

Make bear paws by making hollow fists.

4 Circle back the other way to the right side, back, left side and front.

3 Lean forward slightly and circle your shoulders to the left side, back, right side and front.

5 End by coming to an upright position with arms relaxed by your sides.

Part two – Bear Ambles Forward

1 Start with feet shoulder-width apart with your arms hanging loosely by your sides. Think heavy and weighted into the ground, like a bear.

2 Step forward with your left foot, keeping your hip, shoulder and eyes in line, your chest lifted, your arms swinging naturally, feeling your hip throw your front arm forward. Keep your back heel up.

3 Rock back onto your right heel, letting your arms swing naturally, and stay there for a second.

4 Take one step with your right foot, everything the same as in step 2, but on the opposite side.

Breathing: Breathe in as you step forward. Breathe out as you rock back.

5 Rock back onto your left heel, as in step 3 but on the opposite side.

6 Take one step with your left foot again, everything the same as in step 2.

7 Rock back onto your right heel, exactly as in step 3.

Ending the sequence: The 3 steps forward complete this sequence. To end, step forward with your back foot into a Shoulder-width Stance (see pages 54–5), arms hanging loosely at your sides.

Collect the Qi Energy: Perform this once as shown on pages 270–1, before going on to the next animal.

Monkey

Part one – Monkey Looks

Repetitions: Repeat the sequence 3 times, as follows. First repetition: monkey makes monkey paws, lifts onto toes and looks to the front, left, front, right, front. Second repetition: monkey makes monkey paws, lifts onto toes and looks to the front, right, front, left, front. Third repetition: monkey makes monkey paws, lifts onto toes and looks to the front, left, front, right and back to the front, to finish by dropping the heels and hands.

1 Start with the final posture of Collect the Qi Energy as shown on pages 270–1.

2 Circle your fingers outward in a quick circular snatching action as though making monkey paws.

3 Rise up onto your toes as you lift your monkey paws up to collarbone height, with your index fingers touching and your shoulders lifted up toward your ears. Look cheeky.

4 Look cheekily to your left. Stay on your toes.

MONKEY PAW

Make a monkey hand by bringing your fingers and thumbs together with your fingers pointing downward.

5 Look back to centre. Stay on your toes.

6 Look cheekily to your right. Stay on your toes.

7 Look back to centre. Stay on your toes.

8 Lower your heels as you lower your hands to the starting position.

Breathing: Breathe in as you lift onto your toes and look to each side. Breathe out as you lower your heels and hands.

Part two – Monkey Picks and Eats Fruit

Repetitions:

Repeat the sequence 3 times, as follows. First repetition: as shown. Second repetition: take a large step back to the right to set up your new diagonal and repeat the Steps 2 to 6, but with opposite arms and legs. Third repetition: take a large step back to the left, as for the first repetition.

1 Start with feet shoulder-width apart with palms to the floor and fingertips angled toward each other.

2 Take a large step back with your left foot, on a diagonal to the left, and bring your right foot in on the toes. Looking high up to the right, along your diagonal, at your target fruit as you tip your shoulders to the left, make a monkey paw with your left hand beside your left hip and bring your right palm up near your left shoulder.

5 Put your right heel down and transfer all of your weight to your right leg.

6 Step back along the diagonal with your left foot and bring your right foot in on the toes. Bring your left hand palm up, with the fingers facing back, under your chin, to make a plate to eat from. Bring your right palm up under the left elbow. Take a second to savour your fruit.

3 Step forward with your right foot along the diagonal and imagine that you are brushing branches out of the way with your right arm.

4 Step forward with your left foot, along the diagonal, still looking up at your target fruit, and pluck the fruit with your left hand and make monkey paws with both hands. Keep your back heel up and take a second to enjoy your success at plucking the fruit.

Breathing: Breathe in as you step back. Breathe out as you step forward.

Ending the sequence:
End with a Shoulder-width Stance, arms by your sides.

Collect the Qi Energy:
Perform this once as shown on pages 270–1, before going on to the next animal.

Crane

Part one – Crane Stretches Upward

Repetitions:
Repeat the sequence 3 times. One repetition = bird's beak to front, left leg back with arms, bird's beak to front, right leg back with arms.

1 Start with the final posture of Collect the Qi Energy as shown on pages 270–1.

2 Lift your arms straight ahead with one palm on top of the other, both palms parallel to the floor, to form the bird's beak (see box, below). Stretch your back and arms forward at about a 45-degree angle. Maintain the inward curve in your lower spine when you lean forward. Hold your bird's beak hands higher than your head and look outward from underneath.

Breathing: Breathe in as you lift your arms forward with your bird's beak. Breathe out as you take your arms behind you.

BIRD'S BEAK

Place your right hand over your left hand, and with your arms stretched forward and lifted, bring the palms parallel to the floor. If you feel more natural with the left hand on top, that's fine.

6 Lift your arms straight ahead, forming the bird's beak as in step 2. Stretch your back and arms forward at a 45-degree angle, maintaining the inward curve in your lower spine. Hold your bird's beak hands higher than your head and look outward from underneath.

3 Bend your knees slightly as you bring your arms back to your sides.

4 Transfer your weight to your right leg as you bring both arms back behind, lift up your chest, and bring your left leg back and slightly out to the side with the toes pointed, straightening both legs.

5 Return to a Shoulder-width Stance as you bring your arms back to your sides.

7 Return to a Shoulder-width Stance as you bring your arms back to your sides.

8 Transfer your weight to your left leg as you bring both arms back behind, lift up your chest, and bring your right leg back and slightly out to the side with the toes pointed, straightening both legs.

9 Return to a Shoulder-width Stance as you bring your arms back to your sides.

Part Two – Crane Takes Flight

1 Start with feet shoulder-width apart with your arms by your sides, gently curving, with your palms up and your fingertips toward each other.

2 Transfer your weight to your right leg and bring your left knee up as high as possible into a Crane Stance. At the same time, lift your arms to shoulder height, leading with your elbows.

3 Push through to your palms, creating a graceful, wavelike motion.

Repetitions: Repeat the sequence 3 times. One repetition = right knee up twice + left knee up twice.

Breathing: Breathe in as you lift your arms. Breathe out as you lower your arms.

4 Gracefully lower your wings as you lower your leg and lightly touch the toes to the ground beside your right foot.

5 Lift your left knee up into a Crane Stance and at the same time lift both hands out to the sides in graceful upward arcs until the backs of your hands face each other above your head. Keep your elbows bent outward.

6 Lower both arms down to the sides as you lower your leg and return to Shoulder-width Stance (see pages 54–5) ready to repeat the sequence lifting your right knee.

To close

Now that you have completed performing your Five Animals Qigong, finish with Collect the Qi Energy once (see pages 270–1).

Closing: Finish in the Closing Posture with hands on the Lower Dantian (see page 57).

Smile: A smile is always a good way to end.

PART 5

Qigong in Your Everyday Life

Making Time

Qigong can be viewed as a leisure activity, in which case going to a class once or twice a week would be sufficient. It would be enough to satisfy the needs of many people. However, Qigong can also be used to transform your life, in which case you would need to make it part of your daily routine.

Most of us don't have time to add something additional into our busy lives. We have an excellent list of reasons at our fingertips as to why we don't have time to do anything extra. Sometimes this list consists of the everyday things such as shopping, preparing meals, eating, washing clothes, watching television, keeping up with current news, travelling, working, taking care of the family, visiting friends and relatives, and so forth. Sometimes the list is more unusual, like taking part in special projects, participating in sports activities, having fascinating hobbies or taking special courses involving some type of learning.

We are all busy. Parkinson's Law states that our work expands to fill the time available. Have you ever thought what would happen if suddenly your daily time allowance were cut in half? What would it be like? Would you suddenly be in limbo, or would everything adapt to fit the time available? Would we make better choices about how to spend our time? It's an interesting concept to think about.

Important questions

There are a few questions that are important to ask yourself after completing any activity, whether it be computer games, socializing with friends, attending a class, visiting relatives or indeed anything at all.

- Do I feel better, worse or the same?
- Is this improving my long-term physical and mental health?
- Is this energizing or enervating?
- Is this deeply satisfying and fulfilling?
- Does this enlarge my life or diminish it?
- Do I feel expanded or contracted?

The mere slowing down to ask yourself these questions might be enough to allow change to happen.

Fitting Qigong into your life

One of the great advantages of Qigong is that you don't need much room to practise it. After you understand a few basics, you can practise anywhere without needing much additional time.

Here are a few ideas suggesting how to fit Qigong into your daily life in order to make every day more fun and to reap the benefits of the practice.

Out and about

- Whenever you are outdoors, put your mind on your breathing. The smooth, gentle, abdominal breathing (see pages 67–8) in Qigong is important in daily life.
- Improving your peripheral vision (see page 116) is invaluable whenever you are outside, as it enables you to see more of your surroundings. Not only does this make you more aware of your environment, but this simple measure could add to your overall safety if you notice something before it is close enough to affect you.
- Use your increased leg strength and agility to step aside quickly to avoid stationary or moving obstacles that are in your path.
- If you can't reach something on a high shelf at the supermarket, view this as an opportunity to rise up on your toes slowly and take longer than usual lowering your heels back to the floor on a slow exhalation.
- Whenever you have to wait in line, practise a one-leg stance to improve your balance. If you are in a place where discretion is called for, a Nail Stance (see page 62) or Back Stance (see page 60) usually won't be noticed, as most people are wrapped up in their own thoughts or activities.

LEFT: Connecting to the earth, breathing in Qi energy.

At home

- If you are watching television or listening to the radio or music, practise a simple Qigong move or stance.
- Whenever you have to wait for something to happen at home – such as a delivery to arrive or tea or coffee to brew – strike up a Qigong pose.
- When using your phone, toothbrush or hairdryer, practise a stance on one leg while doing the task.
- In the bath, take time to wriggle and stretch your toes and do ankle flexions, extensions and circling. The water provides warmth and slight resistance, which encourages more mobility.
- When ironing, set the ironing board to a low position so that you can practise your Horse Stance (see pages 58–9). Also, shift your weight from side to side when ironing long items.
- While vacuuming, lunge forward into a Bow Stance (see page 64) when you push the vacuum forward. Transfer your weight back slowly into a Back Stance (see page 60) when you pull the vacuum backward.
- If you are browsing at a library or newsstand, this is a perfect opportunity to hold a stance. A Nail Stance (see page 62) or

small Horse Stance (see page 58) would be an inconspicuous choice.
- When you are on a train or bus and you have to stand, use this time as a balancing opportunity. A Shoulder-width Stance (see page 54), small Horse Stance (see page 58) or Bow Stance (see page 64) will work well in this situation and will rarely be noticed by your fellow travellers.
- Any time you are confined to a room, Qigong comes into its own, because you don't need a large space to practise. If you have enough room to reach out with your arms, you have enough space to practise some form of Qigong. This brings a whole new range of opportunities when, for example, you are by yourself in a waiting room.

With other people

- The Clear Brow of the Sage (see pages 48–9) can be used anytime. Children, animals and some adults are particularly sensitive to moods and facial expressions. If you can appear calm on the surface, as well as actually feeling calm, your interactions will be more rewarding.
- When caring for young children, play a game of "Copy Me", starting with the easier Qigong moves. Most children love this, and in no time Qigong will become a normal part of their lives. A prize for staying

quiet and still for the longest while "Holding a Tree" can turn out to be a peaceful interlude.

- If looking after older children, introduce Qigong to them as a way to improve their concentration and calm their minds. I have taught Qigong in boys' schools and girls' schools, and have found that it helps young people to deal with the anxiety of taking exams and the stress of growing up.

- At work there are plenty of opportunities. If you sit at a desk, most of the Qigong moves can be adapted to a seated position. Resourceful workers are often able to find an empty office, hallway, stair landing or secret hiding spot to do 5 to 10 minutes or more of practice. Fitting Qigong into your daily work pattern makes work more enjoyable.

On the move

- If you go swimming, it adds a further dimension to your practice to do Qigong in water. The resistance of the water makes the moves stronger and more flowing, and when you come back to dry land you can take the memory and feel of it with you to enhance your practice.

- When doing any sport, warm-up time is important to make the joints and tissues of the body more supple, to improve breathing and to prepare the mind. Many top athletes and other sportspeople use Qigong to improve their game.

- When walking up stairs, try using a Bow Stance (see page 64) to go up two or three steps at a time as though you were climbing a mountain.

Anytime, anywhere

- Posture is important anytime, whether you are sitting, standing or moving. Think of your alignment and the way you stand in harmony with gravity, and the way your feet move and roll when walking. See the Posture and Movement Principles chapter, pages 70–3, for more ideas.

Once you decide to think creatively, you can work out so many ways to fit Qigong into your daily life. Qigong practice done on a daily basis will bring health, equanimity and a great deal of fun into each day.

Adaptations to Suit Your Needs

Qigong is adaptable to every need. I have met very few people in my long teaching history whose needs could not be met. It affects all aspects of physical and mental wellbeing and is easy to adapt.

I have taught Qigong to people with the everyday problems that we are all beset with from time to time, such as stress, aches and pains and mild depression. Also, I have worked with people with more serious conditions: stroke, Parkinson's, multiple sclerosis, osteoarthritis, rheumatoid arthritis, psoriatic arthritis, osteoporosis, partial paralysis,

LEFT: Qigong can be practised sitting on a chair.

vision impairment, total blindness, senility, depression, anorexia, obesity, post-traumatic stress disorders, neurological and nervous disorders, psychosis, bipolar disorder, schizophrenia, drug addiction, and bullying and other abuse. All have had positive results.

I have also taught active and physically fit people who want the challenge and mental focus that Qigong can bring. Over the years I have taught people from all walks of life, including school and university students, firemen, doctors, martial artists, business professionals, sports enthusiasts, teachers, gymnasts, dancers, musicians, actors, housewives and househusbands.

Some needs are easy to fulfil. It may be as simple as a person wishing to attend an enjoyable, friendly class. All that is required is that they leave the class feeling better than they did on arrival. The main challenge here is to find a class that suits their personality and time schedule.

Other people have more complex needs, to do with medical conditions, life issues or general confusion. Qigong provides a suitable vehicle within which to address these needs.

How to go about adapting

Every physical ability can be catered for, because every movement can be adapted to be made easier or more difficult. All moves can be performed with fewer or more repetitions. Overall practice time can be as little as two minutes or as much as two hours or more. All moves can be adapted to sitting in a chair or holding on to a support, and some moves can be modified enough to be done lying down. These are all easy ways of adapting Qigong.

Other adaptations are more time-consuming and require working together with a person to identify something that the individual would like to achieve or become. The next step is to agree a course of action and give the person exercises that are suitable and guidelines that will help his or her condition. Ongoing feedback and discussion are important so that programmes can be constantly updated.

Real-life examples

Here are a few examples of how I have worked with people to meet their needs and what adaptations were made. Adaptations can be physical or mental. I have changed people's names.

Helen was a reasonably fit lady in her 60s, but she had weak arthritic knees and was on a long waiting list for a knee replacement. She also had a dog, and one of her pleasures in life was taking her dog for a walk. We identified a goal: she said that if she were able to once again lift her foot up high enough to get over a country stile, she would be satisfied. We did lots of knee-strengthening Qigong exercises and spent time correcting her foot, ankle and knee alignment. It took Helen about one month to understand why her alignment was contributing to her problems, because she had never looked at her body in this way before and it had never crossed her mind. Things often become obvious only after someone has pointed them out, and Helen was keen to make improvements. We worked a lot in front of a mirror until she was able to check her own alignment, restore mobility in her feet and ankles and develop the muscles around her knees. We kept testing different heights to place her foot at, and month by month the height she could manage increased and her balance improved. By the time she was able to hold a high Crane Stance (see page 63), she was also able to place her foot on a stile and have the strength and balance to climb over it. She was delighted.

Kenneth, a young man in his 20s, was completely blind but wanted to learn Taiji. To provide him with a foundation, basic stances and simple Qigong moves were essential. After practising for about six months, he had acquired the balance and stability required to learn a Taiji form. The Qigong had provided him with a starting point, and he continued with his Qigong practice alongside his journey into Taiji.

Barbara was in her 50s and was very lonely. She lived alone and was prone to anxiety. She had read widely about Qigong and wondered if it could improve her quality of life. The first thing Barbara worked on was her breathing, as she had been unaware that she had shallow upper chest breathing which made her more liable to panic attacks. After she had improved her breathing, other things began to change for the better. She loved the flowing movements of Qigong, which brought her more freedom of expression, and she began to smile much more.

George, who was in his 30s, had multiple sclerosis but was determined to delay its progress. Although he was able to walk, he could not maintain a stable position. He was taking part in a hospital research

project where he was measured on a regular basis on a Swaymeter (a device used in tests as a measure of postural control in neuroscience research). George's objective was to beat his previous results. His attitude was key in this and we spent a lot of time practising Standing like a Post Qigong (see pages 170–9). One day, about seven months after he had begun his Qigong practice, he came to his lesson with a big smile on his face. The research project manager had been very surprised because his Swaymeter records had shown marked improvement. George continued to improve.

Sarah was a teenager who had been abused and as a result suffered from depression and low self-esteem. Her goal was to feel confident again and not live in fear. We started with basic Qigong moves to increase her feeling of stability and connection to the earth. We worked together to improve her posture, as she had developed a defeated posture with rounded shoulders, caved-in chest and hanging-forward head. Meditation was also key in her recovery, as she had lost her sense of who she really was. The Standing Meditation postures (see Qigong Meditation chapter) made her feel strong, stable and connected to something worthwhile. After several months she felt confident enough to take part in daily living.

Tom was a martial artist in his early 30s. He wanted to improve his martial arts and also to control his aggression and anger. He lacked rooting and mental resolve, so we started with the Standing like a Post postures (see pages 170–9). He also lacked flow in his body and mind, so the flowing Qigong postures were invaluable. It took about three years for Tom to become strong, rooted and better skilled at controlling his aggression.

I have recounted these real-life examples to demonstrate the varied way in which Qigong can be adapted to suit different needs. Every condition can improve and every need can be addressed. It is important that the person knows what they want and discusses these needs with their teacher, so that they can agree reasonable goals that can be measured in some way and then adapted as the person progresses.

Adaptation to suit someone's needs can be as simple as supplying something to hold on to, or it can be more complex, requiring an understanding of the person's condition, mental attitude toward it and willingness to make changes. Qigong offers many different kinds of benefits and can be adapted to suit your needs. Adaptation is part of living.

RIGHT: Seated Qigong (see Seated Twelve Pieces of Brocade chapter).

Bibliography and Further Reading

Acupuncture and Chinese Medicine: Roots of Modern Practice by Charles Buck, Singing Dragon 2015

Answers to Common Tai Chi and Qigong Questions by William Ting, Xlibris Corporation 2011

Chan Mi Gong by Liu Han Wen, Victory Press 1989

A Chinese-English Dictionary (Revised Edition), Foreign Language Teaching and Research Press 1997

Chinese Medical Qigong by Tianjun Liu, Singing Dragon 2010

Chinese Mythology by Anthony Christie, Newnes Books 1983

Chinese Shamanic Cosmic Orbit Qigong by Master Zhongxian Wu, Singing Dragon 2011

Dao De Jing, Making This Life Significant, a philosophical translation by Roger T Ames and David L Hall, Ballantine Books 2004

Daodejing by Laozi translated by Edmund Ryden, Oxford University Press 2008

The Doctrine of the Elixir by R B Jefferson, Coombe Springs Press 1982

Eastern Philosophy by Kevin Burns, Arcturus Publishing Ltd 2004

The 18 Movements of Taiji Qigong by Lin Housheng, The Qingdao Publishing Company 1996 (primarily in Chinese, with some English)

Fire Dragon Meridian Qigong by Master Zhongxian Wu and Dr Karin Taylor Wu, Singing Dragon 2012

The Illustrated Handbook of Chinese Qigong Forms compiled by Li Jingwei and Zhu Jianping, Singing Dragon 2014

The Illustrated I Ching translated by R L Wing, The Aquarian Press 1987

In a Chinese Garden by Maggie Keswick, Judy Oberlander and Joe Wai, The Dr Sun Yat-Sen Garden Society 1990

Instant Health: The Shaolin Qigong Workout for Longevity by Shifu Yan Lei, Yan Lei Press 2009

The Jade Emperor's Mind Seal Classic translated by Stuart Alve Olson, Dragon Door 1992

Qigong – The Secret of Youth by Dr Yang Jwing-Ming, YMAA Publication Center 2000

Qigong Meditation by Dr Yang Jwing-Ming, YMAA Publication Centre 2003

Reading and Writing Chinese, Third Edition, by William McNaughton, Tuttle Language Library 2005

The Root of Chinese Qigong by Dr Yang Jwing-Ming, YMAA Publication 1997

The Secret of the Golden Flower translated by Thomas Cleary, HarperCollins 1991

Sheng Zhen Wuji Yuan Gong: A Return to Oneness by Li Jun Feng, Lotus Press 2004

The Tao of Power translated by R L Wing, The Aquarian Press 1986

The Taoist Experience by Livia Kohn, State University of New York 1993

The Way of Chuang Tzu by Thomas Merton, Penguin Books Canada Ltd 1965

The Way of Energy by Master Lam Kam Chuen, Gaia Books Ltd 1999

The Way of Qigong by Kenneth S Cohen, Ballantine Books 1997

Yijing, Shamanic Oracle of China translated by Richard Bertschinger, Singing Dragon 2012

Glossary

Abdomen: The area between the chest and the pelvis. It contains the stomach, small and large intestines, pancreas, liver, gall bladder, kidneys and spleen.

Abdominal breathing: Breathing that uses the diaphragm (see entry), a muscle located horizontally below the lungs. The belly expands on inhalation. This is the natural, relaxed form of breathing in all mammals, whenever they are in a state of relaxation.

Acupuncture: A form of treatment in Traditional Chinese Medicine (see entry). Thin needles are inserted at specific points with the intention of adjusting the body's energy flow to a healthier pattern.

Alchemist: A person who practises alchemy (see entry).

Alchemy: A forerunner of chemistry with the aim of transmuting one substance into a different one, for example turning metal into gold or turning various components into an elixir of life (see entry).

Back Stance: A stance where most of the body's weight is on the back leg.

Baduanjin: Eight Pieces of Brocade Qigong, developed from Daoyin techniques. There is a standing style and a seated style.

Baojian: Health Preservation Qigong, developed from Daoyin techniques. Usually practised seated.

Bodhidharma: A Buddhist monk who was of Indian origin. He taught at the Shaolin Monastery in the 6th century CE. Also known as Da Mo, he was credited with establishing in China a form of meditative Buddhism, which, after it spread to Japan, became Zen.

Bow Stance: A stance where most of the weight is on the front leg, and the front knee is bent. It is also called the Bow and Arrow Stance because the front leg is an allusion to the curved front part of the bow and the back leg is straight like the drawstring of the bow.

Buddhism: A philosophy and religion that originated in India c. 6th to 4th century BCE through Gautama Buddha, with the spiritual goal of having a soul free from desire, suffering and sorrow.

Cat Stance: A stance where most of the weight is on the back leg and the toes of the front leg lightly touch the floor.

Centre of gravity: A point in any object around which the force of gravity acts. The best way to visualize this is to balance a small object on your fingertip. The place where you must position your fingertip will be underneath its centre of gravity, which is sometimes referred to as centre of mass. In a human body, the approximate centre is just in front of the second sacral vertebra. The easiest way to get a feel for this is to measure about two fingers' width below the navel when standing with arms down. The exact location varies from person to person, owing to different body proportions and weight distribution. A lower centre of gravity increases stability.

Centreline: An imaginary line that runs down the centre of your body along its vertical axis. It is sometimes called the axis of rotation, because if a person were to rotate in position, the centreline would pass through their body's centre of mass.

Chart of Internal Alchemy: See Neijing Tu.

Cinnabar: A mineral ore composed of mercuric sulphide. Its bright red colour made it valuable as a paint pigment. Used in External Alchemy (see entry) in ancient times, when its toxic properties were unknown, it was an important ingredient in potions and pills claiming to be the elixir of life (see entry).

Confucianism: A system of philosophical doctrines taught by Confucius (551–479 BCE) that focus on the cultivation of virtue and the maintenance of ethics within society. Name of Confucius in Pinyin: Kongfuzi.

Crane Stance: A one-legged stance in which one knee is lifted above waist height in front of the body, with the toes pointed downward.

Dantian: An energy centre in the body, often translated as "elixir field". In Qigong, there are three main Dantians: Lower (below the navel), Middle (heart area) and Upper (between the eyebrows).

Dao: Translated as the way, principle, path, doctrine, source of everything, way of nature.

Daodejing: A classic Chinese text written by Laozi (see entry) in the 6th century BCE. Translations of the title include *The Way and Its Power*, and *The Classic of Virtue and the Way*. It is sometimes referred to as The Five Thousand Character Classic because it is made up of 5,000 Chinese characters.

Daoism: A Chinese philosophical system developed by Laozi in the 6th century BCE. Daoism emphasizes living in harmony with the Dao (see entry). It is sometimes viewed as a religion.

Daoist: A follower of Daoism (see entry).

Daojia Yangsheng: Rejuvenation Qigong developed from Daoyin (see entry) techniques. Yangsheng means nourishing life.

Daoyin: A traditional form of Chinese exercise dating from the Han dynasty or earlier, aimed at preserving and restoring health and youthfulness, with the underlying idea of balancing Qi (see entry). As with many Chinese terms, there is a choice of how to translate this: dao (this is a different dao from The Dao) = to guide, lead, transmit, direct yin (this is a different yin from Yin and Yang) = to draw, pull, stretch, lead, guide.

Daoyin Qigong: Any Qigong based on Daoyin (see entry) techniques.

Daoyin Tu: A silk scroll *c.* 168 BCE consisting of 44 colour drawings of people performing therapeutic exercises.

Dayan: Wild Goose Qigong. A form of Qigong originated by Daoist monks living in the Kunlun mountains in the Jin dynasty.

Diaphragm: The main muscle used in inhalation. It is a dome-shaped sheet of muscle under the lungs.

Dynasty: A succession of Chinese rulers from the same family.

Eight Pieces of Brocade: See Baduanjin.

Eighteen Movements Taiji Qigong: See Shibashi.

Electroencephalogram (EEG): A recording of brain activity. Brain waves are divided into four groups: Beta, Alpha, Theta, Delta.

Elixir of life: A magical potion sought by alchemists (see entry) to prolong life and restore youth.

Embryonic breathing: A state of breathing so subtle that breathing can barely be detected by an observer. This form of breathing sometimes occurs spontaneously in deep meditation.

Emei Qigong: Qigong named after Mount Emei, a sacred mountain in Sichuan Province, China. Developed by a Buddhist monk.

Empty Stance: Any stance where the front leg is empty of weight; for example a Back Stance is an Empty Stance.

External Alchemy: Alchemy (see entry) using resources outside the human body, for example pills and potions concocted from materials such as herbs, gold, silver, cinnabar and arsenic. The ancient Chinese alchemists (see entry) believed that if they could discover the magic elixir of life (see entry), it would produce health and longevity and even immortality.

Fangsong: A modern Relaxation Qigong involving conscious relaxation with visualizations.

Fascia: A type of soft tissue in the body that surrounds every organ, muscle, tendon, ligament, bone and nerve. Every part of your body is connected to every other part through fascia.

Feng Shui: The Chinese system of positioning buildings, furniture and objects to gain a harmonious effect. The most propitious orientation will have a balanced flow of Qi (see entry), and will take all aspects of the surrounding environment into consideration. Literally means wind and water.

Five Elements: Wood, Fire, Earth, Metal and Water are the Five Elements, known as Wuxing. In Chinese philosophy they are viewed as processes, and through interaction each has the ability to increase or subdue any of the other four elements.

Five Animal Qigong: See Wuqinxi.

Flow: Involves the continuous movement of balanced Qi energy throughout the body. It is the ability to move smoothly and continuously, without any jerkiness, with a fluid, soft look to the body. Mentally, it is being completely immersed in what one is doing, with no mental distractions.

Fuqi: Ancient Daoyin Qigong (see entry) involving breathing in Qi (see entry) from nature. Literally means to take Qi.

Horse Stance: A stance where the feet are placed wider than shoulder-width apart, with both knees bent outward. It looks similar to the position you would be in when riding a horse.

Hua Tuo: A famous physician (140–208 CE) credited with formulating Five Animal Qigong (see Wuqinxi).

Hyperextended joint: A joint that goes past a normal range of motion, for example when a knee or elbow joint, which would normally make the leg or arm appear to be in a straight line when fully extended, appears to bow backward.

Intention: A combination of mental and emotional focus, consciously directed inward or outward for some purpose. Intention that comes from a calm mind and a loving heart will have a much different effect than that which comes from an anxious or angry mind and a spiteful heart. The Chinese concept of Yi (see entry) is intention from a calm, focused mind where wisdom is present.

Internal Alchemy: Alchemy (see entry) using resources inside the human body, for example digestion, metabolism, emotion, knowledge, intuition, meditation, Qi energy and everything that can contribute toward the peak performance of the person in terms of physical and mental health and proficiency.

Internal martial arts: There are three main internal martial arts (see Martial Arts): Taijiquan (see entry), Baguazhang, Xingyiquan. The main difference between an internal martial art and an external martial art is in the method of generating power.

Jing: One of the Three Treasures (see entry), it refers to reproductive energy, growth and vitality.

Jingmen: An acupuncture point above the kidneys toward the side of the body. It is the 25th point along the Gall Bladder meridian.

Jingzuo: The practice of Quiet Sitting used in contemplation and meditation.

Labyrinth: A circular path that winds its way into a centre.

Laogong: An acupuncture point on the hand; the eighth point on the Pericardium meridian.

Laozi: The first philosopher of Daoism (see entry), 6th century BCE, credited with writing the *Daodejing* (see entry). His name translates as Old Master.

Lin Housheng: Created Shibashi (see entry) style of Qigong in 1979.

Liuzijue: Six Healing Sounds Qigong. Each sound resonates with different parts of the body.

Locked joint: A joint that is at its end range of movement. Habitually locking a joint puts compressive stress on it, which can damage cartilage.

Longhu: Dragon and Tiger Qigong. The objective is to develop the agility of a flying dragon and the relaxed power of a tiger.

Lü Dongbin: A Tang dynasty scholar and poet who became the best-known of the legendary Eight Immortals in Chinese mythology.

Macrocosmic Orbit: An extension of the Microcosmic Orbit (see entry) to include the arms and legs.

Mandala: A drawing or design that symbolizes the cosmos and is used as a focal point for contemplation.

Martial arts: Any system with a training regime that teaches the student a traditional method of combat and self-improvement. The emphasis in training goals differs according to each tradition, but a common goal is proficiency in self-defence, attack and strategy. Some systems emphasize strength, health and mental and spiritual development.

Meridian: An invisible energy channel in the body, according to Traditional Chinese Medicine (see entry). When you are healthy, the energy pathways distribute balanced Qi energy throughout the body. There are twelve Principal Meridians, Eight Extraordinary Meridians and numerous minor meridian channels.

Microcosmic Orbit: A Qigong method for circulating energy around a circuit of two meridians (see entry): the Conception Vessel (Ren Mai) channel, which runs down the front of the body, and the Governing Vessel (Du Mai) channel, which runs up the back of the body.

Midline: An anatomical term used to divide the body in half. One midline divides the body into equal right and left sides, and in martial arts (see entry) this is usually called the centreline (see entry). The other midline divides the body into front and back, and in martial arts this is usually referred to as the line of your trouser side seam.

Mind: The brain is not the same as the mind, even though the terms are often used interchangeably. The brain is a physical organ. The mind is in every cell of the trillions of cells in our body, and each cell communicates not only with every cell but also with the cells we play host to, like gut bacteria. Also, the autonomic nervous system doesn't connect directly to the brain. It regulates bodily processes such as blood pressure, heartbeat, digestion and breathing, without necessarily feeding back to the brain.

Mindfulness: The daily practice of paying attention to what we are doing, while we are doing it, without any distraction from extraneous thoughts.

Mingmen: An acupoint referred to as the Door of Life, it is a point on the Governing Vessel meridian, which is located on your back opposite your navel.

Nail Stance: A stance in which the majority of your weight is on one leg and the other foot rests lightly on the toes, beside the supporting leg.

Neigong: A type of Daoyin exercise strongly associated with internal martial arts (see entry). Some say it is a form of Qigong because it has the same roots.

Neijing Tu: The Chart of Internal Alchemy. An ancient Chinese illustration of the inner landscape of the human body. (See Internal Alchemy)

Neiyanggong: Internal Nourishing Qigong. A form of Qigong from the Ming dynasty done sitting and lying down.

Perineum: An anatomical term to denote the area between the anus and the genitals.

Peripheral vision: The part of our vision that is outside the central line of view. When we expand our peripheral vision, we see more of what is around us. Peripheral vision can improve with training. Some Qigong exercises train peripheral vision by requiring the person to see both hands at the sides of their head while looking straight ahead.

Pinyin: A method of transcribing Chinese characters into the Roman alphabet. In the 1970s China requested all countries to use this system in preference to older systems such as Wade-Giles, Yale and others.

Proprioception: Our body's ability to sense where parts of the body are in space and in relationship to each other, without having to look.

Qi: A term used in Chinese medicine and philosophy to mean breath, air, energy, spirit, vigour, atmosphere, attitude, life force. One of the Three Treasures (see entry).

Qigong: A Chinese system of holistic health practice, which is often translated as energy cultivation.

Reverse breathing: A form of breathing where the abdomen is pulled in on the inhalation and pushed out on the exhalation. This is opposite to abdominal breathing (see entry).

Seated Twelve Pieces of Brocade: See Shierduanjin.

Shaolin: A place named after the Shaoshi mountain in Henan province, China. *Lin* means forest or woods, and so the name means in a wooded area of the Shaoshi mountain. It is famous for the Shaolin Monastery, a Buddhist monastery that dates back some 1,500 years.

Shaolin Qigong: A form of Qigong based on health exercises taught to the Shaolin monks by the Buddhist monk Bodhidharma (see entry) *c.* 6th century.

Shen: One of the Three Treasures (see entry), referring to mind and spirit.

Shibashi: A Qigong set of eighteen movements developed by Lin Housheng (see entry) in 1979. *Shiba* means eighteen, and Shibashi is often called Taiji Qigong in Eighteen Movements.

Shierduanjin: Seated Twelve Pieces of Brocade. A seated Qigong developed in the Qing dynasty. *Shier* means twelve.

Shoulder-width Stance: Sometimes called Parallel Stance, this is a stance in which the feet are parallel to each other.

Shuigong: Sleeping Qigong. A deep relaxation technique that trains the practitioner to relax at the point which occurs just before sleep.

Stance: The way in which a person stands, especially how he places his feet and distributes his weight.

Standing like a Post: See Zhanzhuang.

Taiji: Used to denote the internal martial art (see entry) of Taijiquan (see entry). Its true meaning is supreme ultimate, which refers to the primal beginning of existence from which Yin and Yang arose. Tai Chi in the Wade-Giles transcription system.

Taiji Tu: The Taiji diagram often referred to as the Yin Yang symbol.

Taijiquan: A Chinese internal martial art (see entry) practised for health, self-defence and self-cultivation. It translates as supreme ultimate fist and is popularly known in the West, using old transcription systems, as Tai Chi, T'ai Chi or T'ai Chi Ch'uan.

Three Treasures: The three energies essential to human life: Jing, Qi and Shen. Jing is life essence and vitality, Qi is breath and life force energy, and Shen is mind and spirit.

Traditional Chinese Medicine: A system of healthcare in China that has developed over thousands of years. It includes acupuncture (see entry), herbal medicine, remedial massage (tuina – see entry), diet and lifestyle advice, and Qigong.

Triple Burner: The Sanjiao meridian. This is a special concept in Traditional Chinese Medicine (see entry) that does not exist in Western medicine. According to the Chinese dictionary, sanjiao is defined as the three visceral cavities housing the internal organs, which would correspond to the lower, middle and upper part of the torso and all of the organs contained. This implies that the Triple Burner affects elimination, digestion and metabolism. It is sometimes associated with the pericardium (the sac enclosing the heart, which has connecting tissue to the heart, and the great vessels, such as the venae cavae, pulmonary artery, pulmonary veins and aorta). It is a topic of debate.

Tuina: Chinese massage. A component of Traditional Chinese Medicine (see entry).

Tuna: An ancient term for Breathing Qigong. *Tu* means to utter, and *na* means to admit.

This refers to exhaling the old and inhaling the new in terms of breath and vital energy.

Ursa Major: A star constellation containing the seven stars popularly known as The Great Bear, The Big Dipper or The Plough. These seven stars have great significance in Chinese cosmology and philosophy.

Vagus nerve: The body's longest nerve. It runs through our brains, chest, diaphragm (see entry), intestines and organs. It is the main part of our parasympathetic nervous system and communicates with our brain through neurotransmitters.

Wujigong: Primordial Qigong, developed by the semi-legendary Daoist sage Zhang Sanfeng who lived in the Wudang mountains during the Ming dynasty.

Wuqinxi: Five Animal Qigong, based on the movements of the tiger, deer, bear, monkey and crane.

Xiangong: Fragrant Qigong. An ancient form of Qigong that became popular in China in the 1990s. "Fragrant" refers to the sweet smell of health.

Xingqi: Circulating Qi (see entry), or an ancient meditative form of Qigong promoting the circulation of Qi.

Xiuzhen Shishu: An ancient Chinese text c. 1300, translated as The Ten Compilations on Cultivating Perfection. Xiuzhen means to cultivate the true character of oneself and is a moral principle in Chinese philosophy.

Yang: The active, dynamic force in the universe.

Yi: A calm focused mind, full of intention (see entry). There is a famous Chinese saying, "The Yi leads the Qi".

Yijinjing: Translated as The Muscle and Tendon Transforming Classic, this is ascribed to the Buddhist monk Bodhidharma (see entry), which he wrote during his stay at the Shaolin Monastery in the 6th century CE.

Yijing: *The Book of Changes*, the oldest Chinese classic, thought to have a history of over 2,500 years, though scholars differ widely on exact dates.

Yin: The passive, nurturing force in the universe.

Yin Yang symbol: See Taiji Tu.

Yongquan: The first acupoint on the Kidney Meridian channel. Often translated as Bubbling Spring (see page 55).

Yue Fei: A famous Chinese General from the 12th century CE whom scholars credit with compiling the Eight Pieces of Brocade Qigong (see Baduanjin). Yue Fei is a Chinese national hero and is honoured to this day.

Zhanzhuang: Standing Post Qigong, or Standing like a Post Qigong, which involves holding stationary positions, often for long lengths of time.

Zhineng: Wisdom Healing Qigong. Developed by Dr Ming Pang who in 1979 founded the Beijing Qigong Research Society. A combination of ancient healing practices including sound vibration, movement and meditation.

Zhongli Quan: One of the Eight Immortals in Chinese mythology.

Zhuangzi: A famous collection of philosophical stories that exemplify the nature of Daoism. Dating from c. 4th century BCE, it is considered to be one of the great treasures of Chinese literature. The book is named after its author, Zhuangzi, which means Master Zhuang.

Zifagong: Spontaneous Qigong. A technique of letting the body move by itself, without interference from the mind of the practitioner.

Index

Acknowledgements

Dan Docherty Director of Practical Tai Chi Chuan International, President and Executive Committee member of The Taijiquan & Qigong Federation for Europe, Chairman and Executive Committee member of The Tai Chi Union for Great Britain. Much gratitude for being my Sifu since 1988 in Qigong and Taijiquan, a long journey blessed with new ways of seeing.

Master Faye Li Yip Co-founder of the Deyin Taijiquan Institute (GB), President of the British Health Qigong Association and Executive Committee member of the International Health Qigong Federation. Thank you for teaching me Seated Twelve Pieces of Brocade and for her support in agreeing to be the model for this chapter.

Gordon Peck Head of Qiworks, Acupuncturist, Qigong expert. My thanks for being available as a consultant concerning Chinese Traditional Medicine.

Norman Allen My gratitude for his valuable, helpful advice and support.

Shifu Yang Rui Head of Shaolin Culture. Thank you for teaching me Shaolin Qigong and being available as an advisor for this chapter.

To the team at Octopus Publishing Group Ltd, to everyone who worked on this book, with special thanks to Leanne Bryan, Senior Editor and Commissioning Editor, without whose help and encouragement I would never have written this book. Special thanks also to Yasia Williams, Art Director, and her design team for their creative input and the stylish layout of the book. Special thanks to Alison Wormleighton, Copy Editor, for her skilful editing suggestions.

To my students who agreed to be models in this book and who are also dear friends: Alina Kisina, who gave me invaluable advice and support. Christine Stevens, who made Modified look chic. Joe Wilson, who brought a big smile and a big heart. Peter Sichel, who contributed calmness and fortitude.

To all of the teachers whose workshops, seminars and courses I have attended over the last two and a half decades, my deepest gratitude for helping me to feel like a perpetual beginner.

To all of my students whose enthusiasm for learning continues to give me great joy.

Picture Credits

LAROUSSE
POCKET
ENCYCLOPEDIA
OF
WINE

General Editor
Christopher Foulkes

LAROUSSE

LAROUSSE POCKET ENCYCLOPEDIA OF WINE
First published in 1995 by Larousse

Managing Editors: CLAUDE NAUDIN, LAURE FLAVIGNY
Art Directors: FRÉDÉRIQUE LONGUÉPÉE, SUSAN JONES
Map Director: RENÉ OIZON
Maps: EUROPEAN MAP GRAPHICS, PALIMPSESTE, MARIE-THÉRÈSE MÉNAGER
Production: ANNIE BOTREL

Edited and Produced by SEGRAVE FOULKES PUBLISHERS
8 King's Road, Kingston upon Thames KT2 5HR, United Kingdom

General Editor: CHRISTOPHER FOULKES
Managing Editor: CARRIE SEGRAVE
Art Editor: NIGEL O'GORMAN
Editors: ALISON FRANKS, MAGGIE RAMSAY, GABRIELLE SHAW MW
Typesetting and Page Makeup: MACGURU
Illustrations: TREVOR LAWRENCE

ACKNOWLEDGMENTS

This book draws upon the resources of the Larousse Encyclopedia of Wine, *produced by the same team, which covers the wine world in much greater detail and with a more thoughtful tone. Renewed thanks to the worldwide team of contributors and experts who worked to shape the* Encyclopedia, *with particular gratitude to those who helped create this book: Alison Franks, John Gilbert, Nigel O'Gorman, Maggie Ramsay, Gabrielle Shaw MW and Carrie Segrave.*

Copyright © Larousse 1995

ISBN 2 03 507 202 6
Sales United Kingdom: Larousse International, 2 Albion Court, Galena Road,
Hammersmith, London W6 0LT
A CIP catalogue record for this book is available from the British Library

ISBN 2 03 507 201 8
Sales USA: Larousse Kingfisher Chambers Inc., 95 Madison Avenue,
New York, NY 10016

Library of Congress Catalog Card Number: 95-80465

ISBN 203 507 203 4
Larousse, Paris

Printed in France

CONTENTS

INTRODUCTION

THE LAROUSSE POCKET ENCYCLOPEDIA OF WINE is just that: a directory of wine names, places, people and terms. The aim is to aid wine choice and enjoyment by offering facts and guidance on as many wines and winemakers as possible.

It is not a compendium of personal tasting notes, with their inevitable quirks of opinion and prejudice. Nor does it reflect the competitive streak in the wine world whereby winemakers vie for medals or awards. This book aims at a balanced picture of what's what in wine, and where possible how wines taste, with the stress on those we are most likely to find in stores, on restaurant lists and when travelling.

The main part of the book is the A–Z, starting on page 33. However, other sections will aid wine choice and enjoyment: there's news from the world of wine; a chapter on Wine and Food discusses wine styles and which food they best go with; an Atlas of Wine Countries has maps showing where the main wine zones are; and at the end of the book are a chapter on Tasting Wine, Vintage Charts, and our list of Value for Money Wines which highlights affordable alternatives to the big names: *rapport qualité : prix*, as the French say.

Future editions will be much improved by feedback from readers: have we missed your favourite wine? Is there a producer of some minor wine who offers the best in quality and value? Let us know!

Christopher Foulkes, General Editor

HOW TO USE THIS BOOK

THE ALPHABET IS CHOSEN as the key access route. Look up what appears on a label – be it a region, grape name, producer or château – and this will lead to some information about the wine. There is no real need even to know which country the wine comes from. Once an entry is found, cross-references (in SMALL CAPITALS) may take you further.

The range covers the world's top wines – Bordeaux classed growths, Burgundy *Grands Crus* and the like – and it also deals with everyday wines: French *vins de pays*, fresh sources of value such as South America and Portugal, Hungary and southern Italy. There are definitions of label terms, summaries of wine rules, and brief sketches of key wine estates and producers.

Each entry in the A–Z starts with a key word in **BOLD CAPITALS**. This is the name, or the part of the name that is easiest to look up. Prefixes such as "de" and "du" in French, and "von" in German, and terms such as Château and Domaine, follow, not precede, the alphabetized word: Château de Fieuzal is listed as **FIEUZAL, CH DE**. *Italics* show the country and region the entry belongs to, and the style of wine (red, white, etc).

ABBREVIATIONS AND CONVENTIONS

Ch	Château	R	Red (wine)
Dom	Domaine	W	White (wine)
NV	Non-vintage	P	Rosé, or pink, wine
VDN	Vin doux naturel	Sp	Sparkling wine

Various official classifications of wine areas are used, and defined in the A–Z, their abbreviations being:

AOC *France*	Appellation d'Origine Contrôlée
DO *Spain*	Denominación de Origen
DOC *Italy*	Denominazione di Origine Controllata
DOC *Portugal*	Denominação de Origem Controlada
DOC *Spain*	Denominación de Origen Calificada
DOCG *Italy*	Denominazione di Origine Controllata e Garantita
QbA *Germany*	Qualitätswein eines bestimmten Anbaugebietes
QmP *Germany*	Qualitätswein mit Prädikat
VDQS *France*	Vin Délimité de Qualité Supérieure
WO *South Africa*	Wine of Origin
VA *USA*	Viticultural Area

Measurements

Wine production is measured in hectolitres, or 100 litres. A hectolitre (abbreviated to hl) is equal to just over 11 cases, or 133 75cl bottles, of wine. Area is measured in hectares, abbreviated to ha. One hectare equals 2.47 acres.

CHOOSING
WINES

WINE NEWS

A PARTIAL – IN BOTH SENSES – tip-sheet: what's new, what's good, what is causing comment and making waves.

BORDEAUX AND NAPA BACK ON FORM

The 1994 vintage saw a decent Bordeaux crop at last: the best vintage since 1990 – which, considering the sad state of '91, '92 and '93, is not saying much. The year was marred by September rain (a recurring pattern this decade), but the wines have turned out well. Caution is needed as Bordeaux *needs* a good vintage, and wish-fulfilment is a well-honed local skill, but independent experts rate the wines fairly high: 1988 is the best parallel.

In California, too, Napa made excellent '94 Cabernets in a cool summer – as good as those of the last good year, 1991.

ORGANIC BEGINS TO MATTER

From a fad to a theory to common sense: that's the progress of organic viticulture and winemaking. Today even respected domaines such as Leroy in Burgundy, Coulée de Serrant in the Loire, and others are to be found practising the extreme form called biodynamism (invoking the moon and stars as well as eschewing chemicals).

An official European Union (EU) definition of "organic wine" is awaited – but broadly, chemicals to combat pests and diseases must have been banned from the vineyard for at least three years. Artificial fertilizers are out. In the winery, additives are avoided: in some cases, egg-white or fish fining is not used, to allow the wine to be truly "vegetarian". The real test is in the taste: organic but horrible is a blind alley. Thankfully, most organic producers take enormous care – and that in any case is the way to make good wine.

ABC: ANYTHING BUT CHARDONNAY...

Look for a resurgence of other white-wine tastes, as wine-makers, and some drinkers, tire of Chardonnay: the greatest white-wine success story since Liebfraumilch. Everyone took to Chardonnay – it's an easy name to say, and the consensus New World style (imitated in eastern Europe and southern France) offers attractive fruity, creamy, slightly sweet tastes, spiced with a touch of oak. Now eyes turn to other grapes: Sémillon can age well, as Australia proves. But Riesling is the chief alternative – better on an absolute scale, some say, than the vaunted Chardonnay. Riesling makes interesting wine where it is given the chance, and deserves better than the sugar-and-water reputation of cheap German exports. Good Germans (QmP wines from classy growers: *see* A-Z section), wines from Alsace, Australia, Austria, New Zealand – Rieslings all – are all worth trying. And keeping, too, for no white wine ages better.

Watch, too, for red-wine developments: ABC can also stand for Anything But Cabernet.

APPELLATIONS EVERYWHERE

The European Union (EU) has been engaged in appellation diplomacy. If you want to sell us your wines, it tells upstart nations like Australia, New Zealand and Chile, think up a wine law that says where the wine comes from. Like Europe's. Thus the Australian bottles with "Produce of South-East Australia" on them, and the more local names such as Coonawarra and Hunter Valley. Chile has come up with a sensible system of five levels, while New Zealand is still working on it. The USA's system of Viticultural Areas is now mature. The A-Z has details: what the new laws mean is that wine behind a label will come from the place stated. That does not guarantee that it will be good wine, any more than wine from the European countries is good because it has an *appellation* or *denominazione*.

WHAT'S NEW

Tokay, wine of emperors, is being re-born. Foreign investors, French, Italian, British and Danish, are reviving the techniques of the pre-communist era and Hungary's great sweet wine is again as good as its reputation. The "classed growths" are back on the map and single-vineyard wines are on their way through the maturing process.

Flying winemakers – often Australians or Australian-trained – have been making waves, and wine, everywhere from Canada to Brazil, from southern France to Hungary. On the plus side: these wines are fresh, free from faults, true to their variety. Debit points are the charge of sameness: dozens of oak-tinged Chardonnays and light, catty Sauvignons. What the footloose winemakers do is raise the standards of everyday wine. Hopefully they will nurture, not submerge, local traditions where these are worth saving.

The magical Midi is "perhaps the most exciting vineyard in Europe" says an American expert. Australian, American and Bordeaux money is funding investment in the South of France, and names like Corbières, Faugères, Minervois and the various *vins de pays* are found on some fabulous (mostly red) wines. There is no hierarchy of quality, only a sprinkling of good producers amid a sea of *ordinaires*. But once found, what character and value…

WINE STYLES

MANY OF THE GRAPE VARIETIES used for wine, and techniques involved, are defined in the A-Z section. These are the main styles of wine, with some notes on how they are achieved.

ORDINARY WINE AND FINE WINE

There is good wine of every sort – and some bad wine too. But there is another question: is the wine ordinary – for everyday drinking, and thus inexpensive; or fine – with special taste qualities, designed for ageing in bottle, and special occasions? Some wines are *always* ordinary: the vineyards, grapes and climates see to that. In other cases – and increasingly – the winemaker has a choice: make ordinary wine, and lots of it, or a small amount of fine wine. Not all quality wine is made to be kept: it can be made to drink young, stressing fruit, freshness and crispness – still good wine, but in a different style.

RED WINES

Reds can be soft, fruity and early-maturing – Beaujolais, many *vins de pays*, ordinary Côtes du Rhône and Bordeaux, Australian branded wines – or more solid and austere in style – higher-level Rhône reds, Médoc, New World Cabernets. Such wines can age in bottle, and develop subtle and interesting flavours: for this they need "structure" in the form of tannin and acidity. The maker will accept a smaller yield of better grapes from his land in return for the extra concentration of taste.

Grapes to make fruity, easy-to-drink, fast-maturing reds: Gamay, Merlot (though it can be made to age), Grenache, Barbera. Grapes which can make long-maturing, fine wines: Cabernet Sauvignon, Nebbiolo, Pinot Noir, Syrah.

Techniques which lead to fruity, drink-young red wines: carbonic maceration; brief, cool fermentation; stainless steel vats rather than wooden casks for storage; filtering; early bottling. Techniques for long-maturing wines: long, warm fermentation; cask-ageing, perhaps in new oak; minimal filtering, bottling at perhaps 1–2 years old.

WHITE WINES: DRY

Most whites are more or less dry. Dry wine results when all natural grape sugar (plus any which may be added) is converted to alcohol (*see* Fermentation). Modern drinkers like freshness, gentle acidity, fruit aromas and flavours, rather than bone-dry, hard whites. Makers use aromatic grape varieties (Sauvignon, Muscats), skin contact, cold and malolactic fermentations to get this style: some leave a little natural sweetness in, by stopping fermentation; some rely on the sweet flavour of ripe grapes. Drink such wines young: the latest vintage is the best. Fewer whites than reds are made to age: examples are Chardonnays and Graves-type whites, where ageing on lees and/or in cask adds structure (*see* Reds); and Rieslings (Germany, Alsace) where bottle-age alters and improves flavour. However, most Chardonnays and Rieslings – and other dry whites – are made to be drunk young. Oak-derived tastes – nuts, butter, vanilla – add to white-wine character, but can also mask the wine's true flavour. Oak chips, even oak essence, are used in cheaper wines instead of costly new casks.

SWEET WHITES

A wide spectrum of styles stems from several ways of making white wine sweet. Simplest, in technique and taste, are those where fermentation is stopped to leave some sugar, and/or some sweetness is added. These include many German wines, Italian Abbocato wines, simple Vouvray from the Loire.

Sweetness gained from over-ripe grapes, including those with noble rot, makes more complex, subtle sweet wines. Here fermentation stops naturally. Examples are Sauternes, German Auslese, Tokaji, New World late-harvest wines. Muscat grapes, strong in aroma and sweetness, make characteristic sweet wines.

SPARKLING WINES

The many ways of putting bubbles into, or keeping them in, a bottle lead to different qualities of sparkling wine. Champagne's method (*see* Méthode Champenoise) is the best: wines improve in bottle, gaining subtlety; the bubbles are prolific, persistent. Tank-method (Charmat) sparklers can be good. Other ways make less subtle, less fizzy wine – but can be good value. Labels will say if the classic method is used, sometimes using terms like "fermented in this bottle". Sparkling wines do not have to be white: Champagne's rosé, pink wines from other areas, and even red fizz (Burgundy and Australia) have their fans.

FORTIFIED WINES

Adding spirit – brandy or a neutral, non-grape spirit – strengthens the wine and made it safer to ship in pre-scientific days. Now, fortification is part of the style. In port and *vins doux naturel*, it is done before the wine stops fermenting, thereby keeping some natural sugar in the wine. Sherry is fortified later in the process; after fermentation and some ageing.

MATCHING
FOOD AND WINE

THE IDEAL FOOD AND WINE partnership is an equal one, in which each enhances the flavours of the other. However, even a very specific recommendation may prove difficult to replicate: wines may taste different from one producer to another, from vintage to vintage, and at various stages of maturity; foods vary in their seasoning, spicing and ripeness. What ultimately counts is personal taste.

Eclectic experimentation may lead you to some fascinating food and wine discoveries, but the following basic principles can act as a starting point.

COLOUR

The old rule of white wine with fish, red with meat is based on sound sense: a tannic red wine can make fish and shellfish taste metallic, while strongly flavoured meat and game overpower most white wine. Some cheeses are much better with white wine than with red.

WEIGHT

The alcoholic strength and depth of flavour of a wine should reflect that of the dish: delicate foods deserve subtle wines, hearty dishes require sturdier wines.

FLAVOUR

Sometimes a contrast in flavours works well – a lemony-scented wine with fried fish – on other occasions a parallel can be drawn: oak-aged wine with smoked food; spicy wine with spicy (but not too spicy) food.

REGION

Many traditional European dishes have a natural affinity with the wine produced in their region of origin: think of Italian wine and pasta; Swiss wine and cheese fondue; Muscadet with shellfish; Cahors with cassoulet.

OCCASION

An everyday supper calls for a simple wine; an elaborate dinner is a chance to show off better wines. But a great wine, worth serious attention, demands fine but simple food. Some foods are difficult: very salty and acidic foods (especially vinegar) leave their taste in the mouth; eggs can clog the taste buds; chillies numb the palate; very sweet puddings make all but the richest dessert wines seem lean.

The following partnerships have all been enjoyed by tasters, but the list is not definitive: use it as a starting point and see page 8 for suggested wines in similar styles.

AIOLI Provence rosé; Australian Chardonnay.

APPLES In savoury cream sauce White Graves, Australian Chardonnay.

Pies, tarts, strudel Sweet German or Austrian *Auslese*, *Beerenauslese*, Tokaji, sweet Vouvray, Quarts-de-Chaume.

ARTICHOKES Vinaigrette Acidic white, eg Muscadet, Sauvignon de Touraine; oaked Chilean Sauvignon Blanc.

Hollandaise Full-bodied dry or medium-dry white, eg Australian or California Chardonnay.

ASPARAGUS Aromatic dry or off-dry white, eg Sauvignon Blanc-based wine or German Riesling.

AUBERGINES Grilled or fried Mediterranean (Sardinian, Valencian, Greek, north African) red or rosé.

Stuffed Red Corbières, Dão, Zinfandel, Barbera.

AVOCADO with shellfish California Riesling or Sauvignon Blanc, South African Chenin Blanc, Sancerre.

Vinaigrette Fino sherry.

Guacamole Mexican Cabernet Sauvignon or California Chardonnay.

BARBECUED FOOD Australian Cabernet/Shiraz, California Cabernet Sauvignon or Zinfandel, Fitou; full-bodied dry rosé, eg Tavel, Rioja, Côtes de Provence; retsina.

BEAN STEW *See* Cassoulet.

BEEF roast St-Emilion, Pomerol, Côte de Beaune *Premier Cru*, Châteauneuf-du-Pape, red Mercurey, Côtes du Rhône.

Grilled steak, hamburger Beaujolais-Villages, Margaux, St-Julien, Chianti, Portuguese country wine, young California or Australian Cabernet Sauvignon, Gamay, Zinfandel.

Casserole Sturdy reds, eg Beaujolais, Mâcon, Côtes du

Chef's Eye View: Phil Vickery

"I do a lot of boiled meats, such as silverside of beef and collar of bacon," says Phil Vickery. *"I serve the bacon with split peas and mash, but there's a strong madeira sauce, and although most people would choose a light red with bacon, I think a big red – a Rioja, for example – would go equally well with the powerful flavours in the sauce."*

Vinegar is said to be the kiss of death to wine, yet a balanced menu often includes it in a dressing for salads, hot vegetables or fish. *"There's a little vinegar in my starter of deep-fried skate with beetroot and saffron mayonnaise, and it's hard to make an objective choice beyond recommending a really crisp dry white."*

His egg custard tart with nutmeg ice cream has been singled out for praise by restaurant reviewers, and is seldom off the menu: *"I don't want to disappoint people who travel a long way to try it. The obvious accompaniment would be a Muscat de Beaumes-de-Venise, but I'd say champagne would be good too."*

Phil Vickery, chef at the Castle Hotel in Taunton, Somerset, produces some of Britain's finest food. Mediterranean and Oriental influences are minimal; instead, he uses the West Country's wealth of ingredients to create immaculate interpretations of traditional English dishes such as spiced potted duck, braised lamb and fish cakes.

Rhône, Châteauneuf-du-Pape, Barbaresco, Chianti, Dão, California Cabernet, Zinfandel, Australian Shiraz blends.

CABBAGE, STUFFED Light but earthy or herb-scented red, eg Beaujolais *crus*, Roumanian Pinot Noir, South African Pinotage.

CAKES Sweet white, sparkling or fortified wine. *See also* Chocolate.

CASSOULET Cahors, Côtes du Frontonnais, Minervois, young red Rioja or Navarra, Zinfandel.

CHEESE Soft cheeses can be difficult to match: their creaminess coats the tongue and any hint of ammonia in a ripe cheese "kills" wine.

Brie (mild) Fine, mature red or white.

Camembert, Brie (ripe) Corbières, St-Emilion, Beaujolais-Villages.

Cheddar Fruity red, eg ruby port, St-Emilion; dry oloroso sherry or vintage port.

Goat's cheese; herbed cheese Dry, fruity white with some acidity, eg Sancerre; dry Languedoc or Provence rosé; light red, eg Saumur, Corbières, Hungarian Merlot.

Gorgonzola, strong blue cheeses Barbera, Dolcetto or Nebbiolo d'Alba, Recioto della Valpolicella, Zinfandel; tawny port, sercial madeira.

Gruyère (young) Swiss white or lively red, eg Beaujolais, Zinfandel; **(mature)** full-bodied dry white or mature red.

Maroilles, pungent cheeses Fragrant red, eg St-Emilion, Côte Rôtie; or aromatic white eg Alsace Gewürztraminer.

Parmesan Barolo, Barbaresco, dry Lambrusco, tawny port.

Port-du-Salut, monastery cheeses Light fruity red burgundy or Bergerac.

Roquefort, soft blue cheeses Sauternes or Monbazillac; Muscat de Rivesaltes; young local red, eg Faugères.

Stilton Vintage or tawny port; dry oloroso sherry;

Monbazillac.

Fondue Swiss dry white, Grüner Veltliner, Sauvignon Blanc wines.

CHICKEN Roast Medium-bodied fruity red, eg burgundy, St-Chinian, Gigondas, Côtes du Ventoux, Chianti, young California Cabernet Sauvignon, Merlot, Zinfandel; dry rosé; crisp white.

Kiev Oaky Chardonnay from Australia or Chile, Alsace Riesling; red Bergerac.

With cream Dry Vouvray, medium-dry Gaillac, Alsace Riesling, white Graves or burgundy; Oregon Pinot Noir.

With tarragon California Chardonnay.

With tomatoes and/or garlic Red Bandol, Crozes-Hermitage; California or South African Chardonnay.

CHILLI CON CARNE Rioja, Argentinian or Chilean Cabernet Sauvignon.

CHINESE FOOD Dry or medium rosé, dry sparkling white; aromatic dry white.

Fish/shellfish with ginger and spring onions *Demi-sec* Vouvray, Gewürztraminer, oaky white Rioja, Australian Chardonnay or Sémillon.

Sweet and sour sauce California or Australian Sauvignon Blanc with good acidity, New Zealand Sémillon/Sauvignon blend.

Peking duck St-Emilion, oaky red or white Rioja, Gewürztraminer.

CHOCOLATE Banyuls, málaga, malmsey madeira, Mavrodaphne, California Black or Orange Muscat, Australian Orange Muscat.

CREAMS, CRÈME BRÛLÉE, FOOLS, TRIFLE, SYLLABUB Sauternes, Monbazillac, Moscatel de Valencia, *Beerenauslese*, Tokaji, sweet oloroso sherry, madeira or marsala, Vin Santo.

DUCK Roast St-Emilion, red burgundy, Côte Rôtie,

Châteauneuf-du-Pape, Cahors, red Côtes de St-Mont, Zinfandel; Riesling *Spätlese*.
With oranges or cherries Loire red, Rosso Conero, Zinfandel, Australian Shiraz.
EGGS Scrambled with smoked salmon Unoaked Chablis or other Chardonnay, non-vintage champagne.
Omelette Beaujolais, Chianti or southern French red or white with tomato or ham; Pinot Noir with mushroom; lightly oaked Australian Chardonnay with smoked fish and cheese; fino sherry with cold Spanish omelette/tortilla.
Quiche Dry, medium-full white, eg Graves, Alsace,

Rheingau *Trocken*; light young red, eg Beaujolais, Chinon, Chilean Cabernet Sauvignon; rosé *vin de pays*.
FISH Generally, the finer the fish, the finer the white wine to accompany it, either crisp and lemony or buttery, oaked styles. Avoid tannic reds; lighter wines based on Cabernet Franc, Gamay and Pinot Noir often work well.
Fish pie Mâcon Blanc, Bianco di Custoza, German *trocken*, Napa Chardonnay.
Freshwater fish White Graves, Anjou, Mosel.
Fried fish Sauvignon Blanc, Muscadet, Alsace Riesling, Pinot Grigio, Verdicchio, Frascati,

Chef's Eye View: Antony Worrall Thompson

"The regional approach seems best with Mediterranean flavours," says Antony Worrall Thompson. *"With roast mullet, served with a stew of white beans and duck confit, I would choose Provençal wine, perhaps Bandol rosé from Domaine de Pibarnon, or a light red like Domaine de Trévallon."*

But in wine, as in cooking, inspiration comes from around the world. With a main dish of duck confit he suggests Barolo, a Barbera, or a Malbec from Mendoza in Argentina: *"Malbec is the same grape used in Cahors, but it's streets ahead of anything you get in France."*

When garlic and chillies are to the forefront, for example as a dressing for char-grilled squid, a powerful Primitivo – or a Zinfandel – springs to mind. *"I'm keen on big reds with these spices; they tend to kick white wine in the teeth."*

Rich desserts like sticky toffee pudding normally demand ultra-sweet wine. After suggesting an Orange or Black Muscat, or a Pedro Ximénez sherry, *"to match syrup against syrup"*, Worrall Thompson had another idea: *"An eau-de-vie such as Mirabelle or Quetsch would provide a strong contrast – and they'd help the digestion of a dish like that."*

Antony Worrall Thompson is one of only five chefs who have been awarded the title Meilleur Ouvrier de Grande Bretagne, yet his London restaurants – Bistrot 190, dell'Ugo, Zoë, Palio – are funky, fun, and light-years away from the solemnity and silver usually linked with highly-acclaimed chefs. Drawing on the peasant cooking of Italy, France, Britain and Ireland, with chillies, Oriental herbs and spices turning up in surprising places, his food is truly eclectic.

English wine; chilled Beaujolais, Chinon.

Mediterranean-style (with olive oil, herbs, garlic, tomatoes, saffron) Southern French rosé or white, Muscadet, Italian Pinot Grigio; retsina; light Beaujolais or other Gamay-based red.

Oily fish (herring, mackerel, sardine, swordfish, tuna) Rich Australian Sémillon or Chardonnay; white Dão, Vinho Verde, Muscadet, Gros Plant, New Zealand Sauvignon Blanc; spicy young Côtes du Rhône.

Salmon, poached White burgundy, Sancerre, Alsace Riesling, Condrieu, California or Australian Chardonnay; Beaujolais, Chinon, Bourgueil; Pinot Noir from Alsace, California, Oregon.

White fish, steamed or grilled Steely, elegant Alsace Riesling; tart, appley Loire Chenin Blanc; lemony Soave.

White fish in creamy/buttery sauce Champagne, Vouvray, Chardonnay-based wine, Muscadet *sur lie*; Mosel. *See also* shellfish, smoked fish.

FRUIT PUDDINGS Sweet white, sparkling or fortified wine.

GAME Lightly hung game, plainly cooked, deserves fine red bordeaux or burgundy (classed-growth Médoc or Graves, *Grand* or *Premier Cru* Côte d'Or, Côte Chalonnaise from a good vintage), or Napa Cabernet Sauvignon.

Well-hung game needs the powerful accompaniment of Hermitage, Côte Rôtie, Châteauneuf-du-Pape, Cornas, Rioja *reserva*, Barolo, Australian Shiraz.

Casserole St-Emilion, Pomerol, Barbaresco, Brunello di Montalcino, Valpolicella Amarone, Dão, California Zinfandel, Australian Shiraz/Cabernet Sauvignon. *See also* Pigeon, Quail, Venison.

GOOSE Assertive red, or sweet

white with good acidity, eg German *Spätlese*, Alsace *réserve exceptionelle*.

HAM Red burgundy or Mâcon, Beaujolais and other Gamays, Dolcetto; Riesling *Spätlese*.

Raw Pinot Grigio dell'Alto Adige, Soave Classico; fino or manzanilla sherry; young Spanish or Italian red.

Smoked German *Spätlese*.

INDIAN FOOD Mildly spiced Alsace Gewürztraminer, Australian Chardonnay, Orvieto *abboccato*.

Tandoori dishes California Cabernet Sauvignon, Australian Cabernet/Shiraz.

KIDNEYS Pomerol, St-Emilion, Zinfandel.

In mustard sauce Morgon or St-Amour.

LAMB Plainly cooked lamb sets off the finest Médoc (especially Pauillac, St-Estèphe) or Graves red, Rioja *reserva*, Ribera del Duero, New World Cabernet Sauvignon. With more herbs, garlic or other flavours, less expensive examples of the above, or try Châteauneuf-du-Pape or Beaujolais.

LIVER Chianti Classico, Chilean or Bulgarian Reserve Cabernet Sauvignon.

With bacon California or Oregon Pinot Noir.

With sage Flowery Nahe Riesling *Spätlese*; Chinon.

MUSHROOMS Pomerol, most Pinot Noir-based wine, South African Pinotage, Merlot.

OXTAIL STEW Spicy red from southern France or Greece.

PAELLA White, rosé or red Rioja, Penedès.

PASTA Almost any Italian red; white with pesto, seafood or creamy sauce.

PÂTÉ, TERRINE Mâcon Blanc, dry Vouvray, Jurançon, Pinot Grigio dell'Alto Adige, California Fumé Blanc; Côtes de Provence rosé; young fruity red.

Chicken liver Dry amontillado sherry.

PEPPERS Pungent Sauvignon Blanc, Alsace Gewürztraminer; Cabernet Sauvignon or Shiraz blend from California or Australia.

PIGEON Good red burgundy, Pomerol, Chianti Classico, Italian Merlot, Sardinian red.

PIZZA Chianti, Sicilian red, Barbera, Zinfandel, Coteaux d'Aix-en-Provence red or rosé.

PORK Medium-bodied red or white, eg Côtes du Rhône, Mâcon, Anjou, Barbera, Douro red, Bulgarian Mavrud; Alsace *Grand Cru* Riesling, Gewürztraminer, Rheingau or Pfalz *Auslese* or *Spätlese*, New World Chardonnay.

QUAIL Pinot Noir from Alsace, Roumania, Oregon.

QUICHE *See* Eggs.

RISOTTO Bianco di Custoza, Trebbiano d'Abruzzo, Pinot Grigio, Grüner Veltliner; young red, eg Dolcetto, Bardolino, Valpolicella.

SALAD White or red with good acidity, eg Loire or New Zealand Chenin Blanc.

SALAMI Barbera, Chianti, dry Lambrusco, Valpolicella, red Beaujolais, Provence red or rosé, Tavel or Corsican rosé, Tempranillo or Garnacha-based wines, eg Rioja, Navarra, Penedès.

SAUSAGES Spicy chorizo Fino or manzanilla sherry.
Grilled Châteauneuf-du-Pape, Cahors, Rioja, Dolcetto, Portuguese red, Merlot from anywhere.

SHELLFISH Wines made from

Chef's Eye View: Michael Romano

One of Michael Romano's signature dishes is a filet mignon of tuna; a 3-inch cube of fish marinaded with soy sauce, ginger, garlic and sherry, then grilled so it is sweetish outside, rare in the centre. "It outsells all other food on the menu, so we've had plenty of chance to experiment – and in New York there's a great selection of wines from all over the world. My two favourites are very different: Cornas, the Rhône red, or Tokay Pinot Gris from Alsace."

A truly memorable food and wine partnership, also based on tuna, is a dish he created to accompany Oregon Pinot Noir. The fish was roasted and served with a spicy, lightly creamy, green peppercorn sauce, and the combination was "so perfect it was almost supernatural".

Michael Romano admits to being excited about the honesty and simplicity of Mediterranean cooking. "Right now on the menu we have a filet mignon of beef with a tomato and anchovy sauce made quickly in the pan. To partner it I would bring in a young, lighter red from southern Italy, perhaps from Friuli in northern Italy, or from Provence, ideally a Bandol."

Michael Romano, of New York City's Union Square Cafe, aims to help Americans become more relaxed about food. "In France and Italy people feel comfortable about food, but here they have an adversarial relationship with it: they worry about health and fitness and slimming. The idea of the restaurant is to present seemingly simple, seasonal food in a casual atmosphere, but with really good, knowlegeable service."

Chardonnay, whether crisply dry or rich and buttery, are good with most shellfish.
Crab, lobster, scallops Champagne; white burgundy (the richer the dish, the better the wine), white Hermitage; Alsace Riesling.
Clams, mussels, oysters Muscadet, Gros Plant, Chablis, red or white Vinho Verde, Verdicchio, Australian Hunter Valley Sémillon.
Prawns, shrimps Muscadet, crisp Sauvignon Blanc; fino or manzanilla sherry.
SMOKED FISH Alsace Gewürztraminer, Rheingau *Spätlese*, oak-aged Spanish whites, manzanilla sherry, Chilean Chardonnay.
Salmon Champagne.
SOUFFLÉS Cheese Fine red burgundy or bordeaux; Alsace Pinot Gris; champagne;

Dornfelder *Trocken*.
Fish Dry white burgundy or bordeaux; Napa Fumé Blanc; South Australian Chardonnay.
TURKEY Light red burgundy, Médoc, Napa Cabernet Sauvignon, Zinfandel.
VEAL Roast Medium-bodied red or white.
With cream sauce A rich Chardonnay.
Osso bucco Barbera, Barbaresco, Valpolicella, Chianti.
VEGETABLES Casseroles Beaujolais-Villages, Rhône and Midi reds, Chianti, Bulls Blood, Zinfandel; Provence white.
Raw Crisp Sauvignon Blanc, rosé or light red, eg Beaujolais, Bardolino.
VENISON Top burgundy; Cahors, Gigondas, Barolo, Australian Shiraz, Zinfandel; late-harvest Tokay d'Alsace, Pfalz *Spätlese*.

Chef's Eye View: Cindy Pawlcyn

Some of the most exciting cooking on the USA's West Coast, with California wines to match, comes from Cindy Pawlcyn.

So close to the heart of America's top wine region, the enthusiasm for matching food and wine should not be unexpected. Even the informally named Buckeye Roadhouse has a "Zinfandel challenge", where half glasses of three different Zinfandels accompany selected dishes. Among several highly successful combinations have been a plate of ribs, smoked duck and smoked chicken, cooked in the restaurant's woodburning stoves. "The fruity but rich wines go really well with the smoky flavours of the food." Equally rewarding with Zinfandel was "100 almond curry duck", based on a traditional Indian spicy almond sauce: the sauce and the wine are apparently even better with squab .

A homely-sounding baked lemon pudding is taken to new heights with the Sauternes-style Dolce, made by Far Niente, but Cindy Pawlcyn also loves the luxury of champagne with dessert. "One of my favourites is Billecart-Salmon's Brut Rosé, which I'd be happy to drink with even a very rich butterscotch crème brûlée."

Cindy Pawlcyn's California restaurants range from the Fog City Diner on San Francisco's Embarcadero and Tra'vigna, an Italian-inspired trattoria in the Napa Valley wine country, to Mustard's Grill, "the American truckstop, deluxe", also in Napa, and the Buckeye Roadhouse on Highway 101 north of San Francisco.

ATLAS
OF WINE
COUNTRIES

FRANCE & BELGIUM

THE WINE REGIONS OF FRANCE extend from cool,
northern Champagne, Alsace and the Loire Valley
to the Mediterranean climates of Provence and the Midi.
Bordeaux and the South-West have Atlantic climates,
while Burgundy's is closer to Champagne. Belgium's
vineyards are mostly in the south,
while Luxembourg's line
the Moselle river.

ANJOU Angers
SAUMUR
Nantes
PAYS
NANTAIS

Loire

Poitiers

la Rochelle

Bastia

*Atlantic
Ocean*

CORSICA

Ajaccio

MÉDOC   BLAYE
BORDEAUX   BOURG
Bordeaux   POMEROL
GRAVES   SAINT-EMILIC
BERGERAC
ENTRE-DEUX-MERS
SAUTERNES

Garonne

SOUTH-WEST

N

Pau

PYRÉNÉES

0		100		200 km
0	50		100 miles	

North Sea

NETHERLANDS

Antwerp

Bruges

Brussels

Maastricht

Escaut

BELGIUM

Mons

Meuse

Liège

Sambre

Meuse

LUXEMBOURG

Luxembourg

Reims

Moselle

CHAMPAGNE

Seine

Paris

Nancy

Strasbourg

F R A N C E

CHAMPAGNE

ALSACE

Seine

Orléans

Auxerre

CHABLIS

Rhin

TOURAINE

SANCERRE

POUILLY

Dijon

Bourges

Beaune

CÔTE DE NUITS

CÔTE DE BEAUNE

JURA

Lake Geneva

BURGUNDY

CÔTE CHALONNAISE

MÂCONNAIS

Mâcon

Clermont-o Ferrand

BEAUJOLAIS

Lyons

SAVOIE

Rhône

CÔTES-DU-RHÔNE

Grenoble

CAHORS

GAILLAC

CÔTES-DU-RHÔNE

Toulouse

COTEAUX DU LANGUEDOC

Nîmes

Avignon

COTEAUX D'AIX - EN-PROVENCE

Nice

Rhône

Montpellier

Marseilles

CÔTES DE PROVENCE

MINERVOIS

CORBIÈRES

Perpignan

CÔTES DU ROUSSILLON

Mediterranean Sea

19

GERMANY

River valleys shape Germany's pattern of wine regions:
the Mosel, Ahr and the eastern regions, being far north,
need the shelter of valley slopes to ripen grapes.
The Rhein and its tributaries shape the other regions,
though the southernmost and warmest, Baden,
has vines beside Lake Constance.

ITALY, SWITZERLAND & AUSTRIA

ITALY HAS VINES FROM the northern Alps right down its Apennine backbone to close to Africa. The north-west (Piedmont) and centre (Tuscany) are the best zones. Switzerland's wine mostly comes from the Vaud and Valais in the west, Austria's from the Danube valley and Burgenland in the east.

WEINVIERTEL
WACHAU Vienna
DONAULAND
CARNUNTUM
THERMENREGION
NEUSIEDLERSEE
SÜD-OSTSTEIERMARK
SÜDBURGENLAND
WESTSTEIERMARK

LIECHTENSTEIN
Salzburg
AUSTRIA
Innsbruck

Danube
Bolzano

Trento

Verona Venice
Trieste

Bologna Ravenna
ALBANA DI
ROMAGNA
CARMIGNANO
Florence
CHIANTI
BRUNELLO DI
MONTALCINO VINO NOBILE DI
MONTE PULCIANO
TORGIANO
Ancona

Pescara

Rome

A d r i a t i c
S e a

ITALY

TAURASI
Naples Bari

T y r r h e n i a n
S e a

I o n i a n
S e a

Palermo
Messina Reggio di Calabria
SICILY Catania

SPAIN & PORTUGAL

SPAIN'S QUALITY WINE ZONES are mostly in the cooler
north: the Catalonia zones inland from Barcelona,
the Rioja zone, and the Ribera del Duero. Jerez in the far
south makes sherry. Portugal's Douro river, in the north,
is the home of port. Vinho Verde comes from the north,
good reds and whites from Bairrada and Dão.

San Sebastián

bao TXAKOLI
(CHACOLI)

Vitoria   oPamplona

groño
RIOJA   NAVARRA

Huesca
SOMONTANO
CAMPO   Ebro   COSTERS
DE BORJA   Zaragoza   DEL SEGRE   CONCA DE
BARBERA   ALELLA

Lérida   PENEDES   Barcelona
CALATAYUD   CARIÑENA   PRIORATO

TERRA ALTA   TARRAGONA   Tarragona
TARRAGONA

Tajo

OS DE
ADRID

UTIEL
MANCHA   REQUENA   Valencia   *Mediterranean*

Sea

ALMANSA   VALENCIA

JUMILLA   ALICANTE

YECLA   Alicante

Murcia

BINISSALEM
Palma   *Majorca*

BALEARIC ISLANDS   N

0	100	200 km
0	50	100 miles

NORTH AMERICA

FEW STATES IN THE USA are without vineyards,
but California, Washington, Oregon and New York
State are the biggest producers. The detail map shows
the West Coast states and their key wine zones.
Canada's vineyards are in southern Ontario,
near the Great Lakes and in western
British Columbia.

Pacific

Ocean

CENTRAL & SOUTH AMERICA

CHILE AND ARGENTINA are the leading wine countries here, though Mexico has the oldest vineyards, and Brazil, Uruguay and Peru make wine. The detail map shows the wine zones of Chile, of which Maipo, Casablanca and Maule are important; and Argentina, led by Mendoza.

AUSTRALIA

WINE IS MADE IN THE SOUTHEAST of the country, and in
Western Australia. The quality zones are in the hilly
districts of New South Wales, in Victoria and in South
Australia. Inland, the Murray River zone makes large
amounts of good everyday wine. In the west,
cool coastal zones are showing promise.

Indian Ocean

NEW ZEALAND

THE SOUTH ISLAND VINEYARDS of Marlborough
are the most noted for quality, though Hawke's Bay,
Bay of Plenty and Gisborne in the North run them
close. Most of the vineyards are very new,
and experiments are still going on to find
the best zones: witness the far-south
vineyard of Central Otago.

Whangarei

Waiheke Island

AUCKLAND
Auckland
Te Kauwhata

North

Island

WAIKATO

Bay of Plenty

BAY OF
PLENTY

GISBORNE

Lake
Taupo

Gisborne

HAWKE'S BAY

Hawke's Bay

Wanganui

Hastings

Tasman

Bay

Nelson

Wellington

NELSON

Martinborough

South

MARLBOROUGH

Blenheim

WAIRARAPA

Clarence

Island

Pacific

Ocean

Christchurch

CANTERBURY
CHRISTCHURCH

CENTRAL
OTAGO

Kawarau

Clutha

Dunedin

Invercargill

Stewart Island

N

| 0 | 100 | 200 km |
| 0 | 50 | 100 miles |

A-Z
WINES OF
THE WORLD

A

ABBOCCATO *Italy* A gently sweet style of wine.

ABELÉ, HENRI *France, Champagne* One of Champagne's oldest houses, owned by the Spanish Freixenet group. Its traditional style, seen in both vintage and NV *cuvées*, is quite rich and full-bodied.

ABRUZZO *Italy* Mountainous area in central Italy where bears can still be found. Mainly R wine from the Montepulciano grape and W from Trebbiano.

AC *France* See APPELLATION D'ORIGINE CONTRÔLÉE.

ACCAD, GUY Consultant winemaker and oenologist, active in Burgundy since the 1980s, who believes in macerating whole bunches of very ripe (red-wine) grapes before fermentation, leading to deep, dark sweet-tasting wines. No-one knows yet if they will age well.

ACKERMAN-LAURANCE *France, Loire, Saumur, Sp; W, P* The first firm to make sparkling Saumur, in 1811. Linked today with the larger firm of Remy-Pannier, it makes a full range of this wine and a Crémant de Loire (Sp; W, P).

ADEGA *Portugal* Winery.

ADELAIDE HILLS *Australia, South Australia* With its high altitude, this cool-climate area makes wines of great elegance and finesse. Leading producers include: Grand Cru Estate, Petaluma.

ADELSHEIM *USA, Oregon, R, W* This estate on the slopes of Chehalem Mountain has Pinot Noir, Pinot Gris, Chardonnay, Pinot Blanc and White Riesling. Ripe black cherry, mushrooms and truffles scent the Pinot Noir; Pinot Gris is a flinty dry W.

AFFENTAL *Germany, Baden, R* Red wine from Spätburgunder, popular in Germany, comes from this valley in North Baden. (The name means "monkey valley".)

AGE, BODEGAS *Spain, Rioja, R, W, P* One of Rioja's main exporters, producing reliable quality wines. Much of their production appears under the Siglo label, although their best wines are the Marqués del Romeral *reservas*.

AGLIANICO DEL VULTURE *Italy, Basilicata, DOC, R* The southern region Basilicata's only DOC and one of Italy's greatest wines. The R Aglianico grape is grown in the volcanic heights of Monte Vulture. Can age very well. Leading producers include: Fratelli D'Angelo, Paternoster.

AHR *Germany, Anbaugebiet, R, W* The Ahr, a tributary of the Rhine near Bonn, is lined by red-wine vineyards, much visited by tourists. Most wine is soft and slightly sweet, made to enjoy on a summer day; but some growers now make more structured, dry wines. Among these are Kloster Marienthal, Weingut Meyer-Näkel, Weingut Brogsitters.

AIRÉN Low-quality white grape; the most widely planted in Spain (and in the world). With careful, modern vinification it produces large quantities of cheap and cheerful wine – sometimes surprisingly good, especially in DO La Mancha.

AJACCIO *France, Corsica, AOC, R, P, W* One of Corsica's top appellations. Its small production is of Rs from the native Sciaccarello grape, plus Grenache, Cinsaut, Carignan. Some Ps and Ws. Leading producers include: Clos Capitoro, Dom Peraldi.

ALABAMA *USA* Hurricanes and humidity try the patience of a few growers, mostly of Scuppernong and other native grapes.

ALBANA DI ROMAGNA *Italy, Emilia-Romagna, DOCG, W* Italy's first DOCG for W wine. From the relatively neutral Albana grape. At its best, it has soft, peachy perfumes. May be dry, *amabile* or *passito*. Grander status than it deserves. Leading producers include: Fattoria Paradiso, Zerbina.

ALBARIÑO/ALVARINHO Quality white grape from north-west Spain and Portugal. In Galicia it makes some of Spain's best whites in the Rías Baixas DO; in Portugal, as Alvarinho, it becomes the best, appley, Vinhos Verdes.

ALCOHOL An important element in wine, but not the only one. Produced during fermentation when yeasts change the sugar content of the grape juice into alcohol, carbon dioxide and heat. The alcohol content of wine varies from around 8° to around 15°.

ALEATICO Red grape with intense perfume, making wine with deep colour, often sweet and strong. Grown in several regions of Italy, and now in Chile (there are also small plantings in Australia and California).

ALELLA *Spain, Catalonia, DO, W, P, R* Wine zone in the north-east near Barcelona, producing all colours of wine but mostly W: fresh wines for drinking young. Experiments with Chardonnay, especially in the hilly, cooler inland areas, are doing well. Leading producers include: Alta Alella, Bodegas Parxet.

ALENTEJO *Portugal, R, W* New wine zone in southern Portugal: full-flavoured R wines from blends of native grapes show more promise than the rather fat, blowzy Ws. Leading producers include: Adega Cooperativa de Borba, Quinta do Carmo, Esporão.

ALEXANDER VALLEY *USA, California, VA* Wine zone in the north of Sonoma, with deep, rich valley soils for good Ws from Riesling and Gewürztraminer and Chardonnay, while Rs from

Cabernet Sauvignon on lighter soils are soft and light. Leading producers include: Clos du Bois, Jordan, Johnson's, Ch Souverain.

ALEXIS BAILLY WINERY *USA, Minnesota, R, W* In the 1970s David Bailly planted some vines on his farm south-east of Minneapolis; a small winery followed. The R vines are the hybrids Maréchal Foch and Léon Millot; produced as varietals, they are dark in colour and in most vintages balanced and flavourful.

ALGERIA *North Africa, R, W, P* Algeria has had a well-developed quality wine system since colonial days, but less wine is made today than hitherto. All vineyards are concentrated in the provinces of Oran and Alger, in the western half of the country. In Oran the best areas are the Coteaux de Tlemcen, making R, W and P wines of fair quality, powerful yet quite soft and the Coteaux de Mascara, producing big, rustic Rs. In Alger, Médéa is a high-altitude zone, making R wines of some finesse.

ALICANTE *Spain, Levante, DO, W, P, R* Hilly wine zone in the region of Valencia with a variety of grapes and wines in all colours. Leading producers include: Eval.

ALIGOTÉ White grape from Burgundy, making dry, fairly acidic wine of varying quality. The best is the Bourgogne Aligoté de Bouzeron, from the Côte Chalonnaise, which has its own AOC. Also grown in Bulgaria, Romania, Moldova, Russia, California.

ALMACENISTA *Spain, Jerez* Term used in Jerez, the sherry country, for wines matured by small wholesalers (also called Almacenistas). These sherries are usually blended, but sometimes sold in bottle: especially by the firm of LUSTAU.

ALMANSA *Spain, Castilla-La Mancha, DO, R, P* Easternmost of four wine zones of Castilla-La Mancha, with vineyards on flatter lowlands. Essentially R wines but also some *rosado*. Leading producers include: Bodegas Piqueras.

ALOXE-CORTON *France, Burgundy, AOC, R, W*
Côte de Beaune village and environs dominated by the Corton hill with its two *Grands Crus:* CORTON (R) and CORTON-CHARLEMAGNE (W). The lower slopes produce the R *Premiers Crus* (less long-lived than the *Grands Crus*) and R village wines (lighter; good value). Leading producers include: Capitain-Gagnerot, Michel Mallard, Prince Florent de Mérode.

ALSACE *France, AOC, W, R, P, Sp* Though northerly, a warm, dry climate produces full-tasting yet dry Ws (most labelled by grape variety) from Riesling, Pinot Blanc, Gewürztraminer, Sylvaner, Pinot Gris, Muscat (Rs and Ps from Pinot Noir). Top vineyards can use village or vineyard names as AOC Alsace *Grand Cru*. Crémant d'Alsace is quality Sp wine, usually Pinot Blanc. Leading producers include: Jean Becker, Hugel, Trimbach, Dom Weinbach, Zind Humbrecht.

ALVARINHO   See ALBARIÑO.

AMABILE   *Italy*   A sweeter style of wine than *abboccato*.

AMIOT, PIERRE & FILS   *France, Burgundy, Côte d'Or, R, W*   This Côte des Nuits estate makes elegant wines for drinking relatively young, from vines in Morey St-Denis and Gevrey Chambertin.

AMIRAL DE BEYCHEVELLE   *France, Bordeaux, Médoc, St-Julien, R*   Second wine of Ch Beychevelle.

AMITY   *USA, Oregon, R, W*   Half of Myron Redford's small vineyard is Pinot Noir, some made in the *nouveau* style: light and fruity, ready just months after harvest. Cinnamon-spiced W Gewürztraminer and the rarely made, peppery R Gamay Noir are noteworthy.

AMMERSCHWIHR   *France, Alsace, Haut-Rhin*   One of the best villages in Alsace, known for Riesling and Gewürztraminer: particularly from Kaefferkopf, a well-known *terroir*, now a *Grand Cru*. Also includes *Grand Cru* Wineck-Schlossberg. Leading producers include: J B Adam, Sparr.

AMONTILLADO   *Spain*   Sherry that has matured beyond the fino stage, developing an amber colour, depth and nutty flavour.

AMOUREUSES, LES   *France, Burgundy, 1er Cru, Côte de Nuits, R*   One of the most attractive Chambolle-Musigny wines. Supremely elegant, with breeding and lovely supple fruit. Leading producers include: Ch de Chambolle-Musigny, Robert Groffier, Georges Roumier, de Vogüé.

AMPEAU, ROBERT   *France, Burgundy, Côte d'Or, R, W*   Skilled W burgundy specialist based in Meursault. Also fine Rs from Volnay and Pommard.

AMPURDÁN-COSTA BRAVA   *Spain, Catalonia, DO, W, P, R*   Catalonia's northernmost wine zone, in the province of Girona on the French border. Vineyards rise from sea level to the Pyrenean foothills. Most wine is *rosado*; also old-style dessert wines. Leading producers include: Cavas del Ampurdán.

ANBAUGEBIET   *Germany*   Wine region: there are 13, such as Pfalz, Baden, Rheingau.

ANCIENNE CURÉ, DOM DE L'   *France, South-West, Bergerac, R, W*   Good R and W Bergerac, plus sweet W Monbazillac and higher-quality R from the Pécharmant zone.

ANDERSON VALLEY   *USA, California, VA*   Zone in Mendocino with a cool climate, good for Chardonnay, Sp wines, Zinfandel (R) and Cabernet Sauvignon. Leading producers include: Navarro, Roederer (Sp), Scharffenberger (Sp).

ANDERSON VALLEY VINEYARDS   *USA, New Mexico, R, W*   In the northern Rio Grande Valley, Anderson, founded in 1973, was the first quality producer in the state, with vineyards around the city of Albuquerque. It has a name for Cabernet Sauvignon, Sauvignon Blanc and other wines.

ANDRÉ, PIERRE *France, Burgundy, Côte d'Or, R, W* Substantial vineyard owner and *négociant* (using the name LA REINE PEDAUQUE): a wide range of wines of varying quality. The best are the Cortons.

ANDRON-BLANQUET, CH *France, Bordeaux, St-Estèphe, Cru Bourgeois, R* Well-sited close to Cos d'Estournel, making strong, rich wines which need time in bottle.

ANGÉLUS, CH L' *France, Bordeaux, St-Emilion, Grand Cru Classé, R* Among the largest of St-Emilion's top properties, with 12,000 cases a year. Recent investment produced a vast improvement in quality. Worth watching.

ANGES, DOM DES *France, Rhône, Côtes du Ventoux, R* Leading estate of the appellation, making complex and tasty wine.

ANGLUDET, CH D' *France, Bordeaux, Margaux, Cru Bourgeois, R* Consistently classed-growth-quality wine: perfumed and elegant, with increasing structure as the vines age. Good value.

ANGERVILLE, DOM MARQUIS D' *France, Burgundy, Côte d'Or, R, W* Top domaine making extremely elegant wines for the medium term from Volnay, Pommard and Meursault. Sole proprietor of the Volnay Clos des Ducs *Premier Cru,* which yields a very classy wine.

ANHEUSER, AUGUST E *Germany, Nahe W* Family estate with four centuries of fine wine behind it: the current list includes wines as old as 1921. Well-structured, long-lived Rieslings from some of the best Nahe vineyards.

ANHEUSER, PAUL *Germany, Nahe, W* Just a century old, another branch of the Anheuser family (*see* above) makes equally good Rieslings but in a lighter, fresher style.

ANJOU *France, Loire, AOC, P, W, R* Within the general Anjou appellation (mostly Rs and dry Ws) are several more specific AOCs. Anjou Villages (R), from Cabernet (Franc and Sauvignon): higher quality than basic Anjou Rouge. Anjou Gamay: light Rs. Anjou Coteaux de la Loire: dry and medium-sweet W wines from Chenin Blanc. Region is best known for simple, slightly sweet, pale pink Rosé d'Anjou, from Groslot grapes; better Ps come from Cabernet Franc grapes, eg CABERNET D'ANJOU. Leading producers include: Aubert Frères, Ch du Breuil, Ch de Fesles, Hervé Papin, Dom de Ste-Anne, Pierre et Yves Soulez, Les Vins Touchais.

ANNEREAUX, CH DES *France, Bordeaux, Lalande-de-Pomerol, R* Good quantities of well-made wine, worth ageing.

ANTINORI *Italy, Tuscany, Chianti, R, W, P, Sp* This famous, top-quality producer makes some of Italy's most innovative wines.

The two main Chianti Classicos, Villa Antinori and Peppoli, are complemented by Cabernet Sauvignon/Sangiovese-based R *vini da tavola* like Solaia and Tignanello. Others include Bolgheri (DOC, P), Galestro (*vino da tavola*, W) and Sp wines.

AOC *France* See APPELLATION D'ORIGINE CONTRÔLÉE.

APPELLATION D'ORIGINE CONTRÔLÉE (AOC) *France* The top grade of French quality wine. The term created by French authorities (the INAO) to guarantee the origin of wines (also cheeses, etc). AOC rules define the specific area of production, grape varieties, minimum levels of sugar in the juice and of alcohol in the wine, maximum yield per hectare, pruning practices, and cultivation and vinification methods.

APULIA *Italy* Huge wine output from Italy's heel. The region has a vast number of DOCs and a bewildering array of grape varieties. Castel del Monte R, W and P is the most famous wine. Locorotondo is one of the best W wines.

AQUÉRIA, CH D' *France, Rhône, Tavel, P* Reliable specialist in this powerful rosé, best drunk young.

ARBOIS *France, Jura, AOC, R, P, W* Jura's main R-wine appellation, using Trousseau, Poulsard and Pinot Noir grapes. Ws are from Chardonnay, with some Savagnin; this local grape also makes VIN JAUNE. Leading producers include: Fruitière Vinicole d'Arbois, Henri Maire, Rolet Père et Fils.

ARBOIS, FRUITIÈRE VINICOLE D' *France, Jura, R, W, P* This major co-op is a leading maker of Arbois wines of all colours, plus VIN JAUNE, using modern facilities: good quality.

ARBOR CREST *USA, Washington State, W, R* Having first gained attention through its creamy, richly-fruited Chardonnays, the Mielke family's south-facing vineyard in the Columbia Valley produces an austere Sauvignon W and a generously fruity, currant-and-berry Merlot R.

ARCHAMBEAU, CH D' *France, Bordeaux, Graves, W, R* In the commune of Illats, a source of impeccably-made, fresh Ws, and soft delicate Rs.

ARCHE, CH D' *France, Bordeaux, Sauternes, 2ème Cru Classé, W* Careful management results in a rich, sweet unctuous Sauternes that, being less well-known than many others, is reasonably priced.

ARGENTINA *South America* Major wine-producing country, ranking fifth in the world, with 208,000ha under vine. Wine has been made here since 1557 and today most is drunk locally, although the export market is expanding. Export wines are from the usual European classic varieties, plus Malbec, which makes dark, characterful Rs and may be blended with Cabernet Sauvignon or Barbera. Main vineyard area is MENDOZA province; quality zones are MAIPU and LUJAN DE CUYO (good Cabernet and Malbec Rs),

Tupungato (Pinot Noir, Merlot, Chardonnay, Gewürztraminer), RIO NEGRO (grapes for Sp wines). Leading producers include: Etchart, Bodegas Flichman, Peñaflor, Bodegas San Telmo, Bodegas Weinert.

ARGILLIÈRES, CLOS DES   *France, Burgundy, 1er Cru, Côte de Nuits, R*   Produces highly-coloured Nuits-St-Georges wines, with a powerful bouquet and a good tannic backbone. Leading producers include: Daniel Rion.

ARIZONA   *USA*   In one corner of a mostly-desert state, south of Tucson, a handful of wineries exploit the high-altitude conditions. Wines from Sonoita (VA and vineyard) and others can be good: Cabernet Sauvignon, Sauvignon Blanc, Pinot Noir.

ARKANSAS   *USA*   Tough climate conditions hinder growers, but some good Ws from Riesling and Chardonnay have joined the mostly-hybrid-grape wines made along the Arkansas River. Leading producer: WIEDERKEHR.

ARLAY, CH D'   *France, Jura, R, W, P*   Old family estate making Côtes de Jura wines, including a Chardonnay/Savagnin W, Pinot Noir R and Corail, a light R from all five local grapes. Also VIN JAUNE and MACVIN.

ARLOT, DOM DE L'   *France, Burgundy, Côte d'Or, R, W*   Nuits-St-Georges estate using clever, modern winemaking techniques to make top-class red and white wines.

ARMAILHAC, CH D'   *France, Bordeaux, Médoc, Pauillac, 5ème Cru Classé, R*   Owned by the Rothschilds of Mouton, and called Mouton-Baronne-Philippe until 1989, this once formed part of the Mouton estate. The wine is classic Pauillac, though with less potential to age than its First-Growth neighbour. A particularly good 1993.

ARROSÉE, CH L'   *France, Bordeaux, St-Emilion, Grand Cru Classé, R*   To the south-west of St-Emilion village, this is one of the less well-known of the *Grands Crus Classés*. A fleshy style, with great concentration: top quality.

ASSMANSHAUSEN   *Germany, Rheingau, R*   Rhine village making R wine from Spätburgunder, both in traditional sweet style (up to EISWEIN) from the State Domaine; and *barrique*-aged dry style from Weingut Kesseler and others.

ATLAS PEAK   *USA, California, VA*   Wine zone in the hills east of Napa Valley, with Rs from ANTINORI's Italian-accented Atlas Peak Winery.

AU BON CLIMAT   *USA, California, Santa Barbara & Southern California, W, R*   This winery in Los Alamos in the Santa Maria Valley buys grapes from some of the best and coolest vineyards in the area, producing stunning, ageable Chardonnays and succulently rich cherry-fruit Pinot Noirs.

AUCKLAND *New Zealand, North Island* New Zealand's oldest wine region, but with a less suitable climate than newer zones further south in North Island and in South Island, which have eclipsed it. Auckland still has some important growing areas like Henderon, Kumeu, Huapai and Waiheke Island. Production is mainly Rs, especially Cabernet Sauvignon.

AUDE, DE L' *France, Vin de Pays, R, W* This *vin de pays* name is mostly used for Rs, from the Aude department in the Midi, using traditional grapes plus some Syrah and Cabernet Sauvignon.

AUSLESE *Germany* German or Austrian wine made from selected bunches of very ripe grapes. Usually a naturally sweet wine, although dry *Auslese* is made. In good vintages, the selection may be of grapes with noble rot (*botrytis cinerea*).

AUSONE, CH *France, Bordeaux, St-Emilion, 1er Grand Cru Classé (A), R* Named after the Roman poet-consul Ausonius, this vies with CHEVAL BLANC as the best St-Emilion. Noticeable in youth for its tannic structure: it can take a decade to soften. Production is tiny.

AUSTRIA Wine is made in the east of the country, with the best quality zones being WACHAU and NEUSEIDLERSEE. Most wines are W, with increasing interest in Rs. The W wines are frequently sweet on the German pattern, but good dry Ws are also made from Riesling and the local Grüner Veltliner grapes.

AUXEY-DURESSES *France, Burgundy, AOC, R, W* Côte de Beaune village and appellation (*see also* ALOXE-CORTON); fine, raspberry-fruited R wines, and deliciously toasty and nutty Ws that bear comparison with Meursault. Leading producers include: Jean-Pierre Diconne, Dom Leroy, Jean-Pierre Prunier, Michel Prunier, Pascal Prunier.

AVA *USA* American Viticultural Area, often abbreviated to VA: an approved vineyard zone which can be as large as a state or as small as a single vineyard: many, but not all, delineate a micro-climate and/or soil zone. US law insists that if a VA is named on a label, 85% of the grapes must originate from there.

AVELEDA, QUINTA DA *Portugal, W* Large producer, with two famous W Vinhos Verdes: Castel Garcia and Aveleda. Grinalda is the top-of-the-range W wine.

AVIGNONESI *Italy, Tuscany, Vino Nobile de Montepulciano, R, W* Pacesetter producer of Montepulciano wines. *Vini da tavola* include Il Marzocco (W) Terre di Cortona (W), and Grifi (R). The Vin Santo is highly regarded, but their star is still the Vino Nobile.

AYALA *France, Champagne* One of the lesser GRANDES MARQUES, based in Ay. The Grande Cuvée vintage is better than the light, biscuity NV.

AZIENDA AGRICOLA *Italy* Wine estate.

B

BACCHUS, CAVEAU DU   *France, Jura, R, W, P*   Traditional attitudes and methods make authentic Jura wines. Rs are from the local Tousseau grape, but Ws use Chardonnay as well as Savagnin.

BACH, MASIA   *Spain, Catalonia, Penedès, R, W, P*   Part of Codorníu (Cava) since 1975, this bodega uses the Extrísimo label for its main wines, both R and W.

BAD DÜRKHEIM   *Germany, Pfalz, W, R*   Wine town making good wine (mostly W, from Riesling, Scheurebe and others) and known for its September wine fair. Leading producers include: Fitz-Ritter, Karst.

BAD KREUZNACH   *Germany, Nahe, W*   The centre of the Nahe vineyards, making good W wine; also the HQ of leading Nahe producers, including the Staatsweingut (State Domaine), August Anheuser, von Plettenberg, Finkenauer.

BAD KREUZNACH, STAATSWEINGUT   *Germany, Nahe, W*   Maker of fine W wines from the best Nahe vineyards, combined with a research centre.

BADEN   *Germany, Anbaugebiet, R, W, P*   Germany's southernmost wine region, made up of several districts (including KAISER-STUHL/TUNIBERG, Ortenau) along the upper Rhine valley and further east. Wines are mostly W, with good amounts of R and Weissherbst, the local rosé. Baden Ws are fuller, often drier, than other German wines; Rs can be good in a "French" style (dry and structured). Producers for the whole region are led by the giant BADISCHER WINZERKELLER (cooperative).

BADIA A COLTIBUONO   *Italy, Tuscany, Chianti, R, W*   The Chianti Classico is a fine wine designed for ageing. The *vino da tavola*, Sangioveto (R), comes from the oldest vines: also a light R, Coltibuono Rosso, and a W wine.

BADISCHER WINZERKELLER   *Germany, Baden, W, R*   Enormous in scale, highly competent in quality: hundreds of wines from thousands of growers. Most are good everyday wines, though a premium range matches Baden's best.

BADISCHES BERGSTRASSE/KRAICHGAU   *Germany, Baden, Bereich, R, W, P*   Zone around Heidelberg, making good light Ws and some modern Rs.

BAHANS HAUT-BRION, CH   *France, Bordeaux, Graves*   Second wine of Ch Haut-Brion.

BAILLY, JEAN-FRANCOIS   *France, Loire, Sancerre, W, R, P*   Bailly is linked via marriage with the Reverdy family, joining two important Sancerre names. The Ws from the 12-ha vineyard are excellent, but Bailly is best known for powerful Rs and light Ps.

BAIRRADA   *Portugal, DOC, R, W, Sp*   Awarded demarcated status in 1979, R Barraida now rivals Dão as one of Portugal's best-known wines. The tannic Baga grape makes a big, ripe, fruity wine, traditionally needing time to soften. Modern versions from larger producers are made for younger drinking. Some W also, plus a little Sp. Leading producers include: Caves Aliança, Luís Pato, Caves São João.

BAJA CALIFORNIA   *Mexico, Central America*   Region where Mexico's greatest vineyard expansion is taking place. More than 10,000ha are currently under vine, with most grapes grown in the Guadalupe Valley and near Ensenada. Very promising Cabernet Sauvignon and Chardonnay.

BALATON   *Hungary*   Wine region south-west of Budapest, around Lake Balaton, Europe's biggest lake, whose tempering effect on viticulture cannot be overstated. On the south shore is the Dél-Balaton area, making still and Sp Ws from Olaszrizling, Sauvignon Blanc and Chardonnay, plus R from Cabernet Sauvignon. Also home to the huge Balatonboglár winery and research station, source of much good W wine under various labels, including Chapel Hill. The Badacsony area makes W wines from Kéknyelü, Szürkebarát and Olaszrizling, among others. Other areas around the lake are Balatonfüred-Csopak and Batalonmellék.

BALBACH, BÜRGERMEISTER ANTON ERBEN WEINGUT   *Germany, Rheinhessen, W*   Top maker of NIERSTEIN wine from the best vineyards of this famous town. Specialist in Rieslings, especially late-harvest ones.

BALESTARD-LA-TONNELLE, CH   *France, Bordeaux, St-Emilion, Grand Cru Classé, R*   This site on the plateau to the east of St-Emilion village produces a richly-coloured Merlot-based wine with lots of body. Needs a good five years in bottle before it begins to mature.

BALLARAT   *Australia, Victoria*   One of the state's cool-climate areas, ideal for Pinot Noir and Chardonnay.

BANDOL   *France, Provence, AOC, R, P, W*   Most Bandol is R, with strong perfume, flavour and colour, from at least 50% Mourvèdre grapes, with Syrah and Grenache. Can age for 20 years. Leading producers include: La Bastide Blanche, Dom de l'Hermitage, Mas de la Rouvière, Moulin des Costes, Ch de Pibarnon.

BANNOCKBURN   *Australia, Victoria, Geelong, R, W*   Producer whose low-yielding, fully mature vineyards and strongly French-influenced winemaking produce superb, complex Sauvignon and Chardonnay Ws, and even more complex Pinot Noir (the estate's speciality) and Shiraz Rs.

BANYULS   *France, Midi, AOC, R, P, W, VDN*   Sweet, lightly forti-fied wine (*vin doux naturel*), from Roussillon, mainly from Grenache Noir: R, W and P wines all become tawny with age, with rich, raisiny, nutty flavours. Leading producer: Dom du Mas Blanc.

BANYULS, GROUPEMENT INTERPRODUCTEURS DU CRU   *France, Midi, Banyuls & Collioure, R, VDN*   By far the largest maker of the R Collioure; also a leader of *vin doux naturel* production.

BARANCOURT   *France, Champagne*   This relatively new house was founded by three young growers. They produce a wide range of champagnes, but their best wine is the rare (still, R) Bouzy Rouge.

BARBADILLO, ANTONIO   *Spain, sherry*   The largest and most important producer in Sanlúcar, founded 1821 and still headed by a Barbadillo. Also a big landowner in Jerez, jointly with **HARVEYS**, for whom it makes a lot of sherry. Most familiar of Barbadillo's huge range are the manzanillas (Eva, Sirena, Solear, Pastora and Don Benigno brands) and a Jerez fino, Balbaina. It has also pio-neered a W table wine, Castillo de San Diego, made from Palomino grapes in a modern, crisp style.

BARBARESCO   *Italy, Piedmont, DOCG, R*   From the Nebbiolo grape, one of Italy's greatest R wines, grown in hilly vineyards east of Alba. Aged for two years, of which one in wood, it has high acidity and tannin, balanced by lush fruit, with a hint of violets. Not quite as massive as neighbouring Barolo, but it ages extremely well. Leading producers include: Ceretto, Pio Cesare, Fratelli Cigliuti, Gaja, Bruno Giacosa, Giuseppe Mascarello & Figlio, Alfredo Prunotto.

BARBE BLANCHE, CH   *France, Bordeaux, Lussac St-Emilion, R*   His-toric château making well-received wines, including an all-Merlot *cuvée*.

BARBE, CH DE   *France, Bordeaux, Côtes de Bourg, R*   Large estate making steadily good wine in the soft, earthy Bourg style.

BARBÉ, CH   *France, Bordeaux, 1er Côtes de Blaye, R*   Not to be con-fused with Ch **DE BARBE**: this is a well-known Blaye property making straightforward, reliable Rs.

BARBERA D'ALBA   *Italy, Piedmont, DOC, R*   Italy's most widely planted R grape is regaining prestige in its native Piedmont, pro-ducing lively, succulent wine with a perfume of blackberries, raspberries and licorice. Best drunk 2–4 years after the vintage. Leading producers include: Aldo Conterno, Giacomo Conterno, Giuseppe Contratto, Bruno Giacosa.

BARBERA   Red grape from Piedmont, now widely planted in Italy and California. Versatile, with good acidity, making a range of styles. Best are the silky-textured **BARBERA D'ALBA** and Barbera d'Asti DOCs.

BARBIER, BODEGAS RENÉ *Spain, Catalonia, Penedès, R, W, P*
Now part of the Freixenet group, Barbier is a reliable producer of
attractive, easy-drinking still wines.

BARDOLINO *Italy, Veneto, DOC, R* Local grape varieties Corvina,
Rondinella, Molinara and others grown near Verona make wine
that is pale in colour, with a cherry perfume and crisp acidity. For
early drinking. Leading producers include: Masi.

BAROLO *Italy, Piedmont, DOCG, R* One of Italy's very greatest R
wines. From the Nebbiolo grape, aged for at least three years, of
which two in wood, before release. Tarry in youth, with high
acidity and tannin, takes on flavours of violets, chocolate, prunes,
tobacco, truffles and autumn smoke. Can age for up to 20 years in
bottle. Leading producers include: Elio Altare, Ceretto, Aldo Conterno, Bruno Giacosa, Giuseppe Mascarello & Figlio, Paolo Scav-
ino, Vietti, Roberto Voerzio.

BAROSSA *Australia, South Australia* Australia's top wine region,
base for many big concerns. Full-bodied dry Rs and Riesling Ws
are perhaps the best wines. Leading producers include: Charles
Melton, Leo Buring, Peter Lehmann.

BARR *France, Alsace, Bas-Rhin* This Alsace village makes good
Sylvaner, with Gewürztraminer and Riesling from the *Grand Cru*
Kirchberg de Barr. Leading producers include: Klipfel, Willm.

BARRELS Wooden barrels (or casks) can be used for fermenting
and/or ageing. Fine reds (and some whites) merit the cost of new
oak to age in: these add tannins and vanilla flavour.

BARRIQUE *France* Barrel mainly associated with Bordeaux, used
for ageing wine, holding 225 litres (24 cases of 12 bottles). The
capacity varies: Muscadet *barriques* hold 228 litres; in Anjou and
Touraine 232 litres. The Burgundy PIÈCE is 228 litres. Barrique-
ageing means the use of new or newish wood: *see* **BARRELS**.

BARSAC *France, Bordeaux, AOC, W* World-class, luscious, sweet
W wine from a commune within AOC **SAUTERNES**. Leading
producers include: Ch'x Climens, Coutet, Doisy-Daëne, Doisy-
Dubroca, Doisy-Védrines, Liot, Nairac.

BARTOLI, DE *Italy, Sicily, W, R* Leading Marsala producer whose
range includes old-style, unfortified 20-year-old Vecchio Samperi
and Joséphine Doré, dry, non-DOC wines; exemplary fortified
Vigna La Miccia and 20-year-old Marsala Superiore. Bukkuram is
a sweet Pantelleria.

BASILICATA *Italy* Area between the heel and
toe of southern Italy, that produces one of the
South's greatest Rs, **AGLIANICO DEL VULTURE**
DOC. Also some good sweet W Moscato.

BASSERMANN-JORDAN *Germany, Pfalz, W* One of the great
estates of the central Pfalz, making Rieslings in classic, elegant
long-lived style.

BATAILLEY, CH *France, Bordeaux, Médoc, Pauillac, 5ème Cru Classé, R*
Long-lived wine in the old-fashioned style from this estate on the
south-west, inland, side of the commune.

BÂTARD-MONTRACHET *France, Burgundy, AOC, W* Côte de
Beaune *Grand Cru*, between Chassagne and Puligny villages and
abutting the *Grands Crus* of **MONTRACHET**, Bienvenues-Bâtard-
Montrachet, Les Criots-Bâtard-Montrachet: all are superbly sited
for making great W wine. Leading producers include: Dom
Leflaive, Dom André Ramonet, Dom Etienne Sauzet.

BAUDRY, BERNARD *France, Loire, Chinon, R* Experimenting with
wood and separation of wines by soil type, Baudry is a serious
producer of Chinon, stressing fruit balanced with oak and ability
to age. He has 25ha at Cravant-les-Coteaux, east of Chinon.

BAY OF PLENTY *New Zealand, North Island* Area south of Auckland, noted for Müller-Thurgau, Sauvignon and Chardonnay Ws.

BÉARN *France, South-West, AOC, R, P, W* Fairly rustic wines from
the Pyrenees. Rs and Ps are from Tannat, with Cabernets Franc
and Sauvignon. Ws, usually labelled Béarn-Bellocq, are from Raf-
fiat de Moncade, a local variety. Leading producer: Les Vignerons
de Bellocq.

BEAU-SÉJOUR-BÉCOT, CH *France, Bordeaux, St-Emilion, Grand Cru
Classé, R* One of the *1ers Grands Crus Classés* before its demo-
tion in the 1985 classification, but quality has certainly improved
since. Mainly Merlot: the overall style is quite soft and silky, but
with enough structure to age well.

BEAU-SITE, CH *France, Bordeaux, St-Estèphe, Cru Bourgeois, R* This
is a finely-sited vineyard indeed, with the view of the river that
locals say good wine demands. The wines are well-made, fleshy
and long-lived.

BEAUCASTEL, CH DE *France, Rhône, Châteauneuf-du-Pape, R, W*
Leading estate in Châteauneuf, making long-lived R and good W.
Also makers of a top Côtes du Rhône, Coudoulet de Beaucastel,
from vineyards adjoining their Châteauneuf land.

BEAUJOLAIS *France, Burgundy, AOC, R, W* Nearly all Beaujolais
is R, from Gamay grapes; a little Chardonnay W is made where
the St-Véran AOC overlaps with Beaujolais. Famous for Beaujolais Nouveau, or Primeur: newly-made wine sold in November
to be drunk within a month or three. Normal Beaujolais is
enjoyed at about a year old: fresh, fruity, an appetizing partner to
country cuisine. Beaujolais Supérieur has a little more alcohol.
Beaujolais-Villages is the best zone: a group of 39 villages; among
them are 10 (the *crus*) that can use their own name: **ST-AMOUR,
JULIÉNAS, CHÉNAS, MOULIN-À-VENT, FLEURIE, CHIROUBLES,
MORGON, RÉGNIÉ, CÔTE DE BROUILLY, BROUILLY.** The rest produce a range of different styles, though none have the keeping
power of the *crus* and are made to be drunk at 1–2 years. Leading
producers of Beaujolais and -Villages include: Trenel et Fils, Loron

et Fils, Pasquier-Desvignes, Georges Duboeuf, Eventail de Vignerons Producteurs, Henry Fessy, Sylvian Fessy, Pierre Feraud.

BEAULIEU *USA, California, Napa, R* This venerable Rutherford house is famed for Georges de Latour Private Reserve Cabernet Sauvignon, which was perfected by winemaker extraordinaire André Tchelistcheff. One of California's world-class Rs, it is 100% Cabernet Sauvignon, matured only in American oak.

BEAULIEU, CH DE *France, Provence, Coteaux d'Aix-en-Provence, W, R, P* This large estate of 300ha makes easy-drinking wines with a herby, southern character. R is from Grenache, Cabernet Sauvignon, Mourvèdre and Syrah; P from Cinsaut and Carignan, W from Ugni Blanc, Clairette, Sauvignon Blanc and Sémillon.

BEAUMES-DE-VENISE *France, Rhône, AOC, R; W, VDN* France's best-known *vin doux naturel* is the sweet W Muscat from this village. It also makes traditional Grenache-based R wine as one of the Côtes du Rhône-Villages. Leading producers include: Dom de Durban, Dom Coyeux.

BEAUMET *France, Champagne* Based in Epernay, this house produces a wide range of champagnes including Cuvée Malakoff, an outstanding *blanc de blancs*.

BEAUMONT DES CRAYÈRES *France, Champagne* This Epernay cooperative has some 210 grower-members with 75ha of vines. It enjoys a very good reputation, in particular for its Cuvée Nostalgie.

BEAUMONT, CH *France, Bordeaux, Médoc, Cru Bourgeois, R* Large, modern and well-placed château in Cussac making solid, good-value wine to keep for five years.

BEAUNE *France, Burgundy, AOC, R, W* Large production and high standards make Beaune a benchmark for good-value R burgundy with elegant perfume and fine, fruity, spicy flavour, best at 6–10 years old. W wines are less distinguished; to be drunk younger. The appellation, named after the medieval centre of Burgundy's wine trade, has no *Grands Crus*, but the largest area of *Premiers Crus* vineyards on the CÔTE DE BEAUNE. Leading producers include: Besancenot-Mathouillet, Dom Machard de Gramont, Dom du Château de Meursault, Daniel Sénard.

BEAUSÉJOUR (DUFFAU-LAGAROSSE), CH *France, Bordeaux, St-Emilion, 1er Grand Cru Classé, R* Perhaps the least well-known of the *1ers Grands Crus*, currently undergoing a revival and worth watching. Innovations include less Cabernet Sauvignon and late harvesting.

BECKER, J B *Germany, Rheingau, R, W* Fine vineyards in the central Rheingau yield good Rs (from Spätburgunder) as well as Riesling Ws in both classic and dry styles.

BECKER, JEAN *France, Alsace, W, R* Old (1610) family firm making all major Alsace wines. The best are Muscat (including a superb botrytized one), Pinot Noir, Gewürztraminer (from *Grand Cru* Froehn) and Riesling.

BEDELL CELLARS *USA, New York, Long Island, R* The first few vintages of Merlot and Cabernet Sauvignon in the early 1980s were so rich and seemingly long-lived that they placed this small winery among the best outside the West Coast.

BEERENAUSLESE *Germany* German or Austrian wine made from individually selected grapes that are always overripe (probably affected by noble rot), and thus very sweet.

BELAIR, CH *France, Bordeaux, St-Emilion, 1er Grand Cru Classé, R* The Dubois-Challon family also own AUSONE next door. Belair is similarly concentrated and quite tannic, but matures sooner.

BEL-AIR, CH *France, Bordeaux, Lalande-de-Pomerol, R* Consistent and long-lived wine, approaching Pomerol in stature.

BELGIUM Wine producer on a small scale, mainly in the Meuse and Sambre valleys, with around 100 growers and a total of 30ha of vineyard. Most wines are Müller-Thurgau whites, with some Pinot Noir reds.

BELGRAVE, CH *France, Bordeaux, Haut-Médoc, 5ème Cru Classé, R* Deservedly obscure till recently, this estate has well-placed land west of St-Julien. Decades of neglect ended in the 1980s with new owners, advice and investment. Results now show.

BELINGARD, CH *France, South-West, Bergerac, R, W* Exciting modern wines from an innovative estate: crisp, dry W Bergerac and substantial R Côtes de Bergerac, sweet W Monbazillac, and top wines under the Blanche de Bosredon label.

BELLAND, DOM ADRIEN *France, Burgundy, Côte d'Or, R, W* Based in Santenay with vineyards throughout the region, including Corton, Puligny and Chambertin. Good, traditional wines.

BELLE-GRAVES, CH *France, Bordeaux, Lalande-de-Pomerol, R* This respected small estate is close to Pomerol in quality.

BELLET *France, Provence, AOC, R, P, W* Tiny zone; wines rarely seen outside Nice. Producers: Ch de Crémat, Ch de Bellet.

BELLEVUE LA FORÊT, CH *France, South-West, Côtes du Frontonnais, R* Leading private estate of the appellation, with good fresh well-made R plus a prestige *cuvée* aged a year in oak.

BENDIGO *Australia, Victoria* This is R-wine country, especially deeply coloured, full-bodied single-variety Shiraz and Cabernet Sauvignon, plus blends of these two grapes. Leading producers include: Jasper Hill, Mount Ida, Passing Clouds, Yellowglen.

BENNWIHR-MITTELWIHR *France, Alsace, Haut-Rhin* These two adjacent villages produce Gewürztraminer and Muscat. *Grands Crus*: Marckrain (Bennwihr) and Mandelberg (Mittelwihr). Leading producers include: Deiss.

BERBERANA, BODEGAS *Spain, Rioja, R, W, P* Established in 1877, this is now one of the largest and most impressive wineries in Rioja. Main labels include Carta de Oro and Carta de Plata, as well as Berberana.

BERCHER, WEINGUT *Germany, Baden, R, W* Modern-minded estate which ages its best Rs and Ws, from Spätburgunder and Grauburgunder, in cask. Most wines are dry.

BEREICH *Germany* Wine district.

BERGER, M *France, Loire, Montlouis, W, Sp* The family's 20ha in St-Martin-le-Beau provides the grapes for this quality-conscious firm. Half their production is Sp, the rest still, ranging from dry to a luscious botrytized *moelleux*.

BERGERAC *France, South-West, AOC, R, W, P* Large area adjoining and east of St-Emilion. Grapes and wine styles are similar to Bordeaux: Cabernet Sauvignon, Cabernet Franc and Merlot for Rs and Ps; Sémillon, Sauvignon Blanc and others for Ws. Modern, crisp dry Ws from Sauvignon Blanc are labelled Bergerac Sec. Côtes de Bergerac Rs have higher alcohol, Ws are medium-sweet, or *moelleux*. PÉCHARMANT is a small zone for good Rs, SAUSSIGNAC for Ws. Leading producers include: Dom de l'Ancienne Curé, Ch Belingard, Ch La Jaubertie, Cave Coopérative de Montravel et Sigoulès.

BERGHEIM *France, Alsace* Bergheim village, and its *Grand Cru* Altenberg de Bergheim, are famous for Gewürztraminer from limestone soils. Leading producers include: Deiss, Lorentz, Gassmann, Sipp.

BERGKELDER *South Africa, Stellenbosch, R, W* Unique to South Africa, the Bergkelder fulfils several roles, which include selling estate wines and producing various ranges of its own (Stellenryck, Fleur du Cap).

BERGSTRASSE, STAATSWEINGUT *Germany, Hessiche Bergstrasse, W* Most important estate in this small region, specializing in EISWEIN, but making a full range of typical soft, generous Ws.

BERLIQUET, CH *France, Bordeaux, St-Emilion, Grand Cru Classé, R* Raised to *Grand Cru Classé* in the 1985 classification, this wine is made under the guidance of the local co-op. Densely structured: best years need about a decade in bottle.

BERLUCCHI, GUIDO *Italy, Lombardy, Franciacorta, W, R, Sp* Italy's largest *metodo classico* producer of Sp wines: Cuvée Impériale Berlucchi Brut, Grand Crémant, Pas Dosé and Max Rosé. Still wines include Bianco Impériale.

BERNKASTEL *Germany, Mosel-Saar-Ruwer, Bereich, W* Zone covering the central, and best, vineyards of the Mosel. Also called the Mittel (middle) Mosel. While several villages – Bernkastel itself, WEHLEN, PIESPORT – have top-class vineyards, there is much poor land within the Bereich. For leading producers see above-named villages and **GRAACH**, **TRABEN-TRARBACH** etc. Bernkastel the village has top vineyards including the famous Doctor, a steep hill above the rooftops making fabulous sweet wine in good vintages; Graben, next to and almost as good as Doctor; Alte Badstube am Doktorberg, ditto. Bernkasteler Badstube is a high-quality *grosslage*; Bernkasteler Kurfürstlay a larger and lesser one. Leading growers in Bernkastel include: Friedrich-Wilhelm-Gymnasium, Lauerburg, Dr Thanisch (both concerns of that name), Wegeler Erben, Loosen, J J Prüm.

BERTAGNA, DOM *France, Burgundy, Côte d'Or, R, W* German-owned domaine with several top vineyards, notably in the Côte de Nuits *Grands Crus* of Chambertin, Clos St-Denis and Clos de Vougeot, that produce elegant, reliable wines.

BERTAUD-BELIEU, CH *France, Provence, Côtes de Provence, W, R, P* Three ranges are produced from this new 50-ha estate near St-Tropez: Cuvée Tradition and Cuvée Prestige, both in R, W and P; and the top R, Ch Villa de Belieu.

BERTINEAU ST-VINCENT, CH *France, Bordeaux, Lalande-de-Pomerol, R* Small estate which is owned by oenologist Michel Rolland's family: excellent winemaking, worth 6-8 years' ageing in good vintages, such as 1990.

BESSAN, CH *France, Bordeaux, 1er Côtes de Bordeaux, R* Family links to Ch **BRETHOUS**; attractive Rs for fairly early drinking.

BESSERAT DE BELLEFON *France, Champagne* Now owned by giant **MARNE ET CHAMPAGNE**. Somewhat light in style, the best wine is the Grande Cuvée Blanc de Blancs.

BEYCHEVELLE, CH *France, Bordeaux, Médoc, St-Julien, 4ème Cru Classé, R* Grand 18th-century château, with large, well-situated vineyard along the edge of the riverside plateau. Lush and delicious, in good vintages it ages well. 2nd wine: Amiral de Beychevelle.

BEYER, LEON *France, Alsace, W* Wine merchants since the 16th century, and producers since the mid-19th, Beyer is known for its dry wine style – particularly Riesling, Gewürztraminer (Cuvée des Comtes d'Eguisheim) and Muscat. Beyer does not produce *Grand Cru* wines.

BIANCO DI CUSTOZA *Italy, Veneto, DOC, W, Sp* From the southern tip of Lake Garda, this wine has a mellow fruitiness often compared to greengages and peaches. Best drunk young.

BIENVENUES-BÂTARD-MONTRACHET See BÂTARD-MONTRACHET.

BIERZO *Spain, Castilla-León, DO, W, R* Fifth and newest wine zone of Castilla-León, owing much in style to neighbouring Galicia. It produces light, fresh, basic wines, made with increasingly modern equipment and methods. Leading producers include: Prada a Tope.

BIGI   *Italy, Central Italy, Umbria, W, R*   Large-scale producer with many single-vineyard wines. Top Orvietos include dry Torricella and sweet Orzalume. Marrano is a dry barrel-aged Grechetto (W). Est! Est!! Est!!! and Aleatico di Gradoli come from Lazio.

BILLECART-SALMON   *France, Champagne*   Small family-owned GRANDE MARQUE at Mareuil-sur-Ay producing superb quality wines which age extremely well. Outstanding.

BILTMORE, CH   *USA, North Carolina, R, W, Sp*
This Ashville winery is part of the historic Vanderbilt estate and mansion built in 1880. Cabernet Sauvignon, Chardonnay and a sparkling Blanc de Blancs are made.

BINGEN   *Germany, Rheinhessen, Bereich, W, R*   The western half of the Rheinhessen region, with some good vineyards at Bingen itself and Iphofen and wide tracts of ordinary ones. The leading producer in Bingen is Weingut Villa Sachsen.

BINISSALEM   *Spain, Majorca, DO, R, W, P*   Spain's first offshore DO, in Majorca, north-east of Palma. Mainly R wines, some better-quality ones aged in oak; W and *rosados* made only as *jovenes*. Leading producers include: Franja Roja.

BIODYNAMIC   A thoroughgoing form of organic viticulture: growing vines according to the cycles of the moon and stars, using balanced plant communities to combat diseases and pests, etc. Some superb wines are made on biodynamic estates: Coulée de Serrant from the Loire, Frick in Alsace, Bize-Leroy in Burgundy, but there is more faith than science in the explanations: sceptics suggest that taking great care of one's vines will bear fruit, whatever the philosophy that inspires the care.

BIONDI-SANTI   *Italy, Tuscany, Brunello di Montalcino, R, W*   Vineyards date back 400 years. Two estates produce Brunello blended wine. Vigna del Fiore is a *riserva*. The Brusco dei Barbi (R) is big and more rustic than the Brunello. Expensive.

BISCHÖFLICHEN WEINGÜTER   *Germany, Mosel-Saar-Ruwer, W*   Charitable estate (like the HOSPICES DE BEAUNE) owning many top vineyards in the Mosel Valley and making fine, elegant Riesling wines.

BIZE, DOM SIMON ET FILS   *France, Burgundy, Côte d'Or, R, W*   Based in Savigny-lès-Beaune, this highly-regarded family-owned and run estate makes mostly R wine in a fruity, elegant style.

BLAGNY   *France, Burgundy, AOC, R, W*   Positive, slightly earthy R from a Côte de Beaune hamlet between Meursault and Puligny; it uses those names for its W wines.

BLANC DE BLANCS   *France*   White wine made from only white grapes. This term is most commonly used for champagne made entirely from Chardonnay.

BLANC DE NOIRS   *France*   White wine made from black grapes.

BLANC FUMÉ DE POUILLY   See POUILLY-FUMÉ.

BLANCHOTS   *France, Burgundy, Chablis, Grand Cru*   The lightest, most accessible and earliest-maturing of the Chablis *Grands Crus*.

BLANDY BROS   *Portugal, Madeira*   Best-known madeira in the UK. The "Duke of" range: Sussex sercial, Cambridge verdelho, Cumberland bual and Clarence malmsey are all 5-year-old wines. Blandy's 10-year-old special reserve wines are among the best. The historic lodges at Funchal are a must for any visitor to the island.

BLANQUETTE DE LIMOUX   *France, Midi, AOC, W*   This Sp W wine is usually made by the method used in Champagne, from local Mauzac grapes (which confer firm acidity and a taste of quince) with some Chardonnay and Chenin Blanc. Crémant de Limoux has more of these two classics. Leading producers include: Cave Coopérative de Limoux, Dom de Martinolles.

BLAYE   *France, Bordeaux, AOC, R, W*   Large appellation (also known as Blayais) on the right bank of the Gironde. Shared a historical reputation for robust, dark, long-lived Rs with neighbour CÔTES DE BOURG (or Bourgeais). Today, these are from Merlot and Cabernet Franc (plus some Malbec and Cabernet Sauvignon), with good fruit and structure. The Ws, from Sémillon, Sauvignon Blanc and Colombard, are akin to Entre-Deux-Mers. Leading producers include: Blaye R, Ch'x Barbé, Haut-Sociondo, Petraud, Segonzac.

BLIN   *France, Champagne*   This dynamic co-op at Vincelles has 85 growers and makes attractive, light, fruity, uncomplicated wines.

BLUE RIDGE MOUNTAINS   *USA, Virginia, VA*   This well-regarded wine zone in central Virginia makes good Ws from Chardonnay and Riesling, and Rs from Cabernet. MONTICELLO is a sub-zone. Leading producers include: Prince Michel, Montdomaine.

BLUSH WINE   Term for pale rosé, mostly used in America.

BODEGA   *Spain*   Cellar. Can also describe the building where wine is made and matured, or the firm that makes it.

BODEGAS FLICHMAN   *Argentina, R, W*   Reliable exporter, making well-aged, highly scented Cabernet Sauvignon under Caballero de la Cepa label. Also good Chardonnay and Syrah.

BODENSEE   *Germany, Baden, Bereich, R, W, P*   Vineyards on Lake Constance (Bodensee) which yield wines of all colours: light, fruity and (the Rs) sometimes pale.

BOIZEL   *France, Champagne*   An old firm, still family-owned. Extensive exports, especially of the NV *brut*, which is a medium-weight champagne with attractive biscuit overtones.

BOLLA *Italy, Veneto, W, R* Verona house making Soave, Soave Classico Castellaro and Vigneti di Frosca; Valpolicella Classico Jago and Amarone Cantina del Nonno; Creso (R) *vino da tavola*.

BOLLINGER *France, Champagne* Leading GRANDE MARQUE with a large vineyard holding. Specialities include fermentation in wood, the use of reserve wines and late disgorgement. Once the youthful austerity has worn off these wines become extremely full, rich and biscuity. Bollinger RD is one of the great champagnes, as is their extremely rare Vieilles Vignes Françaises.

BON PASTEUR, CH LE *France, Bordeaux, Pomerol, R* Owned by the family of Michel Rolland, the oenologist who defined the late-harvest, long-maceration style of Pomerol. Excellent, good value Pomerol, ready at three years in lesser vintages but lasting much longer in the finest years. *See also* BERTINEAU ST-VINCENT.

BONALGUE, CH *France, Bordeaux, Pomerol, R* This is a wine which has to soften before drinking: try it at 5-7 years old.

BONHOMME, DOM ANDRÉ *France, Burgundy, Mâconnais, W* Leading producer of rich, concentrated Mâcon-Viré.

BONNAT, CH LE *France, Bordeaux, Graves W, R* Serious winemaking for oaky, age-worthy Rs and Ws.

BONNEAU DU MARTRAY, DOM *France, Burgundy, Côte d'Or, R, W* Top Corton (R) and delicious, elegant Corton-Charlemagne (W) are made by this Pernand-Vergelesses estate.

BONNES MARES *France, Burgundy, AOC, R* Côte de Nuits *Grand Cru* at Chambolle-Musigny: powerful, solid R wines, among Burgundy's greatest. Leading producers include: de Vogüé, Dom des Varoilles.

BONNET, CH *France, Bordeaux, Entre-Deux-Mers, W, R* André Lurton's lovely château makes pungent, soft W in the modern style plus good AOC Bordeaux R.

BONNEZEAUX *France, Loire, AOC, W* High-class sweet Chenin Blanc Ws from this Coteaux du Layon village. Leading producers include: Ch de Fesles, René Renou.

BONNY DOON *USA, California, Santa Cruz, R, W* Randall Grahm's distinctive wines include a tasty Rhône-style red, Le Cigare Volant, full of cranberry and cherry aromas and flavours; an intensely sweet Muscat Canelli in the style of a German EISWEIN, and several other Rhône and Italy-inspired wines.

BOORDY VINEYARDS *USA, Maryland, R, W* With grapes from its small estate vineyard and from local growers, this winery makes a range from hybrid vines.

BORDEAUX *France, Bordeaux, AOC, R, W, P, Sp* Wine region and appellation. Within the region are 53 appellations in several tiers. Four main groups, MÉDOC, GRAVES/SAUTERNES, ST-EMIL-ION/POMEROL and ENTRE-DEUX-MERS, have sub-divisions of increasingly higher standards. Most of the Gironde *département*, however, is entitled to grow AOC Bordeaux – or Bordeaux Supérieur with slightly higher alcohol. These are mostly R: lively wines showing the personalities of the Cabernet Sauvignon and Merlot grapes. Pale R wine may be labelled Bordeaux Clairet. Sp Ws are sold as Bordeaux *mousseux* and Crémant de Bordeaux. Bordeaux Côtes de Francs, a small appellation east of St-Emilion, makes R and W (dry and sweet) wines.

BORGES & IRMÃO *Portugal, W* Substantial producers and exporters of Vinho Verde W table wines. Gatão is the biggest brand on the home market.

BORTOLI, DE *Australia, New South Wales, Murrumbidgee, R, W* One of the fastest-growing wineries in Australia, producing three million cases a year. Its sweet, luscious botrytized Sémillon W, Noble One, is a great wine and a flagship.

BOSCHENDAL ESTATE *South Africa, Paarl, R, W, Sp* Wide range of wines including a very good blended white, Grand Vin Blanc, and a well-made Sp, Boschendal Brut.

BOSCQ, CH LE *France, Bordeaux, St-Estèphe, Cru Bourgeois, R* An increasingly attractive wine from a château on the northern edge of the area.

BOSSARD, GUY *France, Loire, Muscadet, W, Sp* Organic (since the 1970s) wines of high quality and reputation. His estate wine is Dom de l'Ecu and his top *cuvée* Hermine d'Or. Also **GROS PLANT** and a Sp Muscadet.

BOTRYTIS CINEREA Fungus, known as "noble rot", which shrivels the grapes, concentrating their juice. Botrytized grapes make some of the world's greatest sweet wines: Sauternes, Hungarian Tokaji, *Trockenbeerenauslese*.

BOUCHARD AÎNÉ ET FILS *France, Burgundy, Côte d'Or, R, W* Major Burgundy *négociant*, owning land ranging from *Grand Cru* Chambertin to the Côte Chalonnaise.

BOUCHARD FINLAYSON *South Africa, Walker Bay, R, W* Very small coastal winery recently established in partnership with Burgundy *négociant* **BOUCHARD AÎNÉ ET FILS**. Not surprisingly, their best wine is an elegant, silky Pinot Noir.

BOUCHARD PÈRE ET FILS *France, Burgundy, Côte d'Or, R, W* *Négociant* based in Beaune with world-wide sales. Has major vineyard holdings, with further good land under the name Domaines du Château de Beaune. High and reliable standards, especially in the Côte de Beaune.

BOUCHAUD, HENRI *France, Loire, Muscadet, W, R* The Dom du Bois-Joly in Le Pallet produces classic Muscadets, with all the requisite lightness and freshness; plus **GROS PLANT** and a red **VIN DE PAYS DU JARDIN DE LA FRANCE** from Cabernet Franc.

BOUCHES-DU-RHÔNE, DES *France, Vin de Pays, R, P, W* Wines from the southern Rhône, mostly Rs from Rhône grapes plus some Merlot and Cabernet Sauvignon.

BOUGROS *France, Burgundy, Chablis, Grand Cru* Vineyard yielding firm wines with a certain rustic quality.

BOURDY, CHRISTIAN *France, Jura, R, W, P* Grower and *négociant* making the full range of Jura wines, including Château-Chalon VIN JAUNE, in a traditional style.

BOURG See CÔTES DE BOURG.

BOURGOGNE *France, Burgundy AOC, R, W, P* Burgundy has a complex hierarchy of appellations. At the base are the regional AOCs – wine from approved vineyards anywhere in Burgundy:
Bourgogne R from Pinot Noir, W from Chardonnay or Pinot Blanc, or (rarely) P (the term CLAIRET can be given to Rs, sometimes to Ps); Bourgogne (Grand) Ordinaire also from anywhere in the region, but Gamay (for R and P) and Aligoté (for W) grapes can be used. Bourgogne Aligoté is a brisk W, at its best from BOUZERON in the Chalonnais, where it has its own AOC. Sp wine (Crémant de Bourgogne or Bourgogne *mousseux*) is also made. Some villages (Irancy for Rs, St-Bris for Ws) and some districts (CÔTE CHALONNAISE, HAUTES CÔTES DE BEAUNE, HAUTES CÔTES DE NUITS) may add their name to the Bourgogne label.
Village wines The main villages in the CÔTE D'OR, such as Pommard, Meursault (and a few villages, eg Mercurey in the Côte Chalonnaise and Pouilly-Fuissé in the Mâconnais), which have their own appellations.
Premiers & Crands Crus Certain vineyards within these villages are *Premiers Crus:* these will be mentioned on label, but are not appellations in their own right. The top vineyards or *Grands Crus* are appellations, and use their name alone – for example Chambertin in the Côte de Nuits, Montrachet in the Côte de Beaune.

BOURGUEIL *France, Loire, AOC, R* Good Cabernet Franc Rs from the north bank of the Loire. Akin to CHINON, for drinking young but good vintages age well (up to 10 years). St-Nicolas-de-Bourgueil village has its own appellation. Leading producers include: Pierre-Jacques Druet, Jacques Mabileau, Joël Taluau.

BOUSCASSÉ, CH *France, South-West, Madiran, R* Pioneer of the Madiran revival: keen on oak-ageing, sometimes to excess; these wines need bottle-age too.

BOUSCAUT, CH *France, Bordeaux, Pessac-Léognan, Cru Classé, R, W* Winemaker Lucien Lurton prefers subtlety to flamboyance. The barrel-fermented W is one of the AOC's best; the R is improving.

BOUVET-LADUBAY *France, Loire, Saumur, W, Sp* Most enterprizing and innovative of the sparkling Saumur houses, owned by Taittinger Champagne. Their range includes two top W *cuvées*: Saphir, and Trésor with its high proportion of Chardonnay, partly oak-fermented.

BOUZERON *France, Burgundy, AOC, W* Dry W from Aligoté grape is at its best in Bourgogne Aligoté de Bouzeron, from this Côte Chalonnaise village. Leading producers include: Bouchard Père et Fils, Michel Goubard, A et P de Villaine.

BOYD-CANTENAC, CH *France, Bordeaux, Médoc, Margaux, 3ème Cru Classé, R* Relatively small estate with powerful, long-lasting wine from old vines.

BRACHETTO D'ACQUI *Italy, Piedmont, DOC, R, Sp* Sweet R Sp wine from the Brachetto grape with a distinctive bouquet of roses and sometimes violets. For early drinking. Leading producers include: Ivaldi, Villa Banfi.

BRANAIRE-DUCRU CH *France, Bordeaux, Médoc, St-Julien, 4ème Cru Classé, R* Château is just west of Beychevelle, but its vines are scattered around the commune. The wine does not show the refined "riverside" character of its neighbours, having more body and perfume. A good, elegant 1993.

BRANE-CANTENAC, CH *France, Bordeaux, Médoc, Margaux, 2ème Cru Classé, R* Large well-sited vineyard on the south tip of the Margaux gravel plateau. The Seventies were disappointing, but Prof Peynaud's advice was sought and the decade of the 1980s saw improvement. Wines now show finesse, especially since 1986, and deserve their 2nd-Growth status.

BRANGER, CLAUDE *France, Loire, Muscadet, W* Award-winning, soft yet crisp Dom La Haute Févrie, plus some GROS PLANT. Top *cuvée*, Excellence, is worth ageing: rare for Muscadet.

BRAUNEBERG *Germany, Mosel, W* Village of the Mittel Mosel, close to Bernkastel, with fine Riesling vineyards including the top-class Juffer and Juffer Sonnenuhr. Leading growers include Fritz Haag, Richter, Pauly-Bergweiler, Dr Thanisch.

BRAZIL *South America* After Argentina and Chile, South America's third wine country, in quantity if not quality. Vines were first planted in the 17th century and today it is *labrusca*, rather than classic *vinifera*, which is most widely grown, from the prolific R variety Isabella to Niagara and Dutchess for W. Rio Grande do Sul province in the south is by far the most important. Many international wine companies have been attracted by Brazil's potential wine market. Leading producers include: Vinicola Aurora, Dreher, Marcus James, Riograndense.

BREISGAU *Germany, Baden, Bereich, R, W, P* Light, fresh W wines from the Rhine near Freiburg; the P *weissherbst* is a speciality.

BREJOEIRA, PALÁCIO DE *Portugal, W* Remarkable "first growth" estate producing Vinho Verde, entirely from W Alvarado grapes, typically round and with more body than is customary.

BRENATO'SCHE GUTSWERWALTUNG, BARON VON *Germany, Rheingau, W* Very traditional, a link with the Rheingau's past, making Riesling Ws that stress elegance and fruit.

BRETHOUS, CH *France, Bordeaux, 1er Côtes de Bordeaux* Well-made wine, worth keeping for longer than the appellation would suggest: a good 1990, and a success in '93.

BREUER, BERNARD *Germany, Rheingau, W* Modern pioneer of dry Rheingau Riesling wine under the CHARTA label which Breuer helped start. Dry wines, with structure and fruit, designed to go with food.

BREUIL, CH DE *France, Loire, Anjou, W, R, Sp* The Morgats make fine sweet W COTEAUX DU LAYON-BEAULIEU, R and W Anjou, Sp CRÉMANT DE LOIRE and VIN DE PAYS DU JARDIN DE LA FRANCE (R, W). Sweet wines are deep and rich; the dry benefit from modern techniques.

BRIDGEHAMPTON WINERY *USA, New York, Long Island, W, R* This compact, state-of-the-art winery has made a name with Chardonnay, Merlot and an occasional sweet late-harvest Riesling W.

BRITISH COLUMBIA *Canada* The Okanagan Valley, in the south of the province, is technically a desert, with hot days and cool nights. Irrigation allows grapes (mostly German varieties) for good Ws to be grown. Rs are not yet up to the standard of the Ws. About 30 wineries and 4 wine zones, which include Okanagan and Victoria Island, make wine. Leading producers include: Blue Mountain Vineyard, Brights, Cedar Creek, Dom de Chaberton, Gehringer, Hainle, Lang, Le Comte, Mission Hill, Sumac Ridge, Summerhill.

BRL HARDY *Australia, South Australia, McLaren Vale, R, W* The Renmano/Thomas Hardy merger has created one of the country's biggest wine groups, based in McLaren Vale in South Australia but with vineyards across Australia. Brands are many and various: honest rather than exciting, except for the top wines: eg Eileen Hardy.

BROCARD, JEAN-MARC *France, Burgundy, Chablis, W* Medium-sized producer: mainly *Village* Chablis. No oak used to make good, steely Chablis which ages well.

BROUILLY *France, Burgundy, AOC, R* Largest, most productive and most southerly Beaujolais *cru:* much fairly ordinary R, but also some substantial and long-lived ones. Leading producers include: Ch de la Chaize, J-F Gaget, Ch Thivin.

BROUSSEAU, ROBERT *France, Loire, Muscadet, W* The Dom des Mortiers-Gobin in La Haie-Fouassière has belonged to generations of the Brousseaus. Traditional methods, including some wood maturation, produce wines that can age.

BROUSTET, CH *France, Bordeaux, Barsac, 2ème Cru Classé, W* Despite being large and frankly commercial, this estate makes delicious, spicy, stylish and very well balanced wines, among the bargains of Sauternes. Changed hands in 1994.

BROWN BROS *Australia, Victoria, R, W* Old-established, but still experimenting with (among others) new varieties and high-altitude vineyards. They specialize in single-variety wines.

BRÛLÉSCAILLE, CH *France, Bordeaux, Côtes de Bourg, R* Solid and well-made claret, worth cellaring.

BRUN DE NEUVILLE, LE *France, Champagne* Co-op in the little-known Côte de Sézanne with 145 members and 140ha of vines. The Chardonnay-based wines have lots of fruity appeal.

BRÜNDLMAYER, WILLI *Austria, Kamptal, W, R* One of Austria's top producers, whose family has been making wine since the 17th century. Top quality throughout, from fine dry Grüner Veltliner and steely Riesling to a finely-balanced bordeaux blend and rich, chocolatey Blauburgunder-based R wine.

BRUNELLO DI MONTALCINO *Italy, Tuscany, DOCG, R* From the Brunello grape, a clone of Sangiovese, aged in oak for at least three years. Very full-flavoured and tannic, this expensive wine will age in bottle almost indefinitely. Leading producers include: Altesino, Barbi, Biondi-Santi, Lisini, Villa Banfi.

BRUN DE NEUVILLE, LE *France, Champagne* A cooperative in the little-known Côte de Sézanne district, with 145 members with 140ha of vines. The Chardonnay-based wines have lots of fruity appeal.

BRUT *France* Usually the driest style of champagne and, by extension, other sparkling wines.

BRUT NATURE *France* Very dry sparkling wine style – with no *dosage*.

BUCELAS *Portugal, DOC, W* Less than 30km from Lisbon, produces dry W wines from the acidic Arinto and Esgana Cão ("dog strangler") grape varieties. The best are lemon-fresh. The area is showing sure signs of a revival. Leading producers include: Caves Velhas.

BUENA VISTA *USA, California, Sonoma, R, W* Now German-owned, with 360ha in Carneros; winemaker Jill Davis does well with Chardonnay and Rs such as Pinot Noir, soft, silky Merlot and rich, blackcurranty Cabernet Sauvignon.

BUGEY, VIN DU *France, Savoie, AOC, R, P, W, Sp* Often labelled by grape variety: Jacquère, Molette, Roussette and Chardonnay for Ws; Mondeuse, Pinot Noir and Gamay for Rs. Cerdon is the best of several named *crus*. Roussette du Bugey has its own AOC, with several *crus*. Also many Sp Ws and Ps. Leading producers include: Monin, Caveau Bugiste co-op.

BUHL, VON *Germany, Pfalz, W* Serious Rieslings, made to last, with their balance of fruit and steely acidity.

BUITENVERWACHTING *South Africa, Constantia, R, W* Fairly large ultra-modern winery producing a wide range, including award-winning Merlot and good Chardonnay.

BUJANDA, BODEGAS MARTINEZ *Spain, Rioja, R, W, P* Outstanding producer of meticulously-made wines. A modern style, stressing elegance and balance, is much in evidence here, particularly in their Conde de Valdemar (R).

BULGARIA A drive to make and sell good-value, international-standard wine means Bulgaria has been exporting large quantities to the West since the early 1980s. Cabernet Sauvignon led the way and today 75% of the vineyards are planted with classic varieties. Of the R grapes, a massive 75% are either Cabernet Sauvignon or Merlot. The most widely planted W is Rkatsiteli. Native R varieties like Mavrud, Melnik and Gamza can be good. Mavrud from Assenovgrad in the south is very good; dark and spicy, it can age well. The cooler east and north provide good Ws (Chardonnay, Aligoté) and Rs, especially Cabernet Sauvignon.

BURGAUD, BERNARD *France, Rhône, Côte Rôtie, R* Rising star of Côte Rôtie, making reliable, typical wines.

BURGENLAND *Austria* Some R wines (22%) as well as full-bodied dry Ws. There are four regions: both Neusiedlersee-Hügelland and Neusiedlersee are important for sweet botrytized wines, Mittelburgenland is R wine country, notably Blaufränkisch. The fourth region, Südburgenland, is very small.

BÜRGERSPITAL ZUM HEILIGEN GEIST WEINGUT *Germany, Franken, W* Great charitable estate owning superb vineyards and making a full range of Franken wines.

BÜRGSTADT *Germany, Franken, R* Wine town on the River Main known mostly for serious Rs. Leading producers include: Rudolf Fürst and Weingut der Stadt Klingenberg.

BÜRKLIN-WOLF, WEINGUT DR *Germany, Pfalz, W, R* The top wine estate of the central Pfalz, making both traditional sweet wines and superb modern dry ones from Riesling and a range of other grapes.

BUXY, CAVE COOPERATIVE DE *France, Burgundy, Chalonnais, R, W* Large and well-run concern which produces a wide range of good-value lesser burgundies, but which is especially well known for their Montagnys. Quality may vary, but generally very reliable.

BUZET *France, South-West, AOC, R, P, W* Mostly R wine, from Bordeaux varieties: Cabernet Sauvignon, Cabernet Franc, Merlot, Malbec. Leading producer: LES VIGNERONS DE BUZET.

BUZET, LES VIGNERONS DE *France, South-West, Buzet, R* Quality-biased cooperative making good R Buzet: the top wines spend time in new oak, indeed most wines have some oak-ageing. Its top *cuvée* is the excellent Baron d'Ardeuil.

CABARDÈS   *France, Midi, VDQS, R, P*   Worthwhile Rs and Ps from Cabernet Sauvignon, Merlot and Grenache. Leading producers include: Ch'x de Pennautier, de Rayssac, Rivals.

CABERNET D'ANJOU   *France, Loire, AOC, P*   Rosé, sweet or dry, from Cabernet (Franc and Sauvignon). Better than Rosé d'Anjou.

CABERNET DE SAUMUR   As CABERNET D'ANJOU.

CABERNET FRANC   Red Bordeaux grape: 12–20% of Médoc and Graves wines, but often 50% or more in St-Emilion. Lacks the tannin and acidity of Cabernet Sauvignon, but adds fresh fruit aromas, soft-fruit and earthy tastes. Dominant in Touraine, central Loire, for wines such as Saumur, Chinon, Bourgueil – light reds, mostly for drinking young. Popular in north-east Italy, in the Veneto and Friuli-Venezia Giulia. Some is grown in California.

CABERNET SAUVIGNON   The foundation of red Bordeaux and, although low-yielding, the world's favourite grape for quality red wine. Often blended with Cabernet Franc and Merlot, as 100% Cabernet Sauvignon can prove austere. Wine is dark, tannic, with blackcurrant aromas when young, cedar-wood in mature wines. Reacts well to oak-ageing and well-made wines from a good vintage will improve in bottle for decades.

CÁCERES, BODEGAS MARQUÉS DE   *Spain, Rioja, R, W, P*   This meticulously-run modern winery boasts a justifiably high reputation. Harmonious wines which age very well.

CADET-PIOLA, CH   *France, Bordeaux, St-Emilion, Grand Cru Classé, R*   Small estate on one of the highest points of the St-Emilion plateau. The wines, high in Cabernet Sauvignon for St-Emilion, are quite tannic when young, but begin to soften with a few years' bottle-age, and can be good value.

CADILLAC   *France, Bordeaux, AOC, W*   Near-extinct appellation for sweet W wine made across the river from Sauternes.

CAHORS   *France, South-West, AOC, R*   Fine, tannic R from the Lot Valley, using Malbec grapes (local name Auxerrois), with Merlot and Tannat. Best are capable of long ageing. Leading producers include: Ch du Cayrou, Les Côtes d'Olt, Clos la Coutale, Clos de Gamot, Ch Triguedina.

CAILLERET, LE   *France, Burgundy, Côte de Beaune, 1er Cru, W*   Top Chassagne-Montrachet vineyard, producing fat, weighty mouth-filling wines which age well. Leading producers include: Jean-Noël Gagnard, Bernard Morey, André Ramonet.

CAILLOU, CH *France, Bordeaux, Barsac, 2ème Cru Classé, W* This Barsac estate makes pleasant, but not remarkable, wines.

CALABRIA *Italy* Italy's toe, where quality is still relatively foreign. The only wine known outside the region is R, W and P Cirò DOC.

CALATAYUD *Spain, Aragón, DO, W, P, R* Most recent (1990) of Aragón's four wine zones. High vineyards, little rainfall and thus low yields. All colours of wine produced in *joven* style. Leading producers include: Cooperativa del Campo de San Isidro.

CALIFORNIA *USA* The most important American wine state, with 750 wineries making both world-class premium and good-value mass-produced wines. Quality wines are from coastal zones, including the NORTH COAST counties of NAPA, SONOMA, MENDOCINO; plus SANTA CRUZ, SANTA CLARA and SANTA BARBARA further south. Bulk wines come mostly from the vast CENTRAL VALLEY vineyards. For producers see wine zones.

CALITERRA *Chile, R, W* Ultra-modern winery established in 1986 in MAIPO VALLEY, now owned outright by Errázuris Panquehue. Produces 100,000 cases a year of varietal wines under Calitterra label, including Cabernet Sauvignon, Chardonnay and Sauvignon Blanc.

CALLAWAY *USA, California, Santa Barbara & Southern California, W* The winery, in Temecula, north of San Diego, specializes in a buttery, non-oak-aged Chardonnay called Calla-Lees. Also popular are a complex Fumé Blanc (barrel-aged Sauvignon) and a fruity Sauvignon made in stainless steel.

CALON, CH *France, Bordeaux, Montagne & St-Georges St-Emilion, R* Vineyards in both appellations, so two labels; but the wines are equally good: well-made, supple and enjoyable.

CALON-SÉGUR, CH *France, Bordeaux, Médoc, St-Estèphe, 3ème Cru Classé, R* Most northerly of the Médoc *crus classés*, making long-lasting, solid wines, especially good in the late 1980s.

CAMENSAC, CH *France, Bordeaux, Haut-Médoc, 5ème Cru Classé, R* In St-Laurent, the commune inland from St-Julien. Much investment here: not yet top class, but the wines are honest, and enjoyable with moderate bottle-age.

CAMPANIA *Italy* The region around Naples is best known for its white wines, especially Falerno, a favourite of ancient Rome. R, W, P and Sp Lacryma Christi del Vesuvio is also made here, as is DOCG Taurasi (R).

CAMPO DE BORJA *Spain, Aragón, DO, R, P* One of four of Aragón's wine zones. R and *rosado* are main styles, as well as a sweet (non-DO) mixture of grape juice and spirit called *mistela*. Leading producers include: Bodegas Bordeje and Sociedad Cooperativa Agricola de Borja.

CAMPO VIEJO, BODEGAS *Spain, Rioja, R, W, P* This is Rioja's biggest firm. The quality of its very wide range of wines is generally reliable and can be very good indeed, especially with the Selección José Bezares and Viña Alcorta.

CANANDAIGUA WINE CO *USA, New York, Finger Lakes, R, W, P, Sp* This Orange County wine company is one of America's largest (over 8 million cases a year), and includes its oldest wine label – Virginia Dare. Makes many *labrusca* wines but also some premium varietals, including Muscat.

CANARD-DUCHÈNE *France, Champagne* Owned by the LVMH group, this house produces attractive, good-value wines. The NV has medium weight and an elegantly fruity style.

CANEPA, JOSÉ *Chile, R, W* Family enterprize founded in 1930, one of the first to ferment W wine in stainless steel. Has a good reputation for Sauvignon Blanc, Cabernet Sauvignon and Merlot.

CANNONAU DI SARDEGNA *Italy, Sardinia, DOC, R, P* Elsewhere known as Grenache, the Cannonau grape produces R wines, both dry and sweet, and sometimes Ps. After a year in wood, the wine is high in alcohol, with a soft warm palate. Leading producers include: Giovanni Cherchi, Cantina Sociale di Dorgali.

CANON, CH *France, Bordeaux, St-Emilion, 1er Grand Cru Classé, R* Among the top properties, Canon's wines equal AUSONE and CHEVAL BLANC in best years. Quality has improved hugely since 1982. Made to last, often showing a cedary, elegant character with bottle-age. (For the Fronsac ch of the same name *see* below.)

CANON DE BREM, CH *France, Bordeaux, Canon-Fronsac, R* The famous Libourne merchants J-P Moueix own three "Canons" in Fronsac: Châteaux de Brem, Canon, Canon-Moueix. Each is good, making wines that help push this appellation up the quality ladder, but de Brem is perhaps the best. It deserves bottle-age.

CANON-FRONSAC *France, Bordeaux, AOC, R* Merlot, Cabernet Sauvignon, Cabernet Franc and Malbec grapes make deep-coloured, powerful, supple and long-lasting (10 years or more) wines in this zone on slopes above Fronsac, near Pomerol. Good value. Leading producers include: Ch Canon, Ch Canon de Brem, Ch Canon-Moueix, Ch La Fleur Caileau, Ch Mazeris-Bellevue.

CANON-LA-GAFFELIÈRE, CH *France, Bordeaux, St-Emilion, Grand Cru Classé, R* Totally transformed by its relatively new owners, the Comtes de Neipperg, who brilliantly combine tradition and technology to make outstanding wines.

CANON-MOUEIX, CH *France, Bordeaux, Canon-Fronsac, R* See CH CANON DE BREM.

CANTEMERLE *France, Bordeaux, Médoc, Haut-Médoc, 5ème Cru Classé, R* Very traditional southern Médoc property, modernized in the last decade. High Merlot content gives a soft, early-maturing style. Recent vintages ('88, '89, '90) gained high praise.

CANTENAC-BROWN, CH *France, Bordeaux, Médoc, Margaux, 3ème Cru Classé, R* One of several Médoc estates owned by AXA, the insurance giant, and run by Jean-Michel Cazes (*see* Ch **LYNCH-BAGES**, Pauillac). Vintages since 1988 have improved as modernization and new management take effect. A good 1993.

CANTERBURY-CHRISTCHURCH *New Zealand, South Island* Vines were planted in this district in 1840 but current interest dates from the early 1970s. Produces a wide variety. Leading producers include: Giesen, St Helena, Waipara Springs.

CANTINA SOCIALE *Italy* Cooperative winery.

CAP CORSE, MUSCAT DU *France, Corsica, AOC, VDN* Sweet W *vin doux naturel* from the north of the island.

CAP DE MOURLIN, CH *France, Bordeaux, St-Emilion, Grand Cru Classé, R* Until 1982 there were two properties by this name, but they are now united. The wine is quite rich and generous, with lots of fruit. The same owners as **BALESTARD-LA-TONNELLE**.

CAPBERN-GASQUETON, CH *France, Bordeaux, St-Estèphe, Cru Bourgeois, R* Linked through ownership to **CALON-SÉGUR**; the wines are lighter-style St-Estèphes.

CAPE MENTELLE *Australia, Western Australia, Margaret River, W, R* Majority-owned by Veuve Clicquot of Champagne. Margaret River's cool climate produces outstanding wines from a richly fruity Sémillon/Sauvignon Blanc W blend to a very classy Shiraz R – and a voluptuous Zinfandel R.

CAPEZZANA, TENUTA DI *Italy, Tuscany, R, W* The leading estate of the small Carmignano DOCG makes fine Rs, including a bordeaux-style blend, Ghiaie della Furba, plus normal and *riserva* Carmignano. Also a Chardonnay, Sp Villa di Capezzana Brut and fine Vin Santo.

CARBONNIEUX, CH *France, Bordeaux, Pessac-Léognan, Cru Classé, R, W* Old and beautiful turreted château where white Graves was pioneered. The W improved greatly in the late 1980s under Denis Dubourdieu: at its best rich, toasty, elegant. The R is richly flavoured, firm and often oaky, for medium-term drinking.

CARCAVELOS *Portugal, DOC* Near the estuary of the River Tagus and all but swallowed up by Lisbon. Just one vineyard remains (Quinta dos Pesos) making a fortified wine: sweet and raisiny, with a slight nutty flavour, like a tawny port. Very difficult to find, especially a good one.

CARDONNE, CH LA *France, Bordeaux, Médoc, Cru Bourgeois, R* Large vineyard and impressive facilities in open landscape of the northern Médoc. The wine has improved recently: the 1993 was in a softer, fruitier style.

CAREMA *Italy, Piedmont, DOC, R* Wines here are made from the Nebbiolo grape. Aged for four years, of which at least two are spent in wood. Blackcurrant colour, good acidity, with a fragrance of alpine flowers, mint and tar. Drink at 4 to 6 years old. Leading producers include: Luigi Ferrando.

CARIGNAN, CH   *France, Bordeaux, 1er Côtes de Bordeaux, R*   Old and handsome château making good fresh R with hints of oak, attractive young.

CARIGNAN/CARIÑENA   France's most widely planted red grape, yielding lots of deep-coloured, alcoholic, tannic *vin de table*. New methods produce better wines in the Midi, especially in blends. Grown in North Africa, California, South America and Spain.

CARILLON, DOM LOUIS   *France, Burgundy, Côte d'Or, R, W*   The emphasis at this domaine, which is based in Puligny-Montrachet, is on elegant, stylish white wines from Puligny and elsewhere.

CARIÑENA   *Spain, Aragón, DO, R, W, P, Sp*   Most established of Aragón's four wine zones. Young or *crianza* Rs are best-known wines; also young, fresh Ws and *rosados*. The region is also classified for production of **CAVA**. Leading producers include: Bodega Cooperativa SAN VALERO.

CARMEL   *Israel, R, W, P*   Biggest Israeli company with 70% of the market, only making kosher wines. A growers' cooperative where overdue modernization has recently taken place. Top of the range is the Rothschild series.

CARNEROS, LOS   *USA, California, VA*   Wine zone that straddles the southern ends of Napa and Sonoma. A thin-soiled tract cooled by San Francisco Bay, it is famous for Rs from Pinot Noir and Merlot, and Ws from Chardonnay. Leading producers include: Acacia, Dom Carneros, Saintsbury, Sterling (Winery Lake).

CARRUADES, LES   *France, Bordeaux, Médoc, Pauillac, R*   2nd wine of Ch Lafite-Rothschild. Formerly called Moulin Les Carruades.

CASABLANCA   *Chile, South America, W, R*   New region, north-west of Santiago, benefiting from cool breezes from the Pacific. Chardonnay does very well here, achieving delicate concentrated flavours. Other varieties include Merlot and Sauvignon Blanc.

CASK, CASK-AGEING   See BARRELS, BARRIQUE.

CASSIS   *France, Provence, AOC, R, P, W*   Village near Marseilles with a name for herb-scented W wine from Sauvignon Blanc, Marsanne and Ugni Blanc. Leading producers include: Dom du Bagnol, Clos Ste-Magdelaine, Dom de la Ferme Blanche, Ch de Fontcreuse, Mas Calendal.

CASTEL DEL MONTE   *Italy, Apulia, DOC, R, W, P*   The best-known DOC of Apulia, producing some of its finest wines using a variety of grapes. The P is popular, the R wines can age very well, the W wine is pleasant. Leading producers include: Rivera.

CASTELL *Germany, Franken, W* The centre of the Steigerwald district in the east of Franken, dominated by the Fürst Castell-Castell estate with its dry, solid W wines.

CASTELLANE, DE *France, Champagne* Owned by Laurent-Perrier, and far better known within France than outside. Styles range from an exotic, almost New World, pure Chardonnay *cuvée* to the more restrained and elegant Cuvées Commodore and Florens de Castellane.

CASTRIS, LEONE DE *Italy, Apulia, W, R, P, Sp* Large private producer with a state-of-the-art winery. Famous for the mass-market Five Roses (P). The best of their Salice Salentino DOC wines is Donna Lisa (R). Also Sp wines, Locorotondo (DOC, W) and the sweet, cask-aged Negrino (R).

CATALAN *France, Vin de Pays, R, P, W* Wines from the CÔTES DU ROUSSILLON area, mostly R, using local and classic grapes: a wider range of flavours than the equivalent AOC, and some interesting wines are made.

CATALANS, VIGNERONS *France, Midi, Roussillon, W, R, VDN* Most of the village cooperatives in the Roussillon AOC are members of this large producers' union, which makes a large proportion of the wines of the Roussillon: *vins de pays*, Rivesaltes *vins doux naturels* and the appellation wine.

CATOCTIN *USA, Maryland, VA* Wine zone in the mountains west of Baltimore, showing potential for R and W wines. Leading producers include: Boordy, Catoctin Vineyards.

CATTIN, THÉO & FILS *France, Alsace, W, R* Maker of good Gewürztraminer (from *Grand Cru* Hatschbourg and from Bollenberg *lieu dit*) as well as Pinot Gris and a fine Riesling from *Grand Cru* Hatschbourg, which ages beautifully and for which Théo Cattin is famous.

CAUHAPÉ, DOM *France, South-West, Jurançon, W* Both dry and *moelleux* (sweet) wines from the leading estate of the appellation. There are three grades of each: Vieilles Vignes is the top dry wine, Quintessence the top *moelleux*.

CAUSSES, DOM DES *France, Rhône, Lirac, R* One of the leading makers of this deep R which is made just across the Rhône from Châteauneuf. His 70% Syrah *cuvée* is new-oak-aged; the standard Lirac, also good, is a blend of several grapes. Also owns Dom des Garrigues in the same appellation.

CAVA *Spain & Greece* Cellar in Spanish. Also, by inference, a definition of Spanish *méthode champenoise* sparkling wine, which is made in Catalonia (the vast majority) and elsewhere in Spain.The same word is a Greek term for high-quality table wine.

CAVE COOPÉRATIVE *France* Cooperative winery.

CAVE   *France*   Cellar, either literally or as a storage place for wine.

CAVE SPRING   *Canada, Ontario, W, R*   This model small winery makes top-flight Chardonnay and Riesling.

CAYMUS   *USA, California, Napa, R, W*   The Wagner family began making wine here in Rutherford in 1972. Their Special Selection Cabernet Sauvignon is stunning. Conundrum is a barrel-fermented dry W blending Muscat, Sauvignon, Chardonnay and Sémillon.

CAZANOVE, CHARLES DE   *France, Champagne*   Large family-run house, very well known in France. Their top wine is the Cuvée Stradivarius, a Chardonnay/Pinot Noir blend.

CENCIBEL   *See* TEMPRANILLO.

CENTRAL COAST   *USA, California, VA*   This name is used on labels for wine, usually mid-priced blends, from the California counties south of San Francisco: most important are SANTA CRUZ, MONTEREY, SAN LUIS OBISPO, SANTA BARBARA.

CENTRAL OTAGO   *New Zealand, South Island*   With a mere 35ha under vine, this is the country's smallest grape-growing area, and also its furthest south, tucked into a cool valley in the mountains-Mainly Ws. Leading producer: Chard Farm.

CENTRAL VALLEY   *South America, Chile, R, W*   The heart of the Chilean wine industry: wide irrigated vineyard and farmland. Extends 80km north of Santiago and more than 240km south of the city, with a range of climates and several sub-regions, notably the MAIPO VALLEY, the most concentrated vineyard area. Also the MAULE VALLEY, a much cooler sub-region developed and expanded in the 1980s.

CÉPAGE   *France*   Grape variety.

CERONS   *France, Bordeaux, AOC, W*   Sweet W, lighter and less sweet than Sauternes, from a small zone next to Barsac. Leading producers include: Ch de Cérons, Grand Enclos du Ch de Cérons

CERTAN DE MAY, CH   *France, Bordeaux, Pomerol, R*   On the highest and best part of the Pomerol plateau, making consistently brilliant wines which need several years in bottle.

CÉSAR   Grape variety, now in decline, used in the R wines of Irancy in the Yonne district, near Chablis. Normally blended with Pinot Noir, to which more fashionable variety it is losing ground.

CESARE, PIO   *Italy, Piedmont, R*   Internationally-known R-wine specialist. Barolo, Barbaresco, Barbera and Dolcetto are blended from various vineyards; also a single-vineyard Barolo Ornato.

CHABLIS   *France, Burgundy, AOC, W*   These Chardonnay W wines are typically drier and more austere than those of the Côte d'Or. There are four tiers of quality and status: from the top down are *Grand Cru* (seven of these), *Premier Cru*, simple Chablis and

Petit Chablis (little used). Appealing in youth; good examples of *Premier* and *Grand Cru* Chablis are rewarding after 5–10 years in bottle. Leading producers include: La Chablisienne (co-op), Dauvissat, Durup, Fèvre, Laroche, Michel, Moreau, Raveneau.

CHABLISIENNE, LA *France, Burgundy, Chablis, W* Cooperative with 200 members, making honest, well-made wines at all levels from *Village* to *Grand Cru.*

CHADDSFORD WINERY *USA, Pennsylvania, W, R* This winery in Chester County began in 1982, producing hybrids and blends. Eric Miller buys grapes from the Piedmont region and wins accolades for his barrel-fermented Chardonnays and also makes Cabernet Sauvignon.

CHAIZE, CH DE LA *France, Burgundy, Beaujolais, R* One of the top producers of Brouilly, making good, ripe fruity wines with plenty of body and a rounded finish.

CHALK HILL *USA, California, Sonoma, VA* This white-wine zone is in a warm part of Sonoma: good for Sauvignon Blanc and Chardonnay.

CHALONE *USA, California, Monterey, R, W* The winery, east of Soledad, uses classic Burgundian methods to gain maximum character from Pinot Noir and Chardonnay grapes. Partnered by Ch LAFITE-ROTHSCHILD, Chalone is linked with Edna Valley (San Luis Obispo), Acacia (Napa), Carmenet (Sonoma) and Woodward Canyon (Washington State).

CHALONE *USA, California, Monterey, VA* Wine zone with one estate, CHALONE, in Monterey County.

CHAMARD VINEYARDS *USA, Connecticut, R, W* Small coastal winery concentrating on classic varieties – Chardonnay, Pinot Noir and Cabernet Sauvignon; also Merlot and Cabernet Franc for blending.

CHAMBERT, CH DE *France, South-West, Cahors, R* Good winemaking, using second-hand *barriques* from Ch Margaux, produces a fruity, well-structured concentrated Cahors.

CHAMBERT-MARBUZET, CH *France, Bordeaux, St-Estèphe, Cru Bourgeois, R* This château makes enjoyable, approachable claret which is ready quite quickly.

CHAMBERTIN CLOS DE BÈZE *France, Burgundy, AOC, R* *Grand Cru* adjoining **CHAMBERTIN**; in Clos de Bèze the land is less divided, and the standard is higher. Leading producers include: Dom Bruno Clair, Faiveley.

CHAMBERTIN *France, Burgundy, AOC, R* One of nine *Grands Crus* (the others are Chambertin Clos de Bèze, Chapelle-, Charmes-, Griotte-, Latricières-, Mazis-, Mazoyères- and Ruchottes-Chambertin) in the village of Gevrey-Chambertin in the **CÔTE DE NUITS.**

Quality varies widely, but the greatest have the ability to age for 20 years. Leading producers include: Bouchard Père & Fils, Leroy, Dom Ponsot, Rousseau.

CHAMBOLLE-MUSIGNY   *France, Burgundy, AOC, R, W*   Powerful, elegant, complex Rs, among Burgundy's greatest, come from the *Grands Crus* (**BONNES MARES** and **MUSIGNY**) of this Côte de Nuits village. It has several *Premiers Crus*, and village wines of a good standard. The W is rare. Leading producers include: Hudelet-Noëllat, Mugnier, Mortet, de Vogüé.

CHAMPAGNE   *France, Champagne, AOC, Sp, W, P*   The world's supreme Sp wine, made in a variety of styles from dry to very sweet, usually from a blend of three grapes: Pinot Noir, Chardonnay and Pinot Meunier. Most is non-vintage or NV (ie blended from wines from different vintages), although single-vintage champagne is made in good years. Leading producers include: Bollinger, Charles Heidsieck, Krug, Laurent-Perrier, Moët & Chandon, Perrier-Jouët, Pol Roger, Louis Roederer, Veuve Clicquot Ponsardin.

CHAMPAGNON, DOM LOUIS   *France, Burgundy, Beaujolais, R*   One of the leading producers in the least-known Beaujolais *Cru* of Chénas. Good, rich concentrated wine. Also produces a Moulinà-Vent.

CHANDON, DOMAINE   *Australia, Victoria, Yarra Valley, Sp*   Owned by Moët & Chandon of Champagne, this state-of-the-art winery makes Sp wines of extremely high quality, including the Green Point brand.

CHANSON PÈRE ET FILS   *France, Burgundy, Côte d'Or, R, W*   Vineyard owner and *négociant*. The estate wines, which are mostly R, can be very good.

CHANTEGRIVE, CH DE   *France, Bordeaux, Graves, W, R*   Large estate in Podensac. *Barrique*-ageing yields impressive results. New oak is used for the W Cuvée Caroline and the R Cuvée Edouard.

CHAPELLE-CHAMBERTIN   See CHAMBERTIN.

CHAPELOT   *France, Burgundy, Chablis, 1er Cru*   See MONTÉE DE TONNERRE.

CHAPOUTIER   *France, Rhône, R, W*   Estate owner and *négociant* based at Tain-l'Hermitage: the largest landowner in Hermitage, making much-improved wines since 1990, including the Le Pavillon and Monier de la Sizeranne *cuvées*. Also a good source of Côte Rôtie and other north Rhône AOCs, R and W, and Châteauneuf-du-Pape.

CHAPTALIZATION   Technique of adding sugar to the grape juice before fermentation in order to give the wine a higher alcoholic content. Widely used in Burgundy, Bordeaux, Loire.

CHAPUIS, MAURICE   *France, Burgundy, Côte d'Or, R, W*   This Corton estate is very seriously run. The Corton Charlemagne (W) in particular is extremely fine.

CHARBAUT   *France, Champagne*   Family-owned house that is best known for its pink champagnes, especially the elegant, perfumed Certificate Rosé.

CHARDONNAY   Profoundly adaptable, easy-to-grow white grape from Burgundy and Champagne, now an international classic. It has strong fruit flavours: in hotter climates the fruits move from the citrus of burgundy to pineapple and banana. White burgundy successfully marries the tastes of Chardonnay and oak, a pairing tried everywhere the grape is grown, although Chardonnay with no oak-ageing is made for early drinking

CHARLES MELTON   *Australia, South Australia, Barossa, R, W*   Graeme (Charlie) Melton is at the forefront of the Barossa's rebirth, especially with his velvety, liquorice-and-prune R Nine Popes, blended from Shiraz, Grenache and Mourvèdre.

CHARMES, CH DES   *Canada, Ontario, W, R*   Majestic replica French château with some Burgundian-style Chardonnay, Auxerrois and Gamay, plus good Cabernet in ripe years.

CHARMES, LES   *France, Burgundy, Côte de Beaune, 1er Cru, W*   At the southern end of Meursault, next to Puligny-Montrachet, this vineyard produces top-quality wine with a certain steeliness, for long ageing. Leading producers include: Robert Ampeau, Michelot-Buisson, Guy Roulot.

CHARMES, LES   *France, Burgundy, Côte de Nuits, 1er Cru, R*   One of the top vineyards of Chambolle-Musigny, making wines with good colour and body, and supple elegant fruit. Leading producers include: Barthas-Noëllat, Hudelot-Noëllat.

CHARMES-CHAMBERTIN   *France, Burgundy, AOC, R*   This *Grand Cru* vineyard in the village of Gevrey-Chambertin has a reputation for consistent, early-maturing wines. See also **CHAMBERTIN**. Leading producers include: Bachelet, Rousseau.

CHARTA   *Germany*   Association of Rheingau producers committed to making medium-dry and dry Riesling wines, good with food.

CHARTRON & TREBUCHET   *France, Burgundy, Côte d'Or, R, W*   Both *négociant* and estate (Dom Chartron) with the emphasis on W wines. The estate wines are especially good.

CHASSAGNE-MONTRACHET   *France, Burgundy, AOC, R, W*   The Côte de Beaune village of Chassagne long ago added the name of the *Grand Cru* vineyard MONTRACHET (which it shares with the village of Puligny) to its own; it also shares BÂTARD-MONTRACHET and has its own *Grand Cru*, Les Criots-Bâtard-Montrachet. The *Grands Crus* produce outstanding, long-lived and very expensive W burgundy. W village Chassagne-Montrachet is made to a high standard; Chassagne also makes R wine: soft, fruity, well-structured and can age 10 years in good vintages, yet often over-looked: these can be good value. Leading producers include: Gagnard, B Morey, Ramonet.

CHASSE-SPLEEN, CH *France, Bordeaux, Moulis, Cru Bourgeois, R* One of the best, and best-known, *crus bourgeois*, whose large vineyard makes wine to classed-growth standard. Enjoyable young, but can age for 10 years or longer.

CHASSELAS White grape grown mainly in Switzerland (where it is known as Fendant or Perlan), for a soft, dry white wine. Also grown in the upper Loire, Alsace, Savoie and Germany (where it is called Gutedel).

CHASSENAY D'ARCE *France, Champagne* This cooperative, based in the AUBE district, has 130 growers and takes the grapes from 303ha. Wines are appealing and fruity and there is a 100% Pinot Noir champagne, Cuvée Sélection.

CHÂTEAU *France* Literally castle or country house; in wine terms a unit of land, with or without a dwelling, which is run as a wine estate. Used elsewhere in the world to convey the same message.

CHÂTEAU GRILLET See GRILLET, Ch.

CHÂTEAU-CHALON *France, Jura, AOC, W* The best VIN JAUNE comes from this Jura village. Leading producers include: Christian Bourdy, Jean Macle.

CHÂTEAUMEILLANT *France, Loire, VDQS, R, P* Small production of Rs and Ps from Gamay, Pinot Noir and Pinot Gris, from an area in the southern Cher *département*.

CHÂTEAUNEUF-DU-PAPE *France, Rhône, AOC, R, W* Thirteen grape varieties are allowed in this renowned R of southern Rhône, but most wine is based on Grenache, with Syrah, Mourvèdre and others. A good example from a hot vintage should last for 20–25 years, but will drink well at 5–6. Minor vintages, and most *négociant* wines, are ready at 3–5 years. The W Châteauneuf is also from a blend of grapes, including Clairette, Grenache Blanc and Roussanne. Leading producers include: Ch de Beaucastel, Chapoutier, Ch Rayas, Dom du Vieux Télégraphe.

CHÂTILLON-EN-DIOIS . *France, Rhône, AOC, R, P, W* Remote district east of the Rhône Valley. Rs from Gamay blended with Syrah and Pinot Noir, Ws from Chardonnay or Aligoté.

CHAVE, GÉRARD *France, Rhône, Hermitage, R* The key name in Hermitage today, with wines of elegance and breed. Also small amounts of very good St-Joseph.

CHÉNAS *France, Burgundy, AOC, R* The smallest of the Beaujolais *crus*: next to, and similar to, Moulin-à-Vent. Top Chénas can be quite rich and concentrated. Leading producers include: Guy Braillon, Dom des Brureaux (Daniel Robin), Louis Champagnon, Cave du Ch de Chénas, Dom des Trémont.

CHENIN BLANC   White grape from the Loire with high acidity; can make dry or moderately sweet wine, but the great Chenin-based Loires (Bonnezeaux, Coteaux du Layon, Vouvray) are complex, luscious, long-lived sweet wines. Grown in South Africa, California and New Zealand, for blending or as a medium-dry or dry varietal wine.

CHENONCEAU, CH DE   *France, Loire, Touraine, W, Sp, R*   One of the few historic Touraine châteaux to produce wine. From a 12-ha vineyard on higher ground away from the river, it makes wines with the AOC of Touraine, including dry Ws, Rs and Sp.

CHÉREAU-CARRÉ   *France, Loire, Muscadet, W*   All wines from the four Chéreau-Carré estates that total 74ha are bottled individually *sur lie*. They pioneered wood fermentation and ageing for Muscadet, producing a wine that could easily be mistaken for a white bordeaux.

CHEVAL BLANC, CH   *France, Bordeaux, St-Emilion, 1er Grand Cru Classé (A), R*   Vying with AUSONE as St-Emilion's top property, but with a more consistent record. Relatively large, with 12,000 cases a year. The wine is rich, ripe and intense: often deceptively approachable when young, it can last for 40 years or more.

CHEVALIER, DOM DE   *France, Bordeaux, Pessac-Léognan, Cru Classé, R, W*   Classic R, elegant and long-lived, and a small amount of W which is both very expensive and very fine. Needs 8 years' ageing, but can last for 30.

CHEVALIER-MONTRACHET   See MONTRACHET.

CHEVERNY   *France, Loire, AOC, R, W, P*   Minor zone near Blois, with Ws from Chenin Blanc, Sauvignon Blanc, Chardonnay or the high-acid Romorantin, a grape unique to Touraine; light Rs and Ps from Gamay, Cabernet Franc, Pinot Noir or Cot. Leading producers include: Courtioux, Sauger, Tessier.

CHEVILLON, DOM ROBERT   *France, Burgundy, Côte d'Or, R, W*   This relatively new estate specializes in very good-quality Nuits-St-Georges made in the traditional manner.

CHIANTI   *Italy, Tuscany, DOCG, R*   This broad DOCG currently covers five Tuscan provinces. Sometimes sold in straw-covered flasks, this Sangiovese-based R wine has a fresh cherry aroma and attractive, fruity, sometimes rather light palate. It is best drunk young. Leading producers include: Frescobaldi, Ruffino.

CHIANTI CLASSICO   *Italy, Tuscany, DOCG, R*   The largest of the CHIANTI sub-zones, responsible for some of its best wines, based on the Sangiovese grape. Raspberry and black cherry flavours, combined with dryness and acidity. The best can age well. Leading producers include: Antinori, Badia a Contibuono, Castello di Volpaia, Isole e Olena.

CHIANTI COLLI FIORENTINI   *Italy, Tuscany, DOCG, R*   An important Chianti sub-zone. Not as good as Classico or Rufina, but the wines can be attractive, with supple fruit flavours. Leading producers include: Costello del Trebbio, Il Corno, Parri, Sammastana .

CHIANTI RUFINA *Italy, Tuscany, DOCG, R* The smallest of the Chianti sub-zones and one of the best. Not dissimilar to *classico* but has a higher acidity, often coupled with better fruit and ageing ability. Leading producers include: Frescobaldi, Selvapiana, Villa Vetrice.

CHICAMA VINEYARDS *USA, Massachusetts, R, W, Sp* This estate on the island of Martha's Vineyard grows Chenin Blanc, Chardonnay, Sauvignon Blanc, Gewürztraminer, Cabernet Sauvignon, Merlot and Pinot Noir. The R wines are particularly rated but the Sp Chardonnay, Sea Mist, shows promise.

CHILE *South America* After Argentina, South America's second producer, with 64,530ha. One of the world's few regions with pre-phylloxera vines on their own roots. Two categories of wine are made: for the local market and for export. The former are usually in an old-fashioned style from prolific and low-class varieties, such as País; the latter from French varieties using modern technology. Main region is the **CENTRAL VALLEY**, with its subregions the **MAIPO** and **MAULE VALLEYS**. Came to prominence in the 1980s as a source of reasonably-priced, good wines from Cabernet Sauvignon, Merlot and Sauvignon Blanc. 1995 brought a new appellation system, with five viticultural regions made up of sub-regions, zones and areas. Wines exported to Europe will be at least 85% from the appellation. Leading producers include: Caliterra, Concha y Toro, Errázuriz Panquehue, Cousiño Macul, Santa Rita, Mighel Torres, Undurraga, Los Vascos.

CHINA Although growing wine-grapes is not alien to Chinese culture, historically it has been of little importance. Production is in the north-east and the emphasis is on medium dry, consumer-friendly W wines. The more progressive wineries, however, are beginning to work with international firms to make western-style wines from varieties such as Riesling and Chardonnay.

CHINON *France, Loire, AOC, R* Cabernet Franc Rs from the south bank of the Loire, opposite Bourgueil. Young wines have soft fruit and earthy tastes; from warm years they age to attractive truffle and violet flavours. Leading producers include: Bernard Baudry, Couly-Dutheil, Ch de la Grille, Charles Joguet, Les Caves des Vins de Rabelais, Jean-Maurice Raffault.

CHIROUBLES *France, Burgundy, AOC, R* Most balanced and fragrant of the Beaujolais *crus*, light in colour and style, and the first to be ready: drink within two years. Fashionable and expensive. Leading producers include: Dom Desmoures, Ch de Jauvenard, Dom Passot, Maison de Vignerons Chiroubles.

CHIVITE, BODEGAS JULIÁN *Spain, Navarra, R, W, P* This bodega was the pioneer in establishing Navarra on the export market. Chivite consistently produces very well-made wines, including a range under the Gran Feudo label and a top-quality unwooded R wine, Viña Marcos.

CHOREY-LÈS-BEAUNE *France, Burgundy, AOC, R* Village producing good-value burgundy for early drinking. Leading producers include: J Germain, Maillard Père & Fils, Tollot-Beaut.

CHURCHILL GRAHAM *Portugal, port* Founded 1981, by one of the old-established Graham port family. The wines, labelled Churchills, have been acclaimed by critics and include aged tawnies and an LBV. Also two single-*quinta* wines, Quinta da Agua Alta and Quinta de Fojo.

CIGALES *Spain, Castilla-León, DO, W, P, R* Newest DO (1991) of Castilla-León, but boasts centuries of winemaking experience. Emphasis on excellent *rosados,* though fine Rs promise well for the future. Leading producers include: Avelino Vegas, Hijos de Frutos Villar.

CINSAUT Red grape of medium quality, low in tannin. Likes heat; much used for blending in southern Rhône, Provence, Midi, Lebanon, North Africa, South Africa (where it was crossed with Pinot Noir to make Pinotage).

CINZANO *Italy, Piedmont, W, R, Sp* The major vermouth company also makes Sp Cinzano Brut and Marone Cinzano Pas Dosé under the Asti DOCG. Other Sp wines include Pinot Chardonnay and Principe di Piemonte Brut.

CIRÒ *Italy, Calabria, DOC, R, W* Probably the only DOC of Calabria known outside the region, whose reputation is greater than it deserves. The R can be quite hefty and, at their best, the W wines are attractively fruity. Leading producers include: Librandi, Fattoria San Francesco.

CISSAC, CH *France, Bordeaux, Haut-Médoc, Cru Bourgeois, R* Reliable, good-value claret, dark and tasty, that can age very well.

CITÉ DE CARCASSONE, DE LA *France, Vin de Pays, R* Light, enjoyable Rs from around the famous medieval city in southern France.

CITRAN, CH *France, Bordeaux, Haut-Médoc, Cru Bourgeois, R* On the edge of Moulis. Recent vintages have seen big improvements.

CLAIR, DOM BRUNO *France, Burgundy, Côte d'Or, R, W, P, Sp* Dynamic estate with diverse vineyard holdings in Côte de Nuits. Go-ahead but with a great respect for tradition: very good quality wines.

CLAIRET *France* Red wine, light in body and colour. The word claret is derived from it. Usually used today for pale red wine from Bordeaux.

CLAIRETTE DE BELLEGARDE *France, Midi, AOC, W* Dry W wine from Clairette grapes, made where the Languedoc vineyards meet the Rhône's. Limited production.

CLAIRETTE DE DIE   *France, Rhône, AOC, W, Sp*   Sparkler from the Clairette grape, with some Muscat. There is a traditional *méthode dioise*, but Champagne's technique is increasingly used for the Crémant de Die. Leading producer: Cave Cooperative.

CLAIRETTE DU LANGUEDOC   *France, Midi, AOC, W*   Flavoury dry W from the Clairette grape, recently revived. Leading producers include: Ch la Condamine Bertrand, Dom St-André.

CLAPE, AUGUSTE   *France, Rhône, Cornas, R*   The top maker of this robust Syrah R, with very old vines: a wine to age 10 years.

CLARE VALLEY   *Australia, South Australia*   District with a number of small, well-run, family wineries. Superb, long-lived Riesling Ws. Leading producers include: Jim Barry, Grosset, Knappstein, Mitchell, Skillogalee, Taylors, Wendouree.

CLARIDGE   *South Africa, Wellington, R, W*   Roger Jorgensen gave up fruit farming in Kent, England, for winemaking in the Cape in 1987. He now produces a superb R blend and very good Chardonnay, both innovatively packaged in 50cl bottles.

CLARKE, CH   *France, Bordeaux, Listrac, Cru Bourgeois, R*   Edmond de Rothschild's money has conjured a virtually new vineyard out of a neglected corner. The style is fresh, fruity and relatively fast to mature, though the latest vintages have increasing structure.

CLASSED GROWTH   Translation of CRU CLASSÉ.

CLASSICO   *Italy*   A restricted zone, usually the heart of a wine area. For example; Chianti Classico, Bardolino Classico.

CLEAR LAKE   *USA, California, VA*   Wine zone in Lake County, northern California, making good Sauvignon Ws and Cabernet Sauvignon Rs. Leading producers include: Beringer, Kendall-Jackson, Louis Martini, Sutter Home.

CLERC-MILON, CH   *France, Bordeaux, Médoc, Pauillac, 5ème Cru Classé, R*   The vines are to the east of Ch'x MOUTON and LAFITE. Owned by the Rothschilds of Mouton since 1970, their investment is slowly producing results, with the duo of 1985 and 1986 attracting praise.

CLIMENS, CH   *France, Bordeaux, Barsac, 1er Cru Classé, W*   One of the few estates that can on occasion challenge Ch d'YQUEM, although the wines are very different. Climens is a Barsac: subtle and understated. But after 10 years in bottle it begins, very slowly, to show the majestic elegance of which it is capable. On very good form since 1983.

CLINET, CH   *France, Bordeaux, Pomerol, R*   Michel Rolland is the adviser here. There used to be a fairly high percentage of Cabernet Sauvignon (very unusual in Pomerol), but this has gradually been reduced. Superb wines in good vintages.

CLINTON VINEYARDS   *USA, New York, Hudson River Valley, W, Sp*   This winery specializes in the Seyval Blanc grape, including a Sp version, and also makes good Chardonnay and Riesling Ws.

CLOS *France*   Generally refers to a vineyard surrounded by a wall, in Burgundy particularly. Often they have monastic origins.

CLOS CABRIERE *South Africa, Franschhoek, W, Sp*   Achim von Armin makes some of the Cape's top Sp wines in the Franschhoek Valley from Chardonnay and Pinot Noir.

CLOS CAPITORO *France, Corsica, Ajaccio, W, R, P* Jacques Bianchetti makes prestigious wines under this name: Rs and Ps from Sciacarello and Grenache, and Ws from Vermentino. The R, sold with some maturity, is the best.

CLOS DE LA ROCHE *France, Burgundy, AOC, R*   This *Grand Cru* in Morey-St-Denis produces, along with Clos St-Denis, some of the greatest, longest-lived R wines in the Côte de Nuits. Leading producers include: Bouchard Père & Fils, Dom Dujac, Dom Lignier, Dom Ponsot.

CLOS DE TART *France, Burgundy, AOC, R*   One of Burgundy's original walled, monastic vineyards, this *Grand Cru* in Morey-St-Denis is owned entirely by Mommessin. Rich, dark wine that needs age.

CLOS DE VOUGEOT *France, Burgundy, AOC, R*   Famous *Grand Cru* in a large walled vineyard. With 80 owners, the wine varies in style. Leading producers include: Dom Bertagna, Joseph Drouhin, Jean Gros, Dom Mongeard-Mugneret.

CLOS DES CHÊNES *France, Burgundy, Côte de Beaune, 1er Cru, R*   At the southern end of Volnay, next to Monthélie. Makes elegant, fairly delicate wines which age very well. Leading producers include: Jean-Marc Bouley, Joseph Drouhin, Michel Lafarge, Comtes Lafon.

CLOS DES JACOBINS, CH *France, Bordeaux, St-Emilion, Grand Cru Classé, R*   Owned by Bordeaux *négociant* Cordier, this impeccably-run property consistently makes fine quality wines, with good depth of colour and ripe, plummy fruit.

CLOS DES LAMBRAYS *France, Burgundy, AOC, R*   Côte de Nuits *Grand Cru* in Morey-St-Denis, with (unusually for Burgundy) just one owner, Dom des Lambrays. Replanted in 1980, and the wine has yet to return to the heights.

CLOS DES MOUCHES, LE *France, Burgundy, Côte de Beaune, 1er Cru, R, W*   One of the top vineyards of the Beaune appellation, situated at its southern end. The Ws are quite soft and broad in flavour and the Rs are densely coloured, with a tannic backbone. Leading producers include: Joseph Drouhin.

CLOS DES PAPES *France, Rhône, Châteauneuf-du-Pape, R*   Traditional producer of Châteauneuf, making some of the most elegant and suave wines in the appellation.

CLOS DU BOIS *USA, California, Sonoma, W, R* Large-scale winery making creamy, lemony barrel-fermented Chardonnay; also single-vineyard (Flintwood and Calcaire) Chardonnays and (Briarcrest and Marlstone) Cabernet Sauvignons.

CLOS DU MARQUIS *France, Bordeaux, Médoc, St-Julien, R* 2nd wine of Ch Léoville Las-Cases.

CLOS DU VAL *France, Burgundy, Côte de Beaune, 1er Cru, R* In the commune of Auxey-Duresses. One of the top names in the appellation, producing supple, medium-bodied, raspberry fruited wines. Leading producers include: Michel Prunier.

CLOS DU VAL *USA, California, Napa, R, W* Bernard Portet brings a French flavour to this Stags Leap winery, notably in a blackberry-like Zinfandel R and an unusual silky, oily, dry Sémillon W.

CLOS FLORIDÈNE *France, Bordeaux, Graves W, R* Denis Dubourdieu, master of white winemaking in the Graves and consultant at many Graves estates, owns this small property in Pujols. The results at Floridène are delicious. At present the Ws, aged in new oak, are better than the Rs. *See also* Ch'x REYNON, DU JUGE.

CLOS HAUT-PEYRAGUEY *France, Bordeaux, Sauternes, 1er Cru Classé, W* Elegance and finesse rather than power are the declared aims here. The wine is always good, but scarcely as great as its *premier* rank would suggest.

LES CLOS *France, Burgundy, Chablis, Grand Cru* The largest *Grand Cru* in Chablis, with the longest-lasting, firmest-structured wines.

CLOS PEGASE *USA, California, Napa, R, W* The wines of Clos Pegase, south of Calistoga, are a lean, lemon-pear Chardonnay, a broad, blackcurrant Merlot, a herbaceous Cabernet Sauvignon and a juicy **MERITAGE** red blend of Cabernets Sauvignon and Franc, with Merlot. The property is an architectural showpiece.

CLOS SAINT-JACQUES *France, Burgundy, Côte de Nuits, 1er Cru, R* Top Gevrey-Chambertin vineyard whose wines are densely coloured, powerful and masculine and which require long ageing. Leading producers include: Bruno Clair.

CLOS ST-DENIS See CLOS DE LA ROCHE.

CLOS ST-MARTIN, CH *France, Bordeaux, St-Emilion, Grand Cru Classé, R* This miniscule property is quite a well-guarded secret. Difficult to find, but worth seeking out because of the quality.

CLOUDY BAY VINEYARDS *New Zealand, South Island, W, R, Sp* In large part responsible for New Zealand's world reputation for Sauvignon Blanc, Cloudy Bay is expensive and hard to find. Now owned by Veuve Clicquot and Australia's Cape Mentelle, they make a Sp wine, Pelorus, which is also excellent. They also make Chardonnay and, more recently, R wines.

COASTAL REGION *South Africa, WO* Zone which takes in the best wine areas (WOs) of the Cape: **CONSTANTIA**, Durbanville,

STELLENBOSCH, PAARL, Swartland and Tulbagh.

COCHE-DURY, DOM   *France, Burgundy, Côte d'Or, R, W*   Top estate, making mainly Ws from the Côte de Beaune: excellent Meursault and Corton Charlemagne.

COCHEM   *Germany, Mosel, W*   The centre of one of the better lower Mosel districts, making ripe, attractive Riesling Ws.

COCKBURN SMITHES   *Portugal, port*   Known familiarly as Cockburn's, one of port's most famous names. Wines from its estates Quinta do Tua and Quinta da Eira Velha are occasionally bottled as single-*quinta* vintages. Cockburn's Special Reserve is the UK's leading brand, Fine Ruby almost as popular: both well-made, commercial wines. Aged tawnies are among the best. Cockburn's declares vintages less often than other houses: its 1983 and 1985 releases showed a style which is softer and more velvety than some – although they last as long.

CODORNíU   *Spain, Catalonia, Sp*   Cordoníu, founded in 1872, produced Spain's first Sp wine and is now one of the leading Cava makers, with a wide range that includes a Pinot Noir/Chardonnay blend, Jaume de Codorníu.

COLARES   *Portugal, DOC, R, W*   Three wines may be produced under this DOC, rapidly disappearing because of its proximity to Lisbon. The best is a deeply coloured and austere R, mainly from the Ramisco grape. Also a less good R from a blend of varieties, and a little W from Malvasia which is not worth trying. Leading producers include: António Bernardino, Paulo da Silva.

COLDSTREAM HILLS   *Australia, Victoria, Yarra Valley, R, W*   Founded by author James Halliday, this award-winning winery makes superb Pinot Noir and Chardonnay.

COLLET, JEAN   *France, Burgundy, Chablis, W*   Son Gilles now runs this estate, making rich, stylish oak-aged wines, mainly *Premier* and some *Grand Cru*.

COLLI ORIENTALI DEL FRIULI   *Italy, Friuli-Venezia Giulia, DOC, W, R*   Mainly W wines from the widely-planted Tocai grape, pale in colour with an almond-scented bouquet. Also Pinot Grigio, Chardonnay and many others. R wines from Cabernet Sauvignon and Franc, Merlot, Refosco and Schioppettino. Picolit, the dessert wine, comes from here. Leading producers include: Abbazia di Rosazzo, Livio Felluga, Volpe Pasini.

COLLINES RHODANIENNES, DES   *France, Vin de Pays, R, W*   This zone covers the hinterland of the northern Rhône. Most of the wine is varietal; not only the local Syrah, but also Gamay and Merlot. Can be good value: look for famous Rhône names, estates which use the *vin de pays* name on wine from young vines.

COLLIO GORIZIANO   *Italy, Friuli-Venezia Giulia, DOC, W, R*   Known also as simply "Collio", the wine is similar to neighbouring Colli Orientali, with Tocai dominating but with other good W wines from Pinot Grigio and Pinot Bianco. Leading producers include: Marco Felluga, Gravner, Pra de Pradis, Russiz Superiore.

COLLIOURE *France, Midi, AOC, R* Solid R wine from Grenache, Mourvèdre and Syrah, sharing with Banyuls VDN the steep coastal vineyards near the Spanish border. Leading producers include: Dom du Mas Blanc, Dom de la Rectorie.

COLOMBARD White grape from south-west France, making flowery young wines with crisp acidity. Very successful in California and South Africa.

COLOMBO, JEAN-LUC *France, Rhône, Cornas, R* Maker of good Cornas, plus Vin de Pays and Côtes du Rhône, and a *négociant*. Well-known, too, as a successful consultant oenologist, with radical views (similar to ACCAD's in Burgundy). Bordeaux-trained, he has championed ripe fruit, small-cask, new-oak ageing and an organic regime.

COLORADO *USA* The Grand Valley provides tolerable growing conditions for Riesling, Gewürztraminer and Syrah.

COLUMBIA *South America* Very little table wine is made in Columbia. Most production is of fortified wines, vermouth or tropical fruit blends.

COLUMBIA *USA, Washington State, R, W* This company has some of the Yakima Valley's top vineyards, and makes around 80,000 cases a year, with varietal Rs from Cabernet Sauvignon, Merlot, Syrah and Cabernet Franc, and Ws from Chardonnay, Riesling, Gewürztraminer and Sémillon.

COLUMBIA VALLEY *USA, Washington, VA* The main wine zone of this north-western state, with good fresh Ws (Chardonnay, Riesling, Sémillon) and fruity Rs (Merlot and Cabernet) plus Sp. YAKIMA VALLEY and Walla Walla Valley are sub-zones. Leading producers: *see* WASHINGTON.

COMBETTES, LES *France, Burgundy, Côte de Beaune, 1er Cru, W* At the northern end of Puligny-Montrachet, next to Meursault. Yields wines which are slightly broader than some other Pulignys and a little less elegant. Leading producers include: Robert Ampeau, Leflaive, Sauzet.

COMTÉ DE GRIGNAN, DU *France, Vin de Pays, R* Area on the right bank of the Rhône, around Montélimar. The wines are dominated by southern Rhône grapes such as Grenache. Varietal wines from Gamay, Merlot or Cabernet Sauvignon are allowed.

COMTÉ TOLOSAN, DU *France, Vin de Pays, R, P* Regional *vins de pays* zone covering most of South-West France: not much used, but offering a name for varietal wines now being developed here.

COMTÉS RHODANIENS, DES *France, Vin de Pays, R, W, P* Catch-all *vins de pays* for wines from all over the Rhône-Alpes region, including Provence. Relatively new, and so far little used.

CONCA DE BARBERÀ *Spain, Catalonia, DO, W, P, R* Small, hilly wine zone in central Catalonia. A little experimental Cabernet Sauvignon, but production is 80% *joven* W. Leading producers include: Concavins.

CONCANNON *USA, California, Livermore Valley, R* Founded in 1883, the winery is one of the last to make Petite Sirah, a bold, rustic R, full of plummy flavour.

CONCHA Y TORO *Chile, R, W* Founded in 1883, Chile's largest producer. Makes over three million cases a year under a variety of labels, including modestly-priced Casillero del Diablo range and single-vineyard Cabernet Sauvignon, Merlot and Chardonnay under the Marqués de Casa Concha label.

CONDADO DE HUELVA *Spain, Andalucia, DO, W, P, R* Andalucian wine zone near Portuguese border, producing new-style *joven afrutado* (cool-fermented) wines and old-style fortified.

CONDAMINE BERTRAND, CH LA *France, Midi, Coteaux du Languedoc, W* Quality and production of the various styles of white CLAIRETTE DU LANGUEDOC fell until the Jany family of Condamine Bertrand set out to restore the reputation of the appellation. Today the best wine is lighter and fresher: made at 12°, rather than the previous 13° or 14°.

CONDRIEU *France, Rhône, AOC, W* The Viognier grape achieves perfection in this northern Rhône vineyard. Best drunk between 1½ and 4 years old. Leading producers include: Cuilleron, Delas, Dezormeaux, Guigal, Niero et Pinchon, Alain Paret, André Perret, Georges Vernay.

CONFURON-COTETIDOT, DOM *France, Burgundy, Côte d'Or, R* Followers of the ACCAD style of vinification, producing especially good Nuits-St-Georges and Echézeaux.

CONNECTICUT *USA* Vineyards along the coast and in the west, in the Western Connecticut Highlands area – reckoned the best place for classic vines. Producers include CHAMARD, Haight Vineyards (sited in the west, good for Riesling, Chardonnay and Sp).

CONNÉTABLE DE TALBOT *France, Bordeaux, Médoc, St-Julien, R* Second wine of Ch Talbot.

CONSEILLANTE, CH *France, Bordeaux, Pomerol, R* There is a high percentage of Cabernet Franc in this consistently fine wine, which will age for 20 years or more.

CONSTANTIA *South Africa, WO* The Cape's most historic wine zone, source in the 18th century of great sweet wines, a style revived recently by Klein Constantia. Also a source of Chardonnay, Sauvignon Blanc and Riesling Ws and Cabernet Sauvignon and Shiraz Rs. Leading producers include: Buitenverwachting, Groot Constantia, Klein Constantia.

CONSTANTIN, CH *France, Bordeaux, Graves, W* In Portets, a source for rich, oaky Ws in a commercial but very appealing style.

COOKS *New Zealand, North Island* Now owned by **CORBANS**, a very large winery that did much to put New Zealand on the map. A wide range: both inexpensive and consistently well made: especially their Chenin Blanc.

COONAWARRA *Australia, South Australia* At the southernmost tip of the mainland, and famed for its thin strip of "terra rossa" soil and cool climate. Australia's greatest Cabernet Sauvignons and high-quality Shiraz (R). Leading producers include: Bowen, Brands Laira, Lindemanns, Mildara, Redman, Rouge Homme, Wynns, Zema.

COOPERATIVE Union of grape-growers who jointly own wine-making facilities and sometimes bottle and market wines. Some, but not all, are leaders in their appellations.

CORBANS WINES *New Zealand, North Island, W, R* The second-largest wine firm in New Zealand, ranging from 3-litre boxes to fine estate wines. The best are from Stoneleigh Vineyard in Marlborough, South Island.

CORBIÈRES *France, Midi, AOC, R, P, W* Predominantly R, from Carignan improved by Syrah and Mourvèdre. Large area, from the Mediterranean to the Pyrenees, with many soils, micro-climates and winemakers: 11 *terroirs* are recognized. Some good estates emerging as outsiders invest. Leading producers include: Cave d'Embres et Castelmaure, Ch de Lastours, Ch La Voulte-Gasparets.

CORBIN-MICHOTTE, CH *France, Bordeaux, St-Emilion, Grand Cru Classé, R* One of five properties by the Pomerol border with Corbin in its name. A fairly exotic style of wine, with good depth and body.

CORKED Describes wine that has a strong smell of rotten cork. This rather rare occurrence is caused by the development of certain moulds in the cork: the powerful smell makes the wine clearly undrinkable. Nothing to do with pieces of cork in the glass, which are harmless.

CORNAS *France, Rhône, AOC, R,* 100% Syrah wine from south of Hermitage that can start tough and tannic, but be superb after 10 years. Leading producers include: Auguste Clape, Paul Jaboulet Aîné, Robert Michel, Noël Verset.

CORNEILLA, CH DE *France, Midi, Roussillon, W, R, VDN* Here *vin de pays* and Rivesaltes *vin doux naturel* are made as well as the rich, sturdy **CÔTES DE ROUSSILLON**, R (45% Carignan, 35% Grenache Noir and 20% Syrah), which is made in the classic way.

CORSE, VIN DE *France, Corsica, AOC, R, P, W* General appellation for Corsica, with Rs and Ps from interesting native grapes or imported ones, such as Carignan, Grenache, Cinsaut, Syrah; one bottle in 10 is W, mainly from Vermentino (local name for Malvoisie). Best wines add on the name of a sub-zone: Calvi; Coteaux du Cap-Corse; Figari Porto-Vecchio; Sartène.

CORSIN, DOM *France, Burgundy, Mâconnais, R, W* Elegant, fruity Pouilly-Fuissé and St-Véran.

CORTON *France, Burgundy, AOC, R* The only R *Grand Cru* in the Côte de Beaune. The name is usually linked with a specific vineyard, eg Corton Les Bressandes, Corton Clos du Roi, Corton Les Renardes. Powerfully flavoured, earthy and highly tannic when young; subtlety, perfume and spicy fruit emerge after 6–7 years in bottle. The best wines can last 20 years. Leading producers include: Pierre André, Bonneau du Martray, Capitain-Gagnerot, Dubreuil-Fontaine, Daniel Senard, Tollot-Beaut.

CORTON-CHARLEMAGNE *France, Burgundy, AOC, W* Aloxe-Corton *Grand Cru* for W wines, on the same slope as **CORTON**, yielding some of the world's finest Chardonnays. Their nutty, spicy, sumptuous bouquet and flavour begin to open up after 5 years; will still be great at 15–20. Leading producers include: Bonneau du Martray, Maurice Chapuis, Coche-Dury, Joseph Drouhin, Jaffelin, Louis Latour.

COS D'ESTOURNEL, CH *France, Bordeaux, Médoc, St-Estèphe, 2ème Cru Classé, R* Well-known both for its odd, orientally styled *chai* and for its consistent excellence. There is 40% Merlot, and modern methods are used; but the wines are long-lived and classic in style. Proprietor Bruno Prats is one of the leading winemakers of the Médoc. His wines vie with the region's best. 2nd wine: Ch de Marbuzet.

COS LABORY, CH *France, Bordeaux, Médoc, St-Estèphe, 5ème Cru Classé, R* Next-door to Ch Cos d'Estournel, but different in style: straightforward and early-maturing. Recent vintages have improved.

COSSART GORDON *Portugal, Madeira* Among the major, and oldest, firms: founded in 1745. The style is comparatively light and elegant. Good Company is the basic range, Finest Old the 5-year-old reserve wines, while Duo Centenary is the 15-year-old exceptional reserve range.

COSTERS DEL SEGRE *Spain, Catalonia, DO, W, R, Sp* One of Catalonia's eight wine zones, producing Cava and still wines. Leading producers include: **RAIMAT**, Cellers Castell de Remei.

COSTIÈRES DE NÎMES *France, Midi, AOC, R, P, W* Mainly light R for drinking young (Grenache plus Carignan, Cinsaut, Syrah, Mourvèdre), from Languedoc vineyards by the Rhône. Leading producers include: Dom de l'Amarine, Dom St-Louis la Perdrix, Ch'x de Belle Coste, de Campuget, de Rozier, and de la Tuilerie.

COT See MALBEC.

CÔTE CHALONNAIS   *France, Burgundy, R, W, Sp*   Area south of the Côte d'Or and making similar but lesser wines. The villages of (N to S) BOUZERON, RULLY, MERCUREY, GIVRY and MONTAGNY offer good-value wines: true Burgundian character at sensible prices.

CÔTE D'OR   *France, Burgundy, R, W*   The "Golden Slope" of Burgundy, comprising the CÔTE DE NUITS (northern half) and the CÔTE DE BEAUNE (southern). R wines from Pinot Noir, W from Chardonnay. *See* map (Atlas section) for villages. Also the name of the *département* (county) covering these vineyards.

CÔTE DE BEAUNE   *France, Burgundy, AOC, R, W*   Southern part of the Côte d'Or . Mainly R, but notable exceptions in the W *Grands Crus* of Corton-Charlemagne and Montrachet, the *Premiers Crus* and the village wines from Meursault, Puligny and Chassagne. Simple Côte de Beaune AOC is rarely seen, but Côte de Beaune-Villages may be used for R wine by most of the region's villages and for blends.

CÔTE DE BRÉCHAIN   *France, Burgundy, Chablis, 1er Cru*   See MONTÉE DE TONNERRE.

CÔTE DE BROUILLY   *France, Burgundy, AOC, R*   The Mont de Brouilly rises from the vineyards; those on its slopes form this Beaujolais *cru*. On the Côte the grapes ripen well, yielding generally richer, more characterful wines than BROUILLY. Leading producers include: André Large, Ch Thivin, Ch du Grand Vernay, Les Vins Mathelin, Morin, Viornery.

CÔTE DE FONTENAY   *France, Burgundy, Chablis, 1er Cru*   See FOURCHAUME.

CÔTE DE NUITS   *France, Burgundy, R, W*   Name for the northern half of the Côte d'Or: mostly red-wine vineyards, including famous villages such as Nuits St-Georges and Gevrey-Chambertin. The name Côte de Nuits is only seen on labels when used of the AOC below.

CÔTE DE NUITS-VILLAGES   *France, Burgundy, AOC, R, W*   Mainly R wine from five villages on the north and south edges of this northern part of Burgundy's Côte d'Or. Leading producers include: Dom Allexant, Dom Robert Jayer, Dom de la Poulette, Reine Pedaque, Dom Daniel Rion.

CÔTE, LA   *Switzerland, Vaud*   To the west of Lausanne, a wine-producing district where most of the crop is handled by cooperatives and merchants' cellars. Stylish W wines from the Chasselas grape and Pinot Noir for gentle, drinkable R.

CÔTE ROANNAISE   *France, Loire, AOC, R, P*   Gamay Rs and Ps from Roanne, near the source of the Loire. Best producers: Paul Lapandéry, Félix Vial.

CÔTE RÔTIE   *France, Rhône, AOC, R*   One of the world's great Rs, long-lived and rich. The most elegant expression of the Syrah grape, plus up to 20% of the aromatic W Viognier, from the most northern Rhône vineyards. Leading producers include: Bernard Burgaud, Chapoutier, Marcel Guigal, Joseph Jamet, René Rostaing, Vidal-Fleury.

COTEAUX CHAMPENOIS *France, Champagne, AOC, R, W* Rare still wines from Champagne: the best Rs are from the villages of Ay, Bouzy and Cumières. Both R and (rarer) W wines are like light burgundies. Leading producers include: Barancourt, Bollinger, Gosset, Jacquesson & Fils, Lanson Père & Fils, Laurent-Perrier, Moët et Chandon, Ruinart Père & Fils.

COTEAUX D'AIX-EN-PROVENCE *France, Provence, AOC, R, P, W* Local grapes are now stiffened by Cabernet Sauvignon and Syrah for a modern profile and some interesting R wines are now being made. Leading producers include: Commanderie de la Bargemone, Ch Fonscolombe, Ch Vignelaure.
Les Baux-de-Provence, a sub-zone, has cool, hilly vineyards, welcoming to Cabernet Sauvignon. Leading producers include: Mas de la Dame, Mas de Gourgonnier, Dom des Terres Blanches, Dom de Trévallon.

COTEAUX D'ANCENIS *France, Loire, VDQS, R, P, W* Mainly R wine, from Gamay or Cabernet (Franc or Sauvignon), made around Ancenis in western Loire. Limited production.

COTEAUX DE DIE *France, Loire, AOC, W* Still W wine from Clairette grape, from the same region as the more interesting Sp Clairette de Die.

COTEAUX DE L'ARDÈCHE, DES *France, Vin de Pays, R, W, P* Successful for R from Cabernet, Merlot or Gamay; P, including pure Syrah ones; and W from Chardonnay and Viognier. Growers include several local co-ops and Burgundy *négociant* Louis Latour, whose whites have been especially successful.

COTEAUX DE L'AUBANCE *France, Loire, AOC, W* Medium-sweet to sweet W wines from Chenin Blanc, made in small and declining amounts in the Auibance valley in the Anjou Villages area. Leading producer: Hervé Papin.

COTEAUX DE PEYRIAC *France, Vin de Pays, R, P* Overlapping with the Minervois AOC zone, these wines are Rs from traditional grapes plus imported classic varieties and (increasingly) Ps from Grenache and Cinsaut.

COTEAUX DE PIERREVERT *France, Rhône, VDQS, R, P, W* Large zone along the Durance river; R, W and P wines are closer to Provence than Rhône in style.

COTEAUX DES BARONNIES, DES *France, Vin de Pays, R, W* This zone is east of the Côtes du Rhône region. Rs are from a range of grapes including Merlot and Cabernet Sauvignon, with Ws from Chardonnay and Viognier, alongside the local Clairette and Grenache Blanc.

COTEAUX DU GIENNOIS *France, Loire, VDQS, R, P, W* Gien, between Sancerre and Orléans, makes Ws from Sauvignon Blanc and Chenin Blanc, Rs and Ps from Gamay and Pinot Noir. Limited production.

COTEAUX DU LANGUEDOC *France, Midi, AOC, R, P, W* Large AOC: nearly 100 villages, 14 of them quality *crus*: Quatourze, La Clape (good W wine from limestone hills), St-Chinian (large area, some good Rs), Faugères (increasingly good Rs, worth 4-5 years' ageing, some from Syrah and Mourvèdre), Picpoul de Pinet (W from the local Picpoul grape), Cabrières (P and Rs), St-Saturnin, Montpeyroux, St-Georges d'Orques (good Rs), Pic St-Loup, Méjanelle, St-Drézéry, St-Christol, Coteaux de Vérargues. Leading producers include: Dom d'Aupilhac, Ch Coujan, Ch Grézan, Dom des Jougla, Ch de la Liquière, Ch Rouquette-sur-Mer.

COTEAUX DU LAYON *France, Loire, AOC, W* Luscious sweet Ws made from Chenin Blanc (ideally super-ripe, botrytized grapes). Finest vintages show astonishing depth and richness. Certain villages (eg Chaumes) can add their name to the general appellation. BONNEZEAUX and QUARTS-DE-CHAUME have their own AOCs. Leading producers include: Dom des Baumard, Ch du Breuil, Ch de Fesles, Ch de Belle-Rive, René Renou.

COTEAUX DU LOIR *France, Loire, AOC, R, P, W* Area of diminishing importance, on the Loir (not Loire) river, north of Tours.

COTEAUX DU LYONNAIS *France, Burgundy, AOC, R, P, W* Zone south of Beaujolais making Rs from Gamay plus a very little W (from Chardonnay and Aligoté). Leading producers include: Cave Coopérative de Sain Bel.

COTEAUX DU TRICASTIN *France, Rhône, AOC, R, P, W* Mostly Grenache-based Rs, from southern Rhône. Leading producer: Dom de Grangeneuve.

COTEAUX DU VENDÔMOIS *France, Loire, VDQS, R, P, W* Zone on Loir (not Loire) river, west of Vendôme. Small production, almost all drunk locally.

COTEAUX FLAVIENS, DES *France, Vin de Pays, R, P* Some interesting Rs from non-traditional grapes (Cabernet Sauvignon, Merlot) come from this zone south of Nîmes.

COTEAUX VAROIS *France, Provence, AOC, R, P, W* Wide zone making R wines for drinking young, and reasonable Ps. Leading producers: Dom du Deffends, Dom de Garbelle.

CÔTES D'AUVERGNE *France, Loire, VDQS, R, P, W* Wines from this district around Clermont-Ferrand are similar to Beaujolais: Gamay for R and P, Chardonnay for W. Limited production: most of the wine is drunk locally. Leading producers: Rougeyron, Cave St-Vernay.

CÔTES DE BERGERAC See BERGERAC.

CÔTES DE BLAYE   *France, Bordeaux, AOC, W*   Dry W wine from the same area as BLAYE. Premières Côtes de Blaye covers better Rs and Ws from the same area.

CÔTES DE BORDEAUX ST-MACAIRE   *France, Bordeaux, AOC, W*   Seldom-seen medium-sweet or sweet W wine from the south of Entre-Deux-Mers.

CÔTES DE BOURG   *France, Bordeaux, AOC, R, W*   Best part of the Bourg zone, mostly R, from slopes above the Dordogne. The AOC Bourg has fallen out of use. A little W is also made. Leading producers include: Ch'x de Barbe, Eyquem, Roc des Cambes, Tayac.

CÔTES DE CANON-FRONSAC   See CANON-FRONSAC.

CÔTES DE CASTILLON   *France, Bordeaux, AOC, R*   Rising source of good-value clarets, east of St-Emilion. Leading producers include: Ch Pitray, Ch Thibaud-Bellevue.

CÔTES DE DURAS   *France, South-West, AOC, R, W, P*   Light, early-maturing Rs, and dry and medium-sweet (*moelleux*) W wine from Bordeaux grape varieties. Leading producers include: Duras co-op, Dom de Ferrant, Dom de Laulan.

CÔTES DE FRANCS   *See* BORDEAUX CÔTES DE FRANCS.

CÔTES DE GASCOGNE, DES   *France, Vin de Pays, W, R*   Mostly Ws from the Armagnac country in South-West France: fresh, well-made wines. Most is from the UNION PLAIMONT cooperative, but some private estates are making good wines.

CÔTES DE LA MALEPÈRE   *France, Midi, VDQS, R, P*   Merlot, Cot and Cinsaut grapes, plus Cabernets Franc and Sauvignon, Grenache and Syrah, make wines combining sound structure with Mediterranean warmth. Leading producers include: Ch de Malviès, Ch de Routier.

CÔTES DE MELITON   *Greece, North, R, W*   Wine zone on a peninsula on the north-eastern coast of Greece. The Ws are made from native varieties blended with Sauvignon Blanc and Ugni Blanc; Rs from Limnio and Cabernet Sauvignon. Leading producers include: Ch Carras.

CÔTES DE MILLAU   *France, South-West, AOC, R, W, P*   Small zone in the Tarn valley for Rs, Ws and Ps.

CÔTES DE MONTRAVEL   See MONTRAVEL.

CÔTES DE PROVENCE   *France, Provence, AOC, P, R, W*   The largest AOC of Provence. Two-thirds of the wine is P, made from Grenache, Carignan, Cinsaut, Syrah, Mourvèdre and other grapes, and increasingly Cabernet Sauvignon. Some good Rs from the same grapes from individual estates. Leading producers include: Ch Bertraud-Belieu, Dom Gavoty, Les Maîtres Vignerons de La Presqu'île de St-Tropez, Doms Ott, Commanderie de Peyrassol, Dom Richeaume.

CÔTES DE ST-MONT *France, South-West, VDQS R, W, P* Well-made, good-value country wines come from the same grapes as Madiran (Rs) and Pacherenc du Vic-Bilh (Ws). Leading producer: Plaimont Co-op.

CÔTES DE TOUL *France, Alsace, VDQS, R, P, W* Some of France's most northerly vineyards, in Lorraine, make R and P (Gris de Toul) wine from Gamay and Pinot Noir; small amount of W.

CÔTES DU BRULHOIS *France, South-West, AOC, R, P* Rustic R from the Garonne valley. Little is made.

CÔTES DU FOREZ *France, Loire, VDQS, R, P* Good Rs and Ps from Gamay, made just across the mountains from Beaujolais. Leading producer: Les Vignerons Foréziens co-op.

CÔTES DU FRONTONNAIS *France, South-West, AOC, R, P* This supple, fruity wine is based on the low-tannin Négrette grape, with Cabernet Franc and others. Two sub-areas: Fronton and Villaudric. Leading producers include: Ch Baudare, Ch Bellevue la Forêt, Ch Flotis, Fronton co-op, Ch Montaurio.

CÔTES DU JURA *France, Jura & Savoie, R, P, W, Sp* Mostly W, using Savignan and Chardonnay grapes, from 72 villages. Some R (Pinot Noir and others) and P. Also **VIN JAUNE**. Leading producers include: Ch d'Arlay, Chalandard, Pignier.

CÔTES DU LUBÉRON *France, Rhône, AOC, R, P, W* Mountain area to the east of the southern Rhône: mostly soft, enjoyable Rs, using Syrah and Grenache. W from Clairette grapes can be good. Leading producers include: Dom de Mayol, Ch Val Joanis.

CÔTES DU MARMANDAIS *France, South-West, AOC, R, P, W* Mainly R wines from Merlot, Cabernets Franc and Sauvignon, with Cot, Gamay, Syrah and local Fer Servadou and Abouriou. Leading producer: Cocumont co-op.

CÔTES DU RHÔNE *France, Rhône, AOC, R, P, W* Very varied wines from a huge area of the southern Rhône. Rs are Grenache with Cinsaut, Syrah and others; Ws from Clairette, Roussanne and Marsanne. Leading producers include: Chapoutier, Ch de Fonsalette, Ch du Grand Moulas, Guigal, Jaboulet, Vidal-Fleury.

CÔTES DU RHÔNE-VILLAGES *France, Rhône, AOC, R, W* This AOC is for better wines from 16 communes within the Côtes du Rhône area, which can add their name to the labels:
Beaumes-de-Venise: traditional Rs as well as the famous Muscat dessert wine;
Cairanne: Rs; leading producers include: Dom Rabasse-Charavin;
Laudun: Rs and Ws;
Rasteau: hearty Rs as well as *vins doux naturels*; leading producers include: Dom de la Soumade;
St-Gervais: good Rs and luscious Viognier Ws; leading producers include: Dom Ste-Anne;
Sablet: leading producers include: Dom des Gourbets;

Séguret: some good Rs from close to Gigondas; leading producers include: Dom de Cabasse;

Valréas: leading producers include: Dom des Grands Devers; plus Chusclan, Roaix; Rousset-les-Vignes; Rochegude; St-Maurice-sur-Eygues; St-Pantaléon-les-Vignes; Vinsobres; Visan.

CÔTES DU ROUSSILLON   *France, Midi, AOC, R, P, W*   Sturdy, full-bodied Rs from Grenache, Cinsaut, Syrah and Mourvèdre and a decreasing amount of Carignan. Some Ps, and fairly neutral Ws from Macabeo and Malvoisie. The superior appellation Côtes du Roussillon Villages can only be R; two villages – Caramany and Latour de France – can add their names to the appellation's. Leading producers include: Ch de Cazenove, Dom Cazes, Ch de Corneilla, Ch de Jau, Dom Piquemal.

CÔTES DU TARN, DES   *France, Vin de Pays, R, W, P*   This zone around Gaillac makes robust Rs, some good Ps from Gamay and Syrah, and fresh fruity Ws.

CÔTES DU VENTOUX   *France, Rhône, AOC, R, W, P*   Southern Rhône Rs and Ps (from Grenache, Syrah and many others) and Ws (Clairette and others). Can be good value. Leading producers include: Dom des Anges, Jaboulet, Vieille Ferme.

CÔTES DU VIVARAIS   *France, Rhône, VDQS, R, P, W*   Decent but rather light southern Rhône Rs, Ps and Ws (based on Clairette, Marsanne and Bourboulenc). Leading producer: Dom de Vigier.

COTNARI   *Romania*   Area in the north-east, and well known for its pale, honeyed sweet W wine, similar to Hungary's famous Tokaji. Grapes are left to shrivel on the vine, but noble rot is rare. Made from a blend of varieties, large oak barrels are used for both its fermentation and maturation, and the wine is bottled after a couple of years. Can age very well.

COUHINS-LURTON, CH   *France, Bordeaux, Pessac-Léognan, Cru Classé, W*   Small vineyard, solely Sauvignon Blanc. Fermented and aged in new oak, the wine is distinctive and successful.

COULÉE DE SERRANT, CLOS DE LA   *France, Loire, Anjou, W*   Nicolas Joly combines biodynamic farming and a belief in astrological influence to make a great wine, designed for an immense life, from a single-vineyard appellation in SAVENNIÈRES. The steep vineyard is worked by horsepower.

COULY-DUTHEIL   *France, Loire, Chinon, R*   This is the largest producer of Chinon wines actually based in Chinon, with 65ha of vines, plus grapes from local growers. The top wine is Clos de l'Echo, from a single vineyard that once belonged to Rabelais.

COURANÇONNE, CH DE   *France, Rhône, Côtes du Rhône-Villages, R*   Gabriel Meffre's estate uses mostly Grenache grapes to make an excellent, solid R.

COURCEL, DOM DE   *France, Burgundy, Côte d'Or, R*   Pommard specialist making wonderful, richly coloured, dense, long-lived wines.

COUSINO MACUL *Chile, R, W* On the outskirts of Santiago, a family estate long known for its Cabernet Sauvignon. Since 1990 R wines have been aged in French *barriques*. New additions include Merlot and Chardonnay.

COUTET, CH *France, Bordeaux, Barsac, 1er Cru Classé, W* In the late 1980s Coutet once again found its form, producing tangy wines with the Barsac delicacy behind a great richness of fruit. In great years a special *cuvée* of this sweet wine, Cuvée Madame, is produced.

COUVENT-DES-JACOBINS, CH *France, Bordeaux, St-Emilion, Grand Cru Classé, R* Consistent quality is now ensured by using the lesser vats for a 2nd label. Beautifully perfumed, with lovely, supple fruit. The underground cellars are well worth a visit.

COVEY RUN *USA, Washington State, R, W* This Zillah (Yakima Valley) winery produces Lemberger, an unusual, fragrant, stain-less-steel-fermented R, White Riesling and Chardonnay. La Caille de Fumé is a dry W Sauvignon Blanc/Sémillon blend.

COWRA *Australia, New South Wales* This small, high-up, region of New South Wales is emerging as an important producer of fleshy, buttery Chardonnay. Leading producers include: Cowra Estate, Rothbury.

CRÉMANT *France* Describes gently sparkling wine in Champagne; elsewhere in France a wine made by the *méthode champenoise*.

CRÉMANT DE DIE See CLAIRETTE DE DIE.

CRÉMANT DE LIMOUX See BLANQUETTE DE LIMOUX

CRÉPY *France, Savoie, AOC, W* Delicate dry W wine from Chasselas grapes. Leading producers include: Fichard, Mercier.

CRIOTS-BÂTARD-MONTRACHET, LES See BÂTARD-MONTRACHET

CRIANZA *Spain* See VINO DE CRIANZA.

CROCHET, LUCIEN *France, Loire, Sancerre, W, R* Family firm with 30ha in some of the best Sancerre *crus*: Chêne Marchand and Grand Chemarin for Ws, Clos du Roi for Rs.

CROCK, CH LE *France, Bordeaux, St-Estèphe, Cru Bourgeois, R* Lavish modern equipment and the best advice combine to make increasingly impressive wine at this handsome château.

CROFT *Portugal, port; Spain, sherry* One of the oldest (1678) port shippers. A full range of ports, from Distinction Finest Reserve (sound, commercial quality), up to aged tawnies and vintage wines (including single-*quinta* Quinta da Roeda) that are among the best. Its sister sherry company revolutionized the sherry market in the 1960s with Croft Original Pale Cream, a pale sherry that looked dry, but tasted sweet. Other brands include Delicado fino, Croft Particular medium amontillado and Brandy Croft.

CROIZET-BAGES, CH *France, Bordeaux, Médoc, Pauillac, 5ème Cru Classé, R* Unusually for Pauillac, Cabernet Sauvignon is not the main variety here: it is overtaken by Merlot and Cabernet Franc. Style is thus softer and more open, and wines mature quite quickly.

CROQUE-MICHOTTE, CH *France, Bordeaux, St-Emilion, Grand Cru Classé, R* Near the Pomerol border; this wine is very approachable young. The seductive fruit and soft, supple palate are best enjoyed within a decade.

CROZES-HERMITAGE *France, Rhône, AOC, R, W* Perhaps the best *rapport qualité/prix* of the northern Rhône, with recent dramatic improvements. As in HERMITAGE, Rs are from Syrah, Ws from Marsanne and Roussanne. Leading producers include: Belle, Alain Graillot, Jaboulet/Dom de Thalabert, Etienne Pochon.

CRU *France* Literally meaning growth: an area that reflects a particular soil and climate. In Bordeaux, a wine from a specific estate or château, and from this, the various ranks of wine estates; see below: CRU BOURGEOIS and CRU CLASSÉ

CRU BOURGEOIS *France* The category of château below classed growths in the Médoc.

CRU CLASSÉ Classed growth: in the Médoc, a château placed in one of five ranks by the 1855 Classification (*Premier Cru, Deuxième Cru,* etc).

CRUSIUS, WEINGUT HANS & PETER *Germany, Nahe, W* Small, high-quality estate making long-lived wines from some of the top Nahe vineyards.

CRUZEAU, CH DE *France, Bordeaux, Pessac-Léognan, R, W* Straightforward unoaked W, mostly Sauvignon Blanc, and an austere but stylish oak-aged R.

CUILLERON *France, Rhône, Condrieu, W* Top maker of this rare W, with a standard wine for early drinking and Les Chaillets, a *cuvée* for ageing.

CUMBERLAND VALLEY *USA, Maryland & Pennsylvania, VA* High-quality wine zone, fast expanding, which grows hybrid and classic grapes. Leading producers include: Basignani, Boordy.

CURÉ-BON-LA-MADELEINE, CH *France, Bordeaux, St-Emilion, Grand Cru Classé, R* Relatively unknown property making a wine that is essentially Merlot, backed up with a little Cabernets Sauvignon and Franc. Highly regarded by those who know it well.

CUVE *France* Vat or cask to hold the fermenting grape juice, or to store wine; an alternative for ageing to *barriques*. Can be made of cement or (increasingly) stainless steel.

CUVÉE *France* Signifies a selection of wine that may or may not have been blended. Also describes a batch of wine with the same characteristics.

CVNE (COMPAÑÍA VINÍCOLA DEL NORTE DE ESPAÑA) *Spain, Rioja, R, W, P* One of Rioja's oldest and finest houses, producing good-quality wines throughout their extensive range. Top-of-the-range Imperial and Vina Real (Rs) rank among the finest in the region.

CYPRUS Quality potential as yet is far from realized. Most wine is R, from the alcoholic, tannic, unexciting Mavron grape. W mainly from Xynisteri. The famous dessert wine, Commandaria, can be excellent but is usually simple commercial stuff.

CZECH REPUBLIC The two Czech regions of Bohemia and Moravia make wines, mainly W, of roughly equal quality. A wide range of varieties includes the native, aromatic Irsay Oliver (W). Close in style to those of Austria and Hungary: dry, ripe and crisp, with good fruit. R wines from Pinot Noir can be very good, Sp wine, both W and R, is mader on a large scale and is acceptable. Fine future potential.

D

DAGUENEAU, DIDIER *France, Loire, Pouilly-Fumé, W* Burgundy-trained Dagueneau ferments in new wood as well as stainless steel, for wines (from various – labelled – *terroirs*) that age well. His top *cuvée*, Silex (the name of a type of stony soil), is one of the finest made in Pouilly today.

DAMBACH-LA-VILLE *France, Alsace,* Considered the best wine village in the Bas-Rhin. *Grand Cru* Frankstein is good for Riesling and Gewürztraminer. Leading producers include: Gisselbricht.

DÃO *Portugal, DOC, R, W* Mainly R wine, from one of Portugal's most famous wine areas, from anything up to nine grape varieties. Should be firm, but can taste hard and austere due to old-fashioned winemaking. W wines are also old-fashioned. Modern wineries are beginning to produce better wines: Caves São João, Vinicola do Vale do Dão.

DASSAULT, CH *France, Bordeaux, St-Emilion, Grand Cru Classé, R* This fairly large property makes wine with few hidden depths, but with lots of obvious appeal.

DAUVISSAT, RENÉ *France, Burgundy, Chablis, W* Small, high-quality estate owned by René and son Vincent. Some wines are still vinified in oak and all enjoy some oak ageing. With bottle-age they acquire the flinty mineral taste of the *terroir*.

DAUZAC, CH *France, Bordeaux, Médoc, Margaux, 3ème Cru Classé R* Estate in Labarde, close to the Gironde, making wine that has improved over the last decade but does not yet scale the heights. A new winery, a new *chai* and replanting in the vineyards represent hope for the future.

DEIDESHEIM *Germany, Pfalz, W, R* Top wine village in the Mittelhaardt, the best part of the Pfalz, making serious and long-lived Ws. Top vineyards are Hohenmorgen, Grainhübel and Hergottsackert. Leading producers include: Basserman-Jordan, von Buhl.

DEINHARD, WEINGUT DR *Germany, Pfalz, W* Quality estate based at DEIDESHEIM making good Pfalz W wines, mostly Riesling, in a traditional style

DEISS, MARCEL, DOM *France, Alsace, W, R* One of the region's best winemakers, making concentrated wines of only the highest quality in many varieties and styles, including *vendange tardive* and *sélections des grains nobles*.

DELAFORCE *Portugal, port* The Delaforces are still involved, though the firm is now part of the IDV combine. His Eminence's Choice, an old tawny, is well regarded. Their vintage wines are based on Quinta da Corte: elegant wines, with delicacy and less longevity than some of the blockbusters of the trade.

DELAMOTTE *France, Champagne* Owned by Laurent-Perrier, based in the Côte des Blancs. Quality and elegance are hallmarks, especially in both the vintage *blanc de blancs* and the prestige *cuvée* Nicolas-Louis Delamotte.

DELAPORTE, VINCENT *France, Loire, Sancerre, W, R* Small but top-quality family estate in Chavignol: mainly Ws, small amount of R. The steep slopes, above the village, are worked by hand. Wines are sold around the world, and served in smart Paris restaurants.

DÉLAS FRÈRES *France, Rhône, R, W* Major vineyard owner in the Northern Rhône, with land in Hermitage, Côte Rôtie, St-Joseph and in Condrieu. Wines are correct, not exciting – but they are improving.

DELBECK *France, Champagne* Now owned by François d'Aulun, who used to own Piper-Heidsieck, this house has undergone many changes. Best known for its NV Brut Héritage and a fine rosé.

DELORME, ANDRÉ *France, Burgundy, Chalonnais, R, W, Sp* Good-quality Rully estate producing both R and W wines, especially from Dom de la Renarde.

DEMI-SEC *France* Medium-dry; however in Champagne the term means medium-sweet.

DENOMINAÇÃO DE ORIGEM CONTROLADA (DOC) *Portugal* The top tier of Portugal's appellation system.

DENOMINACIÓN DE ORIGEN (DO) *Spain* The most common grade of Spanish quality wine.

DENOMINACIÓN DE ORIGEN CALIFICADA (DOC) *Spain* A "super-category" for Spanish quality wines meeting special criteria of quality and consistency.

DENOMINAZIONE DI ORIGINE CONTROLLATA (DOC) *Italy* Italian quality wine.

DENOMINAZIONE DI ORIGINE CONTROLLATA E GARANTITA (DOCG) *Italy* Higher grade of Italian quality wine, above DOC. The guarantee is a signal of tighter quality control.

DESCOMBES, DOM JEAN *France, Burgundy, Beaujolais, R* Leading producer of Morgon, the richest and most long-lived of the Beaujolais *Crus*.

DESMIRAIL, CH *France, Bordeaux, Médoc, Margaux, 3ème Cru Classé, R* Recently revived: the land was for many years owned by other châteaux. Results awaited.

DEUTZ *France, Champagne* Family-owned GRANDE MARQUE, at Ay. Overall style quite fruity and forward, although the prestige *cuvée* William Deutz is particularly good.

DEUX ROCHE, DOM DES *France, Burgundy, Mâconnais, R, W* Estate which produces a range of good-quality R and W Mâconnais. The St-Véran in particular is very good.

DEVAUX *France, Champagne* The flagship wine of the dynamic Union Auboise, a group of co-ops in the AUBE district, with 750 growers and 1,400ha of vines. Mainly Pinot Noir, very good value, well-made champagne.

DEZALEY *Switzerland, Vaud, Lavaux, W, R* To the east of Lausanne, a leading wine-producing village making attractive W wine from the Chasselas grape and agreeable but not very complex R from Pinot Noir.

DIAMOND CREEK *USA, California, Napa, R* Estate specializing in R wines with four tiny vineyard plots on Diamond Mountain which yield four distinctive Cabernet Sauvignons: Volcanic Hill, Red Rock Terrace, Gravelly Meadow and Lake – the last released only in top years.

DIAMOND MOUNTAIN *USA, California, VA* Steep hillside vineyards above the Napa Valley form a wine zone making austere, classy Chardonnay and Cabernet Sauvignon. Leading producers include: Diamond Creek, Sterling, Stonegate.

DO *Spain* See DENOMINACIÓN DE ORIGEN.

DOC *Italy* See DENOMINAZIONE DI ORIGINE CONTROLLATA.

DOC *Portugal* See DENOMINAÇÃO DE ORIGEM CONTROLADA.

DOC *Spain* See DENOMINACIÓN DE ORIGEN CALIFICADA.

DOCG *Italy* See DENOMINAZIONE DI ORIGINE CONTROLLATA E GARANTITA.

DOISY-DAËNE, CH *France, Bordeaux, Barsac, 2ème Cru Classé, W* Sauternes in a light and delicate style (except in 1989), with charm rather than power. Can be disappointing in light years, but in good years quintessential Barsac. Also makes a dry white Graves.

DOISY-DUBROCA, CH *France, Bordeaux, Barsac, 2ème Cru Classé, W* Same owners as CH CLIMENS, and the techniques are the same. *Terroir* will out, however, and Dubroca does not have the distinction of Climens; but it is nonetheless classic Barsac that needs bottle-age.

DOISY-VÉDRINES, CH *France, Bordeaux, Barsac, 2ème Cru Classé, W* An outstanding source of fine, complex sweet wine in a relatively full-bodied style.

DOLCETTO Red grape used in seven DOCs in Italy's Piedmont (such as **DOLCETTO D'ALBA**, Dolcetto d'Acqui), usually meant to be drunk within two or three years of the vintage. Prized for easy drinkability, crisp and well structured, with plenty of fruit.

DOLCETTO D'ALBA *Italy, Piedmont, DOC, R* The Dolcetto grape produces wines for which are easy to drink. Mulberry-hued, with bright pink highlights, crisp in taste, with luscious fruit flavours and a rich perfume. Leading producers include: Elio Altare, Ceretto, Giacomo Conterno, Vietti.

DOMAINE *France* Equivalent to château; a wine estate. The inference is that the wine is made, and bottled, by the landowner. Also used in New World countries to convey the same sense.

DOMECQ, BODEGAS *Spain, Rioja, R, W, P* Offshoot of the famous sherry firm, producing soft, agreeable wines. Viña Eguia (R) is good, but the Marqués de Arienzo R, W and P are best.

DOMECQ, PEDRO *Spain, sherry* Famous equally for its flagship La Ina fino sherry and for Fundador and Carlos I brandies. The firm dominates the sherry trade from its spectacular *bodegas* and palace in Jerez. Top of the range, along with La Ina fino, are Rio Viejo dry oloroso, Sibarita Palo Cortado and Venerable Oloroso. The more commercial Double Century range is well regarded.

DOMERGUE, DANIEL *France, Midi, Minervois, R* A newcomer to the Minervois but among the appellation's leaders, Daniel Domergue replanted his land in Le Petit Causse, near Siran, with quality vines: Syrah, Cinsaut, Grenache and Mourvèdre. He makes two wines: Clos Centeilles, destined for long life, and Campagne de Centeilles, for earlier drinking.

DOMEYNE, CH *France, Bordeaux, St-Estèphe, Cru Bourgeois, R* Small, but modern-minded, estate with well-made wine.

DOMINIQUE, CH LA *France, Bordeaux, St-Emilion, Grand Cru Classé, R* On the Pomerol border, and recently a rising star. The wine, which has a very high percentage of Merlot, is outstanding: concentrated but not overly tannic, with a certain opulence.

DON ZOILO *Spain, sherry* The Very Old Fino is the star of the respected Don Zoilo range of Jerez sherries.

DONATIEN BAHUAUD *France, Loire, Muscadet, W* Wine made and bottled *sur lie* at historic Ch de la Cassemichère. This firm of growers and *négociants* also has cellars in La Chapelle-Heulin. Most famous Muscadet is Le Master de Donatien, selected at yearly tastings.

DONNAFUGATA *Italy, Sicily, W, R, P* Their deliciously fresh W wine is entitled to the new Contessa Entellina DOC. Also a P, a rich, barrel-aged R, a Marsala and an apéritif-style Pantelleria.

DOPFF & IRION *France, Alsace, W* Grower and *négociant*: its list includes Riesling Les Murailles (from *Grand Cru* Schoenenberg); Gewürztraminer Muscat Les Sorcières, a powerful, long-lived wine; Muscat Les Amandiers; and Pinot Gris Les Maquisards.

Having distanced itself from the system for years, the company is now marketing *Grand Cru* wines.

DOPFF AU MOULIN *France, Alsace, W* This 400-year-old company continues at the forefront of Crémant d'Alsace production, with Cuvée Julien, Cuvée Bartholdi, Blanc de Noirs and Brut Sauvage among the best. Also some fine still wines under the Domaines Dopff label.

DOUDET-NAUDIN *France, Burgundy, Côte d'Or, R, W* Vineyard owner and *négociant* in Corton and Beaune. Old-fashioned wines for long maturing.

DOURO *Portugal, DOC, R, W* Valley (also the source of PORT) and DOC ,where the production of mainly R and some W table wines is currently undergoing a revival. A wide range of grapes is permitted, with the best producers using Portugal's distinctive native varieties, notably Tinta Roriz and Touriga Nacional for the Rs. Leading producers include: Quinta da Cismeira, Cockburn Smithies, Quinta do Côtto, Ferreira.

DOUX *France* Sweet; applies to wines with a sugar content of over 45 grams per litre.

DOW *Portugal, port* Dow, based at Quinta de Bomfim, is known for its dry style of vintage ports. Owned (since 1912) by SYMINGTON.

DRAPPIER *France, Champagne* Family-run house based in the AUBE district. Wines are rich and biscuity, especially the single-vineyard Grande Sendrée, from old vines.

DROIN, JEAN-PAUL *France, Burgundy, Chablis, W* Young, dynamic producer of *Premier* and *Grand Cru* Chablis: leading exponent of new oak. Some superb wines, others atypically rich and over-oaked.

DROMANA ESTATE *Australia, Victoria, Mornington Peninsula, W, R* The cool Mornington Peninsula climate produces wonderful Chardonnay and Cabernet Sauvignon at this leading estate. Their 2nd label, Shinus, is for wines from bought-in grapes.

DRÔME, DE LA *France, Vin de Pays, R, W* Wines from the Rhône, between Valence and Montélimar. Nearly all R, principally from Grenache, Cinsaut and Syrah. Gamay, Cabernet Sauvignon or Merlot are used for varietal wines. Gamay, in particular, has been successful.

DROUHIN, JOSEPH *France, Burgundy, Côte d'Or & Chablis, R, W* Respected *négociant* and important vineyard owner in the Côte d'Or and Chablis. Strikingly well-made, reliable wines, especially Beaune Clos des Mouches, both R and W.

DRUET, PIERRE-JACQUES *France, Loire, Bourgueil, W, R* Innovative Bourgueil producer, with wines made for ageing but which can also be enjoyed young. The best of the *cuvées,* from the superior

Coteaux zone, is Vaumoureau; the Beauvais and Grand-Mont *cuvées* are also very good.

DRY CREEK VALLEY   *USA, California, Sonoma, VA*   Sonoma Valley wine zone with good conditions for Bordeaux varieties (Cabernets and Merlot for Rs, Sauvignon for Ws), and for Zinfandel Rs. Leading producers include: Dry Creek, Preston, Ridge (especially for Zinfandel).

DUBOEUF, GEORGES   *France, Burgundy, Beaujolais, R, W*   The leading *négociant* of Beaujolais and Mâconnais, who has done more than anyone to raise the profile and quality standards of the region. Duboeuf wines appear both under his own label and those of individual properties and his name, in large print or small, is a surefire guarantee of quality.

DUBREUIL-FONTAINE, DOM   *France, Burgundy, Côte d'Or, R, W*   Top-quality domaine, based in Pernand-Vergelesses, making very serious wines from Corton and Pernand.

DUC DE MAGENTA, DOM DU   *France, Burgundy, Côte d'Or, R, W*   Chassagne-Montrachet domaine whose high-class wines are made by Jadot of Beaune. The Puligny-Montrachets are especially good.

DUCRU-BEAUCAILLOU, CH   *France, Bordeaux, Médoc, St-Julien, 2ème Cru Classé, R*   Well-placed vineyard on the riverside rim of the St-Julien gravel banks. Consistent quality, especially since 1985, is its hallmark; wines, though made in the old-fashioned way, are elegant. A very good 1993. 2nd wine: La Croix.

DUFF GORDON   *Spain, sherry*   Famous sherry house, founded in 1768. Brands include fino Feria and Club Dry amontillado.

DUHART-MILON-ROTHSCHILD, CH   *France, Bordeaux, Médoc, Pauillac, 4ème Cru Classé, R*   Part of the Rothschild jigsaw puzzle on Pauillac's northern plateau, this vineyard (which has no actual château) is owned by the Lafite Rothschilds. Vintages since 1981 have begun to fulfil the site's potential.

DUJAC, DOM   *France, Burgundy, Côte d'Or, R*   Jacques Seysses of Dujac is one of Burgundy's top winemakers: his incredibly elegant wines range from a delicious Morey-St-Denis to great Clos de la Roche.

DULCE   *Italy & Spain*   Term meaning sweet.

DURBACH   *Germany, Baden, W, R*   Village with a good name for Riesling Ws: solid, full of flavour, from steep and spectacular vineyards. Leading producers include: von Nevau, Wolf Metternich, Schloss Staufenberg.

DURFORT-VIVENS, CH   *France, Bordeaux, Médoc, Margaux, 2ème Cru Classé, R*   Very high proportion of Cabernet Sauvignon makes for tough, long-maturing wine. Older vintages are patchy.

DURUP, JEAN *France, Burgundy, Chablis, W* Durup's Dom de l'Eglantière is Chablis's largest estate, mainly *Village* and *Premier Cru* wines, plus some Petit Chablis. Firmly of the anti-oak school, he believes it distorts the true flavour of Chablis.

DUTRUCH-GRAND-POUJEAUX, CH *France, Bordeaux, Moulis, Cru Bourgeois, R* One of a series of châteaux with "Poujeaux" in their name, this structured wine ages well.

DUVAL-LEROY *France, Champagne* Large and dynamic house in the Côte des Blancs which owns 140ha of vines. It sells under many different labels, but under the Duval-Leroy name produces an elegant P and impressive NV.

E

ECHÉZEAUX *France, Burgundy, AOC, R* This *Grand Cru* on the Côte de Nuits above Vougeot makes powerful, scented R wines, maturing in about 10 years. Leading producers include: Drouhin, H Jayer, Mongeard-Mugnerat, Romanée-Conti.

EDEN VALLEY *Australia, South Australia* Wine zone between BAROSSA and the ADELAIDE HILLS. Riesling does particularly well here. Leading producers include: Heggies, Henschke, Hill-Smith, Mountadam, Pewsey Vale.

EDNA VALLEY *USA, California, VA* Wine zone in San Luis Obispo county, known for elegant Chardonnays. Leading producers include: Edna Valley Vineyard, Corbett Canyon.

EGER *Hungary* District in the northern part of Hungary, most famous for the R Bulls Blood (Egri Bikavér) mainly from the Kékfrankos grape. A legendary wine, but today's version is a commercial blend, somewhat light in style. Some good new Rs are appearing under the Eger district name.

EGLISE CLINET, CH L' *France, Bordeaux, Pomerol, R* Very small, mainly Merlot estate making a rare wine but one of Pomerol's finest: full-bodied and generous yet with great finesse.

EGUISHEIM *France, Alsace* This village has *Grands Crus* Eichberg and Pfersigberg, famous for Gewürztraminer. Leading producers include: Léon Beyer, Kuentz-Bas.

EISWEIN *Germany* Literally, "ice-wine". Made from grapes that have frozen on the vine. When the grapes are pressed, still frozen, the water in the grapes remains as ice and the concentrated juice flows out.

ELAN, CH *USA, Georgia, W, R* This winery, restaurant and museum complex, north of Atlanta, attracts over 250,000 visitors a year. The 80-ha vineyard is mainly Chardonnay, Sauvignon Blanc, Riesling, Cabernet Sauvignon and two hybrids, Chambourcin and Seyval Blanc.

ELTVILLE *Germany, Rheingau, W* Leading village of the Rheingau, famous as the HQ of the State Domaine (Staatsweingut). Mostly Riesling Ws, with Sonnenberg rated the top vineyard. Leading producers include: Knyphausen, Schönborn, von Simmern.

EMBRES ET CASTELMAURE, CAVE D' *France, Midi, Corbières, R, W* Cooperative in the forefront of new developments. It has done some wood-ageing since 1980, and in 1992 tried using new barrels for its top wine, Cuvée de Pompadour.

EMILIA-ROMAGNA *Italy* The gastronomic capital of Italy, centred on Bologna, is also home to its most infamous wine, LAMBRUSCO. Other popular varietals include Albana, Sangiovese and Trebbiano.

EN PRIMEUR *France* Wine sold before it has even been bottled. Common in Bordeaux when classed growths are sold in the year after they are made. In America, to buy futures means the same thing.

ENCLOS, CH L' *France, Bordeaux, Pomerol, R* Delicious wines that are relatively inexpensive (for Pomerol) and early-maturing.

ENGLAND Over 1,000ha of vineyards in the south and east make wine, mainly W, on a commercial scale; most is dry, flowery and crisp, though late-harvest Ws and some Rs are appearing. Leading producers include: Adgestone, Barkham Manor, Biddenden, Car Taylor, Denbies, Lamberhurst, Nutbourne, Pilton, Tenterden, Three Choirs, Wootton.

ENTRAYGUES ET DU FEL, VIN D' *France, South-West, VDQS, R, P, W* Rustic Ws from Chenin Blanc; Rs and Ps from local Fer Servadou and Cabernets Sauvignon and Franc, from a tiny zone in the Aveyron *département*.

ENTRE-DEUX-MERS *France, Bordeaux, AOC, W* Dry W wine from Sauvignon Blanc and Sémillon. The Haut-Benauge sub-zone stresses the perfumed Sémillon grape. Leading producers include: Ch Bonnet, Ch le Bos, Ch Grossombre, Ch Haut-Reygnac, Ch Roquefort, Dom de la Serizière, Ch Tour de Mirambeau, Ch la Tuilerie.

EPENOTTES, LES *France, Burgundy, Côte de Beaune, 1er Cru, R* Lying parallel to the N74 highway at the southern end of the Beaune commune, this vineyard produces wines which are densely coloured and perfumed, and with a good tannic structure. Leading producers include: Pierre Bourée & Fils, Michel Bouzereau, Michel Gaunoux, Parent.

ERBACH *Germany, Rheingau, W* Famous wine village with superb, full Riesling Ws from vineyards such as Marcobrunn, beside the Rhine. Leading producers include: the Staatsweingut Eltville, von Simmern, Schönborn.

ERDEN *Germany, Mosel, W* Village on the Mosel, north of Bernkastel, which (like several of its neighbours) has vineyards on the opposite bank: the south-facing Treppchen and Prälat are among the best in the region. Leading producers include: Loosen.

ERMITAGE DE CHASSE-SPLEEN *France, Bordeaux, Médoc, Moulis* 2nd wine of Ch Chasse-Spleen.

ESCHENDORFER LUMP *Germany, Franken, W* Famous Franken vineyard, above the River Main, noted for Silvaner. Leading growers include Juliusspital.

ESER, AUGUST   *Germany, Rheingau, W, R*   Mostly Rieslings in the classic, long-lasting Rheingau style, with a little R.

EST! EST!! EST!!!   *Italy, Lazio, DOC, W*   Fairly innocuous dry W wine based on Trebbiano, sometimes with the addition of Malvasia to increase aroma. Leading producers include: Falesco, Mazziotti.

ESTAING, VIN D'   *France, South-West, VDQS, R, P, W*   France's smallest VDQS zone makes pleasant Ws from Chenin Blanc and Mauzac, fruity P and R (which can be astringent) from Gamay, Cabernet Franc and local Fer Servadou.

ETCHART   *Argentina, R, W*   Partly owned by Pernod-Ricard, this concern produces many good wines. Their Torrontes, sometimes using the brand Cafayate, is flowery and delicious. The range also includes a good-value Malbec.

ETOILE, CH L'   *France, Bordeaux, Graves, W, R*   Well-known Langon estate making structured Rs and fresh, clean Ws.

ÉTOILE, L'   *France, Jura, AOC, W*   Still and Sp W wine from Chardonnay, Savagnin and Poulsard grapes; VIN JAUNE from Savagnin. Leading producers include: Christian Bourdy.

EVANGILE, CH L'   *France, Bordeaux, Pomerol, R*   The Rothschilds of Lafite control this property, always regarded as one of Pomerol's greatest.

EYQUEM, CH   *France, Bordeaux, Côtes de Bourg, R*   Not to be confused with Ch YQUEM , this is a solid R in the Bourg manner.

EYRIE   *USA, Oregon, W, R*   Pioneers of fine wine in Oregon, David and Diana Letts make legendary Pinot Noirs modelled on, and challenging in quality, the best of Burgundy; plus good Ws from Chardonnay and Pinot Gris.

F

FABAS, CH *France, Midi, Minervois, R*   Jean-Pierre Ormières of Ch Fabas was one of the first exponents of *barrique*-matured Minervois, participating in the initial experiments with oak conducted by the *appellation's* oenologist.

FAIVELEY, JOSEPH *France, Burgundy, Côte d'Or, R, W*   Very important Burgundy *négociant* and vineyard owner using modern techniques. Good, reliable quality.

FALFAS, CH *France, Bordeaux, Côtes de Bourg, R*   Ambitious new owners are following organic techniques and making increasingly good claret.

FALL CREEK VINEYARDS *USA, Texas, W, R*   With vines on the shores of Lake Buchanan in Llano County, the Aulers have built a replica of a French château and produce Chardonnay, Cabernet Sauvignon and Sauvignon. A limited amount of Reserve Chardonnay is made and has been impressive.

FARGUES, CH DE *France, Bordeaux, Sauternes, W*   Very small amounts of rich and luscious wine made by the same team as Ch YQUEM (qv). Although half the price of Yquem, Fargues remains the second most expensive wine of the appellation.

FATTORIA *Italy*   Wine estate.

FAUGÈRES *France, Midi, AOC, R*   Appellation within the Coteaux du Languedoc: quite rich, mouthfilling R from Grenache, improved by Syrah and Mourvèdre, gaining from 4–5 years in bottle. Leading producers include: Gilbert Alquier, Ch'x Grézan, Haut Fabregues, de la Liquière.

FAZI-BATTAGLIA *Italy, Central Italy, Marches, W, R*   The single-vineyard Le Moie is one of best wines in the Verdicchio dei Castelli di Jesi Classico zone. Also makes Rosso Conèro and Rosso Piceno.

FENDANT   See CHASSELAS.

FERMENTATION, ALCOHOLIC AND MALOLACTIC   Conversion of the sugar in grape juice into alcohol and carbon dioxide, prompted by yeasts. Malolactic fermentation follows in some wines: malic acid is converted into lactic acid and carbon dioxide. The wine becomes softer and less acidic.

FERNÁNDEZ, ALEJANDRO *Spain, Castilla-León, Ribera del Duero, R*   Former village blacksmith Alejandro Fernández makes long-lived Pesquera (R) from grapes from his own vineyards and matured in new oak casks.

FERRARI *Italy, Trentino, Sp* Large Trento producer of *metodo classico* Sp wine: reliable.

FERREIRA *Portugal, port* Producer best known for aged tawnies: Duque de Bragança is among the finest 20-year-olds; the Quinta do Porto 10-year-old, rich and fruity, is also respected. Vintage wines are quite sweet, Portuguese-style.

FERRIÈRE, CH *France, Bordeaux, Médoc, Margaux, 3ème Cru Classé, R* Small classed-growth leased to CH LASCOMBES, where the wine is made. Though hard to find, it can be very good.

FETZER *USA, California, Mendocino, R, W* Sizeable yet good producer: Barrel Select Cabernet Sauvignon and Chardonnay are much admired. Sundial Chardonnay, fresh with pear and apple flavours, is good value for money. Bel Arbors is a 2nd label.

FEUILLATTE, NICOLAS *France, Champagne* Epernay house owned by 85 co-ops with some 4,000 members and 1,600ha of vines. Their best wine is the prestige *cuvée*, Palmes d'Or.

FÈVRE, WILLIAM *France, Burgundy, Chablis, W* With Dom de la Maladière, Fèvre is the most important owner of *Grand Cru* vineyards. The wines, made and aged in new oak, are austere in youth but with age gain wonderfully rich mineral flavours.

FIEFS DE LAGRANGE *France, Bordeaux, Médoc, St-Julien, R* 2nd wine of Ch Lagrange.

FIEFS VENDÉENS *France, Loire, VDQS, R, W* Vineyards near the Atlantic, south of the Loire, produce R wine from Gamay and Pinot Noir (at least 50%), plus Cabernet Franc and Cabernet Sauvignon. Also some W.

FIEUZAL, CH DE *France, Bordeaux, Pessac-Léognan, Cru Classé, R, W* Star estate in Léognan: the W sensational, though needing bottle-age. The burly R, with its black-cherry flavours and dense structure, can be superb.

FIGEAC, CH *France, Bordeaux, St-Emilion, 1er Grand Cru Classé, R* Among the area's most beautiful estates, lying towards the Pomerol border. Cabernet Sauvignon is approximately one-third of the blend: the wines are generally quite concentrated, yet supple and apppealing. Some vintages lack staying-power.

FILHOT, CH *France, Bordeaux, Sauternes, 2ème Cru Classé, W* Large estate which does well in favourable years, but lesser vintages can lack flair and excitement.

FILLIATREAU, PAUL *France, Loire, Saumur, R, W* Largest producer of Saumur-Champigny Rs. They include a Jeunes Vignes (vines under 50 years old), a Vieilles Vignes, and a special *cuvée*, Lena Filliatreau, from old vines on *silex* soil. Filliatreau also makes Saumur Blanc.

FINGER LAKES   *USA, New York State, VA*   Largest New York State wine zone, with 40 wineries and vineyards along the shores of the lakes. Good hybrid wines; and increasingly, classic-grape ones too: Chardonnay and Riesling Ws are good. Leading producers include: Canandaigua, Glenora, Knapp, Wagner.

FINKENAUER, WEINGUT CARL   *Germany, Nahe, W, R*   Dry wines with flavour and character, worth bottle-age, from one of the best estates in the Nahe, mostly Riesling.

FINO   *Spain*   A pale, dry sherry aged under *flor*.

FIRELANDS WINERY   *USA, Ohio, W, R*   The winery, on the Isle St George (VA) in Lake Erie, is enormously popular with tourists, focusing on Chardonnay, Cabernet Sauvignon and Gewürztraminer.

FIRESTONE   *USA, California, Santa Barbara and Southern California, R, W*   At his winery in the Santa Ynez Valley, Brooks Firestone focuses on apricoty Johannisberg Rieslings Ws (dry and sweet), a rose-perfumed Pinot Noir and a silky, lingering Merlot.

FITOU   *France, Midi, AOC, R*   Earliest appellation of the Midi, R only, made from Carignan, Grenache, Cinsaut, Syrah and Mourvèdre. Fitou has two zones: coastal Fitou-Maritime for lighter, less tannic wines, using a higher proportion of Mourvèdre; Fitou des Hautes Corbières has higher, drier vineyards with more Syrah – wines are sturdier and fuller-bodied. Leading producers include: Mont Tauch co-op, Ch de Nouvelles.

FITZ-RITTER, WEINGUT   *Germany, Pfalz, W, R*   Specialist in dry wines, typical of the Pfalz in their full-flavoured style.

FIXIN   *France, Burgundy, AOC, R*   Village at the north of the Côte de Nuits, with five *Premiers Crus*: powerful burgundies that can age well. Leading producers include: Dom Bart, Bruno Clair, Gelin, Juliet, Morion.

FLEUR CAILEAU, CH LA   *France, Bordeaux, Canon-Fronsac, R*   Small production but elegant and "correct" wine.

FLEUR-DE-GAY, CH LA   *France, Bordeaux, Pomerol, R*   Rare, expensive and superb all-Merlot wine made by Michel Rolland since 1982.

FLEUR-PÉTRUS, CH LA   *France, Bordeaux, Pomerol, R*   Pomerol's most perfumed, elegant wine, which begins to reach maturity in 5-6 years but in a really fine vintage will easily last for 20 years or more.

FLEURIE   *France, Burgundy, AOC, R*   Hilltop village at the heart of the Beaujolais *crus*: attractive, popular and expensive wines. Full of fruit and easy to drink when young, even better after two years. Leading producers include: Fleurie co-op, Dom de Fontabons, Dom de la Grand'Cour, Ch des Labourons, André Metrat, Dom du Pont du Jour.

FLOR *Spain* A particular type of yeast that develops on the surface of FINO sherry, protecting it from oxidation and giving it its distinctive flavour.

FLORIDA *USA* The climate is considered too warm for classic (vinifera) vines, but a handful of wineries make hybrid wines.

FOLIE, DOM DE LA *France, Burgundy, Chalonnais, R, W* One of the top producers of Rully, especially the white Premier Cru, Clos-St-Jacques.

FOLLE BLANCHE High-yielding, highly acidic white grape used for Gros Plant in Muscadet, and in blends in California.

FONPLÉGADE, CH *France, Bordeaux, St-Emilion, Grand Cru Classé, R* This relatively unknown *Grand Cru Classé* deserves greater recognition. Owned by Armand Moueix.

FONROQUE, CH *France, Bordeaux, St-Emilion, Grand Cru Classé, R* Not very well known, but Fonroque consistently produces very attractive, medium-term wines that are reasonably priced.

FONSALETTE, CH DE *France, Rhône, Côtes du Rhône R* Sharing the same owners as Ch RAYAS, this wine is made to the same high standards: possibly the best Côtes du Rhône of all.

FONSCOLOMBE, CH *France, Provence, Coteaux d'Aix-en-Provence, W, R* This 160-ha estate makes good-value, early-drinking wines, predominantly Rs, with a top-range Cuvée Spéciale made from Carignan with Cabernet Sauvignon, Grenache and Cinsaut, oak-matured.

FONSECA GUIMARAENS *Portugal, port* Some of the finest vintage ports, rich, plummy and generally quite sweet: quite different in style from parent company TAYLOR'S. There is also a single-quinta vintage, Quinta do Panascal. Best-known is the vintage-character Bin 27.

FONSECA INTERNACIONAL, J M DA *Portugal, P, Sp* Part of the Grand Metropolitan group, based in Setúbal, producing Lancers medium-dry, slightly sparkling P and the Sp Lancers Brut.

FONSECA SUCCESSORES, JOSÉ MARIA DA *Portugal, R* This Setúbal family firm, dating from 1834, makes Periquita, one of the country's most famous R wines. In the Dão, they select R and W wines from local cooperatives, which are then bottled under the Terras Altas label.

FONTANA CANDIDA *Italy, Southern Italy, Lazio, W* The biggest producer in the region, making predominantly Frascati. Part of the same group as BIGI of Orvieto. The basic Frascati Superiore is consistent, while the single-vineyard Casal Morena and Santa Teresa are among the best of the DOC.

FONTANAFREDDA *Italy, Piedmont, W, R, Sp* Large winery making *metodo classico* Sp wines, such as Contessa Rosa and Gattinera

Brut. Also top-quality, powerful Barolos from nine *crus*, with great ageing potential.

FONTENIL, CH *France, Bordeaux, Canon-Fronsac, R* Michel Rolland's winemaking has made this 90% Merlot wine a star: the 1989 is good, tasting of plums and spice, the 1990 better.

FOPPIANO *USA, California, Sonoma, R, W* Top-quality Cabernet Sauvignon and Chardonnay are sold under the Fox Mountain label, reasonably priced R and W are dubbed Foppiano Vineyards, and the lowest-priced varietals are labelled Riverside Farm.

FORST *Germany, Pfalz, W, R* One of the centres of the Pfalz region, with a name for Riesling Ws, steely and firm in character. Top vineyards include Jesuitengarten and Kirchenstück; leading growers include BASSERMAN-JORDAN, VON BUHL, BÜRKLIN-WOLF, FORSTER WINZERVEREIN (co-op).

FORSTER WINZERVEREIN *Germany, Pfalz, W* Top-quality, good-value wines, mostly Rieslings, come from this growers' co-op at Forst, a leading Pfalz village.

FORTIA, CH *France, Rhône, Châteauneuf-du-Pape, R, W* Highly traditional estate, known for its quality in poor vintages. It has recently been inherited: methods are changing, and the wine style may become more modern.

FORTIFIED WINES Wines to which brandy is added, usually before fermentation is complete. This preserves grape sugar, thus sweetness, in the wine, and adds to the alcohol level. Examples are PORT, SHERRY and VINS DOUX NATURELS.

FORTS DE LATOUR, LES *France, Bordeaux, Médoc, Pauillac, R* 2nd wine of Ch Latour.

FOURCAS-DUPRÉ, CH *France, Bordeaux, Listrac, Cru Bourgeois, R* Rich, gamey claret from the woods of Listrac.

FOURCAS-HOSTEN, CH *France, Bordeaux, Listrac, Cru Bourgeois, R* Serious wine from 40% Merlot. Deserves ageing to bring out the richness.

FOURCHAUME *France, Burgundy, Chablis, 1er Cru* Leading *Premier Cru* Chablis vineyard, facing southwest on the right bank of the River Serein, and thus next to the *Grands Crus*. Refined, charming wines. Vaupulent, Côte de Fontenay, L'Homme Mort and Vaulorent are plots within Fourchaume.

FOURMONE, DOM LA *France, Rhône, Vacqueyras, Gigondas, Côtes du Rhône, R* Roger Combe makes excellent, structured traditional wine in both appellations; also L'Oustau Fauquet, a Gigondas.

FRANCE, CH DE *France, Bordeaux, Pessac-Léognan R, W* Large Léognan estate, recently modernized, with simple though direct and fruity W and velvety, charming R.

FRANCIACORTA   *Italy, Lombardy, DOC, R, W, Sp*   This DOC blends Cabernet Franc, Barbera, Nebbiolo and Merlot for Rs; Ws are from Pinot Bianco and Chardonnay. The highly-regarded Sp includes some Pinot Nero. Leading producers include: Bellavista, Ca' del Bosco, Cavalleri.

FRANCO-ESPAÑOLAS, BODEGAS   *Spain, Rioja, R, W, P*   Part of the same group as Federico Paternina, this bodega makes a wide range of wines: some overtly fruity, others along more traditional, wood-aged lines.

FRANCS, CH DE   *France, Bordeaux, Côtes de Francs, R*   Investment from St-Emilion in an old estate is yielding delicious, fruity but well-structured wines.

FRANKEN   *Germany, Anbaugebeit, W, R*   Region at the heart of Germany, east of the Rhine, along the River Main. Cold winters and springs affect yields, but in warm years the W wines are characterful, intense and long-lasting. Traditionally, Silvaner is the local vine, but many others have been planted. Rs are in a minority. Franken uses a special, squat bottle: the *bocksbeutel*. Leading producers: *see* MAINDREIECK, WÜRZBURG.

FRANSCHHOEK   *South Africa, WO*   Settled by Huguenots three centuries ago and still retaining a distinctly French character, noticeable in its oak-aged wines and the country's best *Cap Classique* (traditional-method) Sp wine at Clos Cabrière. Leading producers include: Clos Cabrière, La Motte.

FRASCATI   *Italy, Lazio, DOC, W*   From the hills around Rome. Main varieties are Malvasia and Trebbiano. Can be very dull but the best are fresh with ripe fruit and a softly rounded palate. Leading producers include: Colli di Catone, Fontana Candida, Villa Simone, Conte Zandotti.

FREEMARK ABBEY   *USA, California, Napa, R, W*   Focuses on Chardonnay and Cabernet Sauvignon; the former makes floral, fruity, fresh Ws, the latter Rs that tend towards cedar, tobacco, cherry and tar, which in good years age remarkably well.

FREIXENET   *Spain, Catalonia, Sp*   This powerful Cava producer also owns a champagne house, Henri Abelé, and makes Sp wine in California. Quality is very high and their best-selling wine, Cordon Negro Brut, very good.

FRESCOBALDI   *Italy, Tuscany, Chianti, W, R, Sp*   Large producer with 500ha of vineyards in Chianti Rufina and Pomino areas. The Pomino Il Beneficio (W) is notable. Other wines include a reliable basic Chianti, Predicato *vini da tavola*, Sp wines and a Brunello di Montalcino.

FRIEDRICH-WILHELM-GYMNASIUM   *Germany, Mosel, W*   Old charitable estate at Trier with a good clutch of well-placed Riesling vineyards which yield traditional flowery, elegant Mosel wines.

FRIULI-VENEZIA GIULIA   *Italy*   In the north-eastern corner of Italy, a mountainous region enjoying a good reputation for crisp dry W wines and fresh, highly-scented Rs.

FRIZZANTE   *Italy*   Term meaning lightly sparkling.

FRONSAC   *France, Bordeaux, AOC, R*   Lighter in style than those from adjoining CANON-FRONSAC, these Rs are made in an area near Pomerol from Merlot, Cabernets Sauvignon and Franc and Malbec. Can be drunk from about two years after the vintage. Leading producers include: Ch'x Fontenil, Moulin Haut-Laroque, de la Rivière, Villars.

FRONTIGNAN, MUSCAT DE   *France, Midi, AOC, VDN*   Aromatic, golden, sweet *vin doux naturel* made entirely from Muscat Blanc à Petits Grains, the best Muscat grape, grown around the town of Frontignan in Languedoc. Leading producer: Ch de la Peyrade.

FUISSÉ, CH DE   *France, Burgundy, Mâconnais, W*   The leading producer of Pouilly-Fuissé. In quality terms more akin to a Côte d'Or wine than a more modest Mâconnais. Good ageing potential.

FUMÉ BLANC   Sauvignon Blanc synonym in California, New Zealand, Australia, South Africa.

FÜRST LÖWENSTEIN   *Germany, Franken, W, R*   Top Franken estate making Silvaner in the classic intense, earthy style, plus Rs.

FÜRSTLICHE CASTELL'SCHES WEINGUT   *Germany, Franken, W*   The largest private estate in Franken, making mostly dry wines, but also late-picked sweet ones when vintages allow.

G

GABILLIÈRE, DOM DE LA   *France, Loire, Touraine, W, R, P, Sp*   The experimental wine school in Amboise makes commercial quantities of high-quality wines from its 16ha of vineyards, notably a concentrated Sauvignon Blanc and a Crémant de Loire (W, Sp).

GAFFELIÈRE, CH LA   *France, Bordeaux, St-Emilion, 1er Grand Cru Classé, R*   The past history of this château was somewhat chequered, but things seem to be on track now. Medium-bodied wines with a good depth of fruit.

GAGNARD, DOM JEAN-NOEL   *France, Burgundy, Côte d'Or, R, W*   Extremely good producer with excellent Chassagne-Montrachets (W); the Rs are very good too.

GAILLAC   *France, South-West, AOC, R, P, W*   One of the most diverse appellations in South-West France. R Gaillac is usually based on the local Duras grape, blended either with local Fer Servadou and Syrah, or with Merlot and Cabernet; generally ready young. W Gaillac can be dry, sweet or *moelleux* (rich and soft); still, Sp (*mousseux*) or *perlé* (very slightly Sp). Sp wine is sometimes made as in Champagne and sometimes by traditional local methods. For Ws, Gaillac's oldest grape variety, Mauzac, can be blended with Loin de l'Oeil (Len de l'El), or with the standard Bordeaux varieties Sémillon and Sauvignon Blanc. A few villages have the appellation Gaillac Premières Côtes for rich, aromatic, sweet W wines. Leading producers include: Ch Clément-Termes, Dom de Labarthe, Cave de Labastide de Lévis co-op, Ch Larroze, Ch de Lastours, Mas Pignou, Técou co-op, Dom des Très Cantous.

GAJA   *Italy, Piedmont, R, W*   Leading Barbaresco producer, with wines including *crus* Sorì Tildìn, Sorì San Lorenzo and Costa Russi, Barolo and Barbera Vignarey. Also a wide range of R and W *vini da tavola*.

GALIL   *Israel, R, W*   This cool-climate area, rising from the Sea of Galilee to the Golan Heights, has been responsible for some very fine quality R and W wines from French varieties. Leading producers include: Golan Heights Winery.

GALISSONNIÈRE, CH DE LA   *France, Loire, Muscadet, W*   The Lusseauds' 30-ha vineyard produces Cuvée Philippe and Cuvée Anne. A GROS PLANT is called Cuvée Valérie. They also own Ch de la Jannière.

GALLANTIN, DOM LE   *France, Provence, Bandol, W, R, P*   Achille Pascal's speciality is his R wines. They are fermented at high temperature, bringing out the colour in the Mourvèdre grapes, and are both long-lived and among the richest in Bandol. A fresh, lively W and a P are also made.

GALLO   *USA, California, Central Valley, W, R, P, Sp*   The world's largest winery, selling 65 million cases a year, ranging from "pop" wines to oak-aged Chardonnay. Most wines are inexpensive but soundly made, though Sauvignon W has star quality.

GAMAY   The red Beaujolais grape, making light red wines with a simple ripe fruit character, mostly for drinking young. Also grown in central France, the Loire and California.

GAMOT, CLOS DE   *France, South-West, Cahors, R*   Old family estate with 100% Auxerrois vines (*see* CAHORS) making solid, tannic wines.

GANDINES, DOM DES   *France, Burgundy, Mâconnais, W*   Delicious fresh fruity Mâcon-Clessé, with some potential to age.

GARD, DU   *France, Vin de Pays, R, P*   The *vin de pays* name of the southern *département* of the Gard, used mostly for Rs.

GARDE, CH LA   *France, Bordeaux, Pessac-Léognan R, W*   Ancient estate recently renovated. Its top Rs, labelled Réserve, are aged in new oak: rich and silky, they can be drunk young but will age. Quality is impressive and prices sensible. Small amount of elegant W from pure Sauvignon Blanc.

GARNACHA/GRENACHE   Spain's (and the world's) most widely planted red-wine grape, Garnacha Tinta/Grenache Noir grows well in hot, dry climates, and is used for blending and for good, fruity P. R wine can be good with careful winemaking. Found in the southern Rhône, Provence, Corsica, Midi, California, Australia, South Africa.

GARRAFEIRA   *Portugal*   Wine (R) from an exceptional vintage that has been matured for at least two years before bottling, with a further year in bottle prior to sale.

GASSMANN, ROLLY   *France, Alsace, W, R*   Well-known winemaker: his wines are rich, with high levels of residual sugar. They include an excellent Muscat Moenchreben (from a single vineyard in Rorschwihr, not the *Grand Cru* in Eichhoffen), a well-regarded Auxerrois, and some good *cuvées*, such as Réserve Rolly Gassmann, from the classic varieties.

GATINOIS   *France, Champagne*   Tiny, quality-conscious firm with 7ha of vineyard at Ay, all of which is *Grand Cru*.

GATTINARA   *Italy, Piedmont, DOCG, R*   Principally made from Nebbiolo, this robust R wine, not dissimilar to Barolo, needs a long time in bottle. Leading producers include: Antoniolo, Luigi Dessilani, Luigi & Italo Nervi.

GAUNOUX, DOM MICHEL   *France, Burgundy, Côte d'Or, R*   Very traditional domaine, specializing in long-lived Pommards.

GAVI *Italy, Piedmont, DOC, W, Sp* From the Cortese grape, crisp and fruity, with hints of lime. Still wines can be quite full, with a silky texture. Best consumed within two years of the vintage, although the finest can last longer. Sp wines are also made. Leading producers include: Michele Chiarlo, La Scolca.

GEELONG *Australia, Victoria* This region of plains and gentle slopes is well suited to fragrant Pinot Noir and Chardonnay. Leading producers include: Bannockburn, Clyde Park, Idyll, Prince Albert, Scotchmans Hill.

GEISENHEIM *Germany, Rheingau, W* Wine village and home of the famous Geisenheim research and teaching college, which has influenced winemaking in Germany and around the world. Also a source of good Riesling Ws from (among others) the Kläuserweg and Rothenberg vineyards.

GENEVA *Switzerland* This Swiss canton has 1,500ha under vine. Half the production is W, mainly from the Chasselas grape (local name Perlan) but also some Aligoté and Chardonnay and light R from the Gamay grape.

GENEVRIÈRES, LES *France, Burgundy, Côte de Beaune, 1er Cru, R* Meursault vineyard which produces highly attractive wines with elegance and finesse. Leading producers include: Louis Latour, Michelot-Buisson.

GENTILE, DOM *France, Corsica, Patrimonio, W, R* This is a new estate reviving old local traditions: R, P and both dry and Muscat-based sweet Ws are made.

GEORGIA *USA* Nearly all the vines grown here are natives or hybrids, but some ambitious experiments may raise the profile of wines from classic *vinifera* vines.

GERMAIN, DOM JACQUES *France, Burgundy, Côte d'Or, R, W* Vineyards in both Chorey-lès-Beaune and Beaune. Very classy, elegant wines.

GERMAIN, HENRI & FILS *France, Champagne* Linked with Bricout and based at Rilly-la-Montagne, with 90ha of vines. Good value, well-made champagne.

GEVREY-CHAMBERTIN *France, Burgundy, AOC, R* Côte de Nuits village with 9 *Grands Crus* (see **CHAMBERTIN**) and 28 *Premiers Crus*. The best Gevrey-Chambertin is powerful, fruity and tannic in character, but not all the wine is worthy of the village name. Leading producers include: Bachelet, Bruno Clair, Drouhin, Dujac, Faiveley, Labouré-Roi, Rousseau.

GEWÜRZTRAMINER In German, *"gewürz"* means spicy, which describes this grape's distinctive aroma; when well made, from ripe fruit, akin to lychees, mangoes or ripe grapefruit. Good examples are fround in Alsace and Baden; the variety is also grown in northern Italy, Austria, eastern Europe, California and New Zealand (sometimes as Traminer).

GEYSER PEAK *USA, California, Sonoma, W, R* Australian wine-maker Daryl Groom makes a brisk, delightful dry W Sémillon/Chardonnay blend at this Geyserville winery. Reserve Alexandre is a complex Meritage R.

GIESEN ESTATE *New Zealand, South Island, W* Canterbury's largest wine estate. The botrytized, late-harvest Rieslings are top quality; also good Chardonnay and Sauvignon Blanc.

GIGONDAS *France, Rhône, AOC, R, P* Some very good R and P wines are made in this southern Rhône area, mainly from Grenache, with Syrah and Mourvèdre. Leading producers include: Dom's des Goubert, des Pallières, Raspail-Ay, St-Gayan.

GIPPSLAND *Australia, Victoria* Flat, often parched, landscape, dotted with small vineyards. Low yields help the production of fine Chardonnay and a few magnificent Pinot Noirs. Leading producers include: Bass Phillip, Briagolong, McAlister, Nicholson River.

GISBORNE *New Zealand, North Island* Historically a bulk wine zone but now regarded as a W wine area with Müller-Thurgau the main variety. Currently promoted as the "Chardonnay capital of New Zealand".

GISCOURS, CH *France, Bordeaux, Médoc, Margaux, 3ème Cru Classé, R* One of the success stories of Margaux, a big estate rescued from dereliction, modernized, extended and replanted. Excellent in the 1970s but less consistent since, apart from the fine 1986 and good 1988, 1989. Style is forward, fruity and attractive.

GITTON PÈRE ET FILS *France, Loire, Sancerre & Pouilly-Fumé, W, R* Vineyard differences are emphasized in this firm's bottlings of ten Sancerres and five Pouilly-Fumés. Its cellars are in Sancerre. Barrel fermentation of the whites gives them strong characters.

GIVRY *France, Burgundy, AOC, R, W* Côte Chalonnaise village noted for its Pinot Noir wine – a powerful, somewhat rustic R, but capable of improvement in bottle for 4–6 years. Leading producers include: Jean-François Delorme, Dom du Gardin-Clos Salomon, Dom Joblot, Louis Latour, Dom Ragot, Dom Thénard.

GLEN ELLEN *USA, California, Sonoma, R, W* The winery made a splash with its affordable Proprietor's Reserve Chardonnay and Cabernet Sauvignon, and makes a quality Sauvignon Blanc. Inventive treatments of unusual R grapes such as Aleatico, Trousseau, Syrah and Cabernet Franc.

GLENORA WINE CELLARS *USA, New York, Fin-ger Lakes, W, R, Sp* The winery emphasizes classic varieties, with grapes from its own vineyard and from local growers. Wines include fine, balanced Riesling; rich, barrel-fermented Reserve Chardonnay; and outstanding *méthode champenoise* Sp (blends of the classic Champagne varities Chardonnay and Pinot Noir).

GLENROWAN *Australia, Victoria* In north-eastern Victoria, better known as Milawa. Glenrowan has an excellent reputation for dessert wines. Leading producers include: Brown Brothers.

GLORIA, CH *France, Bordeaux, St-Julien, Cru Bourgeois, R* One of the success stories of the Médoc, this 48-ha vineyard did not exist until the 1940s. The late Henri Martin assembled the land from small plots bought all around the commune. Despite this the wine gained, and has kept, a fine reputation. Not for long keeping, though the great vintages can be superb.

GOLAN HEIGHTS WINERY *Israel, Galil, R, W* Collectively owned by eight local settlements, this cool-climate winery produces good-quality R and W wines from French varieties. Has three ranges which, in increasing order of quality, are named Gamla, Golan, Yarden. All wines are kosher.

GONZALEZ BYASS *Spain, sherry* Formidable-quality sherries. From spectacular *bodegas* (the shell-shaped La Concha was designed by Eiffel) come the top-of-the-range fino, Tio Pepe, and La Concha amontillado, from 100-year-old *soleras*. Its very old wines – Amontillado del Duque, the dry oloroso Apostoles and the Matusalem sweet oloroso – are some of the finest sherries made.

GOSSET *France, Champagne* An old firm, but a GRANDE MARQUE only since 1992. Family-owned, with an excellent name for wines which age very well in bottle and are not released until several years old. Both the Grande Réserve and Grand Millésime are excellent.

GOULAINE, MARQUIS DE *France, Loire, Muscadet, W* The Ch de Goulaine was founded over 1,000 years ago. The 31-ha vineyard, plus some bought-in wine, produces a prestige Cuvée du Millénaire and a GROS PLANT. Around one-third is bottled *sur lie*.

GOULBURN VALLEY *Australia, Victoria* Centred around the town of Tabilk. Best wines include Shiraz (R), long-lived Cabernet Sauvignon and powerful Riesling. Leading producers include: Mitchelton, Château Tahbilk.

GOURBERTS, DOM DES *France, Rhône, W, R* Family estate making good Gigondas R, an unusual Côtes du Rhône W from Viognier, and Côtes du Rhône-Villages (R and W). All Rs are made with structure to age.

GOURGAZAUD, CH DE *France, Midi, Minervois, R* Roger Piquet, former MD of the *négociant* company Chantovent, experiments with different grape varieties. He first planted Syrah here in the Midi village of La Livinière as far back as 1974.

GRAACH *Germany, Mosel, W* Famous village of the middle Mosel, with vineyards on the great southwest-facing slope upon which also lie ZELTINGEN and WEHLEN. Graach's top vineyards are Domprobst and Himmelreich; leading growers include J A Prüm, S A Prüm, Richter and Wegeler.

GRAF ADELMANN, WEINGUT *Germany, Württemberg, R, W* Top estate of this little-known region, making good Rs in an international style with *barrique*-ageing.

GRAF VON SCHÖNBORN, WEINGUT *Germany, Franken, W* This estate makes typical, traditional Franken Ws with plenty of concentration and flavour.

GRÄFLICH WOLFF-METTERNICH'SCHES WEINGUT *Germany, Baden, W, R* Dry wines in the flavourful Baden style, both Ws (from Grauburgunder and Weissburgunder) and also Rs.

GRAHAM, W & J *Portugal, port* Graham's, based at Quinta de Malvedos, is part of the SYMINGTON group. Rich, sweet wines.

GRAILLOT, ALAIN *France, Rhône, Crozes-Hermitage, R, W* Excellent wines from a patchy appellation: the W is especially good, the R ages well, especially the La Guirande *cuvée*.

GRAMONT, DOM MACHARD DE *France, Burgundy, Côte d'Or, R* Domaine at Nuits-St-Georges using traditional methods, with the emphasis on retaining the individual style of each *cru*.

GRAMPIANS *Australia, Victoria* This area is noted mainly for high-quality Shiraz (R), fleshy Cabernet Sauvignon and peachy Chardonnay. Leading producers include: Best's, Montara, Mount Langi Ghiran, Seppelt Great Western.

GRAN RESERVA *Spain* Red wines, made only in particularly good vintages, that must have spent at least two years in *barricas* (BARRIQUES) and three in bottle.

GRAND CHAMPAGNE NAPOLEON *France, Champagne* This family-owned house is the least known of the GRANDES MARQUES and one of the smallest. Produces top-quality wines, especially the vintages.

GRAND CRU *France* Top-quality French wine: the term is used differently in Bordeaux, Burgundy, Champagne and Alsace.

GRAND MOULAS, CH DU *France, Rhône, Côtes du Rhône, R* Lighter, modern style of R with freshness, fruit and no need to age. The Cuvée de l'Ecu is Syrah.

GRAND ROUSSILLON *France, Midi, AOC, VDN, R, P, W* Rarely-seen *vin doux naturel*, similar to RIVESALTES.

GRAND TINEL, DOM DU *France, Rhône, Châteauneuf-du-Pape, R* Fine R Châteauneuf comes from Elie Jeune's reticent estate.

GRAND VIN *France* The best, or first, wine of a château.

GRAND-MAYNE, CH *France, Bordeaux, St-Emilion, Grand Cru Classé, R* Bought by French insurance giant AXA in the late 1980s, this property should do well under the careful guidance of Jean-Michel Cazes of LYNCH-BAGES.

GRAND-PUY-DUCASSE, CH *France, Bordeaux, Médoc, Pauillac, 5ème Cru Classé, R* New owners have bought more land and have renovated the château, which is in the town of Pauillac, away from the vineyard. Consistent and classic Pauillac, often good value.

GRAND-PUY-LACOSTE, CH *France, Bordeaux, Médoc, Pauillac, 5ème Cru Classé, R* The Borie family, owners of DUCRU-BEAUCAILLOU (St-Julien), took over in 1980 to modernize, improve, and conjure still better wine from the excellent vineyard on the Bages plateau. Style is fruity yet well-structured. A good 1993. 2nd wine: Lacoste-Borie.

GRANDE MARQUE *France* One of the champagne-producing firms belonging to the Institut de Grandes Marques de Champagne. Most – but not all – of the 28 members are the leading champagne houses of today.

GRANDE RUE, LA *France, Burgundy, AOC, R* Côte de Nuits *Grand Cru*, newly-promoted, in Vosne-Romanée.

GRANDS ECHÉZEAUX *France, Burgundy, AOC, R* This *Grand Cru* is smaller than, and reckoned superior to, ECHÉZEAUX. Its wines take even longer to mature. Leading producers include: Joseph Drouhin, Dom de la Romanée-Conti.

GRANDS ÉPENOTS, LES *France, Burgundy, Côte de Beaune, 1er Cru, R* Top Pommard vineyard producing wines of great concentration and structure which age very well. Leading producers include: Michel Gaunoux.

GRANGENEUVE, DOM DE *France, Rhône, Coteaux De Tricastin, R* Elegant and interesting Rs are made here: Grangeneuve is the leading maker of this AOC.

GRATIEN MEYER SEYDOUX *France, Loire, Saumur, Sp: W, P* One of the largest producers of sparkling Saumur, and the only one founded by a Champagne house, Alfred Gratien. Its top wine, Cuvée Flamme (P, W) is a blend of older wines, usually given some bottle-age before release.

GRATIEN, ALFRED *France, Champagne* Traditional house where some wood is still used. Their NV special *cuvée* is mainly Pinot Meunier: quite full-bodied with youthful appeal. Vintage wines last remarkably well.

GRAUBÜNDEN *Switzerland* This canton has 376ha under vine, almost all Blauburgunder (Pinot Noir) which, in a good year, produces full, soft wines, ideal for drinking within two years or so of the vintage.

GRAUBURGUNDER See PINOT GRIS.

GRAVES DE VAYRES *France, Bordeaux, AOC, R, W* From gravel sites beside the Dordogne, in the north of the Entre-Deux-Mers zone.

GRAVES *France, Bordeaux, AOC, R, W* Huge region and appellation south of the city of Bordeaux, with a sub-zone, PESSAC-LÉOGNAN, for fine R and dry W wine. Sauternes, the celebrated sweet W wine, is an enclave within Graves. Graves AOC is for R and dry W wines. The R wines are earthy, supple and appealing, with in richer years hints of black cherries, tobacco or chocolate. Cabernet Sauvignon is the dominant R-wine variety, although in the southern Graves, Merlot is more plentiful, giving wines that evolve more rapidly. W Graves, from Sauvignon Blanc and Sémillon, can be rich, oaky, well-structured wine, delicious in youth but improving in bottle for 10 years or more. Graves Supérieures is W – dry, medium or sweet – with slightly higher alcohol. Leading AOC Graves producers include: Ch d'Archambeau, Clos Bourgelat, Ch de Chantegrive, Ch L'Etoile, Clos Floridène, Dom La Grave, Ch Landiras, Ch Magence, Ch Montalivet, Ch Rahoul.

GREATER CANBERRA *Australia, New South Wales* Australia's Capital Territory enjoys a continental climate, so vineyards are at high altitudes. Cabernet Sauvignon, Riesling and Chardonnay are the best wines. Leading producers include: Brindabella, Doonkuna, Helm's, Lark Hill.

GREEN VALLEY SONOMA COUNTY *USA, California, VA* One of the two sub-zones within Russian River, on the cooler, ocean side of the VA a mere 10 miles from the Pacific. Mainly Chardonnay and Pinot Noir.

GRENACHE See GARNACHA.

GRENOUILLES *France, Burgundy, Chablis, Grand Cru* The smallest *Grand Cru*, making solid, perfumed wines. The vineyard is shared by LOUIS MICHEL, JEAN-PAUL DROIN and LA CHABLISIENNE cooperative.

GRES ST-PAUL, CH DU *France, Midi, Coteaux du Languedoc R; Lunel VDN* The principal independent producer in Lunel takes immense care to retain the freshness and grapiness which is the hallmark of fine Muscat de Lunel. Also known for their R Coteaux de Languedoc: warm and fruity, for early drinking.

GRESSER, DOM ANDRÉ & RÉMY *France, Alsace, W, R* Old-established (1667) company with a young, vibrant image. Reputation founded on *Grands Crus* Rieslings, Brandhof Pinot Noir and Andlau Gewürztraminer.

GRESSIER-GRAND-POUJEAUX, CH *France, Bordeaux, Moulis, Cru Bourgeois, R* Here the good gravel soil yields traditional wines that need plenty of time.

GRESY, MARCHESI DI *Italy, Piedmont, R* Maker of modern-style single-vineyard Barbarescos: Martinenga, Camp Gros and Gaiun.

GRÈVES, LES   *France, Burgundy, Côte de Beaune, 1er Cru, R*   Vineyard in the northern half of the Beaune appellation, producing elegant wines with good structure and length. Leading producers include: Bouchard Père & Fils, Michel Lafarge, Louis Latour, Tollot-Beaut.

GREYSAC, CH   *France, Bordeaux, Médoc, Cru Bourgeois, R*   Large, well-run, recently-developed estate: sound, enjoyable wine.

GRGICH HILLS   *USA, California, Napa, W, R*   Miljenko "Mike" Grgich is noted for his generous, well-proportioned Chardonnays. Also Cabernet Sauvignon and Zinfandel Rs, and Sauvignon and Johannisberg Riesling Ws.

GRILLET, CH   *France, Rhône, AOC, W*   Small, single-château AOC amid the **CONDRIEU** vineyards of the Northern Rhône. Viognier grapes make serious, concentrated W: however, some Condrieus are better and much cheaper.

GRIÑÓN, MARQUÉS DE   *Spain, Castilla-León, Rueda, R, W*   The personable Carlos Falco, Marqués de Griñon, makes an outstanding Cabernet Sauvignon-based R wine under his own name. Also an attractive W wine.

GRIOTTE-CHAMBERTIN   See CHAMBERTIN.

GRIPA, BERNARD   *France, Rhône, St-Joseph R, W; St-Péray W*   Maker of reliable R St-Joseph, and Ws from both St-Joseph and from the little zone of St-Péray.

GRIPPAT, JEAN-LOUIS   *France, Rhône, St-Joseph R, W; Hermitage R*   One of the best R St-Josephs is Grippat's Hospices *cuvée*: both this and his standard wine need bottle-age.

GRIVOT, DOM JEAN   *France, Burgundy, Côte d'Or, R*   Devotee of the ACCAD method, with wines that age well but are not too austere in youth. Very fine *Grands* and *Premiers Crus*.

GROENESTEYN, SCHLOSS   *Germany, Rheingau, W, R*   One of the grand old estates of the Rheingau, 600 years old, today making wood-aged Rieslings in the traditional style that stress natural sweetness, in contrast to the CHARTA dry wines.

GROOT CONSTANTIA   *South Africa, Constantia, R, W*   Established in 1685, this is the Cape's most historic winery. Until 1993 it was Government-owned and run but is now in the hands of a Trust. Their best wine is a bordeaux blend, Gouverneurs Réserve.

GROS PLANT   *France, Loire, VDQS, W*   Dry W from the Muscadet region, made from Folle Blanche grapes: very acidic; good (if the vintage was warm) with local seafood. Sometimes called Gros Plant du Pays Nantais. Leading producer: Les Vignerons de la Noëlle co-op.

GRUAUD-LAROSE, CH   *France, Bordeaux, Médoc, St-Julien, 2ème Cru Classé, R*   This large vineyard has made fashionable and consistent wine for 250 years. In 1815 the Bordeaux *négociant* Lawton described Larose as "substantial, yet fragrant and mellow" – this is still true. The wine needs time to mature. 2nd wine: Sarget de Gruaud-Larose.

GRÜNER VELTLINER   White grape from Austria, making light, peppery wines with firm acidity. Nearly always for drinking young, though in the Wachau region they can be as powerful and long-lived as Rieslings. Also found in the Czech Republic.

GUEBERSCHWIHR   *France, Alsace*   Village producing good Muscat and Riesling. *Grand Cru* Goldert is known for Gewürztraminer as well. Leading producers include: Zind Humbrecht.

GUEBWILLER   *France, Alsace*   With more *Grands Crus* (Kessler, Kitterlé, Saering and Spiegel) than any other village, Guebwiller is famous for Gewürztraminer, Pinot Gris and Riesling. Leading producers include: Schlumberger.

GUENOC   *USA, California, Lake, W, R*   Vineyard overlapping Lake and Napa counties. Langtry Red is a MERITAGE blend of blackcurrant suppleness; Langtry White is oily with olive and licorice. Distinctive Reserve Chardonnay, with rich yet restrained creamy lemon fruit.

GUFFENS-HEYNEN, DOM   *France, Burgundy, Mâconnais, R, W*   Produces top quality Pouilly-Fuissé and Mâcon, which improve with some bottle-age.

GUIGAL, MARCEL   *France, Rhône, R*   Top producer of Côte Rôtie, including the highly expensive special *cuvées* Mouline, Landonne and Turque. His Syrah-dominated Côtes du Rhône is excellent value.

GUIRAUD, CH   *France, Bordeaux, Sauternes, 1er Cru Classé, W*   Restored in the 1980s, this large estate makes Sauternes in a rich, ample style, a creamy confection of peaches and oak.

GUNDERLOCH, WEINGUT   *Germany, Rheinhessen, W, R*   Quality-conscious estate at Nackenheim on the famous, and favoured, Rheinterrasse hillside. Their Riesling wines are full of flavour and local character.

GUNTRUM, WEINGUT LOUIS   *Germany, Rheinhessen, W*   Powerful, fruity, good-value wines with real varietal character from Riesling, Silvaner, Scheurebe etc.

GURGUE, CH LA   *France, Bordeaux, Margaux, Cru Bourgeois, R*   Small vineyard sited just west of Ch Margaux. In the same ownership as Ch CHASSE-SPLEEN and much improved as a result.

GUTEDEL   See CHASSELAS.

H

HAAG, FRITZ *Germany, Mosel, W* Small but top-quality estate making fine, typical Rieslings including a good-value QBA blended from several vineyards.

HAIGHT VINEYARDS *USA, Connecticut, W, Sp* This small hillside vineyard makes Chardonnay, a blend under the Recolte label and a little Sp Blanc de Blancs by the *méthode champenoise*.

HALBTROCKEN *Germany* Term for medium-dry wine.

HAMILTON RUSSELL *South Africa, Walker Bay, R, W* Top-quality Pinot Noir is produced at this coastal winery established over a decade ago by Tim Hamilton Russell. Ws include a good Chardonnay, and an unusual Chardonnay/Sauvignon Blanc blend.

HARGRAVE VINEYARDS *USA, New York, Long Island, R, W* Founded in 1973, this north-coast winery enjoys most success with Rs, notably Cabernet Sauvignon, a good Merlot and Cabernet Franc; its best W, Chardonnay, is slightly inconsistent. Also Sauvignon, Johannisberg Riesling, Gewürztraminer and Pinot Noir.

HARVEY, JOHN *Spain, sherry* The biggest sherry producer. Major brands include all the Harvey sherries (among them the world's biggest seller, Bristol Cream), and the top-quality 1796 range (including a good **PALO CORTADO**).

HATTENHEIM *Germany, Rheingau, W* Town and vineyard centre on the Rhine, with vines in some of the best Rheingau sites. Up the hill is the **STEINBERG**, the famous vineyard of the State Domain, and Kloster Eberbach, the ancient monastery and centre of German wine studies. Leading producers include: Schloss Reinhartshausen, von Simmern, Schönborn.

HAULLER, J, & FILS *France, Alsace, W, R* Relatively large producer of good-value wines from all the Alsace varieties. It stresses Sylvaner, but the best wines include Gewürztraminer *Grand Cru* Frankstein and several Rieslings.

HAUNER, CARLO *Italy, Sicily, W* Painter, architect, designer and winemaker Carlo Hauner makes amber-coloured, aromatic Malvasia delle Lipari and a Catarratto-based dry W wine.

HAUT-BAGES LIBÉRAL, CH *France, Bordeaux, Médoc, Pauillac, 5ème Cru Classé, R* The vineyard is well-placed, with a parcel next to Latour. Modernization and replanting are bringing results: this is now classic Cabernet Sauvignon-flavoured Pauillac. Good vintages (such as 1985, 1986) are long keepers.

HAUT-BAGES-AVÉROUS *France, Bordeaux, Médoc, Pauillac, R* 2nd wine of Ch Lynch-Bages.

HAUT-BAILLY, CH *France, Bordeaux, Pessac-Léognan, Cru Classé, R* Firm and elegant, with discreet oak, this R can be enjoyed early but can age well. Often successful in lesser vintages.

HAUT-BATAILLEY, CH *France, Bordeaux, Médoc, Pauillac, 5ème Cru Classé, R* Run by the Borie family (*see* Ch GRAND-PUY-LACOSTE), a modest-sized property with no château but with a growing name for good wine that matures quickly.

HAUT-BRION, CH *France, Bordeaux, Pessac-Léognan, 1er Grand Cru Classé (1855), R, W* In the commune of Pessac, the sole red *Premier Grand Cru* of the Graves. A wine of breed and consistency, it became more forward and voluptuous by the mid-1980s. Even in modest years (eg 1987, 1991) it produces perfumed, elegant wines. Small quantities of excellent W are made, but are released only in top years. Their Bahans-Haut-Brion (R) is one of the best 2nd wines in Bordeaux.

HAUT-MACO, CH *France, Bordeaux, Côtes de Bourg, R* Reliable quality Rs from a vineyard with (unusually) mostly Cabernet Franc.

HAUT-MARBUZET, CH *France, Bordeaux, St-Estèphe, Cru Bourgeois, R* Well-placed vines, new oak and competent winemaking produce well-regarded deep-coloured and high-flavoured wines.

HAUT-MÉDOC *France, Bordeaux, AOC, R* Southern Médoc appellation covering most vineyards outside Listrac, Moulis, and the more famous communes of St-Estèphe, Pauillac, St-Julien and Margaux; the wines represent good value. Leading producers include: Ch'x Belgrave, de Camensac, Cantemerle, Cissac, Citran, La Lagune, La Tour-Carnet.

HAUT-MONTRAVEL See MONTRAVEL.

HAUT POITOU *France, Loire, VDQS, R, P, W* Gamay, Cabernet Franc and Cabernet Sauvignon Rs and Ps, Sauvignon Blanc and Chardonnay Ws, produced in a zone to the south of the main Loire vineyards. Leading producer: Haut Poitou co-op.

HAUT-SERRE, CHDE *France, South-West, Cahors, R* See VIGOUROUX.

HAUX, CH *France, Bordeaux, 1er Côtes de Bordeaux, R* The large vineyard and new facilities, combined with *barrique*-ageing and modern methods, make prize-winning and attractive claret.

HAWKE'S BAY *New Zealand, North Island* On the east coast of the North Island, a pioneering area. Chardonnay is widely planted, then Müller-Thurgau and Sauvignon. Also top quality Rs. Leading producers include: Esk Valley, Mills Reef, Pask, Te Mata, Vidal, Waimarama.

HEGER, WEINGUT DR   *Germany, Baden, W, R*   Top Baden estate, with a range of fine and age-worthy wines, all dry, including Spätburgunder Rs, Weissburgunder and Riesling Ws and others. Cheaper, good-value wines are sold under the Joachim Heger label.

HEIDSIECK MONOPOLE   *France, Champagne*   This house is a GRANDE MARQUE, but is not among the leaders. The NV is called Dry Monopole; their best is the fruity Diamant Bleu.

HEIDSIECK, CHARLES   *France, Champagne*   Bought by Rémy Cointreau in the mid-1980s and completely transformed by winemaker Daniel Thibault. The NV *brut réserve* is one of the best on the market: rich, weighty, with a lot of Pinot Meunier plus some reserve wines.

HEITLINGER, WEINGUT ALBERT   *Germany, Baden, W, R*   One of the leaders in Baden of the "burgundy style", with oak-aged, dry wines, both R and W, from Spätburgunder, Weissburgunder and Grauburgunder.

HEITZ CELLARS   *USA, California, Napa, R*   Joe Heitz's winery south-east of St Helena, where his son David handles the wine-making, is famous for one of California's most revered red wines: Martha's Vineyard Cabernet Sauvignon, identified by its euca-lyptus scent and classic structure.

HENRIOT   *France, Champagne*   GRANDE MARQUE owned by the LVMH group. Unusually, almost entirely supplied from its own vineyards. The NV Souverain Brut is a Chardonnay-dominated, richly fruity medium-weight wine.

HENRIQUES & HENRIQUES   *Portugal, Madeira*   This is the largest firm outside the MADEIRA WINE COMPANY, and a considerable (for Madeira) landowner. As well as its own wines, it makes HARVEYS' own-label madeiras, and ranges for other wine mer-chants. It also owns other brands: Belem and Casa dos Vinhos de Madeira.

HENSCHKE   *Australia, South Australia, Eden Valley, R, W*   One of the country's greatest small wineries. Founded in 1868, it makes a wide range of outstanding wines, led by the velvety Hill of Grace Shiraz (R), from 120-year-old vines.

HÉRAULT, DE L'   *France, Vin de Pays, R, P, W*   Wines from the prolific vineyards of the south: most is attractive, good-value R, but some seri-ous estates (such as DAUMAS GASSAC) use the name on their wines, as do modern-minded large-scale producers such as Dom de la Baume.

HERMITAGE/ERMITAGE   *France, Rhône, AOC, R, W*   Both R and W wines have been famous since the 17th century. Syrah is the sole permitted grape for Rs; at first the wines can be tough, but after 8

120

years in bottle they begin to reveal a sublimely sensuous fruit. The Ws, from Marsanne or Roussanne or both, are astonishingly long-lived. Leading producers include: Chapoutier, Gérard Chave, Delas Frères, Guigal, Jaboulet.

HERTZ, ALBERT   *France, Alsace, W, R*   Relative newcomer, but already considered to be among the best Pinot Noir producers in the region. The wine is elegant and well-balanced. Gewürztraminer and Riesling Ws are also top quality.

HESSEN, WEINGUT PRINZ VON   *Germany, Rheingau, R, W*   This reliable Riesling specialist, with good vineyards in the Rheingau, stresses late-picked and sweet (rather than Charta-style dry) wines.

HESSISCHE BERGSTRASSE   *Germany, Anbaugebiet, W*   Small wine region specializing in Riesling Ws with flavour and charm, though they are not wines to age. Leading producers: Weingut der Stadt Bensheim, Bergsträsser cooperative, Staatsweingut Bergstrasse.

HEYL ZU HERRNSHEIM, WEINGUT   *Germany, Rheinhessen, W*   One of the top Riesling estates in Germany, with land in the best vineyards of Nierstein. Most wines are dry; all (including the Silvaners and Weissburgunders) show real breed and character, balancing acidity and fruit.

HEYMAN-LÖWENSTEIN   *Germany, Mosel, W*   Small estate at Winningen making spicy, fruity Rieslings.

HIDALGO, VINICOLA   *Spain, sherry*   Manzanilla La Gitana is the most famous wine from this family-owned Sanlúcar *bodega*. Even the amontillados and olorosos have a light, Sanlúcar character, though they also make a heavier Jerez fino.

HOCHHEIM   *Germany, Rheingau, W*   Set apart from the rest of the Rheingau, a village which gave its name to "hock" – the English word for Rhine wine. Today's Hochheim wine is solid, long-lasting yet full Riesling. The top vineyard is Domdechaney. Leading producers include: Aschrott'sche Erben, Ress, Staatsweingut, Werner.

HOFSTÄTTER, J   *Italy, Alto Adige, W, R*   Fine Alto Adige Pinot Nero, notable Gewürztraminer and excellent *vini da tavola*: Yngram Rosso and Yngram Bianco, from this estate.

HOGUE CELLARS   *USA, Washington State, W, R*   The Hogues run a large mixed farm and a 240,000-case winery near Prosser (Yakima Valley), producing a silky W Sémillon, some minty R Merlots, and Rs from Cabernet Sauvignon and Cabernet Franc.

HOMME MORT, L'   *France, Burgundy, Chablis, 1er Cru*   See FOUR-CHAUME.

HOSPICES DE BEAUNE   *France, Burgundy, Côte d'Or, R, W*   The Hospice charity dates from 1443. Now an important vineyard owner whose wines are sold annually at a dramatic auction in

November: this event sets benchmark prices for the Burgundy vintage as a whole. Wines, from named *cuvées* throughout the CÔTE DE BEAUNE, are reliable, if expensive.

HOSPICES DE NUITS-ST-GEORGES, DOM DES   *France, Burgundy, Côte d'Or, R, W*   Small brother of the HOSPICES DE BEAUNE, with top vineyard sites in Nuits.

HOSTENS-PICANT, CH   *France, Bordeaux, Ste-Foy-Bordeaux, R, Entre-Deux-Mers, W*   Newly-revived estate in the eastern corner of Bordeaux region, making good-value, well-constructed R and W.

HÖVEL, WEINGUT VON   *Germany, Saar, W*   Traditional Saar estate, making Riesling wines which (in warm years) reach Auslese levels and above.

HOWELL MOUNTAIN   *USA, California, Napa, VA*   Hill vineyards above Napa Valley which yield fine Zinfandel and Cabernet Sauvignon (Dunn's).

HUDSON RIVER VALLEY   *USA, New York State, VA*   Wine zone north of New York City with 20 wineries, growing hybrid wines plus (increasingly) Chardonnay and Cabernet. Leading producers include: Benmarl, Clinton, Millbrook, Rivendell.

HUET, GASTON   *France, Loire, Vouvray, W, Sp*   The Le Mont vineyard has been recognized as a top Vouvray since the 1600s. Its wines, together with those from Le Haut-Lieu and Clos de Bourg, are made and sold separately. Huet makes Sp and sweet wines, with only a little still dry wine.

HUGEL & FILS   *France, Alsace, W, R*   The 13th generation since 1639 now runs this, the most famous Alsace house. Reliability is the keynote. Gewürztraminer and Pinot Blanc de Blancs are good in the basic range; Cuvée Tradition and Jubilée Réserve Personnelle are superior qualities. Hugel virtually invented, and leads in, *vendange tardive* wines; in its *sélections des grains nobles* the Pinot Gris and Riesling stand out. Wines from their Sporen and Schoenenbourg vineyards are at *Grand Cru* level.

HUNAWIHR   *France, Alsace*   This village produces good Gewürztraminer, but its reputation is for Riesling from Clos Ste-Hune (part of *Grand Cru* Rosacker): possibly the best wine of Alsace. Leading producers include: Sipp-Mack, Trimbach, Zind Humbrecht.

HUNGARY   Bereft of its major export markets after the collapse of communism, Hungary found itself with a massive glut of wine. This potential disaster has been averted by bringing in western (often Australian) expertize to produce clean, well-made Ws from Sauvignon Blanc and Chardonnay, eminently saleable to thirsty hard-currency markets. The most widely planted variety is the Olaszrisling (Laski Rizling or Welschriesling), but the Hungarians are rediscovering native varieties like Furmint. R varieties showing promise include Kadarka. Hungary's most famous wine is

TOKAJI (Tokay), an extraordinary dessert wine made by adding *botrytis*-affected grapes to dry W wine. Incredibly long-lived, it is one of the world's great wines.

HUNTER VALLEY *Australia, New South Wales* The state's best-known region divides into Lower and Upper. In spite of poor weather the Lower Hunter manages to produce Sémillon (W) and Shiraz (R) of outstanding quality. The Upper Hunter offers early-maturing Chardonnay and Cabernet Sauvignon. Leading producers include: *Upper Hunter:* Allandale, Allanmere, Broke, Brokenwood, Drayton's, Evans, Lake's Folly, Lindemans, McGuigan, McWilliams, Murray Robson, Richmond Grove, Rothbury, Tulloch, Tyrrells, Wyndham; *Lower Hunter:* Arrowfield, Reynolds Yarraman, Rosemount.

HYBRID Vines cross-bred from *vitis vinifera* (the classic European grape vine) and another species, usually *vitis labrusca* or *vitis amurensis,* which confers resistance to cold weather. Hybrid vines are grown in the USA and Canada, where their wine can be good, and in England. New plantings of hybrid vines are forbidden for quality wine in EU countries.

I

IDAHO   *USA*   East of **WASHINGTON**, and with similar conditions, the state has a handful of wineries making mostly Ws, with Riesling and Chardonnay among the best grapes. Leading producers include: Ste Chapelle, Hell's Canyon.

IHRINGEN   *Germany, Baden, W, R*   Village in the **KAISERSTUHL** district, the best area of Baden, with good Ws from Silvaner and Rs from Spätburgunder. The Winklerberg is the best vineyard. Leading producers include: Heger, Stigler and the local Kaiserstuhler co-op.

ILE DE BEAUTÉ, DE L'   *France, Vin de Pays, R, P, W*   Wines from Corsica, using both traditional Corsican and classic grapes for R and P wines. Ws from Chardonnay and Chenin Blanc, made in a modern way, are successful: investment from mainland France has rejuvenated mass-production vineyards.

ILLINOIS   *USA*   A small clutch of wineries keep up a long wine tradition here.

INDIA   Wine has been made here for 2,000 years, but even today less than 1% out of the country's 50,000ha of grapes are used for wine. However, western investment and new-wave winemakers are using European varieties such as Chardonnay, Ugni Blanc, Pinot Noir and Merlot. Indian Sp wine, made by the champagne method, can be very good.

INDIANA   *USA*   The Ohio River Valley was a wine zone a century ago, and today several wineries make good Ws from cool-climate grapes such as Riesling and Chenin Blanc.

INDICAÇÃO DE PROVENIENCIA REGULAMENTADA (IPR)   *Portugal*   Wines on the second tier of Portugal's appellation system.

INGELHEIM   *Germany, Rheinhessen, R, W*   Town famous for R wines since Charlemagne's palace stood on this south bank of the Rhine. Also now known for good Riesling Ws.

INGLENOOK   *USA, California, Napa, R, W*   The winery is known for Cabernet Sauvignons that show their Rutherford origins with cedar, eucalyptus and tobacco flavours. Gravion is a dry W bordeaux-style blend of Sauvignon and Sémillon.

INNISKILLIN   *Canada, Ontario, W, R*   Estate known for its vineyard-designated Chardonnays from around Niagara, and for its award-winning Icewine (*see* **EISWEIN**).

IOWA   *USA*   A small and often struggling clutch of wineries today where, pre-Prohibition, there was a flourishing industry.

IPHOFEN   *Germany, Franken, Bereich, W*   Village with a large area of vineyards, the best being the Julius-Echter-Berg. Good, typical Franken W wines. Leading producers include: Johann Ruck, Wirsching.

IPR   *Portugal*   See INDICAÇÃO DE PROVENIENCIA REGULAMENTADA.

IRACHE, BODEGAS   *Spain, Navarra, R, W, P*   Large family-owned business, the quality of whose wines have been somewhat hit-and-miss in the past. Things have improved though, and the wines are attractively fruity.

IRON HORSE   *USA, California, Sonoma, W, R, Sp*   The chilly climes of Green Valley are ideal for Pinot Noir and Chardonnay, used by this Sebastopol winery both for Sp (notably Brut Rosé and Wedding Cuvée) and still wines. Cabernet Sauvignon comes from winemaker Forrest Tancer's vines in Alexander Valley.

IROULÉGUY   *France, South-West, AOC, R, P, W*   Tannat grapes, grown in mountainous terrain in the Pyrenees, give these R and P wines vivid colours, fragrance and richness, although Cabernets Franc and Sauvignon are also important. W Irouléguy is rare. Leading producer: Irouléguy co-op.

ISOLE E OLENA   *Italy, Tuscany, Chianti, R, W*   One of the best Chianti Classicos; the estate also makes Cepparello, an outstanding R *vino da tavola*, a R from (unusually for Italy) the Rhône grape Syrah, and a W from Chardonnay.

ISSAN, CH D'   *France, Bordeaux, Médoc, Margaux, 3ème Cru Classé, R*   Romantic, moated château, with vines on the best east-facing slopes of the Margaux plateau. The wine is approachable quite young but is still long-lived. Smooth, with Margaux sweetness; it is one of the best of the commune and the Médoc. A good 1993.

J

JABOULET, PAUL AINÉ *France, Rhône, R, W*
Reliable *négociant*/grower for all Rhône wines,
especially Hermitage, where La Chapelle is a
top R. Their style is more elegant than some.
Crozes-Hermitage Domaine de Thalabert is a
good buy, as is Parallèle 45 Côtes du Rhône.

JABOULET-VERCHERRE *France, Burgundy, Côte d'Or, R, W* Important Beaune-based *négociant* and estate owners. Reliable wines, especially the Rs.

JACQUART *France, Champagne* Co-op based at Reims calling upon the production of 1,000ha of vineyards. This reliable and very successful brand is especially well-known in France.

JACQUESSON *France, Champagne* Small, 200-year-old firm making an attractive NV and bigger, more austere *cuvée*, Signature, fermented and aged in wood.

JADOT, LOUIS *France, Burgundy, Côte d'Or, R, W* *Négociant* and important vineyard owner based in Beaune. Good Rs and even better Ws, especially those from its own vineyards, though the *négociant* wines are also delicious.

JAFFELIN *France, Burgundy, Côte d'Or, R, W* *Négociant* business with good, reliable wines made for relatively early drinking.

JAMET, JOSEPH *France, Rhône, Côte Rôtie, R* Wines are made here in a wonderfully traditional way by the two young Jamet brothers from their vineyards on the Côte Brune. Their wines are remarkably supple and aromatic, but they take time to reveal their great character.

JAPAN The 1970s saw far-reaching developments here, with European vines and foreign expertize being imported as Japan's interest in wine grew. The Suntory, Mann and Sanraku companies opened wineries, but wine imports are growing and are now more affordable. Today the most widely-planted vines are American hybrids which, together with Japan's native *vinifera*, Koshu, account for 85% of plantings. Some excellent if expensive wines are made in the French style, with the Ch'x Lumière and Mercian labels to the fore. Ch Lion, a Sauternes-style botrytized wine, is also very good.

JARDIN DE LA FRANCE, DU *France, Vin de Pays, R, W, P* This *vin de pays* zone covers the entire Loire Valley, and is used for mainly varietal wines including Chardonnay and Sauvignon Ws, and Gamay, Cabernet Franc and Cabernet Sauvignon Rs.

JASMIN *France, Rhône, Côte Rôtie, R* More elegant than assertive, the Côte Rôtie from here is made in the traditional style and offers good value.

JASNIÈRES *France, Loire, AOC, W* Small AOC for dry Ws from Chenin Blanc, within the larger Coteaux du Loir appellation. Leading producer: Joël Gigou.

JAU, CH DE *France, Midi, Roussillon, W, R, P, VDN* This innovative estate west of Rivesaltes makes a spicy, plummy Côtes de Roussillon (R) and a very aromatic W, as well as a P and a *vin doux naturel*.

JAUBERTIE, CH LA *France, South-West, Bergerac, R, W, P* New World influence and well-placed vineyards offer crisp, fresh W and soft R Bergeracs.

JERMANN *Italy, Friuli-Venezia Giulia, Collio and Colli Orientali, W, R* Superb varietal and blended wines include opulent dry Vintage Tunina (W), a Chardonnay named "Where the Dreams have no End", Engelwhite and Vinnae (both Ws) and the sweet cherry-coloured Vigna Bellina.

JOGUET, CHARLES *France, Loire, Chinon, R* Producer offering several *crus* made from different parts of his vineyard at Sazilly: notably Jeunes Vignes, from vines under 10 years, Clos de la Cure, Varennes du Grand Clos and Clos de Chêne Vert; and the finest, Clos de la Dioterie, which receives considerable wood-ageing.

JOHANNISBERG *Germany, Franken, W* Wine town above the River Main, making good Silvaner and other Ws. Leading producers include: Johann Ruck and Wirsching.

JOHANNISBERG *Germany, Rheingau, Bereich, W, R, Sp* Town in the Rheingau, and also the name for the sole *bereich* or zone of the Rheingau, a label used chiefly for blended and Sp wines. Johannisberg's own vineyards, which include the Hasensprung and Hölle, and the estate of **SCHLOSS JOHANNISBERG**, make top-class Riesling Ws.

JOHANNISBERG RIESLING *USA* Synonym used in America for the "classic" Riesling of the Rhine, as opposed to various lesser grapes with Riesling in their name.

JOHANNISBERG, SCHLOSS *Germany, Rheingau, W* One of the great names in German wine, owning a splendid Riesling vineyard yielding a range of fine, structured wines that (from good vintages) will age for decades.

JOHNER, WEINGUT KARL HEINZ *Germany, Baden, R, W* Johner spent some time running a leading English vineyard, Lamberhurst, and now manages his family estate at Bischoffingen, making excellent R and W Baden wines in the modern style. All are aged in *barriques*; the Rs and the Weissburgunder and Chardonnay Ws in new oak.

JOLYS, CH *France, South-West, Jurançon, W* The largest estate in the AOC, making dry (but unoaked) W, a *moelleux* or sweet W and, in great vintages, the rich W Cuvée Jean.

JORDAN *USA, California, Sonoma, R, W, Sp* Tom Jordan's château-style winery at Healdsburg makes a soft, blackcurranty Cabernet Sauvignon and a Chardonnay oily with licorice and anise; also a small amount of a botrytized, sweet W Sémillon/Sauvignon Blanc and a toasty, apple-fruited, classic-method Sp called "J".

JOVEN *Spain* Term which means young, or un-aged, wine, as opposed to matured wine or **VINO DE CRIANZA**.

JUGE, CH DU *France, Bordeaux, 1er Côtes de Bordeaux, R, W* Prof Denis Dubourdieu (*see* Ch **REYNON**) has family links here so the quality of the wine is no surprise: a good R and an attractive W (AOC Bordeaux).

JULIÉNAS *France, Burgundy, AOC, R* Beaujolais *cru* making Rs from Gamay grapes; wines develop plenty of body after 2–4 years. Leading producers include: Benon, Descombes, Ch de Juliénas.

JULIÉNAS, CH DE *France, Burgundy, Beaujolais, R* François Condemine's estate makes consistently good, perfumed Juliénas with plenty of concentration.

JULIUSSPITAL-WEINGUT *Germany, Franken, W* This large charitable estate makes classic Franken wines: the winemaking stresses the taste that comes from each vineyard and variety.

JUMILLA *Spain, Levante, DO, W, R* One of two Murcia wine zones, in semi-arid country inland from Alicante. Vineyards have been replanted since phylloxera in the 1980s. There is a trend towards *joven* wines, with experiments in cask-ageing. Leading producers include: Bodegas Vitivino.

JURANÇON *France, South-West, AOC, W* Fine, sweet W wines – and dry Ws with the AOC Jurançon Sec – from Gros Manseng, Petit Manseng and Courbu grapes grown in the foothills of the Pyrenees. Leading producers include: Dom Cauhapé, Gan co-op/Ch les Astous, Ch Jolys.

JUSTICES, CH LES *France, Bordeaux, Sauternes, W* Estate making soundly crafted, reliable and affordable Sauternes.

K

KABINETT *Germany* The basic, QMP, level of German and Austrian wines: usually medium-dry to medium-sweet, depending upon the vintage.

KADARKA Red grape native to Hungary; difficult to grow but promising in quality.

KAISERSTUHL TUNIBERG *Germany, Baden, Bereich, R, W, P* Zone of south Baden, taking in the dramatic Kaiserstuhl hill and the adjacent, lower, Tuniberg. The volcanic soil and warm climate of the Kaiserstuhl makes the best wines: flavoursome, even powerful, Ws from Riesling and Grauburgunder; structured Rs from Spätburgunder. Tuniberg wines are less distinguished. Leading producers include: Badischer Winzerkeller, Weinguts Bercher, Dr Heger, Salwey and Stigler.

KAMPTAL *Austria, Niederösterreich* Wine zone north of Langenlois on either side of the River Kamp. W wine dominates, but an increasing number of producers are turning out promising Rs. Leading producers include: Willi Bründlmayer, Jurtschitsch.

KANONKOP ESTATE *South Africa, Stellenbosch, R* South Africa's indigenous grape, Pinotage, is given prominence at this R-only estate, and they show just how good it can be when handled in the right way. Their bordeaux-style blend, Paul Sauer, is amongst the best produced in the Cape.

KARTHÄUSERHOF, WEINGUT *Germany, Ruwer, W* Estate making top-class Rieslings in the elegant, restrained but long-lived style of the Ruwer Valley.

KENDALL-JACKSON *USA, California, Lake, R, W* The original Lakeport winery has grown into a vinous empire producing nearly a million cases a year. The Chardonnay is slightly sweet and pineapply. The Cardinale (R), an expensive **MERITAGE** blend, is big and bold, with cassis, iodine and tobacco fruit.

KENWOOD *USA, California, Sonoma, R, W* The 200,000 or so cases of good, interesting wines made here include pepper-spiced Zinfandel R, refined Artist Series Cabernet Sauvignon, herballemon Sauvignon W, supple Pinot Noir R, crisp, melon-fruited Chenin Blanc and creamy Chardonnay.

KESSELSTATT, WEINGUT REICHSGRAF VON *Germany, Mosel, W* Large estate, all Riesling, with good vineyards in the Middle Mosel, Saar and Ruwer Valleys, making wines which though dry retain fruit and character.

KIENTZHEIM   *France, Alsace*   This village had the first *Grand Cru* (Schlossberg) to be officially recognized. It is famous for Gewürztraminer, but Riesling is also impressive. Leading producers include: Dom Weinbach, Dopff & Irion, Dopff Au Moulin.

KIRWAN, CH   *France, Bordeaux, Margaux, 3ème Cru Classé, R*   The well-placed Kirwan vineyard on the gravel plateau east of Brane-Cantenac, with its high proportion of Merlot and Cabernet Franc, yields Margaux in the softer style, gaining finesse with age.

KLEIN CONSTANTIA ESTATE   *South Africa, Constantia, R, W*   Duggie Jooste makes some of the Cape's finest wines, from the crisp, gooseberry-tinged Sauvignon Blanc to the delicious Muscat dessert wine, Vin de Constance: a modern version of the historic Constantia.

KLÜSSERATH   *Germany, Mosel, W*   Riesling Ws from this village's Brüderschaft vineyard are well regarded.

KNIGHT'S VALLEY   *USA, California, Sonoma, VA*   Warm-climate zone north of (and with similar conditions to) Napa, though within Sonoma county. Good for Cabernet Sauvignon and Merlot (R) and Sauvignon (W). Leading producers include: Beringer.

KNUDSEN ERATH   *USA, Oregon, R, W, P*   Oregon's largest estate winery. Half the production is a mint-spiced, black-cherry-filled Pinot Noir. A honeysuckle-scented Riesling is made both dry and in a Mosel semi-sweet style. Pinot Gris, fermented in French oak and lees-aged, is new; some Pinot Noir is made as a fruity, dry Vin Gris (P).

KOCHER-JAGST-TAUBER   *Germany, Württemberg, Bereich, W*   Small zone of northern Württemberg making mostly W wine.

KOEHLER-RUPPRECHT, WEINGUT   *Germany, Pfalz, W, R*   Long-lived, traditionally-made wines, dry but full, from Riesling, Spätburgunder and other varieties.

KREMSTAL   *Austria, Niederösterreich*   Region which extends on either side of the Danube and its tributary the Krems. Mainly W grapes, including Riesling and Grüner Veltliner, producing very elegant wines. Leading producers include: Malat-Bründlmayer, Mantlerhof, Josef Nigl, Fritz Salomon.

KREUZNACH   *Germany, Nahe, Bereich, W*   The northern part of the Nahe region, making W wine in the Nahe style: earthy, able to age well, showing good acidity. The town of BAD KREUZNACH is the centre. Leading producers include: August Anheuser, von Plettenberg, Staatsweingut Bad Kreuznach.

KRUG   *France, Champagne*   Perhaps the greatest name in Champagne. Big, rich, traditional wines needing years in bottle before they even begin to show of their best. All wines are prestige *cuvées*, using only first pressings and fermenting in wood. Krug NV Grande Cuvée, the most consistently great wine in Champagne, has a high percentage of reserve wine and Pinot Meunier.

KRUG, CHARLES *USA, California, Napa, R, W* Founded in 1861 by Charles Krug, this winery, north of St Helena, is now owned by Peter Mondavi and his sons. It is known for its fine Vintage Selection Cabernet Sauvignons and silky, sweet grass- and hay-scented Chenin Blanc.

KUENTZ-BAS *France, Alsace, W, R* Kuentz began in 1795, and joined André Bas in 1918. Wines of great quality, in particular the *vendange tardive* versions. The top wines are Gewürztraminer, Pinot Gris, Muscat and, increasingly, Pinot Noir. They also make Crémant d'Alsace.

KWV *South Africa, Paarl, R, W* Founded in 1918, the KWV dominates the South African wine scene. It is a huge cooperative producing a wide range of reliable, good-value wines under a variety of labels.

LABASTIDE DE LÉVIS, CAVE DE *France, South-West, Gaillac, W, R, P, Sp* This large cooperative makes the full, diverse range of Gaillac styles, each of them to a good standard.

LABÉGORCE, CH *France, Bordeaux, Margaux, Cru Bourgeois, R* Big improvements over recent vintages make this a château to try.

LABÉGORCE-ZÉDÉ, CH *France, Bordeaux, Margaux, Cru Bourgeois, R* Reliable, good-quality, traditionally made wine.

LABOURÉ-ROI *France, Burgundy, Côte d'Or, R, W* This well-known *négociant* specializes in W wines from all over the Burgundy region. Quality is reliable. Also a range of varietal *vins de pays* from the Languedoc – and a Pinot Noir *vin de pays* from the Aude.

LABRUSCA Vines of the species *vitis labrusca* are grown for wine in the eastern USA. Their wine is reckoned inferior to that of VINIFERA vines, having a strong taste described as "foxy".

LACLAVERIE, CH *France, Bordeaux, Côtes de Francs, R* Owned by the Thienponts of Pomerol, this 50/50 Merlot/Cabernet wine is good, dark, juicy claret. *See also* Ch PUYGUERAUD.

LACOSTE-BORIE *France, Bordeaux, Médoc, St-Julien, R* 2nd wine of Ch Grand-Puy-Lacoste.

LADOIX *France, Burgundy, AOC, R, W* Northernmost Côte de Beaune village; its best vineyards are on the Corton hill and are entitled to be sold as *Grands Crus* or as *Premier Cru* Aloxe-Corton. Wine labelled Ladoix is thus of village status: it can be good value. Leading producers include: Capitain-Gagnerot, Michel Mallard, Prince Florent de Mérode.

LAFAURIE-PEYRAGUEY, CH *France, Bordeaux, Sauternes, 1er Cru Classé, W* With the 1983 vintage new winemaking policies were applied, and since then the wine, aged in 50% new oak, is superb: silky in texture, oaky, elegant: copybook Sauternes. In modest years it can be among the best wines of the vintage.

LAFITE-ROTHSCHILD, CH *France, Bordeaux, Médoc, Pauillac, 1er Cru Classé, R* The large vineyard is superbly placed on the rim of the northern Pauillac plateau. The soil is gravel, the drainage good. Lafite was bought by the famous Paris banking family the Rothschilds in 1868, and is still owned by them. Lafite was the wine to match in the great vintages of the 1980s. It has 70% Cabernet Sauvignon, compared to neigbouring MOUTON-ROTHSCHILD's 85%; and its 15% Merlot (Mouton has only 8%) shows in its lighter style. Lafite is the most graceful, refined, even delicate of the First Growths, though it has the concentration and structure to age for decades.

LAFLEUR, CH *France, Bordeaux, Pomerol, R* Tiny amounts of fabulous – and expensive – pure Merlot wine.

LAFON, DOM DES COMTES *France, Burgundy, Côte d'Or, R, W* Exceptional domaine specializing in Meursault – but their Montrachet is also brilliant.

LAFON-ROCHET, CH *France, Bordeaux, Médoc, St-Estèphe, 4ème Cru Classé, R* The fine vineyard faces south towards Lafite, with old vines, but the wines do not quite reach the heights. There is 80% Cabernet Sauvignon, so most years need keeping. A good 1993.

LAGAROSSE, CH *France, Bordeaux, 1er Côtes de Bordeaux, R, W* Mostly Merlot, the R is solid and structured, ageing in 3 years to elegance; the W (70% Sémillon) is fruity but dry.

LAGEDER, ALOIS *Italy, Alto Adige, W, R* Leading producer of single-vineyard wines from steep sub-Alpine slopes including Alto Adige Chardonnay Löwengang and Erlehof, Cabernet Sauvignon Löwengang and Romigberg, Lagrein Dunkel Lindenburg and Terlano Sauvignon Blanc Lehenhof.

LAGRANGE, CH *France, Bordeaux, Médoc, St-Julien, 3ème Cru Classé, R* The Japanese group Suntory bought the property in 1983 and have spent millions on it, with the vineyards replanted and expanded, new air-conditioned *chai*, etc. Results are now impressive, with enthusiastic notes from critics on the wines from 1985 onwards. 2nd wine: Fiefs de Lagrange.

LAGUNE, LA *France, Bordeaux, Haut-Médoc, 3ème Cru Classé, R* Being outside the famous communes (it is south of Margaux, near Bordeaux) has hidden Lagune's true standing. Excellent wine in the scented, silky Margaux style.

LAKE *USA, California* County in cool-climate northern California with vineyards around the CLEAR LAKE VA and Guenoc.

LALANDE-DE-POMEROL *France, Bordeaux, AOC, R* North of Pomerol two communes, Lalande de Pomerol and Néac, produce Merlot-based Rs which mature faster than most Pomerols and offer a slightly lighter version of the same rich, plummy taste. Leading producers include: Ch'x des Annereaux, Bel-Air, Belle-Graves, Bertineau St-Vincent, Siaurac, Tournefeuille.

LALANNE, JACQUES *France, Loire, Quarts-de-Chaume, W* Lalanne's Ch de Belle Rive estate is dedicated to quality regardless of expense. Yields are low and only botrytized grapes go into this sweet wine, which is fermented in wood before bottling in April/May. The wines, although attractive when young, repay ageing.

LAMBRUSCO *Italy, Emilia-Romagna, R, W, P, Sp* The adaptable Lambrusco grape is usually reserved for R wines which are lightly Sp, sweet and easily quaffable: the best is Lambrusco di Sorbara. It can, however, be vinified dry (and is better for it), though most Lambrusco made for export is medium-sweet. Lambrusco should always be drunk young. Leading producers include: Cavvicchioli, Chiarli, Giacobazzi, Riunite, Villa Barbieri.

LAMOTHE, CH *France, Bordeaux, Sauternes, 2ème Cru Classé, W* There is a new generation taking over here, so quality is likely to improve, but in the past Lamothe has been disappointing.

LAMOTHE-GUIGNARD, CH *France, Bordeaux, Sauternes, 2ème Cru Classé, W* Since new owners took over in the early 1980s the improvement has been spectacular. Since 1986 the wine has been delicious: rich and sweet, lightly oaky, elegant and complex, getting better with every vintage. Now represents one of the few bargains of Sauternes.

LANDIRAS, CH DE *France, Bordeaux, Graves, W, R* Look for Sémillon-dominated Ws in a rich, oaky style from this estate. Rs are impressive too.

LANDWEIN *Germany* Literally country wine; this is a superior sub-category of *Tafelwein*, equivalent to *vin de pays*.

LANGOA BARTON, CH *France, Bordeaux, Médoc, St-Julien, 3ème Cru Classé R* The Barton family has owned and run Langoa- and LÉOVILLE-BARTON for 170 years. The winemaking is traditional, as are the prices, making Langoa a byword for value. The vineyard is quite small: 15ha.

LANGUEDOC *France* This enormous wine region, known generally as the Midi, is strung between the Mediterranean and the inland hills, west of the Rhône. One of the most exciting places in wine today, with many new wines under the various AOC names (MINERVOIS, COTEAUX DU LANGUEDOC, CORBIÈRES etc) and the many *vins de pays*, including the overall VIN DE PAYS D'OC. The most innovative growers often label their wines as simple *vins de pays*, since this frees them from the restrictions the AOC rules put on choice of grape varieties.

LANSON *France, Champagne* Sold in 1990 to giant Marne et Champagne, Lanson's Black Label is one of the world's best-known champagnes. Fresh, citrussy, perhaps a little on the lean side. Vintage wines are better, and can age very well.

LAPATENA *Spain, Ribeiro, W, R, Sp* New winery on a spectacular bend of the River Miño. Production is mainly W, and their best is the Fin de Siglo. R wines include Rectoral de Amandi and Teliro.

LAPORTE, DOMS *France, Loire, Sancerre, W* This 15-ha estate has modern cellars, making high-quality wines. Top *cuvée* is Domaine du Rochoy, from low-yielding vines, left *sur lie* until bottling. Others are Clos la Comtesse and Grand Domaine.

LARMANDE, CH   *France, Bordeaux, St-Emilion, Grand Cru Classé, R*
This old estate to the north of St-Emilion village is planted with
two-thirds Merlot. Very reliable, high-quality wines.

LAROCHE, DOM   *France, Burgundy, Chablis, Corsica, Midi, W*   A
leading (100ha) Chablis estate, also *négociant*, with holdings in
both *Premiers* and *Grands Crus*. Top-quality wines which age well.
Recent ventures in Corsica and LANGUEDOC yield good-value
varietal *vins de pays*.

LAROSE-TINTAUDON, CH   *France, Bordeaux, Médoc, Cru Bourgeois,
R*   Well placed château just inland from Pauillac; a good source
of reliable claret.

LAROZE, CH   *France, Bordeaux, St-Emilion, Grand Cru Classé, R*
This good-sized property, with almost 50% Cabernet Franc, produces attractive, easy wines that mature fairly quickly.

LARRIVET-HAUT-BRION, CH   *France, Bordeaux, Pessac-Léognan, R, W*
Investment in new cellars has brought impressive results: the W
rich and spicy, the R firm and oaky.

LASCOMBES, CH   *France, Bordeaux, Médoc, Margaux, 2ème Cru
Classé, R*   Big vineyard on a grand estate that was restored by
the Franco-American wine merchant and writer, the late Alexis
Lichine, and sold by him to an English brewer. Formerly unexciting wine, but much better in the late 1980s.

LASKI RIZLING   See WELSCHRIESLING.

LASTOURS, CH DE   *France, Midi, Corbières, R*   Estate of international repute, employing handicapped people in the cellar and
vineyard. Classic methods produce several *cuvées* with the
emphasis on the *terroir*, mostly designed for fairly early drinking.

LATOUR À POMEROL, CH   *France, Bordeaux, Pomerol, R*   Very
dense, compact wines from an estate run by the Jean-Pierre
MOUEIX firm.

LATOUR, CH   *France, Bordeaux, Médoc, Pauillac, 1er Cru Classé, R*
The wines of Latour have been sought after since the Middle
Ages. Its old-fashioned Cabernet Sauvignon-based style made it a
legend for longevity. Modernization (it was the first Médoc estate
to install stainless steel vats) has tamed the wine a little, but
hardly changed its deep, dark, sturdy character. The excellence of
the *terroir* allows Latour to make good wines in poor years, and its
microclimate often spares it the region's damaging spring frosts.
In good years it offers up a dark, chewy monster of a wine that
demands patience measured in decades. 2nd wine: Les Forts de
Latour. A 3rd wine, labelled AOC Pauillac, is made in some years.
A very fine 1994, both the *Grand Vin* and Les Forts.

LATOUR, LOUIS   *France, Burgundy, Côte d'Or, R, W*   Major *négociant*
and vineyard owner in Burgundy whose name is known around
the world. The Ws are excellent: their R wines are not quite so
reliable.

LATRICIÈRES-CHAMBERTIN   See CHAMBERTIN.

LAUGEL, MAISON MICHEL   *France, Alsace, W, R*   This large producer is now owned by Rémy-Pannier of the Loire region. Wines are good value, and certain *cuvées* of Gewürztraminer, Pinot Noir, Riesling and Muscat can excel. The Crémant d'Alsace is consistent and good.

LAUREL GLEN   *USA, California, Sonoma, R*   Source of one of the finest Cabernet Sauvignons in the USA, plush with fruit, firmly structured for age.

LAURENT-PERRIER   *France, Champagne*   This leading GRANDE MARQUE is one of Champagne's largest houses. Extremely elegant wines, from bone-dry Ultra Brut to the superb prestige *cuvée* Grand Siècle. The flowery NV is Chardonnay-based.

LAVAUX   *Switzerland, Vaud*   District within the Vaud canton, with steep vineyards overlooking the lake east of Lausanne. Chasselas (W) and Pinot Noir (R) are specialities.

LAVIÈRES, LES   *France, Burgundy, Côte de Beaune, 1er Cru, R*   In the commune of Savigny-lès-Beaune, this vineyard produces wines which are quite light in colour, sport an elegant bouquet and have a supple, soft palate. Leading producers include: Pierre Bitouzet, BOUCHARD PÈRE & FILS, Jean Grivot.

LAVILLE-HAUT-BRION, CH   *France, Bordeaux, Pessac-Léognan, Cru Classé, W*   This is, in effect, the W wine of Ch LA MISSION-HAUT-BRION. Perhaps a little less sumptuous than Ch HAUT-BRION, made by the same team, but an opulent wine by any standards. It needs a decade in bottle.

LAVILLEDIEU, VIN DE   *France, South-West, VDQS, R, P*   Minor country wine of the Tarn valley near Fronton, made from a blend of Négrette, Gamay, Cabernet Franc, Syrah and Tannat grapes.

LAVILLOTTE, CH   *France, Bordeaux, St-Estèphe, Cru Bourgeois, R*   Good, old-fashioned, long-keeping wine that wins prizes in prestigious tastings.

LAZIO   *Italy*   Also called Latium, this region of central Italy is unusual in that the vast majority (90%) of its production is W. Frascati, from the hills south of Rome called the Castelli Romani, is its best-known W wine, though the neighbouring DOCs of Colli Albini and Marino are also good.

LEBANON   Lebanon's name has become synonymous in wine terms with one winery, Ch MUSAR, but there are other vineyards, including the recent Ch Kefraya.

LECCIA, DOM   *France, Corsica, Patrimonio, W, R*   Modern techniques and equipment give the Rs a good fruit flavour with some structure. It also produces a good sweet Muscat.

LEEUWIN ESTATE   *Australia, South Australia, Margaret River, R, W*   Flamboyant promotion and excellent quality made Leeuwin's reputation. Long-lived Chardonnay and classic Cabernet Sauvignon lead the way, though the wine range is wide.

LEFLAIVE, DOM *France, Burgundy, Côte d'Or, W* Together with Domaine Sauzet, Leflaive is the top producer in Puligny-Montrachet: an impressive array of *Premiers* and *Grands Crus* are made, showing elegance and finesse with tremendous staying power.

LEFLAIVE, OLIVIER FRÈRES *France, Burgundy, Côte d'Or, R, W* As *négociant*, and increasingly as a grower, Olivier produces white wines very much in the elegant style of the family estate, DOMAINE LEFLAIVE.

LEITZ, WEINGUT JOSEPH *Germany, Rheingau, W* Young producer of elegant, racy Riesling from good, low-yielding Rüdesheim vineyards.

LEMOINE *France, Champagne* Marque owned by Laurent-Perrier. The main brand, Cuvée Royale, is an extremely well made, good value champagne with an attractive lively palate.

LEO BURING *Australia, South Australia, Barossa, W* Long regarded as the maker of Australia's greatest Rieslings: these are W wines that evolve magnificently for 20 years or more, from citrus and lime in youth to mature toasted aromas and flavours.

LEÓN, JEAN *Spain, Catalonia, Penedès, R, W, P* Pioneer of "new-wave" winemaking in Catalonia, the *bodega* specializes in using classic French grapes and oak fermentation. Their Chardonnay is full-bodied, and the Cabernet Sauvignon-based R ages well.

LÉOVILLE BARTON, CH *France, Bordeaux, Médoc, St-Julien, 2ème Cru Classé, R* Léoville was a large estate on the best vineyard land in St-Julien. It eventually split in three (see below). Barton's 45-ha portion of that original estate is reckoned to make slightly better, more concentrated wine than its sister LANGOA-BARTON.

LÉOVILLE LAS-CASES, CH *France, Bordeaux, Médoc, St-Julien, 2ème Cru Classé, R* This large estate, which includes the original walled Léoville *clos*, is owned and run by Michel Delon, one of Bordeaux's best winemakers. Powerful, concentrated, long in taste and long-lived in bottle, this is one of the great red wines. Comparisons are often made with its 1st-Growth neighbour Latour, across the Pauillac border. 2nd wine: Clos du Marquis.

LÉOVILLE POYFERRÉ, CH *France, Bordeaux, Médoc, St-Julien, 2ème Cru Classé, R* The third portion of the great Léoville property, much improved during the 1980s when Didier Cuvelier took charge and introduced a more rigorous selection. 2nd wine: Moulin-Riche.

LEROY, DOM *France, Burgundy, Côte d'Or, R, W* Proprietior Lalou Bize-Leroy, *négociant* and vineyard owner, is also part-owner of Dom de la ROMANÉE-CONTI. Recently much enlarged, the Leroy estate makes fine, long-lasting wines.

LEY, BODEGAS BARÓN DE *Spain, Rioja, R* New *bodega* where modern technology is intelligently combined with tradition: some experimentation with Cabernet Sauvignon is under way.

LIEBFRAUMILCH *Germany, Rhine, W* German wine, blended by a merchant or cooperative, from at least 70% Riesling, Müller-Thurgau, Silvaner or Kerner grapes grown anywhere in the Rheingau, Pfalz, Nahe or Rheinhessen (usually in the last), of QBA standard. Usually medium-sweet.

LIGURIA *Italy* Cupped around the Gulf of Genoa and bordering Provence in France, most wine from these hilly coastal vineyards is consumed locally. Easy-quaffing W wines and a few long-lived R are made under four DOCs.

LILIAN LADOUYS, CH *France, Bordeaux, St-Estèphe, Cru Bourgeois, R* Impressive wine from this newly restored château. Its hilltop site and apricot walls form a local landmark.

LIMOUX *France, Midi, AOC, W* Appellation for still wines made, like BLANQUETTE DE LIMOUX, from the Mauzac grape plus some Chenin Blanc and Chardonnay. The Chardonnay varietals can be particularly good: the local *cave coopérative* (see below) has identified four different *terroirs* and offers wines from each. Leading producers include: Cave Coopérative de Limoux.

LIMOUX, CAVE COOPÉRATIVE DE *France, Midi, Limoux, W, Sp* Of the annual 666,600 cases of Sp Blanquette de Limoux, 75% comes from this modern, well-run co-op. Its variety of *cuvées* includes Aimery, Cuvée Aldéric and Sieur d'Arques. Also good still Ws from Chardonnay.

LINDEMANS *Australia, New South Wales, Hunter Valley, R, W* Founded in 1870, Lindemans produce good Shiraz (R) plus some Sémillon-based Ws and sophisticated Chardonnays. Production centres also in other parts of Australia, and a wide and reliable range of wines.

LINGENFELDER, WEINGUT K & H *Germany, Pfalz, W, R* Rainer Lingenfelder, who has made wine in Bordeaux and Australia, now runs the family estate and is a leader of modern German R-winemaking, using *barriques* with great success. Noted maker of dry, well-structured Spätburgunder Rs and dry, full-flavoured Riesling Ws.

LIONNET, JEAN *France, Rhône, St-Péray W; Cornas R* Maker of solid, wood-aged Cornas Rs which needs time in bottle to soften, and also excellent St-Péray Ws.

LIOT, CH *France, Bordeaux, Barsac, W* Popular Barsac in a light style, sometimes lacking in *botrytis*, and aged in a mixture of tanks and *barriques*, of which 15% are new. Relatively inexpensive, it makes a sound apéritif Sauternes.

LIQUOROSO *Italy* Fortified dessert wine.

LIRAC   *France, Rhône, AOC, R, P, W*   The best R and W Liracs aspire to the quality of Châteauneuf-du-Pape; the best Ps to that of Tavel. Leading producers include: Jean-Claude Assémat, Dom Duseigneur, Dom Maby, Dom Roger Sabon.

LISTRAC-MÉDOC   *France, Bordeaux, AOC, R*   Solid Haut-Médoc wines that repay keeping. Leading producers include: Ch'x Clarke, Fourcas-Dupré, Fourcas-Hosten.

LIVERMORE VALLEY   *USA, California, VA*   Wine zone south of San Francisco with gravel soils growing Bordeaux varieties: Cabernets, Merlot, Sauvignon. Leading producers include: Concannon, Wente.

LJUTOMER-ORMOZ   *Slovenia, Podravski*   This wine zone has the country's best-quality vineyards and two huge cellars, Ljutomer and Ormoz. Famous for light, pleasant Laski Rizling. Ormoz has the edge over Ljutomer in quality. Wines exported under the Lutomer label come from both. The full potential of the excellent *terroir* has yet to be reached.

LLANO ESTACADO   *USA, Texas, W*   Among the leaders in the Texas wine renaissance, this Lubbock winery averages 75,000 cases a year, producing acceptable Chardonnay, Chenin Blanc and Sauvignon Ws. Cabernet Sauvignon is its next challenge.

LLANOS, BODEGAS LOS   *Spain, Valdepeñas, R, W*   Large producer with 1,200ha of vines. Los Llanos has invested heavily in oak casks, and the best wines include impressive *gran reservas* such as Pata Negra, which is 100% Tempranillo. Also doing good work with Ws from the Airén grape.

LOIRE   *France, Loire, AOC, W, P, Sp*   Most Loire wines go under local names (*see* ANJOU, SAUMUR, MUSCADET, etc), but Crémant de Loire, Sp W or P wine, can be made throughout the vast Loire Valley. Controls for Crémant are stricter than for the straightforward Sp (*mousseux* or *pétillant*) Saumur and Vouvray. Rosé de Loire, a dry P from a minimum 30% Cabernet grapes, can also be made throughout the region. Leading Crémant de Loire producers include: Ackerman-Laurance, Ch du Breuil, Dom de la Gabillière, Langlois-Château.

LOMBARDY   *Italy*   To the east of Piedmont in northern Italy. Wine is less important here than in Piedmont. Oltrepò Pavese is the best-known DOC, though the Valtellina wines – mountain Rs – can be good in warm years.

LONG-DEPAQUIT   *France, Burgundy, Chablis, W*   Unoaked Chablis made to give a true expression of the *terroir*. The flagship wine is from the tiny La Moutonne vineyard.

LONG ISLAND, NORTH FORK OF   *USA, New York State, VA*   Wine zone on a sandy, mild-climate peninsula at the eastern end of the Island, recently burgeoning as a source of good wines: elegant Rs from Merlot and Cabernet; Ws from Sauvignon and

Chardonnay. Leading producers include: Bedel, Bridgehampton, Hargrave, Palmer, Pindar.

LOOSEN, WEINGUT OEKONOMIERAT DR *Germany, Mosel-Saar-Ruwer, W* Ernst Loosen is a modern-minded maker of Mosel Rieslings, using low yields and the latest techniques including experiments with *barriques*. His wines are piquant, spicy and full of taste. The Riesling Trocken (dry) is good value.

LORCH, LORCHHAUSEN *Germany, Rheingau, W* Twin villages officially in the Rheingau wine region, but geographically in the Rhine gorge and thus closer in wine style to the MITTELRHEIN: light, elegant Riesling Ws.

LOUBENS, CH *France, Bordeaux, St-Croix-Du-Mont, W; Bordeaux, R* The leading estate in this sweet-white zone, offering good-value wines akin to minor Sauternes. Also an AOC Bordeaux R.

LOUDENNE, CH *France, Bordeaux, Médoc, Cru Bourgeois, R* Reliable English-owned estate beautifully placed by the Gironde. A light, relatively early-maturing R – and a good W, rare in the Médoc. Also a museum and a respected wine school.

LOUPIAC *France, Bordeaux, AOC, W* Sweet W from a small zone across the Garonne from Barsac. Leading producers include: Ch'x du Cros, Loupiac-Gaudiet, de Ricaud.

LOUPIAC-GAUDIET, CH *France, Bordeaux, Loupiac, W, Bordeaux, R* Old estate making good, light, sweet Ws and a good, fruity AOC Bordeaux R.

LOUVIÈRE, CH LA *France, Bordeaux, Pessac-Léognan, W, R* The W, dominated by Sauvignon Blanc, is a sound oaky wine of some distinction. The R is well structured and ages well. Also made here is Ch Coucheroy: simple but well-made R and W Graves, very good value.

LUGNY, CAVE COOPERATIVE DE *France, Burgundy, Mâconnais, R, W* Very well made lesser burgundies, both R and W – but particularly well known for their good-quality W Mâconnais.

LUJAN DE CUYO *South America, Argentina, R* South of the city of Mendoza, this high-elevation area has a cool microclimate. Cabernet Sauvignon and Malbec do well here.

LUNEL, MUSCAT DE *France, Midi, AOC, VDN* This *vin doux naturel*, from 100% Muscat Blanc à Petits Grains (the best Muscat grape), is made on the eastern edge of the Hérault *département*. Leading producers include: Dom des Aires, Clos Bellevue, Ch du Grès St-Paul.

LUNGAROTTI, CANTINE *Italy, Central Italy, Umbria, W, R* Giorgio Lungarotti is the patriarch of Umbrian wines. The Torgiano DOC, which he instigated, is almost entirely dominated by Lungarotti. His Torgiano (R) is named Rubesco, his W Torre di Giano.

Torgiano *riserva* is a DOCG wine. Miralduolo is the name for R and W *vini da tavola* from Cabernet Sauvignon and Chardonnay. Also has a splendid wine museum.

LUSSAC ST-EMILION   *France, Bordeaux, AOC, R*   North of St-Emilion are several "satellite" villages, of which this is one, whose wines can represent excellent value. Leading producers include: Ch'x Barbe Blanche, Bel-Air, Haut-Piquat, de Lussac, Lyonnat, de Tabuteau, Tour de Grenet; Vieux Ch Chambeau.

LUSTAU, EMILIO   *Spain, sherry*   Innovative firm that launched the ALMACENISTA idea onto the world market, and then followed that with the Landed Age concept (sherries bottled in the country of export and aged in bottle before sale). Also has a growing range of commercial sherries.

LUXEMBOURG   Nearly 2,000ha of vineyards in the upper Moselle valley make crisp, dry W and Sp wines. The quality rating *marque nationale* is equivalent to French AOC.

LYNCH-BAGES, CH   *France, Bordeaux, Médoc, Pauillac, 5ème Cru Classé, R*   Traditional wine from modern equipment is the Cazes family's philosophy. The style is supple and accessible, yet with the concentration and depth of a truly good Pauillac. The large and superbly sited vineyard means that it is in ample supply. A good 1993. 2nd wine: Haut-Bages-Avérous.

LYNCH-MOUSSAS, CH   *France, Bordeaux, Médoc, Pauillac, 5ème Cru Classé, R*   Yet another Médoc château starting to show form after a major renewal programme. The vineyard has 30% Merlot, producing wines in the lighter style which are good value.

M

MABILEAU, JACQUES *France, Loire, Bourgueil, R* Based in St-Nicolas-de-Bourgueil, Jacques Mabileau makes two wines from 13ha on the western edge of the Coteaux zone: a standard *cuvée*, Domaine Jacques Mabileau, and a blend from older vines, Vieilles Vignes, which, for a St-Nicolas, ages well.

MACAY, CH *France, Bordeaux, Côtes de Bourg, R* This recent star of the appellation offers balanced and fruity wines.

MACEDON *Australia, Victoria* This cool-climate area makes Cabernet Sauvignon and Shiraz (R) of note, plus a good range of other single-variety wines. Leading producers include: Hanging Rock, Virgin Hills.

MACÉRATION CARBONIQUE *France* Winemaking technique (used, for example, in Beaujolais) in which R-wine grapes are put into sealed vats without being crushed. Carbon dioxide is pumped in, and fermentation takes place naturally inside the grapes, which split under their own weight. This extracts aroma and colour. After pressing, fermentation is then completed in the normal way.

MACLE, HENRI *France, Jura, W* Specialist in the rare VIN JAUNE of the Château-Chalon AOC: Macle's meticulous winemaking produces long-lived wines.

MÂCON *France, Burgundy, AOC, R, W, P* Wide area in southern Burgundy making mostly modest wines. The Rs are from Gamay or Pinot Noir, Ws from Chardonnay; most wines achieve the extra degree of alcohol needed to qualify for the AOC Mâcon-Supérieur. Both Rs and Ws are best drunk young and fresh. Leading producers include: Cave Coopérative de Lugny, Cave Coopérative de Viré, Trenel & Fils.
Mâcon-Villages AOC for W wines from one of 43 "superior" villages; the village name can be attached, as in Mâcon-Lugny or Mâcon-Viré. Leading producers include: Dom André Bonhomme, Dom des Gandines, Dom Guillemot-Michel, Dom Manciat-Poncet, Dom Jean Thévenet.

MACULAN *Italy, Veneto, R, W* Star Breganze producer, making Cabernet, oak-aged Tocai (W) and Torcolato, a sweet W from dried grapes aged in new oak.

MADEIRA *Portugal, DOC* Island in the Atlantic, 600km west of Casablanca. Its fortified W wine gains uniqueness from the cooking process (*estufagem*) giving the wine its slightly burnt character, together with high acid. Four main styles of Madeira exist, from very dry to very sweet, named after grape varieties used: Sercial, Verdelho, Bual, Malmsey. Basic Madeira (3-year-old) from Tinta Negra Mole is essentially cooking wine. 5-year-old and up can be extremely good and ages very well. Leading producers include: Blandy Brothers, Cossart Gordon, Henriques & Henriques.

MADEIRA WINE CO *Portugal, Madeira* Many of the great madeira names are united in the Madeira Wine Co, formerly an association of shippers but now owned by the **BLANDY** and **SYMINGTON** families. Today it is moving to emphasize the differences between the various companies' wines.

MADIRAN *France, South-West, AOC, R* Wines from the tannic Tannat grape, blended with Cabernet Franc and Cabernet Sauvignon, grown on varied soils in the Pyrenean foothills. Leading producers include: Ch d'Aydie, Ch Bouscassé, Dom du Crampilh, Dom Laffitte-Teston, Ch Montus, Dom Moureou.

MAGDELAINE, CH *France, Bordeaux, St-Emilion, 1er Grand Cru Classé, R* Owned by the Moueix family, Pomerol's leading producers, this beautiful property is among the top *1ers Grands Crus*. The high percentage of Merlot contributes to the wine's opulence and richness.

MAGENCE, CH *France, Bordeaux, Graves, W, R* Well-known estate in St-Pierre-de-Mons in the southern Graves, producing sound Rs and Ws.

MAINDREIECK *Germany, Franken, Bereich*, *W* The heart of the Franken region, vineyards along the Main, particularly around WÜRZBURG and Escherndorf. Leading producers: *see* WÜRZBURG.

MAINE, CH DU *France, Bordeaux, Graves, R* Langon estate making a fine example of traditional R Graves, with ample structure and a hint of austerity, clearly fashioned for a long life.

MAIPO VALLEY *South America, Chile, R, W* Sub-region of the Central Valley, Chile's most important wine-producing area. Maipo was the first sub-region to be developed and still remains its most concentrated vineyard area. Much Cabernet Sauvignon and Merlot is grown for Rs.

MAIPU *South America, Argentina, R* To the south of the city of Mendoza, a high-elevation area with a cool micro-climate. Good Cabernet Sauvignon and Malbec are grown here.

MAIRE, HENRI *France, Jura, R, W, P, Sp* Large-scale *négociant* and grower (with four estates), making over half of all Jura wine. They make good Arbois R and **VIN JAUNE**, though their Vin Fou (Sp W) is not a Jura wine, but a brand drawing upon wine from all over France.

MÁLAGA *Spain, Andalucia, DO, W, R* The few remaining vineyards inland from the city of Málaga furnish grapes for the celebrated fortified wine, which is made sweet, medium-sweet and dry. Lágrima is a sweet version made from free-run juice.

Leading producers include: Hijos de Antonio Barcelo, Lopez Hermanos, Scholtz Hermanos.

MALARTIC-LAGRAVIÈRE, CH *France, Bordeaux, Pessac-Léognan, Cru Classé, R, W* The W, made entirely from Sauvignon Blanc, at its best is rich and aromatic, but can be inconsistent. The Rs are supple with ripe tannins. Both gain from a few years in bottle.

MALBEC Red grape grown for dark, tannic, long-lived wine in Cahors (where it is known as Auxerrois). It is excellent in Argentina, where the wines are deeply aromatic (blackcurrants and spices). Used, in small proportions, in the classic red Bordeaux blend, especially in the Médoc. Malbec is also grown (under the name Cot) in the Loire and Chile.

MALCONSORTS, AUX *France, Burgundy, Côte de Nuits, 1er Cru, R* One of the larger vineyards of Vosne-Romanée, abutting Nuits-St-Georges. Aromatic, supple, elegant wines, needing bottle-age to show their best. Leading producers include: Hudelot-Noëllat, Lamarche, Moillard-Grivot.

MALECASSE, CH *France, Bordeaux, Haut-Médoc, Cru Bourgeois, R* Well-placed estate between Margaux and St-Julien, subject to much investment and recently making very good-value claret. A good 1993.

MALESCOT-ST-EXUPÉRY, CH *France, Bordeaux, Médoc, Margaux, 3ème Cru Classé, R* Known for its tannic, backward youth, this wine blossoms with maturity. It is often rated among the top Margaux.

MALLE, CH DE *France, Bordeaux, Sauternes, 2ème Cru Classé, W* One of the lighter Sauternes, easy and rounded, it usually has attractive fruit. More richness is evident in the 1989 and 1990 vintages, as indeed it should be. 1991 also showed improvement.

MALVASIA/MALVOISIE Good-quality aromatic white grape, producing deep-coloured, full W wines, and in some cases Ps, and adding its character to blends. Grown in Italy, Spain and Portugal. Malvasia gave its name to the sweetest style of madeira, malmsey. (The Malvoisie of Switzerland and some parts of France is actually Pinot Gris.)

MANCHA, LA *Spain, Castilla-La Mancha, DO, W, P, R* This is Spain's largest wine zone. In the southern part of the central plateau or Meseta, its high, dry vineyards produce mainly *jovenes* in all three colours, representing good-value everyday wines. Leading producers include: Rodríguez y Berger, Vinícola de Castilla.

MANZANILLA *Spain* The driest and lightest style of sherry, akin to FINO but made only at the coastal town of Sanlúcar de Barrameda, where (makers say) it gains a salty tang from the sea.

MARANGES *France, Burgundy, AOC, R, W* Rather tough and earthy style of (mostly R) wine from three villages, Cheilly-les-Maranges, Dezizies-les-Maranges and Sampigny-les-Maranges, at the southern end of the Côte de Beaune. These are solid but enjoyable Rs for drinking at 5–8 years old. Leading producers include: Mestre Père & Fils.

MARBUZET, CH DE *France, Bordeaux, Médoc, St-Estèphe, R* 2nd wine of Ch Cos d'Estournel.

MARCHES *Italy* Region of central Italy. Quality has much improved here since the mid-1980s. Best known for the lemony W DOC Verdicchio dei Castelli di Jesi and a promising R, Rosso Conerò DOC.

MARCILLAC *France, South-West, AOC, R, P* Spicy, blackcurranty Rs, mostly for drinking young, from Fer Servadou (Mansois) grapes grown in the Aveyron *département*.

MARCONNETS, LES *France, Burgundy, Côte de Beaune, 1er Cru, R* Vineyard at the northernmost end of the commune of Beaune, visible from the A6 *autoroute*. The wines have good colour, are well-structured and are at their best after a few years in bottle. Leading producers include: Bouchard Père & Fils.

MARCUS JAMES *Brazil, R, W* Brand owned by the Canadaigua Wine Company of the USA, producing almost one million cases of varietal wines including Chardonnay, Cabernet Sauvignon, Merlot and white Zinfandel.

MARGARET RIVER *Australia, Western Australia* Top-quality wines are produced in this cool-climate area, ranging from delicious Sémillon (W), Sauvignon Blanc and Chardonnay to powerful Cabernet Sauvignon which matures gracefully. Leading producers include: Brookland, Cullens, Leeuwin, Cape Mentelle, Moss Wood, Pierro, Vasse Felix, Ch Xanadu.

MARGAUX *France, Bordeaux, AOC, R* The southernmost AOC of the Haut-Médoc, with 22 classed growths. Long-lived R wines with a softer, more opulent and perfumed style than those of Pauillac. Leading producers include: Ch'x Brane-Cantenac, d'Issan, Lascombes, Margaux, Palmer, Prieuré Lichine, Rausan-Ségla.

MARGAUX, CH *France, Bordeaux, Médoc, Margaux, 1er Cru Classé, R, W* The beautiful mansion and some of the best vineyard land in the Médoc make this a true 1st Growth, and since 1978 the wine has matched the status. Bottles a century old attest to Margaux's quality. There is also a W, Pavillon Blanc, (good but expensive) from a vineyard of Sauvignon Blanc west of the main estate. 2nd wine: Pavillon Rouge.

MARGRÄFLERLAND *Germany, Baden, Bereich, R, W, P* Baden's southern, and thus warmest, corner, making soft, enjoyable Ws from Gutedel (the local name for Chasselas) and equivalent Rs from Spätburgunder. Leading producer: Schloss Istein.

MARLBOROUGH   *New Zealand, South Island*   Now the largest grape-growing area of New Zealand. Marlborough enjoys a dry, sunny climate especially suited to Ws from Müller-Thurgau, Sauvignon Blanc, Chardonnay and Riesling. Rs, from Cabernet Sauvignon, tend to be herbaceous. Leading producers include: Cloudy Bay, Le Brun, Hunter's, Jackson, Montana.

MARNE ET CHAMPAGNE   *France, Champagne*   One of the region's giants, owning no vineyards but selling 10 million bottles annually. The name is rarely seen, though: it sells mainly as the buyer's own brand, or under a range of labels including Eugène Clicquot, Gauthier, Gieslier and Alfred Rothschild.

MARQUIS D'ALESME BECKER, CH   *France, Bordeaux, Médoc, Margaux, 3ème Cru Classé, R*   This small estate is typical of the Soussans commune in both size and in the solid, earthy quality of its wine.

MARQUIS DE SÉGUR   *France, Bordeaux, Médoc, St-Estèphe, R*   2nd wine of Ch Calon-Ségur.

MARQUIS DE TERME, CH   *France, Bordeaux, Médoc, Margaux, 4ème Cru Classé R*   New ownership a decade ago brought welcome changes in winemaking, which now more closely matches the quality of the well-placed vineyard.

MARSALA   *Italy, Sicily, DOC, W*   One of the world's great fortified wines. Made from local grapes including Catarratto and Inzolia, it can be dry or sweet. The dry version – "Vergine" – must have 18% alcohol and five years' wood ageing. Leading producers include: De Bartoli, Florio, Carlo Pellegrino.

MARSANNAY   *France, Burgundy, AOC, R, P, W*   In the north of the CÔTE DE NUITS, the village of Marsannay-la-Côte has an AOC for solid and well-coloured R burgundies, and one of the best Ps in France: long-lived, dry and intense. Leading producers include: René & Regis Bouvier, Marc Brocot, Dom Charlopin-Parizot, Bruno Clair, Dom Fougeray de Beauclair, Jean-Pierre Guyard, Louis Jadot.

MARSANNE   White grape (often blended with ROUSSANNE) making dry W wines in the northern Rhône; also grown in the Languedoc for *vins de pays*, Switzerland and Australia.

MARTEAU, JACKY   *France, Loire, Touraine, W, R*   Low yields and high quality are the policy at Marteau's small vineyard south of the River Cher. The usual Touraine grapes are grown for varietal wines: Ws from Sauvignon Blanc, Pineau d'Aunis and Chardonnay; Rs from Gamay and Cabernet Franc.

MARTIN BROTHERS   *USA, California, San Luis Obispo, R, W*   American wines with Italian flavours: the prime Piedmontese grape Nebbiolo is a popular R, with its tar, violet and pomegranate fruit. A supple dry W from Chenin Blanc is distinctive, and a rare Vin Santo is made from Malvasia Bianca grapes.

MARTINENS, CH   *France, Bordeaux, Margaux, Cru Bourgeois, R*   This is a Merlot-dominated vineyard: recent investment has improved an already good, consistent Margaux.

MARTÍNEZ, BODEGAS FAUSTINO   *Spain, Rioja, R, W, P*   Good-quality wines come from this family-owned *bodega*. Both their R and W wines make attractive early drinking, and their *reservas* and *gran reservas* age very well.

MARTINI & ROSSI   *Italy, Piedmont, W, R, Sp*   Largest producer of Asti *spumante* and vermouth; also Sp Riesling and Riserva Montelera Brut by the *metodo classico*.

MARTINI, LOUIS M   *USA, California, Napa, R, W, Sp*   Family-run winery known for Cabernet Sauvignons of finesse and ageability. Martini's Muscato Amabile is a treat: a low-alcohol, fresh, floral, grape-tasting sweet Sp W.

MARTINOLLES, DOM DE   *France, Midi, Limoux, W, Sp*   Owned by the Vergnes family, this is the best of the local private producers of this up-and-coming Sp wine. They have 65ha from which to make stylish Crémant de Limoux and Blanquette de Limoux, and some still W *vin de pays*.

MARYLAND   *USA*   Boordy, founded by Phillip Wagner in 1945, led the way in modern winemaking here: now the state's eastern corner, near Virginia, has several good wineries. The best zone so far is CATOCIN (a VA), in the mountains west of Baltimore. Leading producers include: BOORDY, Catocin Vineyards (Chardonnay and Cabernet Sauvignon), Montbray.

MAS AMIEL   *France, Midi, VDN*   Large estate at Maury planted with 90% Grenache Noir. This *vin doux naturel* is sold in three versions: 6-, 10- and 15-year-old. The last is best, with its flavour of fruit, nuts and prunes, not unlike an old tawny port.

MAS BLANC, DOM DE   *France, Midi, Banyuls, VDN*   The best producer of Banyuls *vins doux naturels*, in three styles. A vintage wine made in top years is aged for a year in 5-hl barrels; a second style has 6 years in 40-hl casks, topped up every 6 months. The third style is made in a kind of *solera* system and is bottled after 6 years.

MAS DE DAUMAS GASSAC   *France, Midi, Languedoc, R, W, Sp*   Estate near Montpellier which produces *vins de pays* at *Grand Cru* quality (and price) levels: some of the most interesting wines in France. Daumas Gassac's success has boosted the quality image of the LANGUEDOC as a whole. A cool microclimate and unusual red glacial powder and limestone soils combine to create unique *terroirs*. Grapes are mainly Cabernet Sauvignon for R and Chardonnay for W, but with a wide selection of others such as Merlot, Syrah, Pinot Noir, Viognier and Gros Manseng. The Rs need bottle-age: up to a decade in good vintages. The Ws are ready sooner. There is also a Sp P wine and a fluctuating list of other wines.

MAS DE LA DAME   *France, Provence, Coteaux d'Aix-en-Provence Les Baux, R, P*   The 55-ha vineyard here has a high proportion of Grenache, but the wines also have a good backbone of Syrah and Cabernet Sauvignon. There are two Rs: Cuvée Réserve and Cuvée Gourmande, and the Rosé du Mas is very fruity.

MASI   *Italy, Veneto, W, R*   Top estate for R wines from Valpolicello. Valpolicellas include Amarone Mazzano, Amarone Campolongo de Torbe and Recioto Mezzanella. *Vini da tavola* include Toar and Campo Fiorin.

MASSACHUSETTS   *USA*   State with a dozen wineries, most close to the ocean, growing classic and native grapes. Leading producer: Chicama Vineyards.

MASTROBERARDINO   *Italy, Southern Italy, Campania, W, R, P*   High-standard wines from near Naples include the finest Fiano di Avellino (W), Greco di Tufo (W) and Taurasi (R). An elegant Lachryma Christi del Vesuvio DOC is made in R, W and P versions.

MATANZAS CREEK   *USA, California, Sonoma, W, R*   There is a wide range here, but the focus is on Chardonnay, rich with butterscotch and vanilla, accented by clove, apple and licorice notes. Also a lean, lasting Merlot R and a Sauvignon, its W equivalent.

MATARO   See MOURVÈDRE.

MÁTRAALJA   *Hungary*   Large and diverse district in the northern part of Hungary. Mostly W wines of all styles from Olaszrisling, Rizlingszilváni and Tramini grapes among others. Also the location of the Gyöngyös estate, where Australian-trained pioneer winemaker Hugh Ryman oversees the making of clean, crisp Ws from Sauvignon Blanc and Chardonnay.

MATUA VALLEY WINES   *New Zealand, North Island, W, R, Sp*   One of the country's most innovative wineries. Wide range includes a good Sp called "M". The top-of-the-range Ararimu wines include Chardonnay and Cabernet Sauvignon.

MAUCAILLOU, CH   *France, Bordeaux, Moulis, Cru Bourgeois, R*   Source of elegant, modern-style wine from a modern *chai* and lots of new oak. Lavish facilities for visitors.

MAUFOUX, PROSPER   *France, Burgundy, Côte d'Or, R, W*   This Santenay *négociant* firm ages all its wines, R and W, in oak, with good results.

MAULE VALLEY   *Chile, South America, W, R*   Sub-region of the Central Valley, Chile's major wine-producing area. Developed and expanded in the 1980s, when it was found that Sauvignon Blanc, Merlot and Chardonnay are well suited to the cool climate.

MAURY   *France, Midi, AOC, VDN*   Mainly R *vin doux naturel* from Grenache Noir grapes, from a tiny AOC within Rivesaltes. It is aged for at least two years, and up to 15, before sale. Some is made in the *rancio* (oxidized) style. Leading producer: Mas Amiel.

MAUVEZIN, CH *France, Bordeaux, St-Emilion, Grand Cru Classé, R* This very small estate has, unusually for St-Emilion, almost 50% Cabernet Franc in the blend. New oak is very important here. A perfumed, elegant wine with supple fruit.

MAVRUD Red grape native to Bulgaria; it is difficult to grow, low-yielding and late-ripening, but when fully ripe and well made it gives dense, tannic and long-lasting wine that can be compared to that from MOURVÈDRE.

MAZIS-CHAMBERTIN See CHAMBERTIN.

MAZOYÈRES-CHAMBERTIN See CHAMBERTIN.

MAZUELO A Spanish name for CARIGNAN.

MCLAREN VALE *Australia, Victoria* To the south of Adelaide, the Vale's name was originally for R wines. While it still yields distinctive Shiraz and Cabernet Sauvignon Rs, many of its vineyards now make very good W wines, too. Leading producers include: Chapel Hill, D'Arenberg, Garrett, Ingoldby, Geoff Merrill, Normans, Wirra Wirra.

MCWILLIAM'S MOUNT PLEASANT *Australia, New South Wales, Hunter Valley R, W* Family-run firm producing top-quality wines, including Elizabeth Sémillon (W), only released when it is 6 years old.

MÉDOC *France, Bordeaux, AOC, R* Clarets from the Left Bank of the Gironde and Garonne rivers, made with a high proportion of Cabernet Sauvignon: refined, austere but appetizing, and long-lived. Within the Médoc peninsula, there is a hierarchy of appellations:
Haut-Médoc (which see) is the southern (better) half of the Médoc. Within Haut-Médoc are MOULIS, LISTRAC and the four renowned riverside appellations: ST-ESTÈPHE, PAUILLAC, ST-JULIEN and MARGAUX.
AOC Médoc covers the northern part of the peninsula. Here there is less of the vital well-drained gravel soil found in the Haut-Médoc. Wines from AOC Médoc typically have less Cabernets and more Merlot, do not need such long keeping (2–5 years) and are good value. Leading AOC Médoc producers include: Ch'x la Cardonne, Greysac, Loudenne, Les Ormes Sorbet, Patache d'Aux, Potensac, La Tour de By, La Tour St-Bonnet.

MEERLUST ESTATE *South Africa, Stellenbosch, R* A beautiful, R-wine only estate where Italian winemaker Giorgio Dalle Cia produces a superbly rich Merlot and a delicious bordeaux blend, Rubicon.

MELINI *Italy, Tuscany, Chianti, R* The third-largest Chianti producer after Ruffino and Antinori. Single-vineyard Chianti Classicos include La Selvanella and Terrarossa.

MELON DE BOURGOGNE/MUSCADET   White grape grown for the light, dry wine of the western Loire, also called Muscadet. Sometimes (erroneously) called Pinot Blanc in California.

MENDOCINO   *USA, California*   County on the north coast of California, with vineyards in **ANDERSON VALLEY** and Ukiah Valley. Rs do well: Zinfandels, Cabernet Sauvignon, Merlot. Anderson Valley is becoming a Sp wine centre.

MENDOZA   *Argentina, South America, R, W, P*   Argentina's winemaking centre is here in the province of Mendoza, some 960km west of Buenos Aires. Responsible for 70% of Argentina's wine.

MENETOU-SALON   *France, Loire, AOC, R, P, W*   Small upper-Loire wine district around villages west of Sancerre, making mainly Sauvignon Blanc W, but also Pinot Noir Rs and Ps. Can be good value. Leading producers include: Chavet, Pelle, Teiller.

MÉNTRIDA   *Spain, Castilla-La Mancha, DO, P, R*   One of four Castilla-La Mancha wine zones, south-west of Madrid, Méntrida is now a mass-production zone – but with scope for great potential. Leading producers include: Bodegas Valdeoro

MERCIER   *France, Champagne*   The LVMH group owns this maker of good, reliable, medium-bodied champagne: particularly popular in France.

MERCIER, CH   *France, Bordeaux, Côtes de Bourg, R*   Perfumed and interesting claret from old vines.

MERCREDIÈRE   *France, Loire, Muscadet, W*   The Futeul family, who are also *négociants*, produce full and powerful Muscadets from 36ha complete with an ancient castle on the banks of the River Sèvre.

MERCUREY   *France, Burgundy, AOC, R, W*   One of the main villages of the **CÔTE CHALONNAISE**, Mercurey makes predominantly R wine from Pinot Noir (and some W from Chardonnay). Good Mercurey can be well-priced and interesting burgundy at 4–6 years. Leading producers include: Dom de Chamerose, Chartron & Trébuchet, Faiveley, Michel Juillot, Mercurey co-op, Antonin Rodet/Ch de Chamirey, Hugues de Suremain.

MEREDYTH VINEYARDS   *USA, Virginia, W, R*   The state's oldest winery, in Middleburg, skilfully produces wines from hybrids and classic grapes. Decent Merlot R recently joined the consistently fine Seyval Blanc.

MERIDIAN   *USA, California, San Luis Obispo, W, R*   This large winery concentrates on a creamy, melon and vanilla Santa Barbara Chardonnay. Cabernet Sauvignon, Syrah and Zinfandel Rs are also made from the Home Vineyard.

MERITAGE   *USA*   Made-up term for a bordeaux-style wine from a blend of the same grapes used in Bordeaux, particularly Cabernet Sauvignon and Merlot for Rs.

MERLOT   The classic red grape of St-Emilion and Pomerol, also used in Médoc blends – and now in southern French *vins de pays*. Unblended, Merlot has a rich colour, a direct aroma and soft, earthy, fruity taste, appreciated in Switzerland, north Italy and increasingly in eastern European and New World vineyards.

METAIREAU, LOUIS   *France, Loire, Muscadet, W*   Nine producers, with 100ha, market their top-quality wines under Metaireau's label. The wines undergo rigorous tastings during vinification and before bottling (*sur lie* in the growers' cellars). Metaireau's own estate is Dom du Grand Mouton.

MÉTHODE CHAMPENOISE   *France*   The method of making sparkling wine that was developed in Champagne in France and has been copied the world over. A secondary fermentation in the bottle results in bubbles of carbon dioxide becoming trapped in the wine. Following an EU directive, the term may no longer appear on the label of any wine from outside the region, although the technique is in use world-wide. Alternative terms include classic method and traditional method.

MÉTHODE RURALE   *France*   Sparkling wine method: the wine is bottled before fermentation is over, producing a sparkle.

METODO CLASSICO, METODO TRADIZIONALE   *Italy*   Terms used in Italy for the MÉTHODE CHAMPENOISE technique for production of sparkling wines.

MEURSAULT   *France, Burgundy, AOC, W, R*   Côte de Beaune village famous for W wines of powerful, persistent flavour and good ability to age. There are no *Grands Crus*, but a large number of *Premiers Crus*. Leading producers include: Bouchard Père & Fils, Comte Lafon, Michelot, Prieur, Ropiteau.

MEXICO   *Central America*   Although Mexico boasts the New World's oldest vineyards, today its climate is considered too hot to be hospitable to wine grapes and the top priority is growing grapes for brandy. There are more than 70,000ha of vines and close to 80% of the wine-grape harvest goes directly into brandy or vermouth production, although table wine production has been on the increase since 1980.

MEYNEY, CH   *France, Bordeaux, St-Estèphe, Cru Bourgeois, R*   The Cordier firm of *négociants* own Meyney and ensure its high standards and wide distribution. One of the best *Crus Bourgeois*, and one of the classic St-Estèphes.

MICHEL, LOUIS   *France, Burgundy, Chablis, W*   The great exponent of unoaked Chablis. Mainly *Premiers Crus*: quintessential Chablis with the classic nerve, steeliness and mineral quality. Michel also uses the label Domaine de la Tour Vaubourg.

MICHIGAN   *USA*   Lake shores provide warm conditions in this Mid-West state for good classic-variety wines. Leading producers include: Ch Grand Traverse, St Julian.

MIGUEL TORRES *Chile, R, W, Sp* Highly innovative venture begun in 1979 by Spain's Torres family: a key stage in Chile's wine renaissance. Miguel Torres concentrates on Sauvignon Blanc and Cabernet Sauvignon, in addition to a Sp wine, Brut Nature. Wines are mainly destined for export.

MILDARA-BLASS *Australia, R, W* Mildara's merger with Wolf Blass unites two of Australia's best-known names. Production, centred in South Australia, includes a wide range of multi-regional, multi-varietal blends such as the succulent R Jamieson's Run. Quality wines are made in Coonawarra and other areas.

MILLBROOK VINEYARDS *USA, New York, Hudson River Valley, W, R* At Millbrook, east of the Hudson, John Dyson grows only classic varieties. Half the production is Chardonnay, a barrel-fermented Reserve. He also features Cabernet Franc and Pinot Noir Rs, and is experimenting with Rhône and Italian varieties.

MILLERIOUX, PAUL *France, Loire, Sancerre, W, R* Clos de Roy (W) and Côte de Champtin (R) are the top wines from Millerioux's well-regarded estate in Crézancy-en-Sancerre. Both are matured in wood.

MILLÉSIME *France* Term meaning year; vintage.

MILLET, CH *France, Bordeaux, Graves, R* This large Portets estate is best known for its fruity if not especially complex Rs, which are best drunk young.

MINERVOIS *France, Midi, AOC, R, P, W* Mostly R-wine appellation: a large and varied area with an improving reputation thanks to better vinification and grapes: eg Grenache, Syrah and Mourvèdre for Rs. W Minervois is being improved by Marsanne and Roussane in addition to Macabeo and Bourboulenc. Leading producers include: Daniel Domergue, Ch Fabas, Ch de Gourgazaud, La Livinière co-op, Dom Ste-Eulalie.

MINNESOTA *USA* Cold winters hamper vine-growing, but ALEXIS BAILLY and a cooperative of small growers keep trying (with some success) with hybrids.

MIREVAL, MUSCAT DE *France, Midi, AOC, VDN* This *vin doux naturel* zone adjoins better-known Frontignan. Very similar wine.

MISSION The name of this R-wine grape variety tells its story: it was grown at the Catholic mission stations of California when the Mexicans ruled. Until the late 19th century it made most California wine, but it is now in decline. Its wine is unimpressive.

MISSION-HAUT-BRION, CH LA *France, Bordeaux, Pessac-Léognan, Cru Classé, R* The same owners as Ch HAUT-BRION, yet the two wines are very different. Rich and tannic, La Mission stresses power and depth of flavour. Sold at 1st-growth prices, it is often worth what is asked.

MISSION HILL *Canada, British Columbia, W, R* New Zealand winemaker John Simes makes rich New World-style Chardonnay and some interesting W blends.

MISSISSIPPI *USA* Native American grapes are the ones to thrive here, making wine with a Southern accent.

MISSOURI *USA* Four VAs and 30 wineries represent the revival of a century-old tradition. Most vines are hybrids, though quality can be good, with a few classic *vinifera* vines. Leading producers include: Hermannhof, Mount Pleasant, Stone Hill.

MITTELHAARDT/DEUTSCHE WEINSTRASSE *Germany, Pfalz, Bereich, W, R* The district which forms the heart of the Pfalz, making good, even great Ws, and some good Rs, in villages such as **FORST** and **DEIDESHEIM**. East-facing slopes and a dry climate give conditions comparable to Alsace. Riesling is joined for Ws by Silvaner, Gewürztraminer, Rulander and other grapes. Leading producers include: Basserman-Jordan, Von Buhl, Bürklin-Wolf, Weingut Dr Deinhard, Weingut Pfeffingen.

MITTELRHEIN *Germany, Anbaugebiet, W* The Rhein valley vineyards north of the Rheingau, lining the Rhine Gorge and side-valleys. W wines, the best from Riesling, are made in scenic but often inaccessible sites. Good, if a touch earthy, wines.

MOELLEUX *France* Describes sweet white wines, particularly those of Vouvray and other Loire vineyards.

MOET & CHANDON *France, Champagne* The largest vineyard owner in Champagne, with 558ha. The NV is the biggest-selling champagne worldwide, although quality has been variable. The vintage wine is consistently fine and Moët also produce one of Champagne's most prestigious wines, the luxury *cuvée* Dom Pérignon.

MOILLARD-GRIVOT *France, Burgundy, Côte d'Or, R, W* Reliable *négociant* and vineyard owner based in Nuits-St-Georges.

MOLDOVA The most western-influenced of the former USSR's winegrowing republics. Its 160,000–200,000ha of vineyards have more European varieties than any other republic, with huge tracts planted to Chardonnay, Cabernet Sauvignon, Sauvignon Blanc, Aligoté and the Pinot family. Native varieties include the rich and spicy Saperavi (R) and the somewhat neutral Rkatsiteli (W). The best wines come from the centre of the country and along the Dniester River. Enormous potential, particularly for Rs. Names to look for include the long-lived Cabernet-dominated Negru de Purkar R.

MOLISE *Italy* In central Italy, one of the smallest and least important wine regions. The main grapes grown are Montepulciano for R and Trebbiano for W. The local DOC, Biferno, is for R, P and W wines.

MOLLEX, MAISON   *France, Savoie, Seyssel, W, R, Sp*   The appellation's leading grower, with vineyards which include the noted Clos de la Péclatte. Makers of still W from Roussette, R (AOC Savoie), and Sp Seyssel. Methods are traditional, results good.

MOMMESSIN   *France, Burgundy, Côte d'Or, R, W*   Large *négociant* based at Mâcon, with a range of Beaujolais, Mâconnais and other wines; also sole owner of the Côte de Nuits *Grand Cru* Clos de LAMBRAYS.

MONBAZILLAC   *France, South-West, AOC, W*   Great sweet W wine of the Dordogne; like Sauternes, it is made from Sémillon, Sauvignon Blanc and Muscadelle. True quality comes from NOBLE ROT. Leading producers include: Ch de Monbazillac, Ch du Treuil de Nailhac.

MONBRISON, CH   *France, Bordeaux, Margaux, Cru Bourgeois, R*   A small vineyard in Arsac with a good name for solid, elegant wines which repay ageing.

MONDAVI, ROBERT   *USA, California, Napa, W, R*   Both company and eponymous founder are among the vital forces in the American wine industry. Famed for its Fumé Blanc (oak-aged Sauvignon Blanc); the Oakville winery also makes structured Cabernet Sauvignon, fruity Chardonnays and supple Pinot Noirs. Reserve wines are among the best made in California. Affordable table wines come from the Woodbridge winery and Mondavi also owns Vichon and Byron.

MONGEARD-MUGNERET, DOM   *France, Burgundy, AOC, R, W*   Expanding domain with holdings of *Grand* and *Premier Cru* vineyards, producing concentrated R wines of quality.

MONIN   *France, Savoie, Bugey, R, W, Sp*   Most important maker of the wines of this VDQS zone: W Roussette de Bugey with a good amount of Chardonnay, R from Mondeuse, and Sp W. Good wines, but most are drunk locally.

MONNIER, DOM JEAN & FILS   *France, Burgundy, Côte d'Or, R, W*   Top-quality R and W wine using traditional methods, from Meursault, Pommard and Puligny.

MONT BOUQUET, DU   *France, Vin de Pays, R*   Zone in the Gard, southern France, making Rs from traditional grapes, often with some added Syrah for spice and interest.

MONT DE MILIEU   *France, Burgundy, Chablis, 1er Cru*   This south-facing vineyard is tucked into a side-valley, earning its *1er Cru* status with powerful, age-worthy Chablis.

MONT-REDON, DOM DE   *France, Rhône, Châteauneuf-du-Pape, R, W*   Reliable producer of R and W Châteauneuf; the R ages well, the W is among the best made.

MONT TAUCH, COOPERATIVE DES PRODUCTEURS DU   *France, Midi, Fitou, R*   The most important of the appellation's co-ops, in the village of Tuchan. It makes six qualities of Fitou, including a selection of the best *terroir* and oldest vines, and wines from various individual domaines.

MONTAGNE ST-EMILION *France, Bordeaux, AOC, R* The largest and probably best of the St-Emilion satellite appellations, sited close to the border with Pomerol. The wines, from varying proportions of Cabernet Sauvignon, Cabernet Franc, Merlot, Malbec and Carmenère, can be supple and fruity with some finesse and good ageing potential. Leading producers include: Ch'x Calon, Croix-Beauséjour, Laroze-Bayard, des Laurets, Maison Blanche, Roudier, La Tour Mont d'Or, Tour-Musset, des Tours, Vernay Bonfort.

MONTAGNY *France, Burgundy, AOC, W, R* Southern village of the CÔTE CHALONNAISE, producing good and sometimes age-worthy Chardonnay Ws. All wines that achieve 11.5° can be labelled *Premier Cru*. Leading producers include: Buxy co-op, Louis Latour, Antonin Rodet, Ch da la Saule, Jean Vachet.

MONTALIVET, CH *France, Bordeaux, Graves W, R* Wines of great consistency: Sémillon-dominated, oaky Ws and juicy Rs. Both should be enjoyed when quite young.

MONTANA WINES *New Zealand, North Island W, R, Sp* The country's largest wine group is also one of the most innovative, and was the first to plant Sauvignon Blanc in Marlborough. Working with Deutz champagne they make the top-quality Sp, Deutz Marlborough Cuvée.

MONTÉE DE TONNERRE *France, Burgundy, Chablis, 1er Cru* Hill of vines next to the *Grands Crus* of Chablis, making wine almost as good and worth bottle-age. Chapelot, Pied d'Aloue and Côte de Bréchain are plots within Montée de Tonnerre.

MONTELENA, CH *USA, California, Napa, W, R* The old stone château, north of Calistoga, excels in richly textured Chardonnays, firm blackberry and blackcurrant Cabernet Sauvignons, zingy, raspberry and peppercorn Zinfandels, and velvety, apricot-laden off-dry Johannisberg Rieslings.

MONTEPULCIANO D'ABRUZZO *Italy, Abruzzo, DOC, R* The best of these good-value Rs are very full-flavoured with lots of warm, ripe fruit. Leading producers include: Barone Cornacchia, Illuminati, Emidio Pepe, Valentini.

MONTEREY *USA, California* County of California's central coast, sunny but dry, yielding good everyday wines from irrigated vineyards in the Salinas Valley, and quality ones from Arroyo Seco, Carmel Valley, CHALONE and Santa Lucia Highlands.

MONTES *Chile, R, W* Estate formed by four partners in 1988, set in the MAIPO VALLEY. The vineyards grow mainly Cabernet

Sauvignon and Merlot for Rs, followed by Sauvignon Blanc and Chardonnay for Ws. Nogales is the label for lower-priced wines, Villa Montes the top-of-the-range export brand.

MONTEVIÑA *USA, California, Sierra Foothills, R* This Amador County winery focuses on Italian-style Rs, including California's most reliable Barbera. New plantings of Nebbiolo share space with trials of Sangiovese, Refosco and Aleatico.

MONTHÉLIE *France, Burgundy, AOC, R, W* Mainly R wines come from this village between Volnay and Meursault in the Côte de Beaune. Increasingly good-value, fragrant, well-structured wines are made from Pinot Noir grapes. Leading producers include: Paul Garaudet, Comte Lafon, Ch de Monthélie.

MONTICELLO *USA, Virginia, VA* Wine zone named after Jefferson's estate, where vines were planted two centuries ago (but without great success). Today, Chardonnay and bordeaux-style Rs are being made. Leading producers include: Montdomaine.

MONTILLA-MORILES *Spain, Andalucia, DO, W* Andalucian wine zone in province of Córdoba, producing *jovenes*, fortified and unfortified wines. The fortifieds, which can be sweet or dry, are similar in style to sherry. Leading producers include: Alvear, Pérez Barquero.

MONTLOUIS *France, Loire, AOC, W, Sp* Still and Sp (*mousseux* and *pétillant*) Ws, from medium-dry to sweet, made across the River Loire from Vouvray. Leading producers include: M Berger, Deletang Père et Fils.

MONTRACHET *France, Burgundy, AOC, W* Côte de Beaune *Grand Cru* which makes the most expensive and often the best W wine in all of Burgundy. Dense, buttery and rich, with a backbone of acidity that means it reaches its potential after 10 years and allows it to last in bottle for 20 years or more. On the slope above Montrachet is the *Grand Cru* of CHEVALIER-MONTRACHET, below it the *Grand Cru* of BÂTARD-MONTRACHET. Leading producers include: Bouchard Père & Fils, Dom de la Romanée-Conti, Drouhin, Leflaive, Jacques Prieur.

MONTRAVEL *France, South-West, AOC, W* Little-known appellation near Bergerac for dry W wine, with sub-zones Côtes de Montravel for medium-sweet and Haut-Montravel for sweet W wines.

MONTROSE, CH *France, Bordeaux, Médoc, St-Estèphe, 2ème Cru Classé, R* The solid, long-lasting wines of this château suggest a St-Estèphe version of Latour, as does the site – though the style has softened since the 1989. In good vintages, among the Médoc's best wines.

MORAVIA *Czech Republic* One of the two Czech regions, the other being Bohemia. Moravia enjoys a slightly warmer climate and has a greater area under vine. R varieties include Frankovka

(Germany's Limberger) and St-Laurent, plus a little Pinot. Ws, which can be good, include Pinot Blanc, Traminer, Laski Riesling and the native, aromatic Irsay Oliver; good Sp wine is also made.

MOREAU, J-J   *France, Burgundy, Chablis, W*   The largest *négociant* house in Chablis, making sound wines, although not always very exciting ones.

MOREY-ST-DENIS   *France, Burgundy, AOC, R*   Long-lived R burgundies in the classic, solid Côte de Nuits style. Those from the five *Grands Crus* (CLOS DE TART, CLOS ST-DENIS, CLOS DE LA ROCHE, CLOS DES LAMBRAYS, BONNES MARES) can be great, while the *Premiers Crus* and village wines offer comparatively good value. Leading producers include: Dujac, G Lignier, Roumier, Rousseau.

MORGEOT   *France, Burgundy, Côte de Beaune, 1er Cru, R, W*   Located in Chassagne-Montrachet around the Abbaye de Morgeot, this vineyard produces fine, full-bodied Ws and deeply-coloured, well-structured Rs. Leading producers include: Blanc-Gagnard, Jean-Noël Gagnard, Olivier Leflaive.

MORGON   *France, Burgundy, AOC, R*   Beaujolais *cru* whose best vineyards share distinctive slate soil, making particularly rich and full, deep-coloured, long-lived wines that develop exotic fruit flavours in age. However, Morgons from less favoured sites can be unsubtle and heavy. Leading producers include: Jonchet, Passot, Savoye, Dom de Thizy.

MORNINGTON PENINSULA   *Australia, Victoria*   Sited south of Melbourne, the cool maritime climate here is proving ideal for winemaking. Results include delicate, elegant W Chardonnays, and Rs from Pinot Noir, Shiraz, Merlot and Cabernet Sauvignon. Leading producers include: Dromana, Elgee Park, Stoniers Merricks.

MOROCCO   *North Africa, R, P*   Wine here is made with a more commercial approach than in neighbouring Algeria. Morocco has 12 wine regions in all, the best and biggest of which is Meknès and Fèz, a high-altitude area beneath the Atlas Mountains, specializing in rich and chewy R wine. Lighter R wines are produced around Rabat, and P wine is made in the regions of Gharb and Semmour.

MOSEL-SAAR-RUWER   *Germany, Anbaugebiet, W*   The wine region taking in the Mosel valley plus its tributaries the SAAR and RUWER. The main valley is divided into (north to south) the Bereichs ZELL, BERNKASTEL, Obermosel and Moseltor. The latter two are of limited interest. Most Mosel wines are W; the best are from Riesling, but many wines at the cheaper end are made from Müller-Thurgau.

MOSELLAND   *Germany, Mosel, W*   The enormous cooperative of the central Mosel, representing many small growers, makes reliable wine at every quality and price level.

MOSELLE, VIN DE *France, Alsace, VDQS, W, R* Mainly W wines from France's most northerly vineyards, along the upper Moselle valley. Main grapes are Rivaner (Müller-Thurgau) and Auxerrois for Ws; and Pinot Noir for Rs.

MOUEIX, J-P *France, Bordeaux, St-Emilion & Pomerol* Well-known firm of *négociants* in Libourne, Bordeaux, owning or part-owning several châteaux in Pomerol, St-Emilion and adjoining districts. They produce reliable blended wines from all these AOCs. Pioneers of the revival of Fronsac, they are now active, too, in the Côtes de Castillon.

MOULIN DE DUHART *France, Bordeaux, Médoc, Pauillac, R* 2nd wine of Ch Duhart-Milon-Rothschild.

MOULIN DES COSTES *France, Provence, Bandol, R, W* The Bunan family own 75ha of vineyards, making this one of the appellation's leading domaines. Rs, blended from different estates, are 65% Mourvèdre, 14% Grenache and 6% Syrah. Cuvée Spéciale, which is made only in the best years, has a higher proportion of Mourvèdre. Also a Cabernet Sauvignon made as Vin de Pays de Mont-Caume.

MOULIN DU CADET, CH *France, Bordeaux, St-Emilion, Grand Cru Classé, R* This estate is now managed by Ets Jean-Pierre **MOUEIX**. The once fairly delicate style of wine is becoming richer, with more body and staying-power.

MOULIN-À-VENT *France, Burgundy, AOC, R* Most serious, most expensive, most age-worthy of the Beaujolais *crus*: deep ruby-R, powerful, well-structured wines that can still impress after 10 years. Leading producers include: Dom la Chevalière, Jean George, Hubert Lapierre, Hospices de Romanèche-Thorins, Dom des Vignes de Tremblay.

MOULIN-À-VENT, CH *France, Bordeaux, Moulis, Cru Bourgeois, R* Good, long-maturing wine in the Moulis style.

MOULIS *France, Bordeaux, AOC, R* Solid, dark, long-lived Médoc Rs from an inland commune, neighbour to **LISTRAC**. Leading producers include: Ch'x Chasse-Spleen, Dutruch-Grand-Poujeaux, Gressier-Grand-Poujeaux, Maucaillou, Moulin-à-Vent, Poujeaux.

MOUNT BARKER-FRANKLAND *Australia, Western Australia* Beautiful cool-climate area which has recently gained a fine reputation for its wines, ranging from Ws from Chardonnay, Sauvignon Blanc and Riesling to Rs from Pinot Noir, Shiraz, Cabernet Sauvignon and Malbec. Leading producers include: Alkoomi, Goundrey, Plantagenet.

MOUNT LANGI GHIRAN *Australia, Victoria, Grampians, R* Trevor Mast is the maker here of long-lived Shiraz Rs which bear comparison with the best of the Rhône.

MOUNT PLEASANT VINEYARD *USA, Missouri, W, R*   Historic winery founded in 1881, revived in 1968, now producing up to 20,000 cases of varietals and sparkling wines. The Vidal Blanc is often top-notch, along with Seyval Blanc, a delicate Riesling W and port-style fortified wine.

MOUNT VEEDER *USA, California, VA*   Area of hill vineyards to the west of Napa Valley, with well-drained volcanic soils yielding good Cabernet Sauvignons and Chardonnays. Leading producers include: Hess Collection, Mayacamas, Mount Veeder, Ch Potelle.

MOURVÈDRE   Sturdy, dark, aromatic red grape, usually blended with Syrah, Grenache and Cinsaut in the southern Rhône, Provence and Midi. Known as Mataro in California and Australia. Spanish in origin, but unknown there now.

MOUTON-ROTHSCHILD, CH *France, Bordeaux, Médoc, Pauillac, 1er Cru Classé, R*   The late Baron Philippe de Rothschild and (since his death) his daughter Philippine have made Mouton the 1st Growth the Baron always believed it to be (he attained its promotion from 2nd in 1973). Cabernet Sauvignon dominates in the vineyard, and the wine style is full, even opulent. A superb museum of works of art showing wine is housed at the estate.

MOUTONNE, LA *France, Burgundy, Chablis*   See VAUDÉSIR.

MUDGEE *Australia, New South Wales*   Not as well known as the Hunter Valley, this region also produces good Sémillon (W) and Shiraz (R), plus Chardonnay and Cabernet Sauvignon. Leading producers include: Botobolar, Craigmoor, Huntington, Stein.

MUGA, BODEGAS *Spain, Rioja, R, W, P, Sp*   Absolutely top quality wines are made along very traditional lines at this leading Rioja *bodega*. The emphasis is on Rs, although W, P and Sp wines are also produced.

MULDERBOSCH VINEYARDS *South Africa, Stellenbosch, R, W*   Larry Jacobs produced his first wines in 1991 but has already achieved international status for both his Ws: a richly exotic Sauvignon Blanc and mouthwatering, buttery Chardonnay.

MULLER, DE *Spain, Catalonia, Priorato, R, W, P*   Established in 1851, De Muller makes hefty, long-lived R wines. A wide range of other wines includes a delicate Moscatel Seco, and the rare but delectable *solera*-aged Priorato wines.

MÜLLER-CATOIR *Germany, Pfalz, W*   Grower whose wide range of grapes, including Gewürztraminer and Grauburgunder, and very traditional techniques make individual, powerful wines.

MÜLLER-SCHARZHOF, EGON *Germany, Saar, W*   Superb, long-lived and expensive Riesling wine (in warm vintages), handcrafted from the fruit of great vineyards including the noble Scharzhofberg hill at Wiltingen.

MÜLLER-THURGAU   Germany's most-planted grape (a crossing: Riesling x Silvaner), producing fairly neutral sweet or dry white wine. Makes ordinary wine in Hungary; better, floral-scented examples in New Zealand, northern Italy, Austria, England and Luxembourg.

MUMM   *France, Champagne*   The largest GRANDE MARQUE, though not the top. Its best-known wine, the NV Cordon Rouge, which has gone through some rough patches, is widely exported. At its best it is attractive, with a delicately fruity palate. The prestige *cuvée*, René Lalou, is very fine.

MURRAY RIVER VALLEY   *Australia, Victoria*   Region yielding more than 80% of Victoria's grapes. Everyday Ws are its life blood.

MURRIETA, BODEGAS MARQUÉS DE   *Spain, Rioja, R, W*   Established in 1870, this Rioja pioneer uses wholly traditional methods. The Rs are oaky, sturdy but capable of ageing to finesse; the Ws are deep and golden but dry in the traditional Rioja style. A small range includes Marqués de Murrieta (R, W) and the expensive, memorable *reserva* Castillo Ygay (R, W), which is only released when mature.

MURRUMBIDGEE   *Australia, New South Wales*   Production in this large, irrigated semi-desert region is mainly bulk Ws, with Sémillon the dominant grape. The only R of significance is Shiraz. Sweet W botrytized Sémillon is a speciality.

MUSAR, CH   *Lebanon, R, W*   Owned by Serge Hochar, who trained in France. Produces top-quality, opulent, long-lived R wine from Cabernet Sauvignon, Cinsaut and Syrah and fine Ws from Chardonnay and Sauvignon Blanc. Despite being in a war zone, 1984 was the only year he did not succeed in making wine.

MUSCADELLE   Aromatic white grape used blended in some white bordeaux, and for rich dessert Liqueur Tokays in Australia.

MUSCADET   *France, Loire, AOC, W*   From the mouth of the Loire, near Nantes. Good Muscadet is fresh, crisp and dry: poor ones are very acidic. With a very few exceptions, these are wines to drink young: the year after they are made. The grape is Melon de Bourgogne, now usually known simply as Muscadet. The region divides into three AOCs:
Muscadet is made mainly in the west, in fairly small quantities.
Muscadet des Coteaux de la Loire comes from east of Nantes.
Muscadet de Sèvre-et-Maine is by far the largest, and best, appellation, from areas around two valleys south-east of Nantes. It is best, fresh and with a hint of bubbles, when it is bottled *sur lie:* straight from the cask, without first racking it off its lees. This gives a rich yeasty flavour as well as a slight natural sparkle. *Sur lie* wines will say so on the label. Leading producers include: Chéreau-Carré, Donatien Bahuaud, Ch de la Galissonnière, Marquis de Goulaine, Louis Metaireau, Ch la Noë, Marcel Sautejeau, Sauvion.

MUSCAT Family of at least 200 grapes; most white, all making distinctively grapey wines. Styles range from light and sparkling Moscato d'Asti and dry Muscat d'Alsace, to sweet golden Muscat de Beaumes-de-Venise and rich dessert Black and Orange Muscats from California and Australia.

MUSIGNY *France, Burgundy, AOC, R, W* Côte de Nuits *Grand Cru,* in the commune of Chambolle-Musigny, whose site and soil produce some of Burgundy's greatest, most refined and subtle R wines. There is also a rare W wine. Leading producers include: Ch de Chambolle-Musigny, Dom Georges Roumier, Dom Comte Georges de Vogüé.

MUSKAT-SILVANER German/Austrian synonym of SAUVIGNON BLANC.

MYRAT, CH DE *France, Bordeaux, Barsac, 2ème Cru Classé, W* For 15 years there were no vines here, but they were replanted in 1988. The first vintage released was the 1991. With young vines, the wine cannot yet match its neighbours.

N

NAHE *Germany, Anbaugebiet, W* Region of vineyards along the Nahe and its tributaries, south of the Mosel and west of the Rhine. Good, even great Riesling Ws from **BAD KREUZNACH, SCHLOSSBÖCKELHEIM, TRAISEN** etc.

NAIRAC, CH *France, Bordeaux, Barsac, 2ème Cru Classé, W* The winemaking here is perfectionist, though the wine is always marked by new oak, excessively for some tastes. The 1990 is a classic Barsac.

NAOUSSA *Greece, R* The Xynomavro grape dominates in this norrthern wine area, producing hefty R wines which have been wood-aged. Leading producers include: Boutari.

NAPA *USA, California, VA* Napa County – as distinct from the Napa Valley which the county includes – has a VA usable by every vineyard there, including some well outside the actual Valley and its watershed. Labels may carry the Napa name or that of a sub-VA such as **STAGS LEAP DISTRICT, RUTHERFORD** or **LOS CARNEROS**.

NAPOLÉON, GRAND CHAMPAGNE *France, Champagne* Family-owned, this is the least-known of the **GRANDES MARQUES**, and one of the smallest. The wines, however, are of top quality, especially the vintage champagnes.

NAUDIN, CLOS *France, Loire, Vouvray, W, Sp* The Foreau family owns 12ha of vineyard, all on the high ground above the village of Vouvray, and makes the usual range of Vouvray wines, from Sp through all sweetness levels of still wine.

NAVARRA *Spain, Navarra, DO, W, P, R* This northern province, which adjoins RIOJA, has been making wine for centuries. The big, powerful *rosados* are among the world's best P wines but the Rs are steadily improving in quality. Research into grapes and microclimates has boosted quality. Leading producers include: **BODEGAS JULIÁN CHIVITE, BODEGAS IRACHE**, Vinícola Navarra, Bodegas Principe de Viana.

NAVARRO *USA, California, Mendocino, W, R* In the cool quiet of remote **ANDERSON VALLEY** the Navarro winery make crisp, dry Chardonnays, supple Pinot Noirs and sweet W botrytized Riesling and Gewürztraminer.

NÉAC See LALANDE DE POMEROL.

NEBBIOLO Classic red grape from Piedmont in northern Italy. Its wine is high in acidity, needing wood-ageing and then many years in bottle to soften the tannins. Makes Barolo, Barbaresco and other northern Italian wines such as Gattinara and Valtellina. Nebbiolo is sometimes grown under other names, such as Spanna and Chiavennasca.

NEDERBURG *South Africa, Paarl, R, W* Home to the annual Nederburg Auction, this huge winery produces an astonishing array, but is most famous for its dessert wines like the Special and Noble Late Harvests and Edelkeur, the latter from Chenin Blanc.

NÉGOCIANT *France* Merchant who buys grapes or wine from growers to mature it and/or sell it to wholesalers or foreign importers.

NELSON *New Zealand, South Island* Small north-coast wine area enjoying a good climate. Mainly W wines are produced, from Chardonnay and Riesling. Leading producers include: Neudorf, Seifried/Redwood Valley.

NEMEA *Greece, Peloponnese, R* St George is the grape variety used in this area near Corinth for making fruity R wines.

NENIN, CH *France, Bordeaux, Pomerol, R* This large estate was until recently making rather old-fashioned wine, lacking the concentration and richness of the top Pomerols. The wine has much improved following investment.

NEUSIEDLERSEE *Austria, Burgenland* Wine zone, split into two districts, around the shores of the wide, shallow Neusiedlersee lake. Almost 20% of Austria's grapes are grown here. Vast quantities of botrytized wines (of mixed quality; some excellent) are produced in the south. Over in Neusiedlersee-Hügelland, on the eastern shore, superb botrytized wines are made. Rust, on the west bank, is its most famous village and Ruster *Ausbruch*, a style of wine generally less sweet than *Beerenauslese*, has been made here for centuries. R wines are increasingly made, from Blaigburgunder and Cabernet Sauvignon, among other grapes. Leading producers include: Anton Kollwentz, Alois Kracher, Willi Opitz, Heidi Schröck, Josef Umathum.

NEW HAMPSHIRE *USA* Harsh winters have killed off attempts to make wine from classic grapes, though hybrids are successful.

NEW JERSEY *USA* Some encouraging wines in European styles come from the small producers in the "Garden State" such as RENAULT and Tewksbury.

NEW MEXICO *USA* The Rio Grande Valley offers a relatively cool climate: grapes were first grown here in 1580. Today wineries in three VAs offer good Cabernet Sauvignon and the record for Sp W wines is impressive. Leading producers include: ANDERSON VALLEY VINEYARDS, Gruet.

NEW SOUTH WALES *Australia* The first Australian state to cultivate grapevines. There are three main regions – HUNTER VALLEY, MUDGEE and MURRUMBIDGEE – Hunter being the best known, especially for Shiraz (R) and Sémillon (W). Vines are also grown at COWRA, noted for Sp and W wines, at MURRUMBIDGEE and elsewhere in the state.

NEW YORK   *USA*   America's second wine state (after California) with wine zones The FINGER LAKES, HUDSON RIVER VALLEY and LONG ISLAND. The first two have track-record of a century or more for both quality and bulk wine, while Long Island is a new zone profiting from the mild ocean climate. New York's wines were mostly from native American (LABRUSCA) grapes until the 1980s, when classic *vinifera* and hybrid vines began to be popular. For producers see named zones mentioned above.

NEW ZEALAND   Wine has nearly two centuries of history here, but only in the 1970s did true quality become the norm. A fast-moving industry incessantly explores new wine zones, grapes and styles. Many vineyards are new, and maturity will boost the quality, particularly of R wines. A cool and variable climate leads to character and finesse but can mean small crops. The Ws are established stars: from Sauvignon Blanc, particularly from MARL-BOROUGH, Chardonnay, Riesling and others. Rs are less success-ful – so far, though there are increasing numbers of interesting ones – but Sp wines are very good. Other wine zones include AUCKLAND, HAWKE'S BAY, NELSON, CENTRAL OTAGO.

NICOLAS FEUILLATTE   *France, Champagne, AOC, Sp*   This Eper-nay house is owned by 85 cooperatives with some 4,000 mem-bers and 1,600ha of vines. Their best wine is the prestige *cuvée*, Palmes d'Or.

NICOLAY, PETER   *Germany, Mosel, W, R*   See PAULY-BERGWEILER.

NIEDERHAUSEN   *Germany, Nahe, W*   Wine town and centre of quality wine in the Nahe, home of the State Domain (STAATS-DOMÄNE) and with top vineyards such as Hermanshölle and Hermannsberg.

NIERSTEIN   *Germany, Rheinhessen, Bereich, W*   Wide and thus diverse zone west and south of Nierstein on the Rhine. Wine with the *bereich* label ("Bereich Nierstein") will be soft, everyday W, usually from Müller-Thurgau grapes. Nierstein the town has excellent vineyards (including Bruderberg, Hipping, Pettenthal) along the RHEINTERRASSE: know wines from these vineyards by the prefix "Niersteiner" in their names, but beware Niersteiner Gutes Domtal, a GROSSLAGE which covers a large area, only 2% of which is within Nierstein, and which is mostly lower-quality vineyards. Leading producers in Nierstein itself include: Anton Balbach Erben, Heyl zu Herrnhausern.

NOBILO VINTNERS   *New Zealand, North Island, W, R, Sp*   This large, family-owned firm uses grapes from both North and South Islands to make mainly Chardonnay, but also a full range of other single variety wines – including a rare for New Zealand planting of South Africa's Pinotage R.

NOBLET, DOM GILLES *France, Burgundy, Mâconnais, W* Very fine producer of rich, generous Pouilly-Fuissé, worthy of bottle-age in good vintages.

NOË, CH DE LA *France, Loire, Muscadet, W* The Comte de Malestroit's historic estate makes Muscadet of good structure, worth keeping for 2–3 years. Curiously, the wine is not bottled *sur lie*.

NOËLLE, LES VIGNERONS DE LA *France, Loire, Muscadet, W, R, P* One of the biggest cooperatives in the Loire, based at Ancenis. Makes **COTEAUX D'ANCENIS** (W, R, P), Muscadet des Coteaux de Loire and *vin de pays*; also an excellent **GROS PLANT**. Labels used include Domaine des Hautes Noëlles for Muscadet.

NORTH CAROLINA *USA* The extravagent **CHÂTEAU BILTMORE** leads a clutch of wineries in a state best known as the home of the native Scuppernong grape, which makes highly individual wines.

NORTH COAST *USA, California, VA* Wine zone taking in Napa, Sonoma and other coastal counties north of San Francisco: the quality heart of California wine.

NOUVEAU *France* Wine of the most recent vintage: after 31 August of the following year, wines can no longer claim this appellation. Beaujolais Nouveau is the most famous.

NOVA SCOTIA *Canada* Three wineries in this cool zone grow hybrid vines, and there are experiments with new kinds of grapes from Russia.

NOVAL, QUINTA DO *Portugal, port* The two vintage ports under this name are from the beautiful *quinta* vineyards: the sweet and fruity regular vintage, a classic Portuguese style; and the Naçional, made in tiny (and expensive) quantities from ungrafted vines. The rest of the range, made from estate and bought-in grapes, is of good quality, from the Late Bottled Noval to the aged tawnies.

NOVELLO *Italy* New wine: see **NOUVEAU**.

NOZET, CH DE *France, Loire, Pouilly-Fumée, W, R* The most famous and most important Pouilly estate, owned by the de Ladoucette family. The top wine from the 52-ha vineyard is Baron de L, which is made only in best years and which commands high prices. Other wines are made from bought-in grapes.

NUITS/NUITS-ST-GEORGES *France, Burgundy, AOC, R* This important wine centre at the heart of Burgundy's Côte d'Or has around 40 *Premiers Crus*. The wines vary in style from scented and opulent to earthy and robust; most are best drunk at 5–8 years. Leading producers include: Dom Georges & Michel Chevillon, Dom Jean-Jacques Confuron, Dom Henri Gouges, Dom Jean Grivot, Dom Jean Gros, Henri Jayer, Dom Mongeard-Mugneret.

NV Non-vintage; often applied to champagne.

OAK, OAK-AGEING   Shorthand terms for the use of oak casks in winemaking and ageing. *See* BARRELS.

OAKVILLE   *USA, California, VA*   Small settlement, the southern neighbour of RUTHERFORD, and like Rutherford also a wine zone within Napa, growing Cabernet Sauvignon and other vines on "bench" – gravel terrace – soils. Leading producers include: Far Niente, Heitz, Robert Mondavi.

OC, VIN DE PAYS D'   *France, Vin de Pays, R, P, W*   This name can be used for *vins de pays* from the entire southern sweep of France, from the Rhône to Spain. Most wines using the name are from named varieties: grapes for Rs and Ps include Cabernet Sauvignon, Merlot and Syrah; for Ws Chardonnay, Sauvignon, Chenin and others. Many successful producers; most of the wine is exported.

OHIO   *USA*   In the 19th century Ohio was a major wine state, and now has 40 producers, most on a small scale. Most vines are along the Lake Erie shore, though the Ohio River VA revives a century-old tradition. Leading producers include: Chalet Debonne, FIRELANDS.

OISLY ET THÉSÉE, LA CONFRÉRIE DES VIGNERONS DE   *France, Loire, Touraine, W, R*   Large cooperative with 52 members and 275ha of vines, producing a high-quality range of Touraine wines. Brand name Baronnie d'Aignan is used for R and W blends. The Sauvignon de Touraine (W) has been very successful.

OLASZRIESLING   See WELSCHRIESLING.

OLIVIER, CH   *France, Bordeaux, Pessac-Léognan, Cru Classé, R, W*   The château is a splendid medieval moated castle, but the wines are not as sensational, though improving.

OLOROSO   *Spain*   Style of sherry that never developed *flor*. True oloroso is dry and rich, but many so-labelled are quite sweet.

OLT, LES CÔTES D'   *France, South-West, Cahors, R*   This co-op makes one bottle in three of Cahors. Styles range from the soft and fruity to more structured wines, eg Ch les Bouysses and Impernal, which are aged in *barriques*.

OLTREPO-PAVESE   *Italy, Lombardy, DOC, R, W, Sp*   Lombardy's most productive DOC. The R is from Bonard and Barbera, a lively blackberry-coloured wine with a bitter cherry flavour. Leading producers include: Castello di Luzzano, Tenuta Mazzolino.

ONTARIO   *Canada*   Main wine province of Canada, with 85% of the country's vineyards, exploiting moderate climate conditions along the shores of Lakes Erie and Ontario. Wines include successful Cabernet Sauvignon and Cabernet-Merlot Rs, Ws from Chardonnay and Riesling and ice wine (see **EISWEIN**). Wines labelled "product of Ontario" come entirely from the state; others may contain imported wine. Leading producers include: Cave Spring, Ch des Charmes, Henry of Pelham, Hillebrand, Inniskillin, Konzelmann, Marynissen, Pelee Island, Reif, Southbrook, Stony Ridge, Vineland.

OPITZ, WILLI   *Austria, Neusiedlersee W, R*   Great inventor of new and highly original wine styles and Austria's king of sweet wines, both R and W. Quality across the estate's range is outstanding and some of his more esoteric offerings include a Trockenbeerenauslese from Grüner Veltliner and a R Blauburger *Eiswein* with delicious toffee flavours.

OPPENHEIM   *Germany, Rheinhessen, W*   Neighbour to **NIERSTEIN**, with its own excellent vineyard the Sackträger. Like Nierstein, Oppenheim has a *grosslage*: a large tract of lesser vines, named Krötenbrunnen, which is allowed to use its name. Leading producers in Oppenheim itself: Guntrum, State cellars (Staatsweingut Domäne Oppenheim).

OREGON   *USA*   State in the Northwest with a cool climate akin to that of Europe's best wine zones. Wine areas include **WILLIAMETTE VALLEY** and **UMPQUA VALLEY**, from which come good Pinot Noir Rs, and Ws from Chardonnay and Riesling. Leading producers include: Adelsheim, Amity, Domaine Drouhin, Eyrie, Knudsen Erath, Ponzi, Tualatin.

ORLANDO   *Australia, South Australia, Barossa R, W*   Owned by Pernod-Ricard, Orlando's wide range of wines under a variety of labels includes the world-famous Jacob's Creek brand.

ORLÉANAIS, VIN DE L'   *France, Loire, VDQS, R, P, W*   Wines made in small amounts on the upper Loire near Orléans. Light Rs and Ps from Pinot Noir and Pinot Meunier, Ws from Pinot Blanc and Chardonnay.

ORMES DE PEZ, CH LES   *France, Bordeaux, St-Estèphe, Cru Bourgeois, R*   Owned by the Cazes family of Ch **LYNCH-BAGES**, this estate makes easy to enjoy, modern-style wines.

ORNELLAIA   *Italy, Tuscany, R, W*   This top estate gives its name to the long-lived R wine based on Cabernet Sauvignon with some Merlot and Cabernet Franc. Poggio alle Gazze (W), from Sauvignon Blanc, is also praised.

ORSCHWIHR   *France, Alsace*   This village has a reputation for Ws from Riesling and Pinot Gris, especially from *Grand Cru* Pfingstberg. Leading producers include: Albrecht, Théo Cattin.

ORTENAU   *Germany, Baden, Bereich, R, W, P*   Zone south of Baden-Baden (the famous spa town) with a good name for Ws from Riesling, and Rs from Spätburgunder. Important villages include DURBACH and Ortenberg; leading producers Freiherr von Nevau, Wolf-Metternich, Schloss Staufenberg.

ORVIETO   *Italy, Umbria, DOC, W*   This well-known wine is currently undergoing a renaissance in quality. The main variety is Procanico and the wine should be fresh, dry and quite concentrated. The best come from the *classico* zone. Semi-sweet (*amabile*) and sweet (*dolce*) versions are also made. Leading producers include: Antinori, Bigi.

OSBORNE   *Spain, sherry, Portugal, port*   Quintessential Puerto de Santa Mariá sherries, soft, elegant and light, come from this famous firm, still family-owned. The firm's large size, modernity and experimentation seem to have done no harm to their Fino Quinta, the dry amontillado Coquerino, or the dry oloroso Bailen. The Osborne port firm was set up in 1967: it makes a full range of ports, most of them exported to western European countries.

OTT, DOMAINES   *France, Provence, Côtes de Provence, W, R, P*   The Ott family's wines command high prices with high standards. R,W and P wines come from the 41-ha Ch de Selle estate, and one top-quality W from the Clos Mireille, based on sandy soils by the coast.

OUDINOT   *France, Champagne*   A wide range of reliable quality wines, with an attractively accessible, fruity style.

P

PAARL *South Africa, WO*   Major wine district, home to the KWV and the annual Nederburg wine auction. Mainly Ws, including Chenin Blanc, Sauvignon Blanc and Chardonnay, but also successful Rs from Cabernet Sauvignon and Pinotage. Leading producers include: Fairview, Glen Carlou, Nederburg, Villiera.

PACHERENC DU VIC-BILH *France, South-West, AOC, W*   Dry, delicate, perfumed Ws from local grapes such as Gros and Petit Manseng, Courbu and Arrufiat (or Ruffiac), grown in the same vineyard area as the Rs of Madiran. Leading producers include: Ch d'Aydie, Ch Bouscassé, Dom du Crampilh, Dom Laffitte-Teston, Ch Montus, Dom Moureou, Union Plaimont.

PADTHAWAY *Australia, South Australia*   Close to Coonawarra, although with a slightly warmer climate, this wine region yields high-quality Ws, especially Chardonnay, Riesling and Sauvignon Blanc. Leading producers include: Padthaway Estate.

PAGLIARESE *Italy, Tuscany, Chianti, R*   On this traditional estate the Sanguinetti family produce an elegant Chianti Classico. They also make the *barrique*-aged Camerlengo R from Sangiovese grapes grown in Montalcino.

PAILLARD, BRUNO *France, Champagne*   Recently founded, Paillard has quickly established a good reputation. A stickler for quality, the date of disgorgement is on every bottle and some wood fermentation is being introduced.

PALETTE *France, Provence, AOC, R, P, W*   Small area just east of Aix-en-Provence making Rs from Grenache, Mourvèdre, Cinsaut; Ws from local Clairette, Sémillon and Muscat. Producers are: Dom de la Crémade, Ch Simone.

PALLIÈRES, DOM DES *France, Rhône, Gigondas, R*   Long-lasting, traditionally made wines with warmth and vigour: good value.

PALMER *France, Champagne*   The 170 members of this highly-regarded co-op own several *Grand Cru* vineyards in the Montagne de Reims. The vintage wines age well.

PALMER, CH *France, Bordeaux, Médoc, Margaux, 3ème Cru Classé, R*   Palmer made better wine than neighbouring Ch Margaux for several vintages in the '60s and '70s. Today Margaux has reasserted itself, but Palmer still makes superb wine, the fruit of a fine site on the same gravel bank as Ch Margaux, plus long fermentation and careful selection. There is 40% Merlot, which shows in the style, but the wines can be very long-lived. 2nd wine: Réserve du Général.

PALMER VINEYARDS *USA, New York, Long Island, R, W* Founded in 1983, great strides have been made with Gewürztraminer W and Merlot R. Also makes Cabernet Sauvignon and Chardonnay.

PALO CORTADO *Spain* A sherry that started life as a FINO, but has the flavour of an OLOROSO.

PALOMINO *Fortified Wines, sherry* This high-yielding white grape is used primarily for sherry (and for sherry-style wines in Australia and New Zealand), but is also grown elsewhere in Spain (and Argentina) for everyday W wines.

PALOMINO & VERGARA *Fortified Wines, sherry* Tio Mateo, the top fino from this firm, is dry and full. It is well known throughout Spain as one of the best made.

PAPE-CLÉMENT, CH *France, Bordeaux, Pessac-Léognan, Cru Classé, R, W* Bordeaux's oldest surviving vineyard, dating from the 14th century. Rich, lush R wine, full-flavoured, with impressive length in the mouth. A tiny but increasing amount of W.

PARDUCCI *USA, California, Mendocino, R, W* John Parducci makes sound affordable wines such as his Petite Sirah (R), with its plum and berry spice flavours.

PARRAS VALLEY *Mexico, Central America, W, R* North of Mexico City, this area is possibly the cradle of American wine, with Bodegas de San Lorenzo, the second-oldest winery in America (founded 1626). The best vineyards are at 1,500m (5,000ft), where the climate is suitable for fine wine production.

PARSAC ST-EMILION *France, Bordeaux, AOC, R* This AOC is no longer seen: its wines use the MONTAGNE ST-EMILION name.

PASADA *Spain* A MANZANILLA sherry that has been aged: it will be dry but full in taste.

PASO ROBLES *USA, California, San Luis Obispo, VA* The largest wine zone in San Luis Obispo County, known for its fruity, soft, accessible Cabernet Sauvignons and its peppercorn-fruited R Zinfandels. Leading producers include: Eberle, Meridian, Ridge.

PATERNINA, BODEGAS FEDERICO *Spain, Rioja, R, W, P* Known as a large-scale producer of good everyday wines; but the W Federico Paternina can be very good as can the R *reservas* and *gran reservas*, which age very well in bottle.

PATRAS *Greece, Peloponnese, W, R* Some W wine is produced here from the pink-skinned Rhoditis grape, but the best-known wine of the area is Mavrodaphne, a fortified R wine of about 15°, matured in oak.

PATRIACHE PÈRE & FILS *France, Burgundy, Côte d'Or, R, W* Beaune-based *négociant* on a very large scale, making mid-rank wines of many Burgundy and other appellations. Patriache also owns the Château de Meursault domaine, whose wines are very good.

PATRIMONIO *France, Corsica, AOC, R, P, W* This serious Corsican appellation has Rs (and Ps) made mainly from the native Nielluccio grape, dry Ws from Vermentino, and sweet Ws from Muscat. Leading producers include: Dom Gentile, Dom Leccia.

PAUILLAC *France, Bordeaux, AOC, R* Clarets from this famed Haut-Médoc commune include 18 classed growths, three of them Firsts. Cabernet Sauvignon dominates, giving a powerful, long-lived wine that smells and tastes of blackcurrants and cedarwood; top wines may need up to 30 years to rise to their full stature, though mid-rank ones can be superb at 8-12. Leading producers include: Ch Lafite-Rothschild, Ch Latour, Ch Mouton Rothschild, Ch Pichon-Longueville Baron, Ch Pichon-Longueville Comtesse de Lalande.

PAULY-BERGWEILER, WEINGUT DR *Germany, Mosel, W, R* This important owner of middle-Mosel vineyards makes fresh, balanced Rieslings using modern techniques. Also owns the estate of Peter Nicolay: similar wines.

PAVIE, CH *France, Bordeaux, St-Emilion, 1er Grand Cru Classé, R* This, the largest of all the St-Emilion *1ers Grands Crus Classés*, with 15,000 cases a year, is owned by the Valette family. Pavie has made a noticeable improvement since 1979: consistently high-quality wines.

PAVIE-DECESSE, CH *France, Bordeaux, St-Emilion, Grand Cru Classé, R* Owned by Jean-Paul Valette, whose family owns **PAVIE**. His wine is quite powerful and noticeably tannic in youth, but starts to mature after 3 years in bottle.

PAVIE-MACQUIN, CH *France, Bordeaux, St-Emilion, Grand Cru Classé, R* Potentially one of the future stars, this well-placed-château made a distinct leap forward in the 1988 vintage, and adopted **BIODYNAMIC** viticulture in 1990.

PAVILLON ROUGE DU CHATEAU MARGAUX *France, Bordeaux, Médoc, Margaux* 2nd wine of Ch Margaux. Pavillon Blanc is Margaux's unusual Sauvignon white.

PÉCHARMANT *France, South-West, AOC, R* Wines from a BERGERAC enclave. Superior soils, Malbec grapes added to the usual Cabernets and Merlot and longer ageing give the wines more structure and potential than AOC Bergerac. Leading producer: Ch de Tiregard.

PÉDESCLAUX, CH *France, Bordeaux, Médoc, Pauillac, 5ème Cru Classé, R* This château is small and little-known, but the wines have been reliable in recent vintages.

PEDRONCELLI *USA, California, Sonoma, R, W, P* Prices at this winery remain reasonable and the following strong. Popular wines include Ws from Chardonnay, Sauvignon and Chenin Blanc; R from Cabernet Sauvignon, and Zinfandel which comes as pale blush, P and R.

PENAFLOR *Argentina, R, W* Argentina's largest producer, with several *bodegas*. The best-known label is Trapiche, including a solid Reserve Cabernet Sauvignon, Malbec (R) and Chardonnay. Other labels include Andean Vineyards and Fond de Cave. The latter is exceptional.

PEÑALBA LÓPEZ, BODEGAS *Spain, Castilla-León, Ribera del Duero, R, P* The latest winemaking technology here produces above-average R and P wines. Their best appear under the Torremilanos label.

PENEDÈS *Spain, Catalonia, DO, W, P, R, Sp* The most important Catalonian wine region, south of Barcelona, producing CAVA Sp wines, a large range of impressive W wines and some good Rs. Leading producers include: Masia BACH, RENÉ BARBIER, Cooperativa Vinícola del Penedès, JEAN LÉON, TORRES.

PENFOLDS *Australia, South Australia, Barossa R, W* Australia's giant of giants. R wines are its strongest suit, with the brilliant Grange, a long-lived Shiraz-based wine, as its ace. Penfolds has made Ws since 1990.

PENNSYLVANIA *USA* Vines are grown in the state's south-east, with classic *vinifera* grapes joining native (LABRUSCA) vines. Leading producers include: Allegro, CHADDSFORD, Naylor.

PERALDI, DOM *France, Corsica, Ajaccio, W, R, P* One of the best-known Corsican estates, owned by the Comte de Poix. The Clos du Cardinal (R) is aged in oak barrels.

PERNAND-VERGELESSES *France, Burgundy, AOC, R, W* Parts of the *Grands Crus* of CORTON and CORTON-CHARLEMAGNE lie within this Côte de Beaune village. Rs (around 80% of production) need 5–15 years in bottle. Leading producers include: Bonneau du Martray, Marius Delarche, P Dubreuil-Fontaine.

PERRIER, JOSEPH *France, Champagne* The NV Cuvée Royale from this GRANDE MARQUE has been somewhat inconsistent in the past. The best wine is the Cuvée Josephine, an almost equal blend of Pinot Noir and Chardonnay.

PERRIER-JOUËT *France, Champagne* One of the oldest champagne houses, now owned by Seagram. Chardonnay is the dominant grape and the wines are consistently elegant with lots of finesse. Their finest wine is Belle Epoque *blanc de blancs* with its distinctive *art nouveau* bottle.

PERRIÈRES, LES *France, Burgundy, Côte de Beaune, 1er Cru, W* One of the best vineyards in Meursault, abutting neighbouring Puligny-Montrachet to the south. Its wines are distinctly classy, displaying lovely buttery character, with an elegance and steeliness behind. Leading producers include: Robert Ampeau, Coche-Dury, Comtes Lafon, Albert Grivault, J & P Matrot, Guy Roulot.

PERU *South America* With less than 250,000 cases annually, Peru is one of South America's lesser producers. However, vines have been grown in the main region, south of Lima, for more than 400 years. The Moquega Valley, near the Chilean border, is another region. Most production goes into brandy.

PESSAC-LÉOGNAN *France, Bordeaux, AOC, R, W* Appellation covering 10 communes in the northern (superior) part of the Graves; all the Graves classed growths are here. Around 75% of the wine is R, to be drunk at 10 years or so. Cabernet Sauvignon is the dominant R grape, blended with Merlot, Cabernet Franc, Petit Verdot and Cot (Malbec). Ws are from Sauvignon Blanc and Sémillon; the best (which are expensive) demand at least 5 years in bottle. Leading producers include: Ch Bouscaut, Dom de Chevalier, Ch'x Couhins-Lurton, de Fieuzal, La Garde, Haut-Bailly, Haut-Brion, Larrivet-Haut-Brion, Laville-Haut-Brion, La Louvière, Malartic-Lagravière, La Mission-Haut-Brion, Pape-Clément, Smith-Haut-Lafitte, La Tour Martillac.

PETALUMA *Australia, South Australia, Adelaide Hills, W, Sp* Famed winemaker Brian Croser makes top-quality wines here, including a fine Sp wine, Croser, good Cabernet Sauvignon and a most interesting Riesling W. Bridgewater Mill is their 2nd label.

PÉTILLANT *France* Term meaning slightly sparkling.

PETIT CHABLIS *France, Burgundy, AOC, W* An appellation within the Chablis district. Seldom seen on a label, as the land in the delimited area is mostly unplanted.

PETIT CHÂTEAU *France* Bordeaux term for an unclassified wine château. It has no official status and is not seen on labels.

PETIT VILLAGE, CH *France, Bordeaux, Pomerol, R* Owned by insurance firm AXA, and managed by Jean-Michel Cazes of Ch Lynch-Bages in Pauillac, this is an estate to watch. Its big, voluptuous style of wine can match some of the best estates in Pomerol. In the finest years the wines will last 20 years or more.

PETIT-FAURIE-DE-SOUTARD, CH *France, Bordeaux, St-Emilion, Grand Cru Classé, R* The Capdemourlin family who own this château also own **BALESTARD-LA-TONNELLE**. This little-known estate produces St-Emilion in a fairly exotic style.

PETITE SIRAH Red grape from California, no relation to the Rhône's **SYRAH**, although it is possibly the same grape as the Durif of southern France. Used in generic blends and as a dark, tannic varietal.

PÉTRUS, CH *France, Bordeaux, Pomerol, R* Very old vines on pure clay, brilliant winemaking and no expense spared make one of the world's most expensive, and best, R wines. Pétrus is virtually pure Merlot. Seductive young, it can age for decades. The estate is part-owned and managed by **J-P MOUIEX**.

PEYMARTIN, CH *France, Bordeaux, Médoc, St-Julien, R* 2nd wine of Ch Gloria.

PEYRASSOL, COMMANDERIE DE *France, Provence, Côtes de Provence, R, P* Françoise and Yves Rigord have made this estate near Flassans one of the best in the *appellation*. There are good Ps, a standard R, Cuvée Eperon, and the top-quality R Cuvée Marie-Estelle, an unusual blend of Cabernet Sauvignon, Grenache and Syrah, which is oak-aged.

PEZ, CH DE *France, Bordeaux, St-Estèphe, Cru Bourgeois, R* The senior *cru bourgeois* of the appellation, very traditional in techniques and in the austere, tannic, spicy style of its wine. The wines need, but reward, patience.

PEZA *Greece, Crete, R, W* Local varieties such as Kotsifali, Liatiko and Vilana are used to produce quite rich and powerful R and W wines in this zone.

PEZINOK *Slovakia* Winery in the Little Carpathians region, making a variety of sound wines under Western supervision.

PFAFFENHEIM *France, Alsace* Wine village with a *Grand Cru*, Steinert, and a growing name for Ws from Pinot Blanc and Pinot Gris.

PFALZ *Germany, Anbaugebiet, W, R* Formerly known as the Rheinpfalz, this southern region makes good W and (increasingly) R wines in a solid, flavoursome style. The best zone is MITTEL-HAARDT, but the Südpfalz or SÜDLICHE WEINSTRASSE makes growing amounts of good wine.

PFEFFINGEN, WEINGUT *Germany, Pfalz, W* Family estate in the heart of the Pfalz specializing in dry, fruity Riesling wines.

PHEASANT RIDGE *USA, Texas, R, W* The winery, in Lubbock, is inconsistent but with flashes of greatness. Owner Bobby Cox produces Ws from Chardonnay, Sauvignon, Chenin Blanc and, most promising of all, R Cabernet Sauvignon.

PHÉLAN-SÉGUR, CH *France, Bordeaux, St-Estèphe, Cru Bourgeois, R* Large and well-known estate, on good form since 1986 and especially in 1990.

PHELPS, JOSEPH *USA, California, Napa, R, W* This winery produces Rhône-style wines, from rose-petal-scented Syrah and delicately spiced Grenache Rs to a tangy W based on Viognier grapes.

PHILLIPPONNAT *France, Champagne* A small house, best known for its fine, weighty, single-vineyard Clos des Goisses.

PHYLLOXERA The *phylloxera vastatrix* aphid, which attacks the roots of the vine, devastated European vineyards in the 19th century after its accidental introduction from America. The only cure was found to be grafting vines onto roots from American vines. Phylloxera, in a slightly different form or biotype, is currently a problem in the USA: US vines are resistant, but not the European varieties they have imported. Failure to graft onto resistant rootstocks has given the pest a chance. Many vines in California and elsewhere are being grubbed up and burnt, to be replaced with vines growing on the correct rootstocks.

PIBARNON, CH DE *France, Provence, Bandol W, R, P* The wines from Comte Henri de Saint-Victor's estate regularly receive awards and taste most attractive, thanks to new wood and a high proportion of Mourvèdre. The P is fruity and fresh, the W crisp and lightly acidic.

PIBRAN, CH *France, Bordeaux, Médoc, Pauillac, Cru Bourgeois* This small estate is under the same ownership as Ch **PICHON-BARON**: the French insurance concern AXA. Jean-Michel Cazes is making deep-coloured wine in a fruity yet muscular style.

PICHON-LONGUEVILLE BARON, CH *France, Bordeaux, Médoc, Pauillac, 2ème Cru Classé, R* The two Pichons glare at each other across the D2 road south of Pauillac. Pichon-Baron's restored château and controversial new *chai* show the investment by insurance giant AXA. Jean-Michel Cazes (owner of Ch **LYNCH-BAGES**) runs the property for AXA, making much-improved, very ripe and solid wine, a worthy contrast to the other Pichon. A good 1993.

PICHON-LONGUEVILLE COMTESSE DE LALANDE, CH *France, Bordeaux, Médoc, Pauillac, 2ème Cru Classé, R* Mme May-Eliane de Lencquesaing has stamped her demanding personality on the wines, and the image, of her estate. The results have been spectacular. A high 35% of Merlot makes the wine softer and more opulent than most Pauillacs. A good 1993, but a small crop. The 2nd wine is Réserve de la Comtesse which, thanks to rigorous selection, contains excellent material and is well-regarded in its own right.

PICQUE-CAILLOU, CH *France, Bordeaux, Pessac-Léognan R* This supple, soundly-made wine is relatively quick to evolve.

PIÈCE *France, Burgundy* Cask of 228 litres, traditional for ageing wine. See also **BARRIQUE**.

PIED D'ALOUE *France, Burgundy, Chablis, 1er Cru* See **MONTÉE DE TONNERRE**.

PIEDMONT *Italy* Together with Tuscany, Italy's most important quality wine area, centred around Turin in the north-west. Long-lived Barolo and Barbaresco are the top DOCG R wines, both made from the Nebbiolo grape. Also produces a wide range of lighter R wines, from Barbera and Dolcetto grapes, and attractive W and Sp wines.

PIEMONTE *Italy* See **PIEDMONT**.

PIEROPAN *Italy, Veneto, W* Prestigious estate which pioneered single-vineyard Soaves. The range now includes single-vineyard Calvarino and the sweet Recioto di Soave Le Colombare.

PIESPORT   *Germany, Mosel, Bereich, W*   Famous village of the Mittel-mosel, with some of its steepest vineyards. Piesport makes top-class wines from Riesling which combine a touch of spiciness with underlying steel. Wines from top producers age very well. The best vineyard is the large Goldtröpfchen. Leading producers here include Bischöflichen Weingüter and Vereinigte Hospitien, both of which are charities, and von Kesselstatt. Much of Piesport's reputation has been lost by Piesporter Michelsberg, a *grosslage* taking in wide tracts of flat north-facing land, producing large quantities of indifferent wine.

PIN, CH LE   *France, Bordeaux, Pomerol, R*   Tiny amounts of prohib-itively priced and reportedly superb wine are made here.

PINDAR VINEYARDS   *USA, New York, Long Island, W, R*   Long Island's largest winery, with 85ha planted at North Fork. The wide range is gaining an international name with its Merlot and Mythology, a R bordeaux-style blend. Chardonnay has also been impressive.

PINOT BLANC   White grape that can make delicately aromatic wines, particularly in Alsace, and makes a good base for sparkling wines. Known as Weissburgunder in Germany and Austria, Pinot Bianco in Italy. Pinot Blanc is increasingly popular in California.

PINOT GRIS   Grape variety that may be red or white; its wine is usually a deep-coloured, full-bodied dry white. Known as Tokay d'Alsace in France, Rülander or Grauburgunder in Germany, Pinot Grigio in Italy, Szürkebarát in Hungary; it is also grown in Romania and Oregon. Pinot Gris is becoming better known as winemakers seek alternatives to the ubiquitous Chardonnay.

PINOT NOIR   The classic grape of red burgundy. Pinot Noir can be difficult to grow and yields must be low to make quality wine. As growers worldwide have found to their frustration, much of the taste of the resulting wine depends upon *terroir* and winemaking. Pinot Noir grown in Oregon, Australia, Italy or eastern Europe can be great – or disappointing. It is also used in Champagne (blended with Pinot Meunier and Chardonnay).

PIPER-HEIDSIECK   *France, Champagne*   Owned by Rémy Coin-treau who also own Charles Heidsieck. The overall style is fairly light and fruity, but the dry Brut Sauvage is one of the finest non-*dosage* (very dry) champagnes and the prestige *cuveé*, Rare, is extremely elegant.

PLAYA, LA   *Chile, R, W*   Wine estate in the **MAIPO VALLEY**, owned by the Pavone family. La Playa produces Rs from Cabernet Sauvignon and Merlot, plus Ws from Chardonnay and Sauvignon Blanc. All but the Chardonnay are estate-grown.

PLETTENBERG, WEINGUT REICHSGRAF VON   *Germany, Nahe, W*   This estate's dry wines, made for the German domestic market, where food-wines are the fashion, complement their beautiful naturally sweet ones, which sell abroad.

POCHON, ETIENNE *France, Rhône, Crozes-Hermitage, R, W* This estate makes quality R wine, with fruit, concentration and plenty of flavour, from an AOC which can be variable. A little W is also made under the same appellation.

PODRAVSKI *Slovenia* Also known as the Drava Valley region, in the north-east near Austria, this zone produces the country's best wines. It has a sub-region, LJUTOMER-ORMOZ. The W wines are at their best reminiscent of Germany and Austria: good Pinot Gris, Rhein Riesling and Traminer, pungent Sauvignon Blanc and *botrytis*-affected dessert wines.

POGGIO ANTICO *Italy, Tuscany, Brunello di Montalcino, R* Maker of modern-style Brunellos designed for earlier drinking. Brunello grapes are also used to make Altero, a R *vino da tavola*.

POINT DU JOUR, DOM DU *France, Burgundy, Beaujolais, R* Elegant feminine Fleurie is produced at this leading Beaujolais estate.

POJER & SANDRI *Italy, Trentino, W, R, Sp* Makers of an innovative range of varietal *vini da tavola* from grapes such as Chardonnay and Pinot Noir, plus *metodo classico* Sp wines, and Essenzia, a sweet late-harvest W.

POL ROGER *France, Champagne* Traditional, family firm whose wines are of consistently high quality. The Cuvée Sir Winston Churchill, whose favourite champagne it was, is all elegance and finesse; the special *cuvée*, PR, is richer with greater body.

POMEROL *France, Bordeaux, AOC, R* Superb wine from a small area north-west of St-Emilion. Merlot is the dominant grape, followed by Cabernet Franc and a small amount of Cabernet Sauvignon. Generally the wines are ready at 4–6 years, with a plummy appeal and fullish, well-rounded palate. The finest are richer and more concentrated, and can mature for 40 years or more, taking on a gamey character. Leading producers include: Ch'x Le Bon Pasteur, Bonalgue, Certan de May, Clinet, La Conseillante, L'Evangile, La Fleur-de-Gay, La Fleur-Pétrus, Lafleur, Latour à Pomerol, Petit Village, Petrus, Trotanoy; Vieux-Ch-Certan.

POMINO *Italy, Tuscany, DOC, R, W* High-quality DOC which owes much to the Frescobaldi family. Cabernet and Merlot are combined with Sangiovese for the R wine. Pinot Bianco, Chardonnay and Trebbiano are used for the W. Leading producers include: Frescobaldi.

POMMARD *France, Burgundy, AOC, R* Burgundies of deep colour, intense aroma, concentrated flavours, full body and complex structure that can improve in bottle for 10 years, especially from the best *Premiers Crus* (Epenots, Rugiens, Clos de la Commeraine). Leading producers include: Robert Ampeau, Dom Jean-Marc Boillot, Dom de Courcel, Dom Bernard Glantenay, Dom de Montille, Ch de Pommard.

POMMERY & GRENO *France, Champagne* Owned by the LVMH group, this **GRANDE MARQUE** has 300ha of vines. There has been some inconsistency in the NV, but both the Louise Pommery Brut and Rosé are outstanding.

PONIATOWSKI, PRINCE *France, Loire, Vouvray, W, Sp* The family has owned Le Clos Baudoin since 1910. The 22-ha vineyard is the source of traditional Vouvray, with emphasis on dry and Sp wines, sold under the name Aigle d'Or, with sweet wines made only in exceptional years.

PONTET-CANET, CH *France, Bordeaux, Médoc, Pauillac, 5ème Cru Classé, R* A large and well-placed vineyard, just south of Mouton's, promises more than the wine has always delivered. However a slow process of improvements has showed results, especially since 1989.

PONZI *USA, Oregon, W, R* Racy Riesling Ws and taut, richly built Pinot Noir Rs (tasting notes cite black cherry, mushroom, clove) are well regarded. Chardonnay is barrel-fermented in Allier oak, stressing the wine's sweet lime fruit.

PORTO *Portugal, DOC* One of the world's great fortified wines, from the Douro Valley of northern Portugal. Essentially R, although a tiny quantity of W is also made. R port comes in a variety of styles but is always sweet. Cask ageing is a critical aspect of most port production., with lesser wines like Ruby and Vintage Character spending several years in wood. Aged tawnies can spend up to 40 years or more in wood. Vintage and Single Quinta ports, however, are bottled after two years and mature in bottle (for at least 15 years and up to 50). Leading producers include: Croft, Delaforce, Dow, Ferreira, Fonseca Guimaraens, Quinta do Noval, Sandeman, Smith Woodhouse, Taylor Fladgate & Yeatman, Warre.

POUGET, CH *France, Bordeaux, Médoc, Margaux, 4ème Cru Classé, R* Little-known classed growth making good wine.

POUILLY-FUISSÉ *France, Burgundy, AOC, W* Five southern Mâconnais villages share land well suited to growing Chardonnay. Old vines and new oak can make this W burgundy a rich, long-lived and serious wine. Other wines, especially from *négociants*, are made to be drunk young. Not all Pouilly-Fuissé lives up to its reputation. Leading producers include: Dom Coursin, Dom Jeanne Ferret, Dom Michel Forest, Ch de Fuissé, Dom Gilles Noblet, Dom Guffens-Heynen, Dom Roger Saumaize.

POUILLY FUMÉ *France, Loire, AOC, W* World-famous dry W wine from Sauvignon Blanc grapes; fuller and longer-lasting than **SANCERRE** on the opposite bank of the Loire. The name "fumé" encapsulates the typically smoky flavour of the grape, which reaches perfection on Pouilly's flint and chalk soils. Leading producers include: Didier Dagueneau, Masson-Blondelet, Ch du Nozet, Ch de Tracy.

POUILLY-LOCHÉ   *France, Burgundy, AOC, W*   This village east of POUILLY-FUISSÉ makes similar but usually cheaper W wines, also from Chardonnay grapes.

POUILLY-SUR-LOIRE   *France, Loire, AOC, W*   Wines made from Chasselas grapes; a declining appellation. Do not confuse with the Sauvignon-based POUILLY FUMÉ which is made in the same area. Leading producers include: Bernard Blanchet, Patrick Coulbois, Jean-Claude Dagueneau.

POUILLY-VINZELLES   *France, Burgundy, AOC, W*   Chardonnay W wines, made in a village neighbouring POUILLY-FUISSÉ.

POUJEAUX, CH   *France, Bordeaux, Moulis, Cru Bourgeois, R*   This large château contends with Maucaillou and Chasse-Spleen as the best in the commune. Good traditional claret: dark, flavoursome and long-lived.

POUSSE D'OR, DOM DE LA   *France, Burgundy, Côte d'Or, R*   Leading Volnay estate, producing balanced and elegant red burgundies which age well. Also makes good Pommard and Santenay.

PREDICATO   *Italy*   Term for Tuscan quality wines, R and W, meeting certain local criteria.

PREMIER CRU   *France*   Officially-defined vineyard or estate in a ranking system. Definitions vary; the term is used in Bordeaux, Burgundy and elsewhere. In Burgundy it signifies a vineyard below *Grand Cru* in status.

PREMIERES CÔTES DE BLAYE   See CÔTES DE BLAYE.

PREMIERES CÔTES DE BORDEAUX   *France, Bordeaux, AOC, R, W*   Good R wines and sweet Ws from hillside vineyards on the north bank of the Garonne River. Leading producers include: Ch'x Brethous, Gourran, de Haux, du Juge, Lagarosse, Mestrepeyrot, Ch de Plassan, Reynon, Tanesse.

PRESTON   *USA, California, Sonoma, R, W*   Sauvignon W and Zinfandel R are this winery's mainstays, but the latest wines are from Rhône varieties such as W Marsanne and Viognier, and R Carignane, Syrah, Mourvèdre, Grenache and Cinsaut; there is also a particularly tasty R Barbera.

PREUSES   *France, Burgundy, Chablis, Grand Cru*   Vineyard making wine considered to be more feminine and elegant than LES CLOS. It shares LA MOUTONNE with VAUDÉSIR.

PRIEUR, DOM JACQUES   *France, Burgundy, Côte d'Or, R, W*   Dynamic domaine with an impressive array of *Grand* and *Premier Cru* vineyards throughout the Côte d'Or, including land in Montrachet and Chambertin. Rising quality.

PRIEURE-LICHINE, CH   *France, Bordeaux, Médoc, Margaux, 4ème Cru Classé, R*   Alexis Lichine (*see* Ch LASCOMBES) built up this estate, which consists of widely scattered plots, and it is now run by his son Sacha. The wine is a good monument to the estate's creator.

PRIMEUR *France* Wines made to be drunk very young; they are marketed from 21 November of the year they are made till 31 January of the following year. (Not to be confused with *en primeur*.)

PRIMORSKI *Slovenia* One of Slovenia's three major wine zones, on the Adriatic coast, influenced in wine styles and grapes by Italy's proximity. Primorski has good Rs from Merlot and Cabernet Sauvignon, and often excellent Ws from Pinot Gris and Blanc, Chardonnay and Malvasia. The local speciality is Refosk (R), dark and acidic.

PRIORATO *Spain, Catalonia, DO, W, R* One of eight Catalonian wine zones, with mountain vineyards producing a range of light *joven* W to heavy, powerful R. Leading producers include: DE MULLER, Cellers Scala-Dei.

PRISSÉ, CAVE COOPERATIVE DE *France, Burgundy, Mâconnais, R, W* Good, reliable producer of R and W Mâconnais wines.

PROSECCO DI CONEGLIANO-VALDOBBIADENE *Italy, Veneto, DOC, Sp* Wine zone to the north of Venice, home of a Sp wine with a slightly almondy flavour, crisp acidity and lowish alcohol.

PRULIERS, LES *France, Burgundy, Côte de Nuits, 1er Cru, R* One of the top Nuits-St-Georges vineyards. The wines are densely coloured, very aromatic, well-structured with a good tannic backbone. Leading producers include: Henri Gouges, Jean Grivot.

PRÜM, J J *Germany, Mosel, W* This leading middle-Mosel estate owns superb plots in Wehlener Sonnenuhr and other vineyards. The wines are classics, especially the AUSLESEN. Lesser (QBA) wine use the Dr M Prüm label.

PRÜM ERBEN, S A *Germany, Mosel, W* Estate with a traditional approach making cask-aged, classic Mosels from fine vineyards in Graach, Wehlen etc.

PRUNOTTO, ALFREDO *Italy, Piedmont, R* One of the leading *négociants* of the wine town of Alba, producing single-vineyard Barolo Bussia and Cannubi, Barbaresco Montestefano, Barbera d'Alba Pian Romualdo and Nebbiolo d'Alba Occhetti.

PUCELLES, LES *France, Burgundy, Côte de Beaune, 1er Cru, W* One of the best Puligny-Montrachet vineyards, making lovely, elegant wines with a nice steely acidity which age very well. Leading producers include: Leflaive, Henri de Villamont.

PUISSEGUIN ST-EMILION *France, Bordeaux, AOC, R* Among the "satellite" zones to the north-east of St-Emilion. It can equal St-Emilion in quality and offers good value. Leading producers include: Ch'x l'Abbaye, Durand, Guibeau, Laplagne, des Laurets, de Roques, Teillac, Teyssier.

PULIGNY-MONTRACHET *France, Burgundy, AOC, W* Côte de Beaune village which concentrates on great W wines from its four *Grands Crus* – MONTRACHET, CHEVALIER-MONTRACHET, BIENVENUES-BÂTARD-MONTRACHET and BÂTARD-MONTRACHET – and a clutch of excellent *Premiers Crus*. Vineyards are ideally sited and the wine is often the best W burgundy – and expensive. The *Grand Cru* wines reach their best in 10 years, as do some of the elegant *Premiers Crus*. Village Puligny-Montrachet is less special, although still expensive. Leading producers include: Adrien Belland, Dom Henri Clerc, Dom Leflaive, Olivier Leflaive Frères, Dom Michelot-Buisson, Dom Jean Monnier & Fils, Dom Etienne Sauzet.

PUYGUERAUD, CH *France, Bordeaux, Côtes de Francs, R* The Thienponts of Pomerol own this château as well as nearby Ch LACLAVERIE and have given the appellation a boost. The wine is dark and solid, showing the potential of the area.

PYRENEES *Australia, Victoria* This region enjoys a temperate climate ideally suited to full-bodied, textured R wines from Shiraz and Cabernet Sauvignon.

PYRÉNÉES-ORIENTALES, DES *France, Vin de Pays, R, P, W* Wines from the hilly country close to the Pyrenees: solid, powerful Rs are in the majority.

Q

QBA *Germany* See QUALITÄTSWEIN EINES BESTIMMTEN ANBAU-GEBIETES.

QMP *Germany* See QUALITÄTSWEIN MIT PRÄDIKAT.

QUADY *USA, California* Andrew Quady's winery makes a fascinating range of sweet wines, including Muscats both orange and black and a port-style wine which he calls Starboard.

QUALITÄTSWEIN EINES BESTIMMTEN ANBAUGEBIETES (QBA) *Germany* Quality wine from a defined region. The lower of two bands into which all German quality wine is divided.

QUALITÄTSWEIN MIT PRÄDIKAT (QMP) *Germany* Quality wine with distinction. The higher of the two bands for German quality wine. QmPs are made from grapes sweet enough to need no added sugar. Each QmP wine falls into one of six levels, in ascending order of sweetness: KABINETT, SPÄTLESE, AUSLESE, BEERENAUSLESE, TROCKENBEERENAUSLESE, EISWEIN.

QUARTS-DE-CHAUME *France, Loire, AOC, W* Luscious sweet W wines from Chenin Blanc grapes are produced from this enclave within the Coteaux du Layon zone. Leading producer: Jacques Lalanne/Ch de Belle Rive.

QUEBEC *Canada* A small area 50 miles south of Montreal manages to make wine, mostly Ws from Seyval Blanc, in this cold-winter province.

QUEENSLAND *Australia* State in the north-east corner of Australia which has a small area in the south under vine, but serious wines have been made only since 1970. Sémillon (W) and Shiraz (R) do well here, though Cabernet Sauvignon and Chardonnay are also planted.

QUÉNARD, RAYMOND *France, Savoie, R* Leading maker of the rare R of Chignin, in the Alps.

QUINCY *France, Loire, AOC, W* Dry W wines from Sauvignon Blanc, produced on the south bank of the Cher not far from Sancerre. Can be good value. Leading producers include: Joseph Mellot, Dom Sorbe.

QUINTA *Portugal* Farm, estate or vineyard.

QUINTARELLI *Italy, Veneto, R, W* Estate with a range of rich, complex wines include a *ripasso* Valpolicella and Recioto Amarone. *Vini da tavola* include *passito* Amabile del Cerè (W), Alzero (R) and Molinara (R).

R

RABASSE-CHARAVIN, DOM *France, Rhône, Côtes du Rhône-Villages, R* Excellent Syrah-based R wine made to age, plus a good W.

RABAUD-PROMIS, CH *France, Bordeaux, Sauternes, 1er Cru Classé, W* Since 1983 this estate has made some of the most delicious wines in the region: not too oaky, with charm not power and, in top years, a delectable freshness and raciness.

RAIMAT *Spain, Catalonia, Costers del Segre, R, W, P, Sp* Extremely well-run, large and innovative winery, using both French and Spanish grape varieties. Their Sp Chardonnay is excellent. The blended Clos Abadia (R) and the single-variety R wines are also very good.

RAMONET, DOM ANDRÉ *France, Burgundy, Côte d'Or, R, W* Top quality W burgundies, including some Le Montrachet, emerge from this leading estate based in Chassagne-Montrachet.

RANCIO A pungent taste found in old, maderized, fortified wine.

RANDERSACKER *Germany, Franken, W* This village just upstream from Würzburg has a good cooperative cellar and some good estates, including Weingut Robert Schmitt. The Pfulben vineyard includes some of the best sites in Franken, suited to Riesling, Müller-Thurgau and Silvaner.

RASTEAU *France, Rhône, AOC, R, P, W, VDN* Grenache-based dessert wine (*vin doux naturel*); most is sweet W, but the R is generally better. Rasteau village also produces hearty R wine under the Côtes du Rhône-Villages appellation. Leading VDN producer: Dom de la Soumade.

RATTI-ANTICHE, RENATO *Italy, Piedmont, R* The late Renato Ratti was a leading maker of Barolo. His family now run the estate, which makes a range including Barolo Marcenasco, Barbera, Dolcetto and Nebbiolo d'Alba.

RAUENTHAL *Germany, Rheingau, W* In the hills above the Rheingau, this village makes good wines in warm years. The Baiken vineyard is noted for fine Riesling Ws.

RAUSAN-SÉGLA, CH *France, Bordeaux, Médoc, Margaux, 2ème Cru Classé, R* An example of the dramatic improvements in the Médoc in the 1980s: new stainless steel, better vines, a new team – and the estate is back where it was last century, a true 2nd Growth. A good 1993, and in 1994 David Orr, ex-head of Latour, took over for new owners Chanel.

RAUZAN-GASSIES *France, Bordeaux, Médoc, Margaux, 2ème Cru Classé, R* Less in the limelight than the other half of the old Rausan estate *(see* RAUSAN-SÉGLA), and less consistent.

RAUTENTRAUCH'SCHE WEINGUTSVERWALTUNG *Germany, Ruwer, W* Estate which is a source of some of the best Ruwer wines: Rieslings of restrained but long-lived elegance.

RAVENEAU, FRANÇOIS AND JEAN-MARIE *France, Burgundy, Chablis, W* Small estate making some of Chablis's finest *Premiers* and *Grands Crus*: wines with great weight, nerve and flintiness, developing complexity with age.

RAVENSWOOD *USA, California, Sonoma, R, W* Joel Peterson's intense, berry-laden Zinfandel R makes up over half the production at his winery. A Merlot R and a Meursault-like Chardonnay, both intense, are also made.

RAYAS, CH *France, Rhône, Châteauneuf-du-Pape, R, W* Many feel this is the top wine of the appellation. Low yields, 100% Grenache vines and superb winemaking contribute: sadly, the estate is so small there is little of it. Also excellent white Châteauneuf and Ch de Fonsalette, a Côtes du Rhône far better than the modest appellation would suggest.

RAYMOND-LAFON, CH *France, Bordeaux, Sauternes, W* Meticulous winemaking yields sumptuous sweet wines that require long ageing. By harvesting as late as possible, excellent wine is made even in modest years. Raymond-Lafon is the most expensive Sauternes after Yquem and Fargues, but superb and well worth the price.

RAYNE-VIGNEAU, CH DE *France, Bordeaux, Sauternes, 1er Cru Classé, W* Standards have greatly improved here recently, and Rayne-Vigneau is once again a reliable source of some fine Sauternes. The wines of the late 1980s and 1991 were very good.

REAL COMPANHIA VINÍCOLA DO NORTE DO PORTUGAL *Portugal, W, R* Table wine arm of the port house Royal Oporto. Evel brand R and W wines are generally good value.

REBHOLZ, WEINGUT *Germany, Pfalz, W, R* This estate is at Siebeldingen in the up-and-coming southern part of the Pfalz, the SÜDLICHE WEINSTRASSE. Rebholz makes good Rs, plus Ws such as well-made dry but powerful Rieslings and excellent Müller-Thurgaus.

RECIOTO *Italy* Sweet red wine from grapes that have been left to dry for a time after picking, to concentrate their juice. High in alcohol and velvety in texture, it is akin to port.

REDDE, MICHEL ET FILS *France, Loire, Pouilly-Fumé, W* Important producers, with a large estate of 27ha. They make a straight *cuvée*, and in the best years a deluxe wine, Cuvée Majorum. Winemaking equipment is modern and these wines are designed for early drinking.

REGALEALI   *Italy, Sicily, W, R, P*   The island's premier estate, producing high-quality *vini da tavola* in all three colours. The top W, Nozze d'Oro, contains Sauvignon Blanc; the Rosso del Conte R is aged in new wood.

RÉGNIÉ   *France, Burgundy, AOC, R*   Beaujolais *cru*: the 10th and most recent to be delineated. The wines reflect their location: in the north the *cru* adjoins **MORGON**; in the south **BROUILLY**. In general Regnie is a light and elegant wine for a *cru* Beaujolais, but with a pronounced and pleasant aroma. Leading producers include: Dom de Bel Air, Caveau des Deux Clochers, Georges Duboeuf.

REINE-PÉDAUQUE, LA   *France, Burgundy, Côte d'Or, R, W*   This firm is a *négociant* and landowner, with the same owners as **PIERRE ANDRÉ**, with fine sites, mostly around Corton.

REINHARTSHAUSEN, SCHLOSS   *Germany, Rheingau, W, R*   The Prince of Prussia owns this large estate, which has Riesling in some top Rheingau vineyards and Chardonnay on an island in the Rhine. Most wines are dry, though there are traditional sweet wines too.

REMOISSENET, PERE & FILS   *France, Burgundy, Côte d'Or, R, W*   Beaune is the headquarters of the *négociant* and vineyard owner. The Ws are extremely good, the Rs less reliable.

RENAULT WINERY   *USA, New Jersey, Sp, W, R*   One of the oldest and most successful wineries in the state, located in Egg Harbor City, producing some 25,000 cases of assorted wines. Sp wines, such as Spumante, head the list.

RENOU, RENÉ   *France, Loire, Bonnezeaux, W, R*   One of the great advocates of the wines of the Layon Valley and président of the Syndicat des Vins de Bonnezeaux, M Renou makes Bonnezeaux and R wines from his 18ha in Thouarcé.

RESERVA   *Spain*   Red wines that must spend three years in the *bodega*, of which at least one must be in *barricas* (**BARRIQUES**). W and R *reservas* must spend two years in the *bodega*, of which six months must be in *barricas*.

RESERVE   *France*   Term used for special *cuvées* put aside for ageing and future use.

RÉSERVE DE LA COMTESSE   *France, Bordeaux, Médoc, Pauillac, R*   2nd wine of Ch Pichon-Lalande.

RESS, BALTHASAR   *Germany, Rheingau, W, R*   This leading Rheingau estate has good vineyards at Rüdesheim and elsewhere. Ress is a member of **CHARTA** and a specialist in dry wines.

RETSINA   *Greece, W*   Greek speciality, dating from Classical times, which is now made like other W wines, except that small pieces of resin from the Alep pine are added to the must and removed at the first racking of the young wine. Retsina should be drunk very cold. Leading producers include: Boutari.

REUILLY *France, Loire, AOC, R, P, W* Dry Ws from Sauvignon Blanc, and Rs and Ps from Pinot Noir and Pinot Gris, made in the Upper Loire region near Bourges.

REVERCHON, WEINGUT *Germany, Saar, W, R* Harmonious and elegant are words used of the Reverchon estate's Saar Rieslings, which though light show the concentration of low yields from fine vineyard sites.

REVERDY, JEAN, ET FILS *France, Loire, Sancerre, W, R, P* One of the traditional names of Sancerre since the 17th century, Reverdy makes Ws from Clos de la Reine Blanche in Verdigny; also R and P Sancerre from a 2-ha plot.

REYNON, CH *France, Bordeaux, 1er Côtes de Bordeaux, R, W* Prof Dubourdieu of Bordeaux University here practices what he preaches: good Rs, well above the status of the appellation, and a W under the Bordeaux AOC.

RHEINGAU *Germany, Anbaugebiet, W, R* Generally reckoned Germany's top wine region, a band of mostly south-facing vineyards overlooking the Rhine west of Weisbaden. Riesling is the classic grape, for W wines traditionally sweet (Auslese etc.) and increasingly dry (see **CHARTA**). Some Rs are made at the western end of the region, around Assmanshausen. Important villages include **ELTVILLE, GEISENHEIM, HOCHHEIM, JOHANNISBERG, RÜDESHEIM** etc. Leading producers include: Becker, Breuer, Eser, Schloss Groenesteyn, Prinz von Hessen, Schloss Johannisberg, von Mumm, Schloss Reinhartshausen, Balthasar Ress, Schloss Schönborn, Staatsweingut Eltville, Schloss Vollrads.

RHEINHESSEN *Germany, Anbaugebiet, W, R* Large region of flat vineyards making mostly everyday wines, including large amounbts of **LIEBFRAUMILCH**. There are islands of high quality at **BINGEN** and the **RHEINTERRASSE** around **NIERSTEIN**.

RHEINTERRASSE *Germany, Rheinhessen, W, R* Long slope overlooking the Rhein, providing good vineyard sites which produce the finest wines of the region. Famous villages here include **NACKENHEIM, NIERSTEIN** and **OPPENHEIM**, although two Grosslagen, Niersteiner Gutes Domtal and Oppenheimer Krotenbrunnen, are best known for mass production wines. Leading producers include: Anton Balbach Erben, Gunderloch, Louis Guntrum, Kühling-Gillot, and Heyl zu Herrnsheim.

RHODE ISLAND *USA* This small state with a moderate climate has a handful of producers and some good wines from classic varieties. Leading producer: **SAKONNET**.

RÍAS BAIXAS *Spain, Galicia, DO, W* The newest wine zone of Galicia, in north-west Spain, is investing in modern technology and makes excellent W wine from the Albariño grape. Albariño is rich but dry wine which is among the best Ws in Spain. Leading producers include: Granxa Fillaboa, Bodegas Morgadío-Agromiño.

RIBEAUVILLÉ   *France, Alsace*   Overlooked by three castles, this village makes splendid wines from *Grands Crus* Geisberg, Kirchberg de Ribeauvillé and Osterberg. The Rieslings produced are among the best in Alsace. Leading producers include: Trimbach, Faller.

RIBEIRO   *Spain, Galicia, DO, W, R*   Galician wine zone, producing light, fresh *joven* R and W, and *enverado* from under-ripe grapes. New investment is under way and great potential is apparent. Leading producers include: BODEGAS LAPATENA, Cooperativa Vitivinícola del Ribeiro.

RIBERA DEL DUERO   *Spain, Castilla-León, DO, P, R*   The most important wine zone in Castilla-León and one of the best in Spain for R wines. It takes in part of the upper Duero Valley, which has limestone soils and a cool climate. The zone makes high-quality *rosado* and R wines, mostly *crianzas*, with some superb *reservas* and *gran reservas*. The sole grape is Tinta Fino – the Tempranillo of Rioja. Leading producers include: ALEJANDRO FERNÁNDEZ, BODEGAS PEÑALBA LÓPEZ, BODEGAS RIBERA-DUERO, BODEGAS VEGA SICILIA.

RIBERA-DUERO, BODEGAS   *Spain, Castilla-León, Ribera del Duero, R, P*   The oldest cooperative in the area, producing reliable quality wines from cellars at Peñafiel. It also uses the labels Peñafiel and Protos (for its best wine).

RICASOLI   *Italy, Tuscany, Chianti, R, W*   The Ricasoli family were the creators of modern-style Chianti in the 19th century. Their Chianti Classico, Riserva del Barone, which is aged for five years, is very reliable. Barrique-ageing helps shape the R *vino da tavola*, San Ripolo. Ricasoli is also the largest maker of VIN SANTO in Tuscany.

RICAUD, CH DE   *France, Bordeaux, Loupiac, W, Bordeaux, R*   The long-lived, complex sweet W from this château is better than the appellation would suggest. Also makes AOC Bordeaux R.

RICCADONA   *Italy, Piedmont, W, Sp*   Large producer of vermouth, Asti and *metodo classico* Conte Balduino Extra Brut and Riserva Privata Angelo Riccadona.

RICEYS, ROSÉ DES   *France, Champagne, AOC, P*   Rare Pinot Noir still P wines from a small AOC in the Aube. Leading producers include: Alexandre Bonnet, Morel Père & Fils.

RICHEAUME, DOM DE   *France, Provence, Côtes de Provence, R, W, P*   Henning Hoesch produces excellent local R wines, practising strict organic techniques. Of three styles of R, the best is Cuvée Tradition, and there is also a little P and W. The wines spend up to 18 months in small wooden barrels.

RICHEBOURG   See ROMANÉE.

RICHOTEY, CH *France, Bordeaux, Fronsac, R* Estate with a good reputation for solid, well-flavoured wines.

RICHTER, MAX-FERDINAND *Germany, Mosel, W* Producer of a range of high-class Mosels, the best being cask-aged, including regular supplies of Eiswein.

RIDGE *USA, California, Bay Area, R* One of the best names in California. Based at Cupertino, this winery is now Japanese-owned. Veteran R specialist Paul Draper produces great Cabernet Sauvignons and distinctive Zinfandel R from disparate vineyards (Sonoma, Paso Robles, Amador). A collectors' favourite is the dense, almost black York Creek (Napa) Petite Sirah.

RIESLING Classic white grape from Germany, which in careful hands makes dry or superb sweet wines that perfectly balance acidity and sweetness, for early drinking or to age for decades. Grown in the best vineyards of the Mosel and Rhine valleys, in Austria, northern Italy and Alsace, where its wine is typically higher in alcohol and drier than in Germany. It also does well in California (sometimes called Johannisberg or White Riesling), New Zealand and Australia (Rhine Riesling).

RIESLING ITALICO See WELSCHRIESLING.

RIEUSSEC, CH *France, Bordeaux, Sauternes, 1er Cru Classé, W* Owned since 1984 by the Rothschilds of Lafite, Rieussec has recaptured its reputation as one of the great Sauternes: powerful and rich, though balanced.

RIO NEGRO *South America, Argentina, Sp, W* Argentina's southernmost wine region, and one of the coolest, its grapes mainly used for Sp wines.

RIOJA *Spain, La Rioja, DOC, R, W, P* Spain's best-known wine region, subdivided into Rioja Alavesa, Rioja Alta and Rioja Baja. Many large-scale bodegas, or wineries, produce a vast range of good to outstanding wines, in all three colours, by a process which stresses cask-ageing. W wines are from Viura grapes, and the majority are made to be fresh and light. P wines too are for drinking young. Traditional oak-aged W Rioja – still made by some bodegas – has some Malvasía to add weight to the Viura. R grapes are Tempranillo, Garnacha and Graciano. Styles of R are *joven* – sold without wood-ageing; *crianza* – with at least a year in cask; *reserva* – at least 4 years old; and *gran reserva* – at least 6 years old. Most Rioja is ready to drink when sold, though the top Rs will gain from extra bottle-age. Leading producers include: **BODEGAS CAMPO VIEJO, CVNE, BODEGAS MUGA, MARQUÉS DE MURRIETA, BODEGAS FEDERICO PATERNINA, BODEGAS LA RIOJA ALTA.**

RIOJA ALTA, BODEGAS LA *Spain, Rioja, R, W* One of the very top names for quality in the Rioja region, concentrating mainly on *reservas* and *gran reservas*. Viña Ardanza is an elegant and well-balanced R and the Reserva 904 is a bigger, more concentrated R wine.

RION, DOM DANIEL   *France, Burgundy, Côte d'Or, R*   Estate with widespread vineyard holdings in the Côte de Nuits making wines in a modern, fruit-dominated style.

RIQUEWIHR   *France, Alsace*   Ancient and lovely village that includes two *Grands Crus* – Schoenenbourg and Sporen – known for Ws from Riesling, Gewürztraminer and Muscat. Leading producers include: Deiss, Dopff Au Moulin, Hugel.

RISCAL, MARQUÉS DE   *Spain, Rioja, R, P, W*   Quality has been somewhat patchy at this *bodega* in the past, but recent investment means that wines from the late 1980s onwards are much improved. Riscal also produces wines in Rueda, from French varieties including Sauvignon Blanc as well as Spanish staples.

RISERVA   *Italy*   DOC or DOCG wines with additional ageing in cask or bottle or both.

RIVENDELL WINERY   *USA, New York, Hudson River Valley, W, R*   The high reputation of Rivendell is built upon Ws such as Chardonnay, barrel-fermented Seyval Blanc and Vidal Blanc, Rs including Cabernet Sauvignon and blends.

RIVERA   *Italy, Southern Italy, Apulia, W, R, P*   The leading producer of the Castel del Monte DOC, making R, W and P wines. Il Falcone is a *riserva* R. The Terre al Monte range includes an interesting Aglianico *rosato*.

RIVERINA   *Australia, New South Wales*   A vast inland area encompassing the Murrumbidgee region. Production is mainly bulk Ws, especially Sémillon and Trebbiano. Rs are mainly Shiraz.

RIVESALTES   *France, Midi, AOC, VDN*   This name covers a wide range of *vins doux naturels*: Ws (*blanc* or *doré*) tend to darken, and Rs become lighter, with age. Best is the RANCIO style, achieved by ageing for at least 9 months with some exposure to oxygen; such wine is often sold as Vieux Rivesaltes. The W Muscat de Rivesaltes, on the other hand, should be drunk within 1-2 years: it may have a lemony, honeyed flavour, or a fuller, richer, orangey taste. Leading producers include: Dom Cazes, Ch de Corneilla, Mont Tauch co-op, Dom Sarda-Malet.

RIVIÈRE, CH DE LA   *France, Bordeaux, Fronsac, R*   The largest Fronsac estate: a splendid château with ancient cellars and long-lived, opulent wines.

ROBERTSON   *South Africa, WO*   In the Breede River Valley, this region enjoys a hot, arid climate tempered by sea breezes from the Indian Ocean. Its estates and co-ops produce good Chardonnay and Shiraz, as well as Sp wines. Leading producers include: Graham Beck, Van Loveren, Weltevrede, De Wetshof.

ROBOLA   *Greece, Islands, W*   A big dry W wine from the island of Cephalonia from the native Robola grape.

ROC DES CAMBES, CH   *France, Bordeaux, Côte de Bourg, R*   François Mitjavile's St-Emilion, **LE TERTRE RÔTEBOEUF**, is well known: this, his second estate, makes equally uncompromising and (for the AOC) costly wine in a rich, heady style.

ROCAILLES, DOM DU   *France, Savoie, W, R*   Leading maker of Ws from the best Savoie villages (*crus*), Abymes and Apremont, as well as R Vin de Savoie.

ROCCA DELLE MACIE   *Italy, Tuscany, Chianti, R, W*   Maker of a good-value range of fruity wines. The basic Chianti Classico and the *riserva* are designed for relatively early drinking. The *vino da tavola* Ser Gioveto (R) needs age.

ROCHEMORIN, CH DE   *France, Bordeaux, Pessac-Léognan R, W*   Large estate with a fine fleshy R and sound W, both enjoyable young; medium-priced and very good value.

RODERN   *France, Alsace*   Known historically for R from Pinot Noir, this village now produces Gewürztraminer and Pinot Gris Ws, and includes most of *Grand Cru* Gloeckelberg. Leading producers include: Gassmann, J Sipp.

RODET, ANTONIN   *France, Burgundy, Chalonnais, R, W*   An important *négociant* firm, producing wines from the whole of Burgundy and also making an excellent Mercurey from the Château de Chamirey vineyards.

ROEDERER   *USA, California, Mendocino, Sp*   Champagne house Louis Roederer started making classic Sp in California in 1985. The goal is 100,000 cases from almost 162ha of vines. The oak-aged Estate Brut is elegant, with lemon and bread-dough aromas.

ROEDERER, LOUIS   *France, Champagne*   Founded over 200 years ago, this family-owned **GRANDE MARQUE** makes some of the greatest champagnes. Reserve wines and long ageing before sale are two keys to the consistent quality of the NV Brut Premier. The prestige *cuvée*, Cristal, created for a Tsar, is one of the great luxury champagnes.

ROLET PÈRE ET FILS   *France, Jura, R, W, P, Sp*   Estate which concentrates on single-variety wines, including a P (Poulsard), Rs (Pinot Noir and Trousseau) and Ws from Chardonnay (including an oak-aged *cuvée*) and Savagnin. Sp, **VIN JAUNE** and Macvin complete the range.

ROMANÉE, LA   *France, Burgundy, AOC, R*   The five *Grands Crus* of La Romanée, **ROMANÉE CONTI**, Romanée-St-Vivant, **RICHEBOURG** and **LA TÂCHE** form a block on the hillside above the Côte de Nuits village of Vosne-Romanée. Their wines are known for their phenomenal cost as well for their spicy opulence and capacity to age for 10–15 years or more. Leading producers include: Bouchard Père et Fils, Alain Hudelot-Noéllat, Domaine de la Romanée-Conti, Ch de Vosne-Romanée.

ROMANÉE CONTI   See ROMANÉE (La).

ROMANEE-CONTI, DOM DE LA *France, Burgundy, Côte d'Or, R, W* Sole owners of Romanée-Conti and La Tâche and major owners of other top *Grands Crus*. These are the wines by which all other red burgundies are judged. Rich, heady and incredibly deep in taste, they are destined for a long life. Greatly sought after, their very limited production on occasion ensures ridiculously high prices. Have been known to disappoint.

ROMANÉE-ST-VIVANT *See* ROMANÉE (LA).

ROPITEAU FRÈRES *France, Burgundy, Côte d'Or, R, W* Estate owner and *négociant*, whose Ws are generally better than Rs. Their best wines are the Meursaults.

ROSADO *Spain* Rosé or pink wine.

ROSATO *Italy* Rosé or pink wine.

ROSEMOUNT ESTATE *Australia, New South Wales, Hunter Valley W, R* Rosemount, founded in 1969, produces remarkably consistent wines. Chardonnays are rich and fruity, R wines enjoyable and with character. Roxburgh Chardonnay and Show Reserve wines are the flagships.

ROSETTE *France, South-West, AOC, W* Tiny enclave within the Bergerac zone which offers a name for local sweet W wine. Often these are sold as Côtes de Bergerac.

ROSSO CONERO *Italy, Marches, DOC, R* This coastal zone near Ancona is increasingly promising, yielding flavoursome meaty wines from the Montepulciano grape. Leading producers include: Fazi-Battaglia, Garofoli, Monte Schiavo, Umani Ronchi.

ROSSO DI MONTALCINO *Italy, Tuscany, DOC, R* Little brother to Brunello di Montalcino. May be sold after one year's ageing, so much less tannic than the Brunello. Leading producers include: Tenuta Caparzo, Col d'Orcia, Villa Banfi.

ROSSO PICENO *Italy, Marches, DOC, R* Broad DOC whose best wines come from the *superiore* zone. Mainly Sangiovese with some Montepulciano. Leading producers include: Fazi-Battaglia, La Torraccia, Villa Pigna, Villamagna.

ROT, NOBLE *See* BOTRYTIS CINEREA.

ROTHBURY ESTATE *Australia, New South Wales, Hunter Valley W, R* Created by wine guru Len Evans, this estate is now a public company. Its annual 250,000 cases include buttery Chardonnays, dense Shiraz Rs and fine Sémillon Ws.

RÔTI *France* Literally "roasted". A characteristic of sweet wines with aromas of dried grapes resulting from noble rot (BOTRYTIS CINEREA.)

ROTY, JOSEPH *France, Burgundy, Côte d'Or, R* Leading producer in Gevrey-Chambertin, making densely concentrated, fruity, oaky, long-lived R wines.

ROUDIER, CH *France, Bordeaux, Montagne St-Emilion, R* A top estate of the St-Emilion "satellites" making rich, solid wine worth a few years' cellaring.

ROUFFACH *France, Alsace* This village's vineyards encompass the *Grand Cru* Vorbourg, which includes the noted Clos St-Landelin. Pinot Noir (for Rs), Riesling and Pinot Gris (Ws) all do well. Leading producers include: Dopff and Irion, Schlumberger.

ROUMANIA Although it has a long winemaking history, most wine is drunk locally. The best wines come from four main regions: Tîrnave, Cotnari, Dealul Mare and Murfatlar. W wines with good aromas and firm acidity are made from a wide range of grapes including Muscat Ottonel, Sauvignon Blanc and Pinot Gris. For Rs, Pinot Noir, Cabernet Sauvignon and Merlot do well in Dealul Mare. The best Cabernet Sauvignon comes from the warmest region, Murfatlar. Cotnari is known for its pale, honey-eyed sweet wine which gained fame alongside Hungarian Tokaji.

ROUSSEAU, DOM ARMAND *France, Burgundy, Côte d'Or, R* Estate with vineyards in Morey-St-Denis and Gevrey-Chambertin. Traditional, benchmark wines.

ROYAL OPORTO WINE COMPANY *Portugal, port* Originally set up in 1756 by the Portuguese government as the controlling body for the port trade, today it is by far the largest producer of port. The wines are mainly very commercial and often appear in supermarkets as own-label wines.

ROZAY, CH DU *France, Rhône, Condrieu, W* Quality wines, from old vines, that can be among the appellation's best.

RUCHOTTES-CHAMBERTIN *See* CHAMBERTIN.

RÜDESHEIM *Germany, Rheingau, W* Town situated below its famous vine-covered hill, the Rüdesheimer Berg. The steep Berg Schlossberg vineyard yields Riesling Ws with a distinctive flavour from the slaty soil. Leading producers include: Dr. Heinrich Nägler, Bernard Breuer, Balthasar Ress.

RÜDESHEIM *Germany, Nahe, W* Village (as opposed to the town of the same name in the Rheingau) which is the centre of the *grosslage* Rosengarten. The district produces pleasant, everyday wine.

RUEDA *Spain, Castilla-León, DO, W, Sp* One of the fine wine zones of Castilla-León, owing its modern prominence to the Marqués de Riscal brand, and now producing many styles of wine including W DO Rueda Superior and new Sp wine DO Rueda Espumoso. W Rueda is usually crisp, dry and fresh – very much a modern W wine. There are plans to extend the DO to include R and *rosados*. Leading producers include: Castilla la Vieja, Marques de Griñon, Marqués de Riscal, Vinos Blancos de Castilla.

RUFFINO   *Italy, Tuscany, Chianti, R, W*   One of Chianti's giants with some of its best *riservas*, such as Riserva Ducale. The firm was instrumental in creating Predicato wines. Nero del Tondo is a R from Pinot Nero; their prestige W wine is called Libaio.

RUGIENS, LES   *France, Burgundy, Côte de Beaune, 1er Cru, R*   This Pommard vineyard is divided into Rugiens Bas and Rugiens Haut, the former in particular producing wines of exceptional quality with great ageing potential. Leading producers include: J-M Boillot, de Courcel, Michel Gaunoux, de Montille, Pothier-Rieusset.

RUINART   *France, Champagne*   This relatively unknown small GRANDE MARQUE was founded in 1729 and is now owned by the LVMH group. Very well-made, elegant and flowery; and good value: especially the *blanc de blancs* prestige *cuvée*, Dom Ruinart.

RULÄNDER   See PINOT GRIS.

RULLY   *France, Burgundy, AOC, R, W*   Village in the CÔTE CHALONNAIS district. Rully makes elegant, spice-accented Chardonnay Ws and clear, pleasing Pinot Noir Rs. Some, but not all, of the best vineyards are *Premier Cru*. Leading producers include: Dom Belleville, Jean-Claude Brelière, Chartron & Trébuchet, Pierre Cogny, André Delorme, Dom de la Folie, Dom de la Hermitage, Paul & Henri Jacqueson, Dom de la Renarde, Ch de Rully/Antonin Rodet.

RUPPERTSBERG   *Germany, Pfalz, W, R*   Wine village in the central or Mittelhaardt zone of the Pfalz region. Produces fine W Riesling, Silvaner and Scheurebe from the Hoheburg and Linsenbusch vineyards.

RUSSIAN REPUBLIC   W and Sp wines are made in the south and east of the republic from varieties including Muscatel (for dessert wines), Silvaner, Riesling, Aligoté and the ubiquitous Rkatsiteli. R wines are made in the south and east. The greatest potential is for Rs from Cabernet Sauvignon.

RUSSIAN RIVER VALLEY   *USA, California, Sonoma, VA*   In Sonoma County, a cool climate wine zone producing interesting Rs from Pinot Noir, Ws from Chardonnay, flinty White Riesling and nutmeg-spiced W Gewürztraminer. Also some crisp Sp wines. Leading producers include: Gary Farrell, Korbel, Piper Sonoma, Sonoma Cutrer.

RUSSIZ SUPERIORE   *Italy, Friuli-Venezia-Giulia, Collio and Colli Orientali, W*   Estate producing some very stylish varietal wines. Two *vini da tavola*, Roncuz (W) and a sweet wine Verduzzo (W), have received acclaim.

RUST-EN-VREDE   *South Africa, Stellenbosch, R*   This R-only estate is owned by former Springbok Jannie Englebrecht. His Shiraz, with its rich, roasted quality, is distinctly reminiscent of the northern Rhône. Shiraz also appears in the estate's best wine, a blend of R grapes called Rust-en-Vrede.

RUSTENBERG ESTATE   *South Africa, Stellenbosch, R, W*   Outstandingly beautiful, and one of the Cape's oldest estates, Rustenberg has a fine reputation notably for its Rs, including a fairly restrained Cabernet Sauvignon and a good bordeaux blend, Rustenberg Gold.

RUTHERFORD   *USA, California, VA*   In the heart of the Napa Valley, this area, sometimes called the Rutherford Bench, is the wide, flat, low terrace along the side of the valley. Rutherford is famous for its distinctive Cabernet Sauvignons with firm, tannic structure and somewhat herbaceous flavours. Leading producers include: Beaulieu, Caymus, Grgich Hills, Heitz Cellars, Inglenook.

RUTHERGLEN   *Australia, Victoria*   Vines were first planted here in Victoria's north-east in the mid-19th century. This region now enjoys an excellent reputation for liqueur Muscats. Leading producers include: Baileys, Morris.

RYMAN, HUGH   A name appearing on millions of wine labels. An Australian-trained oenologist, son of Nick Ryman, formerly of Ch Jaubertie in Bergerac, Ryman works in Eastern Europe, Spain, southern France and elsewhere, conjuring good modern wines out of backward areas by use of straightforward modern techniques.

S

SAALE-UNSTRUT *Germany, Anbaugebiet, W* Region in the east of Germany, around Leipzig, making mostly dry W wines. The former monastic estate now called the Staatsweingut (state cellars) Naumberg is the main producer, along with the Freyburg/Unstrut co-op.

SAAR-RUWER *Germany, Mosel-Saar-Ruwer, Bereich, W* Zone along two small rivers, the Saar and Ruwer, tributaries of the Mosel. Top-class Riesling Ws are made in warm years. Ordinary wines carry the **WILTINGER SCHARZBERG** name. Leading producers include: Karthäuserhof, von Schubert (both Ruwer); Bischöfliche Weingüter, Egon Müller-Scharzhof, von Hövel, Reverchon, Bert Simon, Vereinigte Hospitien.

SAARSTEIN, SCHLOSS *Germany, Saar, W* Rieslings with pronounced acidity, balanced by fruit, are the aim of this Saar estate.

SABLES DU GOLFE DU LION *France, Vin de Pays, P, R, W* This is the *vin de pays* for the sandy coastal plain where the Listel firm (*see* **SALINS DU MIDI**) have a successful venture making P wines from Grenache, plus Rs (Cabernets, Syrah, Cinsaut etc), and Ws from Sauvignon and Muscat as well as local grapes.

SACHSEN *Germany, Anbaugebiet, W* Region in eastern Germany around Dresden and Meissen, making dry W wines. Leading producers: Meissen co-op, Schloss Wackerbarth.

SAGET, GUY *France, Loire, Pouilly-Fumé, W* Familiar throughout the Loire Valley as *négociants*, the Sagets started in Pouilly, where they still farm. Their wines, especially the Pouilly-Fumé, can be attractive and age well.

SAINT-GEORGES, LES *France, Burgundy, Côte de Nuits, 1er Cru, R* Leading vineyard in the Nuits-St-Georges appellation, with great bouquet and a full, satisfying palate. Leading producers include: Robert Chevillon, Henri Gouges.

SAINTSBURY *USA, California, Napa, R, W* In the heart of the Carneros district, this estate grows R Pinot Noir and W Chardonnay. Garnet is a lighter, fresher Pinot Noir R bursting with cherry fruit.

SAKONNET VINEYARDS *USA, Rhode Island, W, R* The 17.5-ha vineyard provides Ws from Vidal Blanc, Chardonnay and Gewürztraminer and Rs from Pinot Noir and Cabernet Franc. The best-selling wines are two blends, America's Cup White and Spinnaker White.

SALES, CH DE   *France, Bordeaux, Pomerol, R*   Pomerol's biggest estate and the only real château in the region: not great wine, but enjoyable and early-maturing.

SALINS DU MIDI, LES   *France, Midi, Gard, R, W, P*   Enormous enterprise with three estates on the Carmargue sand dunes, and two in Provence, at the forefront of new developments, including organic viticulture. The flagship wine, a Vin de Pays des Sables du Golfe du Lion, is a delicate P using the Listel name.

SALON   *France, Champagne*   Owned by Laurent-Perrier, this miniscule **GRANDE MARQUE** has just one hectare of vines in the Côte des Blancs. Its sole vintage wine, expensive and extremely sought after, ages beautifully.

SALWEY, WEINGUT B   *Germany, Baden, R, W, P*   This estate is a specialist in Rs, ageing all wines in oak. A dry Weissherbst P is another speciality.

SAMOS   *Greece, Islands, W, VDN*   The Aegean island of Samos produces sweet wines from the Muscat grape. They can be *vin de liqueur, vin doux naturel* or Samos Nectar, a very sweet W from sun-dried grapes, capable of long wood-ageing. Leading producers include: Cambas.

SAN FELICE   *Italy, Tuscany, Chianti, R, W, P*   Estate making good basic Chianti Classico and single-vineyard Pogio Rosso and Villa la Pagliaia *riserva* Chiantis. San Felice is also known for fresh, young Bianco Val d'Arbia (DOC, W), fruity Rosé di Canaiolo *vino da tavola* and blended Vigorello (R).

SAN JUAN DEL RIO   *Mexico, Central America, R, W, Sp*   Recently developed, this vineyard region is 160km (100 miles) north of Mexico City. Most plantings are at a cool 1,800m (6,000ft). Some Cabernet Sauvignon and Pinot Noir Rs are made, also Sp wines.

SAN PEDRO   *Chile, R, W*   Based in the **MAULE VALLEY**, this is one of Chile's oldest wineries, founded in 1865. San Pedro is one of the country's largest producers with roughly 770,000 cases a year. It is best known for its good-value Gato Nero and Gato Blanco wines which account for 50% of exports. Other labels include Castillo de Molina and Santa Helena.

SAN VALERO   *Spain, Aragón, Cariñena, R, W, P*   The largest cooperative in this wine zone, producing wines from everyday young Rs and Ws to prizewinning *gran reservas*.

SANCERRE   *France, Loire, AOC, W, R, P*   Dry W wine with vibrant acidity, grassy bouquet and gooseberry or blackcurrant flavours; a model Sauvignon Blanc wine now emulated around the world. It tends to be lighter and earlier-drinking than its twin, **POUILLY FUMÉ**. Rs and P are from Pinot Noir. Leading producers include: J-F Bailly, J-M Bourgeoise, Lucien Crochet, Gitton, Alphonse Mellot, Clos de la Poussie, Prieur, Reverdy, J-M Roger, J-L Vacheron, A Vatan.

SANDEMAN *Portugal, port, Spain, sherry* George Sandeman began in London in 1790, with initial capital of £300. Today his firm is owned by Seagram but still family-run and is one of the largest port producers. Much of the range, eg Founder's Reserve, is standard commercial port, but there are also fine wines, from attractively fruity 10-year-old Royal Tawny to soft, relatively fast-maturing vintage wines. House of Sandeman sherry has seen a considerable increase in quality of brands such as Don Fino, and wines like Royal Ambrosante amontillado and Imperial Corregidor oloroso, based on long-established *soleras*.

SANFORD *USA, California, Santa Barbara & Southern California, R, W, P* From vines on the bank of the Santa Ynez River, Rich Sanford makes butter- and grapefruit-tasting Chardonnay, black cherry-rich Pinot Noir R, herbaceous Sauvignon W which ages well, and tangy orange-peel and rose-petal Pinot Noir Vin Gris P.

SANGIOVESE The main red grape for Chianti. Clones are found all over Italy, making wines of varying quality.

SANTA CAROLINA *Chile, South America, R, W* Established in 1875 in the MAIPO VALLEY, one of the first wineries to develop vineyards in the new CASABLANCA area. The firm enjoys a good reputation for Cabernet Sauvignon, Sauvignon Blanc and Sémillon, especially for the Special Reserve versions of the first two.

SANTA MONICA *Chile, South America, R, W* Owned by well-known winemaker Emilio de Solminihac and his wife, Monica, this firm produces export wines only from Cabernet Sauvignon and Merlot (Rs), Chardonnay, Sauvignon Blanc, Sémillon and Riesling (Ws).

SANTA RITA *Chile, South America, R, W* Chile's leading exporter to both the UK and North America. Founded in 1880, it has recently developed vineyards in the new CASABLANCA region. Santa Rita sells under three different labels, the best of which is Medalla Real, headed by Cabernet Sauvignon and Chardonnay.

SANTA YNEZ VALLEY *USA, California, Santa Barbara, VA* Wine zone in Santa Barbara County, where Chardonnay and particularly Pinot Noir seem perfectly suited. Also Sauvignon Blanc and Merlot. Leading producers include: Firestone, Sanford.

SANTENAY *France, Burgundy, AOC, R, W* Here R wine reasserts itself in this village south of the famous W-wine vineyards of Montrachet. There are several *Premiers Crus*, and some good wines are made in a rather tough, earthy style. Try them at 5–8 years. Leading producers include: Adrien Belland, Ch de la Charrière, Fleurot-Larose, Mestre Père & Fils, Piieur-Brunet, Roussot.

SANTENOTS, LES *France, Burgundy, Côte de Beaune, 1er Cru, R, W* The R wines from this vineyard are under the appellation Volnay-Santenots and combine breeding and elegance. The Ws appear as Meursault-Santenots and are full-bodied with a long finish. Leading producers include: Marquis d'Angerville, Comtes Lafon.

SANTORINI   *Greece, Islands, W*   The volcanic soil here produces a powerful dry W wine from the Assyrtiko grape, in addition to a sweet wine called Vissanto.

SARDINIA   *Italy*   This Mediterranean island continues to make wines from native varieties such as R Cannonau and Girò and W Nuragus and Torbato in addition to more modern styles. Leading producer Sella & Mosca is a driving force.

SARGET DE GRUAUD-LAROSE   *France, Bordeaux, Médoc, St-Julien, R*   2nd wine of Ch Gruaud-Larose.

SARTRE, CH LE   *France, Bordeaux, Pessac-Léognan, R, W*   With the same owners as Ch Carbonnieux, this small Léognan estate offers the Carbonnieux style at half the price. The R here is better than the W.

SASSICAIA   *Italy, Tuscany, DOC, R*   Legendary wine, the brainchild of Mario Incisa della Rochetta, first made in 1968. It is from 75% Cabernet Sauvignon and 25% Cabernet Franc, *barrique*-aged. Superb and very long-lived.

SAUMUR   *France, Loire, AOC, R, W, P, Sp*   The basic AOC is for R and W still wines from the Cabernets (Franc and Sauvignon) and Chenin Blanc grapes, made around Saumur on the south bank of the Loire. Also crisp, Sp (*mousseux* or *pétillant*) W wines. Saumur-Champigny (from Cabernet grapes) is one of France's most fashionable light R wines, from nine communes east of Saumur. Leading producers include: Ackerman-Laurence, Bouvet-Ladubay, Ch de Chaintre, Paul Filliatreau, Gratien Meyer Seydoux, Ch de Targé, Philippe et Georges Vatan.

SAUSSIGNAC   *France, South-West, AOC, W*   Enclave within Bergerac for medium-sweet or rich sweet W wine. Often sold as Côtes de Bergerac. Leading producers include: Pierre Sadoux.

SAUTEJEAU, MARCEL   *France, Loire, Muscadet, W*   Firm based at Dom de l'Hyvernière near Le Pallet, which, along with Dom de la Botinière at Vallet, is the source of their Muscadet. Its turnover of more than a million cases a year includes wines from Anjou, Saumur and Vouvray.

SAUTERNES   *France, Bordeaux, AOC, W*   World-famous, luscious sweet W wine from the southern Graves region. The most common blend of grapes is 80% Sémillon, 20% Sauvignon Blanc. Great Sauternes – rich, viscous, honeyed wine that retains a dash of acidity that helps it improve for decades – is made only from grapes that have been attacked by **BOTRYTIS CINEREA** ("noble rot"). The châteaux were classified in 1855, into *Premier Cru supérieur* (of which there is only one, Ch d'Yquem), *Premiers Crus* (11 châteaux) and *Deuxièmes Crus* (14 châteaux). Leading producers include: Ch Filhot, Ch Guiraud, Ch Lafaurie-Peyraguey, Ch Rieussec, Ch de Suduiraut, Ch d'Yquem.

SAUVIGNON BLANC   White grape used in Bordeaux blends for both dry and sweet wines, and for dry whites such as Sancerre and Pouilly Fumé in the upper Loire. Most are designed to be drunk young, in the fresh, acidic and assertive yet fruity style of the Loire wines: New Zealand Sauvignon Blancs are often excellent. A short period of oak-ageing emphasizes the smokiness of the grape, and has led to its alternative name, Fumé Blanc, being widely used in California. Also grown in Chile, Austria, Slovenia and Bulgaria.

SAUVION   *France, Loire, Muscadet, W, R, P*   One of the most dynamic *négociants* in the region, based at the Ch du Cléray in Vallet. Brands include Sauvion du Cléray, Cardinal Richard and Carte d'Or. Despite buying 80% of its grapes from growers, it ensures quality by basing purchases on tastings, selling some wines as *cuvées*, known as Découvertes.

SAUZET, DOM ETIENNE   *France, Burgundy, Côte d'Or, W*   Together with Domaine Leflaive, Sauzet is the top producer in Puligny-Montrachet, making classic W burgundies in the *Grands* and *Premiers Crus*.

SAVENNIÈRES   *France, Loire, AOC, W*   Bone-dry Ws from Chenin Blanc, made on the north bank of the Loire. There are two high-quality single-vineyard appellations: **COULÉE-DE-SERRANT** and **ROCHE-AUX-MOINES**. Leading producers include: Dom des Baumard, Clos de la Coulée de Serrant, Dom Mme Laroche, Pierre et Yves Soulez.

SAVIGNY/SAVIGNY-LES-BEAUNE   *France, Burgundy, AOC, R, W*   For Côte d'Or burgundies, these are very reasonably priced R wines. The *Premiers Crus* are notable for their appealing scent and clean, fruity taste; they are best drunk between 4–10 years old. Some Ws are also made. Leading producers include: Dom Simon Bize & Fils, Dom Pierre Guillemot, Dom Antonin Guyon, Dom Rapet Père & Fils, Dom Seguin.

SAVOIE, VIN DE   *France, Savoie, AOC, R, P, W, Sp*   Still or Sp (*mousseux* and *pétillant*) dry W wines, and some Rs and Ps, from large mountainous area. 17 villages or *crus* can use their name on the label: the most important are Abymes, Apremont, Arbin, Ayze, Chautagne, Chignin and Jongieux. The W grape Roussette has its own AOC, in which it may be used alone or blended with Chardonnay. Other local W-wine grapes are Jacquère, Gringet, Chasselas and high-acid Molette, which is used for Sp wine. The characteristic R-wine grape of Savoie is Mondeuse; Gamay and Pinot Noir are more recent arrivals. Leading producers include: Louis Magnin, Raymond Quénard, Ch de Ripaille, Dom des Rocailles, Le Vignerons Savoyard.

SAVOYE, DOM RENÉ   *France, Burgundy, Beaujolais, R*   One of the top producer of Chiroubles, the most fragrant of the Beaujolais Crus and best drunk young.

SCHARFFENBERGER *USA, California, Mendocino, Sp, W, P* Champagne firms Pommery and Lanson are partners with John Scharffenberger in this Sp wine producer at Philo. The Sp W leans towards the austere, though the Brut P has rich, fruity aromas, and plum and strawberry tastes.

SCHEUREBE White grape (Silvaner x Riesling) from Germany, making good-quality wine, especially in the Pfalz, where the strong bouquet and high acidity can result in characterful wine for long-term keeping. Also grown in England.

SCHLOSS BÖCKELHEIM *Germany, Nahe, Bereich, W* Zone covering the southern half of the Nahe, including fine vineyards at TRAISEN, NIEDERHAUSEN and SCHLOSSBÖCKELHEIM and rather ordinary ones elsewhere. Mostly W, the best from Riesling, which can from good sites be concentrated and long-lived. Leading producers include: Paul Anheuser, Crusius, Dönhoff, Staatliche Weinbaudömane.

SCHLOSS STAUFENBERG, MARKGRÄFLICH BADISCHES WEINGUT *Germany, Baden, R, W, P* Fruity, intense Rieslings and Rs of high quality keep up the reputation of this old estate.

SCHLUMBERGER, DOM *France, Alsace, W, R* This family firm has amassed many vineyard plots over the years and now has the largest holding in Alsace and one of the most important in France. It includes steeply terraced plots which are expensive to cultivate, but the *terroirs* are worth it. Their Gewürztraminers made their name – especially Cuvée Christine (now defined as a *vendange tardive*) and Cuvée Anne, a *sélection des grains nobles*. Also of top quality are Pinot Gris and Rieslings from *Grands Crus* Kitterlé and Saering.

SCHMITT, ROBERT WEINGUT *Germany, Franken, W* This estate stresses natural viticulture and winemaking, yielding well-balanced, long-lived wines in the traditional Franken style.

SCHOLTZ HERMANOS *Spain, Málaga* Probably the best málaga producer; certainly the most familiar in export markets, and also the oldest (founded 1805). Its most famous brand is Solera 1885: essentially a dry wine, although with considerable richness. Moscatel Palido is very sweet; Seco Añejo is intensely dry, like an old amontillado sherry. Dulce Negro is very dark, concentrated and sweet.

SCHÖNBORN, SCHLOSS *Germany, Rheingau, W, R* Estate producing classic Rheingau Rieslings, with well-balanced acidity and fruit, and *barrique*-aged Rs.

SCHRAMSBERG *USA, California, Napa, Sp, W* Jack Davies and his wife Jamie founded this specialist Sp wine estate in 1965 on an old Calistoga winery. Their Blanc de Blancs, with lemon and bread-dough aromas, and Blanc de Noirs, with flinty, berry flavours, both age beautifully.

SCHRÖCK, HEIDI *Austria, Neusiedlersee-Hügelland, W, R* One of a small coterie of female winemakers, based in Rust, Schröck produces a wide range of wines, including Welschriesling and Weissburgunder (Ws), a grippy P from Cabernet Sauvignon and the rare Ausbruch (sweet W). One of her best wines is the R Blaufränkisch with its fine, ripe, silky-fruit palate.

SCHUBERT, WEINGUT VON *Germany, Ruwer, W* The estate's beautiful labels stress the name of the Maximin Grünhaus vineyard, all three parts of which it owns. Superb, long-lived Rieslings with balance and style.

SCHUSTER, EDUARD WEINGUT *Germany, Pfalz, W* Traditional maker of Rieslings and other Ws, which show all the Pfalz fullness and character.

SEBASTIANI *USA, California, Sonoma, W, R* Once a bulk producer, the stress has switched to high quality, notably the flinty, floral dry W from the rare vine Green Hungarian.

SEC *France,* **SECO** *Spain and Portugal,* **SECCO** *Italy* All mean dry. In champagne, however, sec means medium-dry.

SECOND VIN The second wine of a château, as opposed to its *grand vin*. Often made from young-vine fruit.

SEGONZAC, CH *France, Bordeaux, 1er Côtes de Blaye, R* One of the top châteaux of Blaye: large amounts of well-made claret.

SEKT *Germany* Sparkling wine, made by a variety of methods. "Deutscher (German) Sekt" is despite the name usually made from non-German base wine, and is medium-dry and bland. Better-quality Sekt is labelled *brut* and has a district name on the label: the best are made from Riesling or Weissburgunder and will say so, while Winzersekt is made by a grower or estate.

SÉLECTION DE GRAINS NOBLES *France* Luscious, sweet wines with a natural concentration of sugars from late-picked BOTRYTIZED grapes or from grapes which have begun to dry on the vine. Term used particularly in Alsace; also Sauternes, Monbazillac and Coteaux du Layon.

SELVAPIANA *Italy, Tuscany, Chianti, W, R* Chianti Rufina estate known for its long-lived wines: normal, *riserva* and *cru*, Vigneto Bucerchiale (R), plus Borro Lastricato (W).

SÉMILLON Useful but unfashionable white grape, best known for its partnership with Sauvignon Blanc in great sweet wines such as Sauternes. Sémillon is particularly prone to rot – good news if the rot is "noble" BOTRYTIS CINEREA, bad if it is grey rot. Sémillon is also blended with Sauvignon Blanc in dry Bordeaux whites, and alone has made some superb, long-maturing dry wines in Australia's Hunter Valley. Also grown in Chile, Argentina and South Africa.

SÉNARD, DOM DANIEL   *France, Burgundy, Côte d'Or, R*   Now a follower of Guy ACCAD's style of vinification, this domaine produces top-quality red Cortons.

SETÚBAL   *Portugal, DOC*   Peninsula in southern Portugal known
for Moscatel de Setúbal, a sweet, fortified wine, but also for exciting new styles of R and W wine. Leading producers include: J P
Vinhos.

SEYSSEL   *France, Savoie, AOC, W, Sp*   The best-known wine of
this appellation is the Sp Seyssel Mousseux, made mainly from
Molette grapes, but usually with a little Roussette for finesse,
made as in Champagne. Leading producers include: Maison
Mollex, Varichon & Clerc.

SEYVAL BLANC   Hybrid white grape with high acidity, making dry
wine with neutral or grapefruity character in England, New York
State and Canada.

SHIRAZ   Synonym for the Syrah grape grown in Australia and
South Africa.

SHOMRON   *Israel, R, W, P*   One of Israel's main wine-production
areas using grapes produced in the Carmel Valley. Leading producers include: Carmel.

SIAURAC, CH   *France, Bordeaux, Lalande-de-Pomerol, R*   The leading
estate of the appellation; quite large, with delicious, early-maturing wine.

SICHEL, H   *Germany, Rheinhessen, W, R*   Large merchant house,
known for its Blue Nun Liebfraumilch brand and for a range of
good wines from all German regions.

SICILY   *Italy*   The Mediterranean's largest island is paying increasing attention to quality. Although some international varieties
have infiltrated, native grapes such as Grillo and Inzolia remain
important for the mainly W wine production. Also home to one
of the world's great fortified wines, MARSALA.

SIEGRIST, THOMAS   *Germany, Pfalz, R, W*   Red-wine specialist,
noted for his *barrique*-aged Spätburgunder and Dornfelder, and
also Ws from Weiss- and Grauburgunder.

SIERRA FOOTHILLS   *USA, California, VA*   Wine zone along the
eastern edge of the Central Valley, producing densely-fruited R
wines from Zinfandel and Cabernet Sauvignon, plus Ws from
Chardonnay and Sauvignon, and some fortified and dessert
wines. Leading producers include: Boeger, Monteviña, Renaissance.

SIGALAS-RABAUD, CH   *France, Bordeaux, Sauternes, 1er Cru Classé,
W*   Not much new oak is used here, and bottled young, Sigalas
is delicious: intensely fruity and racily elegant. Drink at 8-10
years old. Bought in 1994 by Cordier: standards should further
improve.

SIGOLSHEIM *France, Alsace* Wine village long known for its Riesling, Muscat and Gewürztraminer; the latter especially in *Grand Cru* Mambourg. Leading producers include: Sick-Dreyer, Pierre Sparr.

SILVANER/SYLVANER White grape making wine high in acidity, low in aroma, except from good producers in Alsace and Franken in Germany. Useful in blends.

SILVER OAK *USA, California, Napa, R* This Oakville winery makes just Cabernet Sauvignon. The Napa Valley, Alexander Valley (Sonoma) and Bonny's Vineyard Cabernets are all powerful and violet-scented.

SIMI *USA, California, Sonoma, W, R* The Healdsburg winery built in 1890 was refurbished by Russ Green and Moët-Hennessy of France. Chardonnays feature ripe clove, apple and anise flavours, the Cabernet Sauvignons are round and soft with violet scents and Sendal, a new W Sémillon/Sauvignon blend, is fleshy with ripe fig and honeydew-melon fruit.

SIMMERN, LANGWERTH VON *Germany, Rheingau, W, R* Traditional-style Rheingau Rieslings which respond beautifully to bottle-age.

SIMONE, CH *France, Provence, Palette, W, R* The leading producer in this small AOC, with very old vines (Grenache, Mourvèdre, Cinsaut for Rs; Clairette, Sémillon, Muscat for Ws). Traditional methods, and wine that can age for many years.

SIN CRIANZA *Spain* Wines that have spent no time in oak, or less than the legal minimum for *crianza* wines.

SIRAN, CH *France, Bordeaux, Margaux, Cru Bourgeois, R* This showplace château makes smooth silky wines that can age well.

SLOVAKIA The country has 28,000ha under vine, representing two-thirds of the former Czechoslovakia's vineyards. Mainly makes W wines from a wide number of varieties, including the native, aromatic Irsay Oliver, which at their best can be very attractive, with good fruit, very ripe and crisp. Of the small amount of R wine made, Pinot Noir stands out.

SLOVENIA There are 21,500ha under vine, divided into three major regions: **PRIMORSKI**; **PODRAVSKI** (the best) in the northeast which includes the Ljutomer sub-region; and (less important) Posavski. Production is fairly evenly divided between Ws (including Pinot Gris, Traminer, Sauvignon Blanc and Laski Rizling) and Rs (good Merlot and Cabernet Sauvignon and the local Refosk).

SMITH-HAUT-LAFITTE, CH *France, Bordeaux, Pessac-Léognan, Cru Classé, R, W* This large estate changed hands in 1990, with much money spent since. The first vintages under the new régime show the results. The W in particular, an all-Sauvignon Blanc wine, shows real concentration and breed. The (R) 2nd wine is Hauts de Smith.

SOAVE   *Italy, Veneto, DOC, W*   Well-known W from north Italy. Pale straw in colour, it has crisp acidity balanced by delicate fruit flavours that hint of toasted almonds. The main variety is Garganega. The best wines come from the *classico* zone. Recioto di Soave is sweet. Leading producers include: Anselmi, Bolla, Masi, Pieropan.

SOCIONDO-MALLET, CH   *France, Bordeaux, Haut-Médoc, Cru Bourgeois, R*   Serious, long-lived wine with the structure to repay patience. A good 1993.

SOGRAPE   *Portugal, W, R*   Portugal's largest winemaker, based at Vila Real, produces balanced R and W wines including Gazela, one of the best W Vinhos Verdes, and the whistle-dry Chello.

SOLERA   *Spain*   The system of blending sherry, across years as well as between casks. The aim is to maintain consistency and character. A solera may carry a date: its year of foundation.

SOMANTANO   *Spain, Aragón, DO, W, P, R*   Aragón wine zone, with up-to-date equipment and exciting prospects, producing highly individual R and light, fruity W and *rosados*. Both French and Spanish grape varieties are grown. Leading producers include: COVISA (COMPAÑÍA VITIVINÍCOLA DE SOMANTANO), Cooperativa Comarcal Somontano de Sobrarbe.

SONOMA   *USA, California*   County north of San Francisco, between Napa and the coast. Essentially a cool-climate zone, it has eight major viticultural areas (VAs): LOS CARNEROS, SONOMA VALLEY, SONOMA MOUNTAIN, RUSSIAN RIVER VALLEY, GREEN VALLEY, CHALK HILL, SONOMA COAST, KNIGHTS VALLEY, ALEXANDER VALLEY and DRY CREEK VALLEY. Together with Napa, Sonoma is California's major quality-wine region, well suited to growing a wide variety of grapes.

SONOMA COAST   *USA, California, Sonoma, VA*   At its best a wine zone where cool conditions make for intense, vine-matured fruit flavours. Something of a political creation, however, and the areas within it are linked only by their contact with the seashore. Wide range of varieties including Cabernet Sauvignon, Chardonnay, Merlot and Sauvignon Blanc.

SONOMA MOUNTAIN   *USA, California, Sonoma, VA*   Small subzone at the north-western end of Sonoma Valley. Best suited to Cabernet Sauvignon, Zinfandel and Sauvignon Blanc.

SONOMA VALLEY   *USA, California, Sonoma, VA*   About 2,450ha are mainly devoted to Cabernet Sauvignon, Merlot and Sauvignon Blanc on the valley floor, whereas the upper slopes are home to radiant, raspberry-fruited Zinfandel.

SOPRON   *Hungary*   North of Lake Balaton, this zone enjoys a more temperate climate than the rest of Hungary. Mainly R wines from Kékfrankos, with some Pinot Noir and Cabernet and Ws from Zöldveltelini, Tramini and Leányka.

SOUMADE, DOM DE LA *France, Rhône, Côtes du Rhône-Villages R, VDN* Good Syrah-dominated Rs and an excellent Vin Doux Naturel come from this Rasteau estate.

SOUTARD, CH *France, Bordeaux, St-Emilion, Grand Cru Classé, R* One of St-Emilion's oldest estates, run organically along traditional lines. Wines are dark, quite tannic when young and of very fine quality: the best will last more than 20 years.

SOUTH AUSTRALIA *Australia* Quality R, W and Sp wines are made in this state which boasts some of the country's finest regions, including BAROSSA VALLEY – birthplace of Australia's great R wine, Grange – the ADELAIDE HILLS, MCLAREN VALE, COONAWARRA and PADTHAWAY.

SOUTH CAROLINA *USA* A big wine region in pre-Revolutionary days, wine is being revived here by a few growers.

SOUTH-WEST COASTAL *Australia, Western Australia* This narrow coastal strip, 250km long by 20km wide, is noted for its unusual soil, a fine Tuart sand. Wine styles are diverse. Leading producers include: Capel Vale.

SOUVERAIN, CH *USA, California, Sonoma, R, W* Now part of Nestlé, Souverain produces fine Sonoma wines that are undervalued and hence underrated. Winemaker Tom Peterson's wines include spicy Zinfandel R, supple Pinot Noir R and silky Chardonnay.

SPARR, PIERRE *France, Alsace, W* Wines have a rich fruit flavour, sometimes with a hint of sweetness, with Pinot Gris, Riesling and Gewürztraminer the best. There are also some top-quality blends, such as Kaefferkopf (Gewürztraminer/Pinot Gris) and Symphonie (Riesling/Pinot Gris/Pinot Blanc/Gewürztraminer), as well as sparkling wine.

SPÄTBURGUNDER German synonym for PINOT NOIR.

SPÄTLESE *Germany* Literally, late-picked. QMP wine from riper grapes than *Kabinett*. *Spätlese* can be sweet, but is increasingly the basis for drier wines.

SPRING MOUNTAIN *USA, California, Napa, VA* Wine zone of Napa Valley, on the hills west of St. Helena where old vineyards yield densely-flavoured fruit. Main varieties include Cabernet Sauvignon, Merlot (R) and Johannisberg Riesling (W). Leading producers include: Cain Cellars, Robert Keenan, Smith-Madrone.

SPUMANTE *Italy* Term meaning sparkling.

ST AMOUR, CH DE *France, Burgundy, Beaujolais, R* One of the leading estates in St-Amour, making delicately fruity wines which also age well in bottle.

ST HALLETT *Australia, South Australia, Barossa, W, R* Top-quality winery with a meticulous eye for detail. The superb Old Block Shiraz R is from vines at least 60 years old and the wine is aged in

American oak. Other stars include Poachers White, a tangy Sémillon/Chardonnay/Sauvignon Blanc blend.

ST HUBERTS *Australia, Victoria, Yarra Valley, W, R*   The first of the Yarra Valley revivalists, and now owned by **ROTHBURY ESTATE** (of the Hunter Valley), St Huberts makes excellent Chardonnay and Cabernet Sauvignon.

ST JEAN, CH *USA, California, Sonoma, W, R*   Chardonnay accounts for 70% of the 225,000-case output: the Robert Young Vineyard wine is creamy and toasty, that from the Belle Terre Vineyard toasty and pear-like. Rs include an earthy, meaty Pinot Noir; Ws a honeyed, botrytized Riesling and Gewürztraminer.

ST JULIAN WINE CO *USA, Michigan, W*   Founded in 1921 in the Paw Paw region, the company has success with a wide range of wines including Sp from hybrid grapes.

ST-AMAND, CH *France, Bordeaux, Sauternes, W*   Charming, traditionally-made Sauternes; never very concentrated, but elegant: good value for money.

ST-AMOUR *France, Burgundy, AOC, R*   Most northerly of the Beaujolais *crus* (strictly speaking, it is part of Mâconnais), and one of the smallest, St-Amour makes light, delicately fruity Gamay Rs. For drinking young, or after 2–3 years in bottle. Thanks to the atractive name, they can be expensive. Leading producers include: Jean-Paul Ducoté, Dom des Ducs, Dom Dufour, Dom de la Cave Lamartine/Paul Spay, Dom du Paradis, Dom Jean Pâtissier, Ch de St-Amour/Pierre Siraudin.

ST-AUBIN *France, Burgundy, AOC, W, R*   Tucked behind the Côte de Beaune, this village's well-sited, south-facing vineyards make light, fresh, delicious and good-value W and R wines. Leading producers include: Jean-Claude Bachelet, Gérard Thomas.

ST-BRIS, SAUVIGNON DE *France, Burgundy, VDQS, W*   Dry W wine made from the only Sauvignon Blanc grown in Burgundy, south-west of Chablis. Leading producers include: Caves de Bailly, Dom Bersan, Luc Sorin.

ST-CHINIAN *France, Midi, AOC, R*   Large area of the COTEAUX DU LANGUEDOC in the Cévennes foothills. Its varied soils and microclimates makes light, fruity Rs for early drinking and more substantial ones that gain from ageing. Grenache, Syrah, Mourvèdre are the main grapes, with Carignan which can provide acidity and backbone as well as perfumed fruit. Leading producers include: Berlou co-op, Ch Cazal-Viel, Ch Coujan, Dom des Jougla.

ST-EMILION *France, Bordeaux, AOC, R*   Important Bordeaux region making enjoyable, sometimes splendid, Rs from Merlot, Cabernet Franc and some Cabernet Sauvignon. Typical St-Emilion has youthful appeal after 3–6 years, with supple plummy fruit. Top wines can easily last 15 years or more, depending on the vintage. The best châteaux are classified into 11 *Premiers Grands Crus Classés* and 64 *Grands Crus Classés*, though this is reviewed every 10 years. Lesser châteaux are awarded *Grand Cru* status. To the north are the "satellite" villages of LUSSAC, MONTAGNE, PUISSEGUIN and ST-GEORGES.

ST-ESTÈPHE   *France, Bordeaux, AOC, R*   Haut-Médoc commune north of Pauillac; with five classed growths and many other châteaux: wines are generally less prestigious than Pauillac. Top châteaux may be slow to mature, but much wine is now made in a faster-maturing style with more Merlot in the blend.

ST-ESTÈVE, CH DE   *France, Rhône, Côtes du Rhône, R, W, P*   Experimental attitudes here produce a range of unusual, characterful wines, including a Viognier W, two Rs and a P.

ST-GAYAN, DOM   *France, Rhône, Gigondas, R*   Big, sometimes agressively tannic wines which age well.

ST-GEORGES   ST-EMILION   *France,   Bordeaux, AOC, R*   Wine from this small St-Emilion satellite may also be sold as MONTAGNE ST-EMILION. Leading producers include: Ch'x Belair St-Georges, Calon, Macquin St-Georges, St-André Corbin, St-Georges, Tours du Pas St-Georges.

ST-GEORGES, CH   *France, Bordeaux, St-Georges St-Emilion, R*   Large and beautiful château and a well-placed vineyard: quality wine well up to St-Emilion standards and worth ageing.

ST-JEAN-DE-MINERVOIS, MUSCAT DE   *France, Midi, AOC, VDN*   This *vin doux naturel* is from 100% Muscat Blanc à Petits Grains (the best Muscat variety), picked when almost overripe; thus with high potential alcohol. Producers aim for a delicate grapey Muscat flavour. Leading producers include: Dom Barroubio, Dom Sigé, St-Jean-de-Minervois co-op.

ST-JOSEPH   *France, Rhône, AOC, R, W*   Northern Rhône district across the river from Hermitage and Crozes-Hermitage. Rs are from Syrah, Ws from Marsanne, Roussanne or both. Variable in quality, but the best wines are good value. Leading producers include: Clos de l'Arbalestrier, Courbis, Jean-Louis Grippat.

ST-JULIEN   *France, Bordeaux, AOC, R*   Smallest of the great Médoc communes, with 11 classed growths. Ch Talbot makes a rare W ; the rest are all R, dominated by Cabernet Sauvignon: consistent, concentrated wine. Leading producers include: Ch'x Ducru Beaucaillou, Léoville Barton, Léoville Las-Cases, Léoville Poyferré.

ST-NICOLAS-DE-BOURGUEIL   *See* BOURGUEIL.

ST-PÉRAY   *France, Rhône, AOC, W*   Still or Sp W from Marsanne or (rather better) Roussanne grape, or a blend of both. The best still St-Péray is like a good, minor W Hermitage. Leading producers include: Bernard Gripa, Jean Lionnet, Alain Voge.

ST-PIERRE, CH *France, Bordeaux, Médoc, St-Julien, 4ème Cru Classé, R* Small estate with the same owners as Ch **GLORIA**. The wine is solid, dark and flavoursome and can take a long time to mature. The 1986 is superb, the 1993 good.

ST-POURÇAIN *France, Loire, VDQS, R, P, W* Zone between the Loire and Burgundy making wine from Burgundian grapes: Tressallier, Chardonnay, Aligoté (and Sauvignon Blanc) for Ws, Pinot Noir and Gamay for Rs and Ps.

ST-ROMAIN *France, Burgundy, AOC, R, W* Fresh crisp W wines and firm, cherry-flavoured Rs come from this village on the edge of Hautes Côtes de Beaune. Leading producers include: Bernard Fèvre, Maison Jean Germain, Alain Gras, René Gras Broisson, Louis Latour, Leroy, René Thévenin, Charles Viénot.

ST-SAPHORIN *Switzerland, Vaud, Lavaux, W, R* Leading wine-producing village to the east of Lausanne whose steep vineyards produce easy-drinking W wine from Chasselas and appealing R from Pinot Noir.

ST-VERAN *France, Burgundy, AOC, W* Chardonnay W, grown in south Mâconnais, which overlaps with Beaujolais: the wine can also be called Beaujolais Blanc. Cheaper than Pouilly-Fuissé, St-Véran can easily equal it in quality. Leading producers include: Dom des Deux Roches, Prissé co-op, Dom Vincent.

STAATLICHE WEINBAUDOMÄNE NIEDERHAUSEN-SCHLOSSBÖCK-ELHEIM *Germany, Nahe, W* The State Domain of the Nahe, a famous maker of Rieslings, concentrated and long-lived wines from the famous Kupfergrube vineyard and light, elegant and fresh ones from Niederhausen and Schlossböckelheim.

STAATSWEINGUT ELTVILLE *Germany, Rheingau, W, R* The State Domain, based in Eltville, inherited monastic vineyards and owns the famous Steinberg and many others, including R-wine plots at Assmanshausen. High standards, with the stress on typicity from the various sites. Eiswein is a speciality.

STAGS LEAP DISTRICT *USA, California, Napa, VA* Wine zone of Napa Valley, east of Yountville, known for the "iron-fist-in-velvet-glove" style of Cabernet Sauvignon, whose herbal, violet and black pepper flavours surround a sturdy core of fruit. Leading producers include: Clos Du Val, Shafer, Pine Ridge, Silverado, Stag's Leap Wine Cellars, Stags' Leap Vineyard.

STAG'S LEAP WINE CELLARS *USA, California, Napa, W, R* Warren Winiarski makes Chardonnays that are neither over-oaked nor flabby with ultra-ripe fruit, and Cabernet Sauvignons with a firm tannin backbone underlying a silky, olive-pepper cloak. World-class wines.

STE MICHELLE, CH *USA, Washington State, R, W, Sp* The Yakima Valley winery makes a range of varietal wines (Riesling and Cabernet Sauvignon) and Domaine Michelle Sp.

STE-ANNE, DOM *France, Rhône, Côtes du Rhône-Villages, R, W* The R wines from here, made from Syrah and Mourvèdre grapes, have inspired a generation of local winemakers with their structure and ageing ability. The Viognier W is also very good.

STE-CROIX-DU-MONT *France, Bordeaux, AOC, W* Sweet W wine from zone opposite Sauternes on the north bank of the Garonne. Leading producers include: Ch'x La Grave, Loubens, La Rame.

STE-EULALIE, DOM *France, Midi, Minervois, R* This abandoned estate in La Livinière was bought in 1979 by Gérard Blanc. He replanted and re-equipped; the favoured technique is *macération carbonique*, and there is also some oak ageing.

STE-FOY BORDEAUX *France, Bordeaux, AOC, R, W* These wines from the far east of the region are often sold under the more widely-known AOC Bordeaux.

STEEN South African synonym for CHENIN BLANC.

STEIERMARK *Austria* For wine Styria is split into three unequal parts: Süd (south), Süd-Ost (south-east) and West Steiermark. The Süd makes the finest wines. In quality and price its Ws equal those of the Wachau, although different in style: delicate in structure and high in acidity. Many grapes are grown, including Weissburgunder (Pinot Blanc), Riesling and Morillon (Chardonnay). Weststeiermark is known for a rare P, Schilcher, from the indigenous Blauer Wildbacher grape, it can be refreshing if the acidity is not too high. The Süd-Ost is very small. Leading producers include: Alois Gross, Erich Kuntner, Manfred Platzer, Manfred Tement.

STEINBERG *Germany, Rheingau, W* Famous walled, ex-monastic vineyard owned by the Staatsweingut, the state domain of the Rheingau.

STELLENBOSCH *South Africa, WO* The most important area of South Africa. Many of its top wines are blended Rs, from the two Cabernets, Merlot and Shiraz, often aged in oak. The best Pinotage comes from here. Also good Ws from Chardonnay and Sauvignon. Leading producers include: Meerlust, Mulderbosch, Rustenberg, Rust-en-Vrede, Vriesenhof, Warwick.

STERLING *USA, California, Napa, R, W* Perched atop its Calistoga hilltop, Sterling makes an exquisite Merlot R, dense and focused Diamond Mountain Ranch Cabernet Sauvignons and Chardonnays, and the lush, supple Winery Lake Pinot Noir R.

STIGLER, WEINGUT RUDOLF *Germany, Baden, R, W* Quality estate making both the traditional Ws of Baden – dry, fruity and characterful – and good Rs.

STONE HILL WINE CO *USA, Missouri, W, R* Produces a wide range of wines, apart from its own 25-ha vineyard. Catawba and

Norton (*labrusca* wines) remain popular, while respectable hybrids include Seyval Blanc, Vidal and Vignoles, among Ws, Villard Noir among Rs.

SUAU, CH *France, Bordeaux, 1er Côtes de Bordeaux, R* The large vineyard, equally Merlot, Cabernet Sauvignon and Cabernet Franc, plus intelligent winemaking yields claret worth ageing. Also a W, fresh and soft.

SUCHOTS, LES *France, Burgundy, Côte de Nuits, 1er Cru, R* This large vineyard in the commune of Vosne-Romanée yields full, elegant, supple wines with a touch of spice. They develop very well in bottle. Leading producers include: Robert Arnoux, Jean Grivot, Hudelot-Noëllat, Mongeard-Mugneret.

SÜDLICHE WEINSTRASSE *Germany, Pfalz, Bereich, W, R* The southern part of the Pfalz, just north of the French border. Here mass-produced wines are the norm, but good, estate-bottled Ws (from Weissburgunder, especially) and *barrique*-aged Rs are on the increase. Leading producers (apart from co-ops) include Becker, Hohenberg, Rebholz, Siegrist.

SUDUIRAUT, CH DE *France, Bordeaux, Sauternes, 1er Cru Classé, W* A byword for power and opulence, it can also be coarse and unpredictable: 1983 and 1986 were disappointing, 1990 magnificent. No wine was made under the château label in 1991, '92 & '93 due to bad weather. Now owned by AXA and run by Jean-Michel Cazes, Suduiraut's standards should be maintained.

SULFITES *See* SULPHUR DIOXIDE.

SULPHUR DIOXIDE Used as a disinfectant in winemaking. Too much produces a smell of rotten eggs in the wine, and induces headaches. EU wines may have no more than fixed maximum levels of the product. *See* Tasting Wine p242.

SUMAC RIDGE *Canada, British Columbia, W, R* Specialist in Ws with high-quality Pinot Blanc, Gewürztraminer and Riesling.

SUPERIORE *Italy* Describes wine that has a higher alcohol content (or a little extra ageing) than the standard DOC wine.

SUR LIE *France* On the lees (unracked). Used of wines (especially Muscadet) bottled without being racked.

SUTTER HOME *USA, California, Napa W, R* In the last decade Sutter Home has grown from a 50,000-case Zinfandel-only winery to one making nearly five million cases, including the enormously popular White Zinfandel, the light, fruity R Soleo, and new alcohol-free wines.

SWAN VALLEY *Australia, Western Australia* Pioneer region of the West: hot and dry in summer, but the deep alluvial soils have very good water-holding capacity. It has undergone a recent decline in production as new areas have emerged. Leading producers include: Haughton, Sandalford.

SYMINGTON   *Portugal, port*   The Symingtons sell the single-quinta vintage Quinta do Vesuvio under their own name, but this family firm also own a host of other familiar port houses: GRAHAM'S, DOW'S, WARRE'S, Gould Campbell, Smith Woodhouse.

SYRAH   Red grape from the Rhône, making deep-coloured, smoky, peppery, complex, long-lived wines such as Hermitage and Côte Rôtie. Australians call it Shiraz, and often blend it with Cabernet Sauvignon to make a relatively soft, accessible wine. Used alone and to add interest to blends in Provence and the Midi, and also grown in varying amounts in Italy, Spain, New Zealand and California.

T

TÂCHE, LA *France, Burgundy, Côte de Nuits, Grand Cru, R* Top R-wine vineyard in the group headed by La ROMANÉE. La Tâche is owned by Domaine de la ROMANÉE-CONTI.

TACORONTE-ACENTEJO *Spain, Canary Islands, DO, R, P, W* The vineyards of this zone, situated in north-west Tenerife, in the Canary Islands, enjoy a sub-tropical climate. Most production is R in the *joven* style, and there is some W and *rosado*.

TAFELWEIN *Germany* Table wine. The lowest grade of German wine. The prefix Deutscher or German means the wine is actually grown in Germany. Some modern wines of high quality are sold as *Tafelwein* because their producers do not submit them for official testing.

TAHBILK, CH *Australia, Victoria, Goulburn Valley, R, W* Family-owned, historic winery with some Shiraz vines dating from 1862 which still produce. Wines include elegant W Marsanne and long-lived, sometimes tannic but always concentrated Shiraz and Cabernet Sauvignon Rs.

TAILLEFER, CH *France, Bordeaux, Pomerol, R* Large (for the area) property which makes a light, early-maturing style of Pomerol.

TAITTINGER *France, Champagne* This is a GRANDE MARQUE whose style stresses delicacy and elegance, although the wines become richer and weightier after several years in bottle. The NV *brut* reserve is mainly Chardonnay and the luxury *cuvée*, Comtes de Champagne, is 100% Chardonnay.

TALBOT, CH *France, Bordeaux, Médoc, St-Julien, 4ème Cru Classé, R, W* Large estate owned by the Cordier family and run with great attention to detail. The wine, soft, full and rich, has many friends. In great vintages it can age well; in minor ones it is reliable. A good 1993. 2nd wine: Connétable de Talbot. Also, unusually, a white: Caillou Blanc, made from Sauvignon Blanc grapes grown in St-Julien.

TARGÉ, CH DE *France, Loire, Saumur-Champigny, R* Edouard Pisani-Ferry makes one of the best wines of the AOC in his spectacular caves and modern cellars. His only wine is a blend of Cabernet Franc with a little Cabernet Sauvignon. It ages well.

TARRAGONA *Spain, Catalonia, DO, W, P, R* One of eight wine zones in Catalonia, formerly known for sweet R fortified wine, but now producing mainly light wines in all colours, mostly in *joven* style, but also some heavier R. Main producers include: DE MULLER, Pedro Rovira.

TASMANIA *Australia* A small island off the south-east coast, with a tiny wine production. Its cool climate ensures that Pinot Noir for Rs does well, and some very good Chardonnay is also made. Sp wines are another speciality.

TAURASI *Italy, Campania, DOCG, R* Campania's best R wine, and some of Italy's best value: tannic when young but after many years evolves into a fine, rich wine with pruney fruit. Leading producers include: Mastroberardino.

TAVEL *France, Rhône, AOC, P* Big, alcoholic P from southern Rhône, with a high proportion of Grenache Noir in the blend. Leading producer: Ch d'Aquéria.

TAYAC, CH *France, Bordeaux, Côtes de Bourg, R* Several *cuvées* are made: the top one, "Prestige" is mostly Cabernet Sauvignon. Not typical of the AOC, but good (if expensive) claret.

TAYAC, CH *France, Bordeaux, Margaux, Cru Bourgeois, R* This large vineyard yields solid, traditional wine.

TAYLOR FLADGATE & YEATMAN *Portugal, port* For many the epitome of vintage port. Taylor (known as Taylor Fladgate in the USA) was founded in 1692 and is still a family-controlled partnership. Grapes are still trod at Quinta de Vargellas: next door to computerized stainless steel. The range goes from the classic vintages (among the finest), through the single-quinta Quinta de Vargellas, excellent aged tawnies (especially the 20-year-old) and the first (and the best-selling) Late Bottled Vintage. Quinta de Terra Feita has recently been released as a single-quinta wine. Basic wines are never less than well made.

TE MATA *New Zealand, North Island, W, R, P* The oldest New Zealand winery, and among the most prestigious. Top wines are the Coleraine Cabernet Sauvignon/Merlot R blend, and the rich Elston Chardonnay. Also good-value P and dry W blends.

TELMONT, DE *France, Champagne* Good value, well-made champagnes from a family-owned producer.

TEMECULA *USA, California, VA* Sited north of San Diego, this is a wine zone whose sandy soil is well suited to Chardonnay for both still and Sp wine. Leading producers include: Callaway, Thornton.

TEMPIER, DOM *France, Provence, Bandol, R, P* Lucien Peyraud of Tempier is an influential local figure. Traditional techniques rule; the wines possess huge tannins and fruit, and can age for many years. The two Rs are a normal *cuvée* and a Cuvée Spéciale.

TEMPRANILLO Red grape used in Spain's best red wines, including Rioja, Ribera del Duero, Navarra and Penedès. Aromatic and subtly flavoured, with an affinity for oak-ageing, it goes under many names in Spain (Ull de Llebre, Cencibel) and Portugal (Aragonez, Tinta Roriz).

TENNESSEE *USA* Fifteen producers, most of them along the Tennessee valley, combat a tough climate to make wine here.

TENNESSEE VALLEY WINERY *USA, Tennessee, W* Loudon County winery using native American varieties, hybrids and classic vines. The best wines are Aurora (W), de Chaunac (R) and Maréchal Foch (R). Chardonnay and Sauvignon Blanc have been erratic in quality.

TENUTA IL POGGIONE *Italy, Tuscany, Brunello di Montalcino, R, W* Estate making a large range of wines include Brunello and Rosso di Montalcino DOC, Moscadello, Vin Santo and Bianco di Sant'Angelo (W).

TENUTA *Italy* Wine estate; holding.

TERLANO *Italy, Trentino-Alto Adige, DOC, W, Sp* This wine zone enjoys a good reputation for its fine, still varietal Ws. Dry Sp wine is also produced, predominantly from Pinot Bianco. Leading producers include: Alois Lageder, Castel Schwanburg.

TERRA ALTA *Spain, Catalonia, DO, W, R* The highest and most southerly wine zone in Catalonia, bordering Aragón, producing the traditional sweet, oak-aged *rancio* Rs, but also lighter, fresher wines. Experimental plantings of French grapes. Leading producers include: Pedro Rovira.

TERRES BLANCHES, DOM *France, Provence, Coteaux d'Aix-en-Provence Les Baux, W, R, P* Noël Michelin uses no herbicides or insecticides on his vines and few chemicals in the *chai*. He makes a W, an attractive P and a R of elegance after a few years' bottle-ageing.

TERROIR *France* The winegrowing environment, covering soil, site and local climate.

TERTRE DAUGAY, CH *France, Bordeaux, St-Emilion, Grand Cru Classé, R* Comte Léo de Malet-Roquefort also owns LA GAFFE-LIÈRE. This estate's somewhat chequered history is now behind it: worth seeking out.

TERTRE, CH DU *France, Bordeaux, Médoc, Margaux, 5ème Cru Classé, R* This estate has a large amount of Cabernet Sauvignon on its inland outcrop of gravel. The wines have improved markedly over the last few years.

TESCH, WEINGUT ERBHOF *Germany, Nahe, W* This estate has a good name for dry wines from Riesling and other varieties.

TESSIER, PHILIPPE *France, Loire, Chevernay, W, R* Run by the Tessiers for three generations, this estate makes R and (better) W wines, with a soft spot for the local Romorantin grape, which here produces a crisp, rather than piercingly acidic, W wine.

TETRE-ROTEBOEUF, CH LE *France, Bordeaux, St-Emilion, Grand Cru, R* This superb small property makes roughly 2,000 cases a year. Meticulous vineyard management and winemaking by François

Mitjavile results in an almost pure Merlot wine with wonderful depth and longevity. ROC DES CAMBES (Côte de Bourg) has the same owner.

TEXAS *USA* New vineyards on a grand scale make Texas the fourth US wine state. Most vines are in three cool-climate zones: on the High Plains near Lubbock, the Hill Country (VA) west of Austin, and in West Texas. Good wines from Cabernet Sauvignon and other French varieties show the potential. Leading producers include: Cap Rock, FALL CREEK, LLANO ESTACADO, PHEASANT RIDGE.

THANISCH, DR *Germany, Mosel, W* Two famous estates, with the same name, each own part of the great Doctor vineyard at Bernkastel, plus other fine Riesling vineyards. Those who can afford the wines will know them apart.

THANN *France, Alsace* The southernmost wine village of Alsace has been renowned for wine since the 12th century. Looming above is the famous *Grand Cru* Rangen. Steep, south-facing slopes produce Pinot Gris, Riesling and Gewürztraminer. Leading producers include: Zind-Humbrecht.

THELEMA MOUNTAIN VINEYARDS *South Africa, Stellenbosch, R, W* Gyles Webb is one of the Cape's top winemakers. Elegance and balance sum up his wines, from his Cabernet Sauvignon, easily the best in the Cape, to the citrussy, classy Chardonnay.

THERMENREGION *Austria, Niederösterreich* Region south of Vienna. Production is small, but the area is famous for the village of Gumpoldskirchen, much of whose wine is made from two local grapes, Zierfandler (or Spätrot) and Rotgipfler. W wine is rich, broad and spicy, usually semi-sweet and strong. R wines are also gaining a reputation, notably from St-Laurent and Zweigelt.

THEUILEY, CH *France, Bordeaux, Entre-Deux-Mers W, Bordeaux R* Good-value fruity light R and increasingly impressive Sauvignon Blanc W.

THIVIN, CH *France, Burgundy, Beaujolais, R* Delicious Côte de Brouilly is produced at this property, rich, weighty and round with lovely fruit and finesse.

THOUARSAIS, VIN DU *France, Loire, VDQS, R, P, W* This small Loire zone south of Anjou produces Rs and Ps from Cabernet Franc, Cabernet Sauvignon or Gamay, Ws from Chenin Blanc.

TICINO *Switzerland* Italian-speaking canton in southern Switzerland, especially well known for its soft, easy-drinking R wine from the Merlot grape. Some Cabernet Sauvignon has been recently introduced and there is a little W and P too. Leading producers include: Delea, Tamborini.

TIEFENBRUNNER *Italy, Alto Adige, W, R* Estate with fine Alto Adige Pinot Nero, notable Gewürztraminer W and excellent *vini da tavola*: Goldmuskateller, Feldmarschall and Linticlarus (R, W).

TINHOF, ERWIN *Austria, Neusiedlersee-Hügelland, W, R* Young producer who studied in France and achieves elegance and balance in all his wines, from a classy, steely Muskat Ottonel W, through a superb almost Viognier-like Neuburger W (called Fuchsenriegl) fermented and partly aged in new oak to a delicious, red-fruited Blaufränkisch R.

TINTA RORIZ See TEMPRANILLO.

TINTO *Spain and Portugal* Red.

TIO MATEO *Spain, sherry* Palomino & Vergara's top fino, Tio Mateo, is known throughout Spain: a classic Jerez fino, dry and full.

TIREGAND, CH DE *France, Southwest, Bergerac, R, W* Classic Pécharmant Rs, one from young vines, and a *grand vin* from Merlot, both Cabernets and a little Malbec, are aged in a proportion of new oak.

TOKAJI *Hungary* This region in the north-east of the country produces Hungary's most famous wine, hailed by Louis XIV of France as the king of wines. Botrytis-affected grapes are added to a dry white wine and the mixture begins to referment very slowly, resulting in an intense sweet wine with highish alcohol, rich in both extract and glycerol. The more *puttonyos* (maximum six) on the label the sweeter the wine. Main grape varieties are Furmint, Hárslevelü and Sárga Muskotály (Muscat Lunel). Also a dry version (Dry Szamorodni) and extremely sweet Aszú Eszencia. Single-variety Furmint is a good dry wine. Currently undergoing a renaissance, thanks to foreign investment and expertise.

TOKAY D'ALSACE See PINOT GRIS.

TOLLOT-BEAUT ET FILS *France, Burgundy, Côte d'Or, R* Large family-owned estate around Corton and Beaune, producing robust, long-lived R wines.

TONDONIA *Spain, Rioja, R, W, P* Probably the most traditionalist of all Rioja producers. Wines – R and W– are full and oaky and can age well. The best is Tondonia but Bosonia and Cubillo are also very good.

TONNERRE *France, Burgundy, Chablis, 1er Cru* See FOURCHAUME.

TORGIANO *Italy, Umbria, DOC, W, R* Much is owed to the LUNGAROTTI family for raising the quality levels of this DOC. It offers well-balanced W from Trebbiano and Grechetto; while the R is mainly Sangiovese. The *riserva* has DOCG status. Leading producers include: Cantine Lungarotti.

TORO *Spain, Castilla-León, DO, R, W, P* One of the Castilla-León wine zones, producing Toro, a heavy, heady R wine, mainly from the Tinta Toro grape, R *crianza* wines and a small quantity of *rosado* and W wines. Leading producers include: Bodegas Fariña, Bodegas José-María Fermoselle.

TORRACCIA, DOM DE *France, Corsica, Porto-Vecchio, R* Experimentation and traditional varieties (Syrah, Mourvèdre and Corsican R grapes) combine to make interesting wines reflecting the island's true character.

TORRE QUARTO *Italy, Southern Italy, Apulia, R* Renowned for its Malbec and Uva de Troia-based wine (R). Malbec is now replaced by Montepulciano grapes.

TORRES, MIGUEL *Spain, Catalonia, Penedès, R, W* Brilliant, innovative winemaker who took over the family bodega in the early 1960s and subsequently put Catalonia firmly on the international map. He uses Spanish and French grapes to great effect, notably with Vina Sol (W), Sangre de Toro (R) and full-bodied Gran Coronas (R) – especially the Black Label. Also active in Chile: *see* MIGUEL TORRES.

TOUCHAIS, LES VINS *France, Loire, Anjou, W, R, P* Large *négociant* and estate based at Doué-la-Fontaine. The sweet Layon wines, sold as Anjou Blanc Moulin Touchais, can be extraordinary, showing the ageing ability of Chenin Blanc. But most sales are of straightforward Rs and Ps.

TOUR BLANCHE, CH LA *France, Bordeaux, Sauternes, 1er Cru Classé, W* The wines of the 1970s and early 1980s were dire, but happily standards have risen: since 1988 again worthy of its *Premier Cru* status.

TOUR-CARNET, LA *France, Bordeaux, Haut-Médoc, 4ème Cru Classé, R* Sited in St-Laurent, the commune inland from St-Julien, this château used to make wine in a rather rustic, tough style. Recent vintages here have been softer, though still well-structured.

TOUR DU BIEF, DOM DE LA *France, Burgundy, Beaujolais, R* One of the finest producers of Moulin-à-Vent, the most powerful of the Beaujolais Crus, with a powerful structure that ages well.

TOUR MARTILLAC, CH LA *France, Bordeaux, Pessac-Léognan, Cru Classé, R, W* Consistent maker of plump, fleshy yet elegant Rs, and impeccably balanced Ws that are oaky but retain their youthful fruitiness for many years.

TOUR-DE-MONS, CH LA *France, Bordeaux, Margaux, Cru Bourgeois, R* Well-known property making reliable, smooth, enjoyable wine from, almost equally, Merlot and Cabernet Sauvignon.

TOUR-DU-PIN-FIGEAC (MOUEIX), CH *France, Bordeaux, St-Emilion, Grand Cru Classé, R* Much better than the other property of the same name. Fairly full-bodied, with lots of fruit.

TOURAINE *France, Loire, AOC, R, P, W, Sp* Large appellation south of Tours for W (still or Sp), R and P wines. The best wines are from three village appellations: Touraine-Amboise, Touraine-Azay-le-Rideau and Touraine-Mesland. Some varietal appellations are grouped under the Touraine AOC: Sauvignon for Ws, Gamay for Rs. Leading producers include: Paul Chainier, Ch de

Chenonceau, Dom de la Gabillière, Jacky Marteau, J M Monmousseau, Vignerons de Oisly et Thésée co-op, Jacky Preys.

TOURELLES DE LONGUEVILLE, LES   *France, Bordeaux, Médoc, Pauillac, R*   2nd wine of Ch Pichon-Baron.

TRACY, CH DE   *France, Loire, Pouilly-Fumé, W*   The Comte d'Estutt d'Assay's family has been here since the 16th century. Recent modernization of the cellars has produced some very fine Pouilly-Fumé from their 24ha.

TRAISEN   *Germany, Nahe, W*   Village in the heart of the Nahe. The most famous vineyard, planted exclusively with Riesling, is the Bastei, whose W wines are full of character and incredibly intense in flavour and bouquet. Riesling from the larger Rotenfels is almost as good. Leading producers include: Crusius, Staatliche Weinbaudomäne.

TREBBIANO   White grape of central Italy: prolific, acidic, often characterless, widely planted throughout the world, and used for blending and distilling. Grown as Ugni Blanc in France, particularly in Cognac.

TREFETHEN   *USA, Napa*   The fine wooden Eshcol winery just north of Napa city is one of the valley's oldest. It now makes good Chardonnay and Cabernet and a popular, good-value pair of blended wines, Eshcol R and W.

TRENTINO   *Italy, Trentino-Alto Adige, DOC, R, W, Sp*   This DOC covers a wide range of wines. W varieties include Nosiola, Chardonnay and Pinot Bianco. Rs are Marzemino and Teroldego. Fine sweet Vin Santo is also made. Leading producers include: Concilio Vini, Ferrari, Pojer & Sandri, De Tarczal.

TRENTINO-ALTO ADIGE   *Italy*   Mountainous region of north-east Italy combining two distinct areas. Alto Adige is particularly well known for its fine dry W wines from French and German varieties. In lower-lying Trentino the wines tend to be mellower and broader in flavour.

TRÉVALLON, DOM DE   *France, Provence, Coteaux d'Aix-en-Provence Les Baux, R*   Acclaimed as the finest estate in Les Baux, and one of the top few in Provence. All methods are organic. Eloi Durrbach's one wine is 60% Cabernet Sauvignon; it needs at least 5 years in bottle, then develops gradually.

TRIGUEDINA, CH   *France, Southwest, Cahors, R*   Prince Probus, the top *cuvée* from this old family estate, is among the best-known Cahors. A quarter of the vines are Merlot, which are felt to add suppleness to the traditional Auxerrois (Malbec).

TRIMBACH, F E   *France, Alsace, W, R*   With Hugel, Trimbach has done more than anyone to promote Alsace. Wines include W Gewürztraminer (especially Cuvée des Seigneurs de Ribeaupierre) and Pinot Gris; but the Rieslings are undoubtedly the best of the region. Cuvée Frédéric-Emile, from *Grand Cru* Osterberg, is bettered only by Clos Ste-Hune, their vineyard (for the last 200 years) within *Grand Cru* Rosacker. A world-class wine (though not legally *Grand Cru*), Clos Ste-Hune epitomizes Riesling and is considered by many to be the best wine in Alsace.

TRITTENHEIM   *Germany, Mosel, W*   Famous town in the Mittelmosel, whose Riesling Ws can have much finesse and breeding, The most noted vineyard is Trittenheimer Apotheke.

TROCKEN   *Germany*   Dry wine. Do not confuse with TROCKENBEERENAUSLESE.

TROCKENBEERENAUSLESE   *Germany*   The top QMP grade. As with *Beerenauslese*, it is made from individually selected grapes, which are always overripe and thus very sweet; in this case the grapes are shrivelled and dry, their juice concentrated from the action of noble rot.

TRONQUOY-LALANDE, CH   *France, Bordeaux, St-Estèphe, Cru Bourgeois, R*   A familiar wine in export markets, made in the solid St-Estèphe style. The late-1980s' vintages were very good, though these wines always need patience.

TROPLONG-MONDOT, CH   *France, Bordeaux, St-Emilion, Grand Cru Classé, R*   Beautiful property, and one of St-Emilion's largest. Run by Christine Valette since 1980: a superb run of vintages in 1988, 1989, 1990. A future star.

TROTANOY, CH   *France, Bordeaux, Pomerol, R*   Ranks as one of Pomerol's top dozen estates and in its finest years the wine can be almost as dense as Pétrus, with virtually the same potential lifespan at a fraction of the price.

TROTTEVIEILLE, CH   *France, Bordeaux, St-Emilion, 1er Grand Cru Classé, R*   There has been noticeable improvement here since the mid-1980s. Before, wines lacked concentration and aged too quickly, but are now much more serious. Medium rather than long-term drinking.

TUALATIN   *USA, Oregon, W, R*   The 34-ha estate in the tiny town of Forest Grove produces flinty, apricot Riesling W, smoky-clove Pinot Noir R and toasty, clear clove Chardonnay; also Ws from Sauvignon, Gewürztraminer, Flora (a Sémillon/Gewürztraminer crossing) and Müller-Thurgau.

TUNISIA   *North Africa, R, W, P*   Tunisia's vineyards are concentrated in the north-east sector of the country, around the capital of Tunis. Her best wines are Ws from the Muscat grape which can be sweet or dry. Also makes fairly reliable R and P wine. A system of AOC control is similar to that of France.

TURCKHEIM   *France, Alsace*   Village with a name for some of the best Pinots Noir Rs in Alsace. *Grand Cru* Brand yields Ws from Pinot Gris, Riesling and Gewürztraminer. Leading producers include: Dopff Au Moulin, Meyer, Zind-Humbrecht.

TURKEY   The vast country has an extremely long winemaking history, but since most of the population is Muslim, only 2% of the produce of its 600,000ha of vines is turned into wine. 40% of production is state controlled. Production is split almost equally between R and W, with only a very little P.

TURSAN   *France, South-West, VDQS, R, P, W*   The W wine is from Baroque grapes, with Sauvignon Blanc, Gros and Petit Manseng and Sémillon to provide flavour and vitality. R Tursan, from Tannat, Cabernet Sauvignon and Cab Franc, tends to be rustic in flavour.

TURSAN, LES VIGNERONS DE   *France, South-West, Tursan, W, R*   Leading maker of these obscure but tasty W and R wines from the Landes.

TUSCANY   *Italy*   Together with Piedmont, Italy's leading region for quality wine production. Sangiovese is the great Tuscan grape for R wine and the mainstay of CHIANTI, Italy's best-known wine. It is here that the renaissance in Italian winemaking has made its greatest mark with wines like SASSICAIA and Ornellaia. Tuscany also has some fine traditional wines like BRUNELLO DI MONTALCINO (R), VINO NOBILE DI MONTEPULCIANO (R) and VIN SANTO.

TXAKOLI (CHIACOLÍ)   *Spain, Basque Country, DO, W, R*   Spain's northernmost wine region, in the Basque country, produces light, dry W and light R, both in the *joven* style. Leading producers include: Txakoli Eizaguirre, Txomin Etxaniz.

TYRRELLS   *Australia, New South Wales, Hunter Valley, R, W*   One of the great Hunter names, where tradition and commerce are intelligently balanced. Excellent Sémillon and Chardonnay Ws.

U

UGNI BLANC   French synonym for TREBBIANO.

UKRAINE   The speciality here is W and Sp wine, the latter especially in the Crimea (which once had a quality wine industry, and could do again). Principal varieties are Rkatsiteli and Aligoté, with some Rhein Riesling and Sauvignon Blanc. Quality is fairly indifferent. Sp wine may be made by the champagne method, *cuve close* or the Russian "continuous" system.

ULL DE LLEBRE   See TEMPRANILLO.

UMANI RONCHI   *Italy, Central Italy, Marches, W, R*   Large, innovative private producer. Ws include Verdicchio dei Castelli di Jesi, fine single-vineyard Verdicchios and Le Busche, a barrel-fermented Verdicchio. Rosso Conèro wines are Casal di Serra, San Lorenzo and top-quality Cùmaro.

UMATHUM, JOSEF   *Austria, Neusiedlersee, W, R*   Producer of very attractive W wines including a Welschriesling with lees-ageing and a good, spicy Ruländer fermented and partly aged in new oak. He uses new oak for his Rs too, including a delicious St-Laurent with attractive strawberry fruit and his top R wine, a heady blend of Zweigelt, Cabernet Sauvignon and Blaufränkisch.

UMBRIA   *Italy*   This small, landlocked region in the very centre of Italy is most famous for its W wines, notably Orvieto DOC. Its best known R wine is Torgiano from the LUNGAROTTI stable.

UMPQUA VALLEY   *USA, Oregon, VA*   One of Oregon's three wine zones, to the south of the Willamette Valley. Varieties which do well here include Pinot Noir and Chardonnay.

UNDURRAGA   *Chile, R, W*   One of the first Chilean producers to export, it also dominates the domestic market. The firm produces more than one million cases a year, of which exports are 40%, mainly Chardonnay and Sauvignon Blanc Ws. Merlot and Pinot Noir are recent additions to the list.

UNGSTEIN   *Germany, Pfalz, W, R*   Village in the MITTELHAART. Rich, fruity and fiery are among terms used for Ungstein's wine. R is quite important, but the best wines are Riesling Ws. Leading producers include: Pfeffingen.

UNION PLAIMONT   *France, Southwest, Côtes de St-Mont, W, R*   This co-op dominates the area, using the latest techniques to make three ranges with increasing amounts of oak-ageing: Tradition, Privilège and Collection. Also makes lots of good-value Vin de Pays des Côtes de Gascogne (R, W and P).

URUGUAY *South America* The fourth-largest wine producer in South America, with 14,000ha of vines in the south and west of the country. More than half the vineyard area is classic vines. Production totals eight million cases.

URZIG *Germany, Mosel, W* Town on a bend in the river in the MITTELMOSEL zone, where the top vineyards begin. Noted vineyards here are Prälat and Treppchen. Urzig's Würzgarten ("spice garden") is known for the spicy notes in its wine. Leading producers include: Dr Loosen, Mönchhof-Robert Eymnael and Dr Pauly-Bergweiler.

UTIEL-REQUENA *Spain, Levante, DO, W, R* Hilly wine zone of Valencia, producing W and R wines characteristic of the province. Leading producers include: C. Augusto Egli.

V

VACHERON, DOM JEAN-LOUIS *France, Loire, Sancerre, W, R* This firm specializes in R Sancerre, of which it makes fine examples, some matured in new wood. The 30-ha domaine produces Les Cailleries (R), Les Romains (P) and Le Paradis (W).

VACQUEYRAS *France, Rhône, AOC, R* Southern Rhône grapes (eg Grenache, Syrah) make Rs with good depth of colour and flavour. Leading producers include: Dom Le Couralou, Dom la Fourmone.

VAL JOANIS *France, Rhône, Côtes du Luberon, R, W* Reliable and large estate making good, fresh Ws for drinking young, and a fruity, flavoursome R.

VALAIS *Switzerland* The most important wine-producing canton of Switzerland with 5,000ha under vine, much of it at extremely high altitudes. Fendant (the local name for the Chasselas grape) is the main W wine and Dôle, a blend of Pinot Noir and other varieties the most important R. Leading producers include: Charles Bonvin, Simon Maye, Rouvinez.

VALDEORRAS *Spain, Galicia, DO, R, W* The easternmost wine zone of Galicia, contiguous with Bierzo, making similar light, fresh *joven* style R and W wines. Leading producers include: Bodega Cooperativa Jesús Nazareno.

VALDEPEÑAS *Spain, Castilla-La Mancha, DO, W, R* Of the four wine zones of Castilla-La Mancha, this has consistently produced good-quality wines from its hilly, south-facing vineyards. W wines are in *joven* style, but better Rs are made up to *gran reserva* level. Leading producers include: Bodegas Los Llanos.

VALDESPINO *Spain, sherry* Not the best-known or biggest firm; but for many, the small, high-quality Valdespino range of sherries is the very best. Their finest, the full but elegant fino Inocente, comes (uniquely for Jerez) from just one ancestral vineyard. Valdespino is also known for the dry, nutty amontillado Tio Diego, the sweet but not overwhelming 1842 Oloroso – and for fine sherry vinegar.

VALENÇAY *France, Loire, VDQS, R, P, W* Wines from the edge of Touraine, seldom found outside the area. Ws are from Menu Pineau (or Arbois), Sauvignon Blanc, Chardonnay, Chenin Blanc and Romorantin, a local high-acid variety. Rs and Ps are from Cabernets Sauvignon and Franc, Gamay and Pineau d'Aunis (a Loire original, also known as Chenin Noir).

VALENCIA *Spain, Levante, DO, W, P, R* East coast province which has vineyards from sea level up to more than 800m, producing a wide range of wines in all colours, from everyday blends to some reasonably impressive *crianza* and *reserva* Rs, as well as sweet wines. Leading producers include: C Augusto Egli, Bodegas Levantinas-Españolas, Bodegas ViniVal.

VALLE D'AOSTA *Italy* A very small and relatively unimportant wine producing region in Italy's north-west mountains. Most of the wine is drunk locally.

VALLÉE DU PARADIS, DE LA *France, Vin de Pays, R* The attractive name of this *vin de pays* ensures wide sales of the attractive Rs from the hills of Roussillon, in the far south of France.

VALMUR *France, Burgundy, Chablis, Grand Cru* One of the lighter *Grand Cru* wines, for drinking earlier than Les Clos.

VALPOLICELLA *Italy, Veneto, DOC, R* Mainly from Corvina, Rondinella and Molinara, a zesty, light ruby-R wine, with an appealing grapey flavour. Also made as the richer, darker *ripasso*, sweet *recioto* and dry *amarone*. Leading producers include: Allegrini, Bolla, Masi, Quintarelli.

VALTELLINA *Italy, Lombardy, DOC, R* Mountain-valley wine from the Nebbiolo grape, known locally as Chiavennasca. Garnet in colour with floral and herbal fragrances. For early drinking, although the *superiore* version is best at 5–10 years. Leading producers include: Enologica Valtellinese, Nino Negri.

VARICHON ET CLERC *France, Savoie, Seyssel, W, Sp* Leading maker of Sp Seyssel, using the classic method aided by modern equipment. Their top Sp is Royal Seyssel. They also make a still W under the Roussette de Savoie AOC.

VARIETAL Term for a wine made from a single variety of grape.

VAROILLE, DOM DE *France, Burgundy, Côte d'Or, R* Both *négociant* and vineyard owner, the estate wines of this domaine are very serious indeed, with lots of ageing potential.

VASCOS, LOS *Chile, R, W* Famous vineyard dating from 1750, now part-owned by Ch Lafite-Rothschild. Cabernet Sauvignon makes up more than half the production. Some Chardonnay and Sauvignon Blanc.

VATAN, PHILIPPE ET GEORGES *France, Loire, Saumur, W, R* Philippe Vatan makes one of the best wines in Saumur-Champigny as well as a memorable Saumur Blanc. Also a standard Saumur-Champigny, a Vieilles Vignes and a rare sweet Saumur Moelleux (W).

VAUCRAINS, LES *France, Burgundy, Côte de Nuits, 1er Cru, R* Nuits-St-Georges vineyard, which produces richly-coloured, highly-structured wines which require long bottle ageing. Leading producers include: Robert Chevillon, Henri Gouges.

VAUD *Switzerland* After Valais, Switzerland's most important wine-producing canton, with 3,700ha under vine, divided into five districts. Main grape varieties are Chasselas for W and Pinot Noir for R. The wines produced make attractive, easy drinking, and are best consumed young. Leading producers include: Badoux, Chevalley, J & P Testuz.

VAUDÉSIR *France, Burgundy, Chablis, Grand Cru* Solid, long-lived and lively wines. Vaudésir includes part of La Moutonne, a vineyard on the *Grands Crus* slope, but without the status of a *Grand Cru*: a 2.3-ha parcel within Vaudésir and Preuses that once belonged to the nearby Cistercian abbey of Pontigny. LONG-DEPAQUIT are the principal producers, making a stylish wine of considerable finesse.

VAULORENT *France, Burgundy, Chablis, 1er Cru* See FOURCHAUME.

VDN *France* See VIN DOUX NATUREL.

VDP *Germany* The Verband Deutscher Prädikatsweingüter, an association of top wine estates: the VDP seal is a good sign of quality.

VDQS *France* See VIN DÉLIMITÉ DE QUALITÉ SUPÉRIEURE.

VECCHIO *Italy* Wine that has been aged for a longer period than most in cask and/or bottle.

VEGA SICILIA, BODEGAS *Spain, Castilla-León, Ribera del Duero, R* Established in 1864, and at the time a lone pioneer of quality winemaking in the Duero Valley. Meticulous care and traditional methods combine to produce carefully crafted wines which age supremely well, from the Valbuena (R) to Vega Sicilia Unico (R) which may have spent up to 10 years in oak.

VENDANGE *France* Vintage time. *Vendange tardive*, late harvest, refers mainly to sweet Alsace wine.

VENEGAZZÙ *Italy, Veneto, R* The first famous Venegazzù from this estate was a classic bordeaux-style blend needing long ageing. These wines now come in a range of styles.

VENETO *Italy* The most geographically diverse of all Italy's regions, offering a broad range of styles. Best-known wines include Soave (DOC, W), Valpolicella and Bardolino, both of which DOCs make R.

VENOGE, DE *France, Champagne* Good value and quality from this old firm whose luxury *cuvée* Des Princes is well regarded.

VERDICCHIO DEI CASTELLI DI JESI *Italy, Marches, DOC, W, Sp* Verdicchio is the main W grape of the Marches, producing light, lemony wines which go well with seafood. Can be Sp. Leading producers include: Fazi-Battaglia, Fratelli Bucci, Monte Schiavo, Umani Ronchi.

VEREINIGTE HOSPITIEN   *Germany, Mosel, W*   Centuries old, this charity, equivalent in status and intent with the HOSPICES DE BEAUNE, owns former monastic vineyards in the Middle Mosel and Saar Valleys where it makes fine traditional Rieslings.

VERGELESSES, ILE DE   *France, Burgundy, Côte de Beaune, 1er Cru, R, W*   Vineyard in the commune of Pernand-Vergelesses. The W wines are aromatic and quite delicate and the Rs have lovely supple, strawberry fruit. Leading producers include: Dubreuil-Fontaine, Laleure-Piot, Louis Latour.

VERNACCIA DI SAN GIMIGNANO   *Italy, Tuscany, DOC, W*   From vineyards near the medieval town of San Gimignano, the Vernaccia grape produces a slightly honeyed wine with just a hint of crisp acidity. Leading producers include: Castello de Montauto, Fattoria di Cusona, Montenidoli.

VERNAY, GEORGES   *France, Rhône, Condrieu, W*   The leading maker of this rare and fashionable W: several grades of wine, all excellent.

VEUVE CLICQUOT PONSARDIN   *France, Champagne*   One of the top GRANDS MARQUES. The NV blend, with its distinctive yellow label, is consistently good and the flagship wine, La Grande Dame, is a rich, weighty blend of Pinot Noir and Chardonnay.

VICCHIOMAGGIO, CASTELLO   *Italy, Tuscany, Chianti, R, W*   Estate making mainly Chianti Classico (labels are San Jacopo, Vigna Petri and La Prima); and also a Chardonnay-based *vino da tavola* (Ripa delle Mimose, W) and a Sangiovese/Cabernet blend (Ripa delle More, R).

VICTORIA   *Australia*   The most southerly state of mainland Australia. Produces an enormous variety of wines and, increasingly, some of very high quality.

VIDAL BLANC   Hybrid white grape derived from TREBBIANO, used in a range of reasonable wines, including ice wines (EISWEIN), in north-eastern USA and Canada.

VIDAL WINE PRODUCERS   *New Zealand, North Island, W, R*   This Hawke's Bay winery makes good-quality, classy wines.

VIDAL-FLEURY   *France, Rhône, R, W*   This respected grower of Côte Rôtie Rs is also a *négociant* making a range of wines: the R and W Côtes du Rhônes stand out.

VIEILLE FERME   *France, Rhône, Côtes du Ventoux, R*   The same ownership as Ch BEAUCASTEL, which lends class to this large-scale maker of easy-to-enjoy Rs.

VIEUX TÉLÉGRAPHE, DOM DU   *France, Rhône, Châteauneuf-du-Pape, R, W*   Noted estate in Châteauneuf: reliable, quality wine. The R is mosly Grenache, with some Syrah and Mourvèdre.

VIEUX-CHATEAU-CERTAN   *France, Bordeaux, Pomerol, R*   Once considered Pomerol's finest wine, now eclipsed by PÉTRUS. The largest of the top properties in the appellation. The Cabernet Franc and Cabernet Sauvignon in the blend can make it taste quite Médoc-like.

VIGNA, VIGNETO   *Italy*   Vineyard.

VIGNELAURE   *France, Provence, Coteaux d'Aix-en-Provence, R, W, P*   George Brunet's estate remains the best in the appellation. The R, in a bordeaux style, is 60% Cabernet Sauvignon, 30 Syrah and 10 Grenache, with long ageing in Hungarian oak. A second wine, La Page de Vignelaure, continues the bordeaux parallel.

VIGNERON   *France*   A wine-grower or vineyard worker.

VIGNOBLE   *France*   Vineyard, which can be just one plot or an entire region, as in "the Bordeaux *vignoble*".

VIGOUROUX   *France, Southwest, Cahors, R*   This *négociant* firm owns four Cahors estates, including Ch de Haut-Serre, on the plateau land where Cahors gained its reputation, which they helped revive. Vigouroux make good use of oak-ageing.

VILLA BANFI   *Italy, Tuscany, Brunello di Montalcino, R, W*   Spectacular modern winery producing Brunello, Rosso di Montalcino DOC, a R blend, Castello Banfi, a pure Cabernet Sauvignon, and two varietal W wines.

VILLA MARIA ESTATE   *New Zealand, North Island, W, R*   New Zealand's third-largest producer makes a full range of R and W wines, including botrytized Riesling W.

VILLA SACHSEN, WEINGUT   *Germany, Rheinhessen, W*   Based at Bingen, on the Rhine, this estate offers well-made, cask-matured wines, mostly Riesling.

VILLAINE, A & P DE   *France, Burgundy, Chalonnais, R, W, P*   Aubert de Villaine is part-owner of Dom de la ROMANÉE-CONTI, but at his estate in the Côte Chalonnaise he makes excellent Aligoté from old vines.

VILLÁNY-SIKLÓS   *Hungary*   To the west of the Great Plain, this is Hungary's southernmost wine district, making plummy, earthy Merlot and Cabernet Sauvignon Rs for export. Local specialities are the (R) Kékfrankos and Kékoportó grapes. Siklós is known for Ws.

VILLARS, CH   *France, Bordeaux, Fronsac, R*   Leading estate of Fronsac with a good record in the 1980s and especially 1990 for fruity, well-structured wine.

VILMART   *France, Champagne*   A small, top-quality grower with 11ha at Rilly-la-Montagne making all its wine in oak. Weighty, rich champagne.

VIN DE L'ANNÉE *France* Wine of the most recent vintage.

VIN DE PAILLE *France* Literally, straw wine. Sweet wine made from grapes dried on straw mats.

VIN DE PAYS *France* Country wine: A superior grade of *vin de table* produced according to regulations concerning grape varieties, yields and localities.

VIN DE TABLE *France* The lowest grade of wine defined in French law. It cannot claim a specific origin and is usually sold under a brand name.

VIN DÉLIMITÉ DE QUALITÉ SUPÉRIEURE (VDQS) *France* The grade of French quality wine below AOC.

VIN DOUX NATUREL (VDN) *France* Literally, naturally sweet wine. Wines that are rich in natural sweetness are fortified to preserve residual sugar.

VIN GRIS *France* A pale P wine made as W wine, but from R grapes.

VIN JAUNE *France* Wine made in the Jura which is affected by FLOR.

VIN ORDINAIRE *France* Everyday wine that is included in the classification *vin de table*.

VIN SANTO *Italy* A wine made from dried grapes, aged in small barrels. Can be sweet or dry.

VIÑA DE VERO *Spain, Aragón, Somontano, R, W, P* Name used by a relatively new company producing good-quality wines from both Spanish and French varieties, including Pinot Noir and Gewürztraminer.

VINCENT, DOM *France, Burgundy, Mâconnais, W* Maker of very fine St-Véran, in quite an opulent style.

VINCOR INTERNATIONAL *Canada, Ontario & British Columbia, W, R* North America's eight-largest winery, also owning Brights, Cartier and Inniskillin. A vast portfolio of wines from imported blends to single-vineyard bottlings.

VINELAND ESTATES *Canada, Ontario, W, R* Riesling specialist, with a range from bone-dry wines to Late Harvest and Icewine (EISWEIN).

VINHO VERDE *Portugal, DOC, W, R* The term means "green wine" but Vinho Verde can be either W or R (the R is rarely exported). It is so named because it is made to be drunk young and fresh, retaining a slight *pétillance* or sparkle. It should be low in alcohol and high in natural acidity. Leading producers include: Quinta da Aveleda, Borges & Irmão, Palácio de Brejoeira.

VINHOS, J P *Portugal, W, R* Look for fresh, grapey João Pires Dry Muscat and ripe-tasting R Tinto da Anfora from this firm.

VINIFERA   Vines of the species *vitis vinifera* – the classic grape vine of Europe – are sometimes so-named in the USA and Canada to distinguish them from hybrid or **LABRUSCA** vines.

VINO DA TAVOLA   *Italy*   Table wine. Much of it is ordinary, but some *vini da tavola* are superior wines made in DOC areas but not according to DOC rules.

VINO DE CRIANZA   *Spain*   Literally, wine of breeding. Quality wine that must have two full years' storage (one for W and P *crianzas*), with a minimum of six months in barrel.

VINO DE LA TIERRA (VDT)   *Spain*   Country wine (like the French *vin de pays*) from one of 28 areas that have shown their own character.

VINO NOBILE DI MONTEPULCIANO   *Italy, Tuscany, DOCG, R*   Mainly made from Prugnolo, a local Sangiovese clone, softened by Canaiolo Nero and lent fragrance by Mammolo. This wine must be aged in wood for two years. It can be lean, but the best have hints of spice and sandalwood. Leading producers include: Avignonesi, Boscarelli, Tenuta Trerose.

VINOS DE MADRID   *Spain, Madrid, DO, W, P, R*   The vineyards of this zone produce good, everyday wines for the capital, mostly in *joven* style but also some *crianza* R. Leading producers include: Bodegas Orusco.

VINTAGE   Originally the grape harvest; as there is only one per year, the term has come to refer to the wine made from the harvest of a particular year.

VIOGNIER   White grape of the northern Rhône, fabulously scented, often tasting of sweet, ripe peaches and apricots, it reaches perfection in the Condrieu and Château Grillet AOCs. Also grown in the Midi and California.

VIRÉ, CAVE COOPÉRATIVE DE   *France, Burgundy, Mâconnais, R, W, Sp*   One of south Burgundy's best- run cooperatives, producing wines of consistently reliable quality.

VIRGINIA   *USA*   Winemaking here started in 1609, and Thomas Jefferson's Monticello estate had vines in the 1770s. Today there are 50 wineries, and 7 VAs, the most important the Blue Ridge Mountains and Monticello. Leading producers include: **MEREDYTH**, Montdomaine (Chardonnay, and Bordeaux-style Rs from Monticello), Piedmont Vineyards (good Ws), Prince Michel (Chardonnay).

VOARICK, DOM MICHEL   *France, Burgundy, Côte d'Or, R*   Domaine based in Aloxe-Corton: low yields and fine Corton vineyards combine to produce concentrated wines for long ageing.

VOGE, ALAIN   *France, Rhône, St-Péray W, Sp; Cornas, R*   An important grower of long-lived, massive Cornas, in three *cuvées*, and a maker of good, dry Sp St-Péray.

VOGÜÉ, DOM COMTE GEORGES DE *France, Burgundy, Côte d'Or, R*
Major owner of *Grands* and *Premiers Crus*, mostly in Chambolle-Musigny. Top-class wines.

VOLKACH *Germany, Franken, W* Town in the
Steigerwald zone to the east of the region. The
Escherndorfer Lump vineyard, immediately
south of Volkach, is one of the few known outside Franken. Good Riesling, Müller-Thurgau
and Traminer Ws are produced at one of the
good smaller co-ops at nearby Nordheim.
Leading producers include: Schloss Halburg.

VOLLRADS, SCHLOSS *Germany, Rheingau, W* Ancient aristocratic
estate with its vineyard set high above the Rheingau, yielding
Riesling wine in a balanced, racy style.

VOLNAY *France, Burgundy, AOC, R* Côte de Beaune R, from Pinot
Noir. The appellation's hallmark is delicate, silky, violet- and
strawberry-scented wines from *Premiers Crus* such as Caillerets,
Champans, Clos des Chênes and Clos des Ducs. Drink from 4–5
years old, though they can age much longer. Leading producers
include: Marquis d'Angerville, Jean-Marc Bouley, Joseph
Drouhin, Dom Lafarge, Hubert de Montille, Dom de la Pousse
d'Or, Joseph Voillot.

VOLPAIA, CASTELLO DI *Italy, Tuscany, Chianti, R, W* Maker of elegant, perfumed, long-lived Chianti Classico; also Bianco Val d'Arbia (DOC, W), the W oak-aged Torniello, and two *vini da tavola*:
Coltassala and Balifico (R).

VON MUMM, G H *Germany, Rheingau, W, R* Important vineyard
owner in Johannisberg, making classic Rieslings which are dry
but solid and full of character.

VOSNE-ROMANÉE *France, Burgundy, AOC, R* Côte de Nuits village, with five *Grands Crus* and a clutch of excellent *Premiers Crus*:
(Aux Malconsorts, Les Suchots, Les Chaumes Aux Brûlées, Les
Beaux Monts), which produce outstandingly opulent wines that
can age for 10–15 years. The village AOC also produces elegant,
reliable wines.

VOUGEOT *France, Burgundy, AOC, R* Besides the famous *Grand
Cru* Clos de Vougeot, other Vougeot wines include some *Premiers
Crus* and village wines: some divided from the *Grand Cru* only by
the Clos wall. Leading producers include: Domaine Bertagna.

VOUVRAY *France, Loire, AOC, W, Sp* High-quality Ws, dry,
medium and sweet; still or Sp, from east of Tours, on the north
bank of the Loire. Styles vary from vintage to vintage: in a warm
year, most wines will be sweet; if the weather is not so good,
drier wines will result. Good sweet wines can age very well.
Leading producers include: Philippe Brisebarre, Dom Bourillon
d'Orléans, Gaston Huet, Ch Moncontour, Clos Naudin, Prince
Poniatowski.

VRANKEN   *France, Champagne*   Large house with 153ha of vines. The wines stress Chardonnay and are light and elegant. Brands include Charles Lafitte, Sacotte and Demoiselle.

VRAYE CROIX-DE-GAY, CH   *France, Bordeaux, Pomerol, R*   Small but well-placed vineyard making long-lived and well-regarded wines.

W

WACHAU *Austria, Niederösterreich* Vineyards along the Danube gorge form one of the smallest Austrian regions, but the source of the best W wines. Grüner Veltliner and Riesling dominate. Wachau has its own quality categories which appear on the label; lightest is *Steinfeder*; richest are *Smaragd*; *Ried* on the label denotes a vineyard of singular merit. Leading producers include: Franz Hirtzberger, Emmerich Knoll, Nikolaihof, F X Pichler, Franz Prager.

WACHENHEIM *Germany, Pfalz, W* Fine-wine village in the MITT-ELHAARDT, with famous vineyards such as Gerümpel and Altenberg. Solid-long-lasting W wine is the local tradition. Some estates also make drier wines in a modern style. Leading producers include: Bürklin-Wolf.

WAGNER VINEYARDS *USA, New York, Finger Lakes, W* Premier maker of Chardonnay. All wines are estate-grown; about half of 20,000-case annual production is of classic-grape wines, including Pinot Noir R and Riesling and Gewürztraminer Ws. Also makes barrel-fermented Seyval Blanc and Reserve White.

WAIKATO *New Zealand, North Island* South of Auckland, this area is noted for Müller-Thurgau, Sauvignon Blanc and Chardonnay. Leading producers include: De Redcliffe.

WAIRARAPA *New Zealand, North Island* Small, recently-planted area internationally renowned for its Rs from Pinot Noir. Also grows some W varieties. Leading producers include: Ata Rangi, Dry River, Palliser, Te Kairanga.

WALKER BAY *South Africa, WO* Cool-climate coastal area benefitting from Atlantic breezes, ideal for Pinot Noir and Chardonnay in a subtle, Burgundian style. The potential here is very exciting. Leading producers include: Bouchard-Finlayson, Hamilton Russell.

WALLHAUSEN, SCHLOSS, PRINZ ZU SALM-DALBERG'SCHES WEIN-GUT *Germany, Nahe, W* Modern-minded, though aristocratic, this estate does not use vineyard names except for a few top ones, the rest of the wine being blended as one *cuvée*.

WALNUT CREST *Chile, R, W, Sp* Highly ambitious company founded in 1986 by several major shareholders of Concha y Toro in partnership with Banfi Vintners. Produces about one million cases a year, including a Sp wine. Best wines include Merlot, Cabernet Sauvignon and Sauvignon Blanc.

WARRE *Portugal, port* Wines of immense power from the oldest of the British port houses, founded 1670. A Symington became a partner in 1892, and they still own it.

WARREN-BLACKWOOD *Australia, Western Australia* A very new wine region better known by its two sub-regions Manjimup and Pemberton. Thought to have great potential, especially for Pinot Noir and Chardonnay. Leading producers include: Donnelly River, Gloucester Ridge, Mounford, Piano Gully, Smithbrook, Warren.

WARWICK ESTATE *South Africa, Stellenbosch, R, W* Essentially an R-only estate with a particular penchant for Cabernet Franc, produced as a rich, grassy single varietal and also included in the outstanding bordeaux blend, Trilogy.

WASHINGTON *USA* Major grape-growing state, though most grapes end up as juice, not wine. The wine zones, which include the COLUMBIA VALLEY and YAKIMA VALLEY, are east of the Cascade Mountains and thus dry (meaning irrigation), warm in summer and cold in winter. Crisp, fresh Ws from Chardonnay and Riesling are the mainstays; with soft, fruity Rs from Merlot and Cabernet Sauvignon. Leading producers include: ARBOR CREST, COLUMBIA, COVEY RUN, HOGUE, STE-MICHELLE, WOODWARD CANYON.

WEGELER-DEINHARD *Germany, Rheingau & Mosel, W* Owner of part of the Bernkasteler Doctor and other fine vineyards, making classic Mosels that age well in bottle, and a large estate in the Rheingau making good-value, characterful Rieslings, many dry. Increasingly, the Rheingau wines are sold by village, not vineyard, name.

WEHLEN *Germany, Mosel, W* Town in the MITTELMOSEL, whose most famous vineyard, Wehlener Sonnenuhr, meaning sundial, enjoys a superb, southwest-facing site. Leading producers include: J A Prüm, S A Prüm and Max-Ferdinand Richter.

WEIL, ROBERT *Germany, Rheingau, W* Estate making very fine Rieslings from top Rheingau vineyards, both dry ones to partner food and superb sweet ones for sipping alone.

WEINVIERTEL *Austria, Niederösterreich* Largest of the Austrian wine regions, north and north-west of Vienna, accounting for 31% of total production. Most wines are in a light, easy-to-drink style although some producers concentrate on *eiswein*. Leading producers include: Richard Luckner, Roman Pfaffl, Fritz Rieder.

WEISSBURGUNDER See PINOT BLANC.

WELSCHRIESLING White grape, unrelated to Riesling, which makes light, aromatic dry and sweet wines of variable quality in Austria, northern Italy (Riesling Italico), and throughout southeast Europe (where its synonyms include Laski Rizling and Olaszriesling).

WENTE   *USA, California, Bay Area, W, Sp, R*   The Wentes started winegrowing in the Livermore Valley in 1883 and the estate remains family-owned, the former Cresta Blanca winery now remodelled into a restaurant and Sp wine centre. Wente's Sémillon W has lovely melon-fig fruitiness.

WERNER'SCHES WEINGUT, DOMDECHANT   *Germany, Rheingau, W* Fine, elegant traditional Riesling Ws from an old family estate at Hochheim. These are wines worth bottle-age.

WEST VIRGINIA   *USA*   Promising wines are being made in the east of the state, close to the expanding areas of Virginia.

WESTERN AUSTRALIA   *Australia*   The country's newest wine state has already an exciting reputation for quality. The cool-climate areas of MARGARET RIVER and MOUNT BARKER-FRANKLAND produce an excellent range of Rs and Ws, though the hot, dry SWAN VALLEY has undergone a recent decline.

WESTHALTEN   *France, Alsace*   Distinctive Pinot Blanc and Pinot Gris Ws come from this village, which includes the *Grands Crus* Vorbourg and Zinnkoepflé. Leading producers include: Frick.

WETSHOF ESTATE, DE   *South Africa, Robertson, W*   Chardonnay specialist Dannie de Wet produces a wide range of very good-quality Ws under both the De Wetshof and Dannie de Wet labels. The main difference is the amount of oak influence, from the fresh lemony Finesse, with just a touch of oak, to the bigger, more full-flavoured Chardonnay d'Honneur.

WIEDERKEHR VINEYARDS   *USA, Arkansas, W, R*   Founded in Altus by the Swiss Wiederkehr family in 1880, now one of the largest producers east of the Rockies. With two-thirds of the 263-ha vineyard containing classic varieties, the company produces a wide range, the list topped by Riesling W and several Muscat-based Ws.

WIEN   *Austria*   The capital (Vienna in English) is surrounded by 700ha of vines and almost all the wine is drunk locally. Around Vienna are dozens of *Heurigen*, inns where growers sell their own wines; mainly light, racy W wine from the last vintage. Grüner Veltliner is the most popular grape, also excellent Riesling and Weissburgunder (Pinot Blanc). Leading producers include: Fuhrgassl-Huber, Franz Mayer, Herbert Schilling.

WILLAMETTE VALLEY   *USA, Oregon, VA*   Oregon's most important wine zone, extending south and west from Portland to Eugene. A cool-climate area, providing up to three-quarters of the state's wine-grapes. This is home to extremely elegant Pinot Noir Rs (accounting for nearly half of the land under vine) and Ws from Chardonnay, Riesling and Pinot Gris. Leading producers include: Knudsen Erath, Oak Knoll, Ponzi.

WILTINGEN   *Germany, Mosel-Saar-Ruwer, W*   Town in the Saar, surrounded by vineyards. Cheaper Saar QbA wine is sold under the *grosslage* name Wiltinger Scharzberg, but much wine with a high level of acidity finds its way to the makers of Sekt, Germany's sparkling wine. The best vineyard site is Scharzhofberg, not to be confused with the *grosslage*. Leading producers include: Egon Müller-Scharzhof.

WINKEL   *Germany, Rheingau, W*   Top Rieslings, marked by a pronounced fruity-acid style, are produced in this village. The best vineyard is Winkeler Hasensprung and the most famous producer is Schloss Vollrads.

WINNINGEN   *Germany, Mosel, W*   One of the largest wine villages on the Mosel. Shares the top-quality terraced vineyard Winninger Uhlen with its neighbour, Kobern. Winningen is known for its characterful, strongly-flavoured Riesling wines. Leading producers include: von Heddesdorff, Richard Richter, von Schleinitz.

WINTZENHEIM   *France, Alsace*   This village has one of the most famous vineyards, *Grand Cru* Hengst, which produces Ws from Gewürztraminer plus Pinot Gris and Riesling. Leading producers include: Meyer, Zind-Humbrecht.

WIRSCHING, WEINGUT   *Germany, Franken, W*   Characterful dry wines, much appreciated with food, come from good vineyards at Iphofen.

WISCONSIN   *USA*   Wine is made here in commercial quantities, with Riesling and Pinot Noir among the successful varieties. Leading producers include: Wollersheim.

WOODWARD CANYON   *USA, Washington State, R, W*   At his winery in Walla Walla Valley, Rick Small specializes in R from Cabernet Sauvignon (blackcurrant and dill flavours) and Merlot (coffee and tobacco), but also makes a W Burgundian-style Chardonnay (clove and butter). His Meritage (bordeaux-style) R is called Chabonneau.

WORCESTER DISTRICT   *South Africa, WO*   District of highly efficient cooperatives making 25% of country's total output, including good Ws from Riesling, Sauvignon Blanc and Colombard. Also important for brandy production. Leading producers include: Nuy Cooperative.

WÜRTTEMBERG   *Germany, Anbaugebiet, R, W, P*   Region around Stuttgart and Heilbronn in the Neckar Valley, specializing in soft, sweet R wines, all drunk locally. Ws from Riesling, and modern-style, sometimes *barrique*-aged, Rs, are more in the international taste. Leading producers include: Graf Adelmann, Robert Bauer, von Neipperg.

WÜRZBURG   *Germany, Franken, W*   The capital of Franken, containing its three greatest wine estates: the Bürgerspital, noted for its intense Trockenbeerenauslesen; the Juliusspital, regarded as best at the moment; and the Staatlicher Hofkeller with its prime sites in the Stein vineyard.

WÜRZBURG STAATLICHER HOFKELLER *Germany, Franken, W, R* Great estate whose cellars beneath the Residenz in Würzburg are as famous as the wines, which are made in classic Franken style.

WYNNS COONAWARRA ESTATE *Australia, S Australia, Coonawarra, R, W* Possibly the most famous, certainly the most successful, producer in this southernmost area. Very good, reliable quality – and some outstanding wines under the John Riddoch and Michael labels.

Y

YAKIMA VALLEY *USA, Washington State, VA* Sub-zone of the Columbia Valley, growing varieties like Riesling and Chardonnay for Ws; Merlot and Cabernet Sauvignon for Rs.

YALUMBA *Australia, S Australia, Barossa, R, W* This family firm is best known for its Sp wine, Angas Brut, the Oxford Landing range and its well-priced brands.

YARRA VALLEY *Australia, Victoria* A beautiful, cool-climate area of Victoria, noted especially for top-quality Pinot Noir R in a style to challenge Burgundy. Also makes very good Chardonnay, Shiraz (R), Merlot and Cabernet Sauvignon. Leading producers include: de Bortoli, Domaine Chandon, Coldstream Hills, St Huberts, Yarra Yering.

YECLA *Spain, DO, Levante, W, P, R* One of two wine zones in Murcia, inland from Alicante, recently investing in new technology to make a wider range of distinctive wines to attract new markets. Leading producers include: Bodegas Castaño.

YORK MOUNTAIN *USA, California, VA* In San Luis Obispo County, and a mere 12ha in size, this is the exclusive domain of York Mountain Winery, founded in 1882.

YQUEM, CH D' *France, Bordeaux, Sauternes, 1er Cru Supérieur, W* For many years the only Sauternes château to follow the highest standards, Yquem still leads with its hand-crafted, long-lived, enormously complex (and costly) wine.

Z

ZELL/MOSEL *Germany, Mosel-Saar-Ruwer, Bereich, W* Also called the Lower Mosel, a zone rather in the shadow of the Mittelmosel (*see* **BERNKASTEL**) but making good-value W wines.

ZELTINGEN *Germany, Mosel, W* Village in the Mittelmosel, opposite Wehlen, with some superb, south-west facing vineyards, the famous vineyards being Himmelreich, Schlossberg and Sonnenuhr.

ZIND HUMBRECHT *France, Alsace, W* Leonard Humbrecht has campaigned tirelessly for lower yields. His 30ha are extremely well sited and include four *Grand Cru* holdings. Methods are natural and traditional; Pinot Gris and Gewürztraminer excel.

ZINFANDEL Versatile red grape from California, probably related to southern Italy's Primitivo. Can make long-lived, complex, deep red wines, but also very pale P or "blush" wines.

ZÜRICH *Switzerland* This important wine-producing canton in German-speaking Switzerland makes W wines mainly from Riesling-Sylvaner (Müller-Thurgau) and R from Blauburgunder (Pinot Noir, also known as Clevner or Beerli). Most production is handled by two large local cooperatives although a few very small estates do exist.

TASTING
WINE

DESCRIBING A TASTE

WINETASTING IS NOT DIFFICULT: it only needs concentration in order to make full use of the memory, which is our main tasting tool. The words used to describe a taste – or a smell – are those which trigger the memory.

The process of tasting has a few simple steps. First, pour a little wine into a clean glass. Look at the colour, against a white background if possible. Is the wine dark or pale, dense or light? Is it clear and bright, or muddy and dull? Clear your mind, concentrate hard. Then sniff: what does the wine's smell remind you of? Maybe another wine, or something quite different. Finally, take a good taste and hold the wine in your mouth, letting it coat the palate and tongue. The mouth is less subtle than the nose: look for weight, acidity, sweetness, astringency and texture.

The key to learning – if that, rather than appreciation, is the aim – is to make notes straight away.

TASTING TERMS

This is a basic glossary of words for describing wine. Words that describe the principal components of wine – acid, alcohol and tannin (in **CAPITALS**) – are grouped under their respective entries.

Acetic   *See* Volatile.

ACID/ACIDITY   Gives life and freshness. Also helps define and prolong wine flavours. Words for acidity (from too little to too much) include: flat, flabby, soft, supple, fresh, lively, crisp, firm, hard, sharp, green, tart, acid.

ALCOHOL   Gives wine its characteristic "weight". Described as (from inadequate to excess): watery, thin, light, medium-bodied, full-bodied, ample, generous, heady, heavy, alcoholic, hot.

Aroma   Smells that come from the grape rather than from ageing in barrel or bottle, or from vinification. *See also* Bouquet.

Aromatic   Wines from grapes with a particularly pronounced aroma (eg Gewürztraminer, Muscat, Sauvignon Blanc, Cabernet Sauvignon).

Astringent   The drying, gripping sensation on the gums produced by tannin (*qv*).

Austere   Hard, unyielding impression given by wine with high tannin or acid, which needs time to soften.

Backward   Not ready to drink; needs more bottle-age to mellow.

Balanced   Wine whose component parts "balance" each other nicely, so that no element appears lacking or obtrusive for its type.

Blackcurrant   The smell and taste usually associated with Cabernet Sauvignon wines .

Body   Combined impression of weight and consistency,

due mainly, but not solely, to the level of alcohol.

Botrytis   See Noble rot.

Bouquet   General term to describe the smell of wine, but particularly used for smells deriving from vinification and barrel- or bottle-age. *See also* aroma.

Buttery   A smell and taste often associated with rich, oaked Chardonnay.

Cedary   Cedar-wood smell found in wines aged in new French oak.

Closed   Muted but promising bouquet or flavour.

Cloying   Sweetness that is "sticky" because it is not balanced by enough acidity.

Coarse   Used to describe texture, tannin in particular. Also describes a harsh mousse in sparkling wines.

Complex   Indicates quality: variety and subtlety in both flavour and bouquet.

Corked wine   Smell of damp and mould completely dominates the bouquet and flavour of the wine. Nothing to do with harmless fragments of cork in the glass.

Drying out   Mature wines that are losing their flavour, so allowing their acid, alcohol or tannin to appear obtrusive.

Dumb   *See* Closed.

Earthy   Usually a positive term; recalling damp earth on nose and palate.

Elegant   Finesse, harmony, no harsh impressions.

Fierce   Harshness, from high levels of alcohol and/or acidity.

Fine   High-quality wine.

Finish   Tastes and aromas that linger on after the wine has been swallowed. *See also* Length, Short.

Fleshy   Rich in flavour, supple in texture. Refers mainly to reds.

Flinty   Mineral taste in crisp dry white wines, such as Chablis and Sancerre.

Fruity   Many wines smell or taste of a specific fruit (eg peach, apple, blackcurrant, cherry); others have a pleasant general "juiciness" of aroma and flavour. A term difficult to avoid, easy to over-use.

Gooseberry   A taste and smell mostly associated with Sauvignon Blanc.

Grapey   Used to suggest a taste of fresh grape juice. Muscats are almost the only wines to smell and taste just like the fresh grape.

Green   Unripe, young. Also refers to acidity.

Grip   A firm, dry feel on the gums; produced by tannin in red wine.

Harsh   Refers to texture.

Herbaceous   A smell reminiscent of green plants, or freshly cut grass.

Hollow   Empty of flavour and noticeably short.

Lean   Used critically, means a lack of ripe fruit.

Length/Long   The hallmark of a high-quality wine. *See also* Finish.

Maderized   *See* Oxidized wines

Mature   Ready to drink.

Mellow   With a soft, agreeable texture.

Noble rot *Botrytis cinerea*, the rot on ripe grapes that concentrates natural flavours. Tasters spot this intensity and a honey-and-lemon character.

Nutty A smell and taste often found in mature white burgundy, good-quality dry marsala, amontillado sherry.

Oaky Smells (vanilla, cedar wood, caramel, toast) and sometimes slight dryness of texture that derive from ageing in new oak barrels.

Oxidized wines So-called because excess contact with oxygen has spoiled their taste. White wines look dull, with a darker colour than normal for age/type: lacklustre straw to brown. Flat, stale smell; dull, sharp taste. Also called maderized. Red wines too have a dull appearance, browner than normal for age/type. Flat, stale nose with a "sweet and sour" or caramelly smell and taste.

Peppery Smell of ground black pepper, in port and Rhône wines especially.

Pétillant Lightly sparkling.

Petrolly Agreeable petroleum smell in mature Rieslings.

Raw Harsh impressions from alcohol, acid and tannin in immature wine.

Reduced *See* Sulphur-related faults.

Rich Describes flavour and texture.

Ripe A sweetness of flavour in wines made from very ripe grapes.

Rustic Coarse; a result of primitive or careless winemaking techniques.

Short Lacking in persistence of flavour on the finish. *See also* length.

Smoky Smell and/or taste; eg in white Sancerre and northern Rhône reds.

Stewed Like tea brewed too long: dull, vegetal smell; coarse, astringent.

Sulphur-related faults The pungent, acrid, suffocating smell of sulphur dioxide: like a safety match on being lit; shows as a sharp, dry prickling sensation in throat on tasting. The smell of Hydrogen sulphide is bad eggs, rubber, garlic, rotting vegetation, with tastes to match. Also called reduced.

Supple Soft and gentle, without being flabby.

TANNIN Substance from grape skins that gives red wine its dry, mouth-puckering feel. Described as (from a little to a lot): fine-grained, soft, matt, dry, rich, firm, tough, coarse, vegetal, stemmy, astringent.

Thin Dilute and meagre in flavour.

Tired Lacking freshness.

Vanilla The smell and taste most often associated with wines that have been aged in new oak barrels.

Volatile wines Have a noticeable sour vinegar smell from the "volatile" acid: acetic acid, ie vinegar. Thin, sharp, sour taste.

Wet wool Smell in unoaked Chardonnay (Chablis) and Sémillon (Sauternes). Also found in wines with too much sulphur.

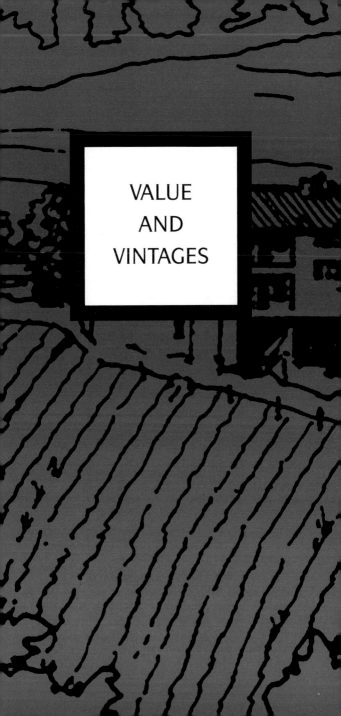

VALUE
AND
VINTAGES

VALUE-FOR-MONEY WINES

WHICH WINES TODAY OFFER the best *rapport qualité:prix*, in the expressive French phrase? They may be new areas, striving for recognition, or classic ones unjustly overlooked. Here are some suggestions, grouped by wine style, for wines which offer both quality at their various levels, and good value.

VALUE DRY WHITES

Here the value-hunter has to search hardest, for while the world's winemakers vie to make look-alike Chardonnays, wines with real interest are harder to find.

CÔTE CHALONNAIS
White wines from the village appellations Rully, Montagny and Givry offer real burgundy flavours, and quite a lot of finesse, at sensible prices. Wines come from the excellent local cooperatives and from private estates.

RHONE WHITES
Rhône reds get the limelight, but skilled winemakers can conjure excellent whites from the sunny valley: Condrieu is expanding, and its Viognier-grape wine is better value; White Crozes-Hermitage can be well made and good value. White Hermitage and Châteauneuf are serious and age-worthy wines yet far cheaper than burgundies of equivalent stature.

VIN DE PAYS D'OC
This French "country wine" name covers the whole of the Midi and is used on some good, modern wines such as Chablis expert Domaine Laroche's whites from Sauvignon, Chardonnay (oak-aged) and Viognier; the Fortant de France range; and the wines made by Australian wine giants Penfolds, working with Midi cooperatives.

RIESLING FROM AUSTRALIA
The obsession with Chardonnay is wearing off, and Australia's better winemakers are trying their skills on Riesling, another classic white grape. Styles tend to be fruity yet acidic, clean and with a touch of sugar on the finish. Good young, but can age well.

IRSAY OLIVIER

This grape variety, native to Hungary and Slovakia, is being taken seriously by western- (and Australian-) trained winemakers working in these Danube countries. It produces extremely fresh, flowery, perfumed white wines with an attractive appealing palate.

BADEN WHITES

Wines with more weight and flavour than most white Germans are found in the relatively warm zone of Baden. They range from soft and refreshing everyday wines, often labelled just Baden, to solid, dry Grauburgunders (Pinot Blanc) from individual estates. And – unlike the more usual German wine styles – all are good with food.

VALUE REDS

Red wine is less troublesome to make than white, and thus value is easier to find. Character, and that imponderable called personality, are more apparent in the following wines than in the average reds at mid-market prices.

PÉCHARMANT

This superior sub-zone within Bergerac in South-West France makes good Bordeaux-like reds with substance and structure, worth bottle-age. They are a little more fruity, and less austere, than clarets of similar stature.

CÔTES DU RHÔNE-VILLAGES

Wines from this southern French appellation offer much more flavour and character than straight Côtes du Rhône for a moderate amount more. The best villages are Séguret, Rochegude, Cairanne.

MONTEPULCIANO D'ABRUZZO

Rich, soft and enjoyable, these R wines from one of Italy's wildest mountain areas are pleasant drunk young yet can improve with a year or two in bottle.

TEMPRANILLO

Rioja's main grape also makes interesting, age-worthy reds (under the name Tinto Fino) in Ribera del Duero; and is also starting to appear as a varietal wine from other parts of Spain.

DOURO

From the port country of northern Portugal, these red table wines were once the exclusive meal-time drink of the port shippers – before they started on the port. Now more widely available, they are dark, solid yet fruity.

SHIRAZ
Wines from Australia's Shiraz grape (France's Syrah), either alone or blended with Cabernet Sauvignon, offer flavourful yet soft reds akin to Bordeaux from a hot vintage. Everyday examples are excellent value: spend some more and real character can be found.

CABERNET FROM CHILE
Cabernet Sauvignon thrives in Chile, and in recent years winemaking techniques have improved to take advantage of it. Everyday wines are black-cherry-red, fruity and good slightly chilled. Most producers also offer more serious age-worthy wines akin to mid-rank Médocs.

VALUE SWEET WHITES

Sweet wines at moderate prices are fast shaking off their headachy image as modern winemakers take control of the process. These suggestions cover a wide range of styles. All should be served well chilled, and all are enjoyable with or without food.

SAUTERNES ALTERNATIVES
Bordeaux and its surrounding areas produce some extremely good, value-for-money, lesser sweet wines, which may or may not be *botrytis*-affected. Cérons is the best known, followed by Loupiac, St-Croix-du-Mont, Monbazillac and Saussignac.

VENDANGE TARDIVE
Alsace has refined this traditional wine which uses very ripe grapes, usually picked after the main harvest. It is normally sweet, but can be dry. These are top-quality wines from either Gewürztraminer, Pinot Gris, Riesling or Muscat, and they are never cheap, but they are unusual, intense and clean in taste, thus good value.

JURANÇON
In the vineyards of the Pyrenees, grapes are allowed to dry on the vine until well into the autumn to concentrate sweetness, and the wine is then oak-aged. The result is like fine Sauternes, although developing greater complexity with bottle-age.

TOKAJI

Hungary's classic zone (also called Tokay) is reviving. The technique is complex: the result is a rich, heady mix of extract, alcohol and glycerol. The more "puttonyos" on the label (maximum 6), the sweeter the wine. As Tokaji is still regaining prestige and thus price, it is currently good value.

RECIOTO DI SOAVE

This northern Italian speciality is made from semi-dried grapes, and is much richer in taste and texture than dry Soave, with a higher alcohol content.

EISWEIN (ICE WINE) FROM CANADA

A well-kept secret, Canada's Ontario vineyards are the largest producer of rare, sweet white Eiswein, made from Riesling and the hybrid Vidal. The late-harvest grapes are frozen solid by the cold, and the resulting wine has wonderfully intense flavours.

MUSCAT

One of the world's most adaptable and appealing vine varieties, immediately recognizable for its grapiness. Muscat wines offer refreshing pleasure from the lighter style of Valencia in southern Spain and France's Midi, to the more exotic Orange and Black Muscats of California and Australia's even richer Rutherglen Liqueur Muscats.

DESSERT WINES FROM ENGLAND

Not fully exploited yet, but England has very good potential for producing lusciously sweet, botrytized wines, with a fine balance of flavours. Leading producers include: Chiltern Valley Vineyards, Denbies, Northbrook Spring, Pilton Manor, Westholme.

VALUE SPARKLING WINES

It will never be cheap to make sparkling wine, as getting the bubbles in means more work than leaving the wine still. Industrial-scale methods allow fizz of a sort to be made quite cheaply, but these use very ordinary base wine, and can rarely offer much in the way of flavour to go with the froth. Champagne is the benchmark, and for occasions when only champagne will do there are some suggestions below. As for the rest, look for sparklers made in the champagne method, or the Charmat technique, and look widely: the whole world seems to be trying to gain a slice of the celebration market.

CRÉMANT

The name used for French sparkling wines made outside Champagne by the same method: mainly in the Loire, Burgundy, Alsace and Bordeaux (labels say Crémant de Loire, d'Alsace, etc). Quality can be extremely good.

CHAMPAGNE'S SOUTHERN ZONES

Previously little-heard-of areas in the south of the Champagne region are beginning to forge an identity for themselves as producers of well-made, good-value champagnes. Mainly Chardonnay is grown in the Côte de Sézanne, ripening very well and making rich, slightly exotic wines. Over in the Aube Pinot Noir dominates, giving wines of finesse and staying power. These zones offer the magic name Champagne on the label, plus some real character and flavour: qualities that really cheap champagnes may lack.

CAVA

Spain's premium sparkling wine, Cava is made from native grape varieties like Macabeo (Viura) and Parellada, and offers high standards, broad fruit flavours and low acidity. Some of the premium *marques* have Chardonnay in the blend.

ASTI SPUMANTE

Famous but sadly maligned. If well-made, Asti from Northern Italy these days offers a deliciously refreshing soft grapey mouthful of flavours, combined with low alcohol. Look also for Moscato d'Asti, with even lower alcohol and an unusual Muscat-grape flavour.

PROSECCO DI CONEGLIANO-VALDOBBIADENE

This wine, usually called just Prosecco, is from near Venice. Clean but fairly neutral, with a slightly almondy flavour, it has snappy acidity and lowish alcohol. Unpretentious, for drinking young.

SPARKLING WINE FROM NEW ZEALAND

With its cool European-style climate, New Zealand produces some seriously good champagne alternatives made by the same method and with the same grape varieties, resulting in rich, weighty flavours balanced by good acidity.

SPARKLING WINE FROM AUSTRALIA

With a wide range of prices and qualities, from basic party fizz (Angas Brut, Seaview, Yalumba) to some serious classic-method wines, often made by companies linked with champagne houses (Domaine Chandon's Green Point, Petaluma's Croser), Australia has plenty of value. All offer fair value, plenty of fruit and an interesting alternative to European sparklers. Look for classic grapes (Pinot Noir, Chardonnay) on labels for more European-style wines.

VALUE FORTIFIED WINES

Fortified wines take time, skill and money to make. Success demands that the maker hold large stocks of slowly maturing wine: a challenging task financially. Areas with long traditions – port, sherry, South Africa – have the reserves of blending wine and the skills to offer interesting fortified wines, especially if the obvious names are bypassed.

SINGLE QUINTA PORTS

These are ports from a single estate made by some of the leading shippers, sometimes using just one or two of the top port grape varieties. Bottled two years after the vintage, they always bear a vintage date, age very well in bottle and represent an excellent alternative to vintage port.

MANZANILLA

This style of dry sherry can only be made on the coast at Sanlúcar de Barrameda, where moist conditions ensure that *flor* grows all year round. Manzanilla has a deliciously salty tang. The best is like a fine Fino, but less expensive.

AUSTRALIAN LIQUEUR MUSCATS

Fermentation is stopped almost before it has begun by the addition of spirit, ensuring that the finished wine retains wonderfully fresh, grapey aromas and flavours.

CAPE FORTIFIEDS

The South African tradition of making wines in the style of sherry and port has left a legacy: cellars full of superb old wines at value-for-money prices. Some are blends: Muscat styles, some like rather sweet chocolaty port, others like sherries. Fifteen-year-old wines can be had at very reasonable prices.

VINTAGE CHARTS

VINTAGE CHARTS MADE MORE SENSE when there were fewer wines: now, nothing can be that simple. However most wines are designed to be drunk young: it is the exceptions which are discussed below.

Ratings (the first figure) are out of 10. D means drink now; (D) means probably past its best; K means drink now, but can be kept; L means lay down for the future: the figure (eg L 10+) gives an estimate of likely time to maturity from the vintage.

RED BORDEAUX

Ordinary Bordeaux AC red will be good at 2 years old, *petits châteaux* of the Médoc and other areas at 2–5 years, though in great vintages they can surprise by lasting longer. Ratings are for classed growths or their equivalent; other wines will mature sooner. Recent vintages are proving to be attractive earlier than is traditionally the case, but good years will still have a long life.

1994	8	L 5 +

Rain in September again dashed the highest hopes, but wines promise well: first tastings show dark, solid wines, especially where careful selection has weeded out poor vats

1993	7	L 4 +

September rain spoilt prospects, in St-Emilion most of all, but still fair to good: early-maturing wines

1992	6	K

Large crop; best wines from Pauillac and St-Estèphe, light and simple wines elsewhere

1991	5	D

Poor weather – frost and rain – ended the run of good years

1990	10	L 8 +

Another hot, dry vintage: the best wines ripe and superb

1989	9	L 8 +

Large, ripe, opulent vintage: elegant and consistent wines

| **1988** | **9** | **L 10 +** |

Wines with structure and balance for long life

| **1987** | **6** | **D** |

Poor weather, moderate wines, best in St-Emilion/Pomerol

| **1986** | **8** | **K** |

Fine wines; the best are for keeping: Médoc better than St-Emilion/Pomerol

| **1985** | **7** | **K** |

Ripe, delicious, early-maturing wines

| **1984** | **5** | **D** |

Tough Cabernet-based wines in the Médoc and Graves: almost total failure across the river in St-Emilion

| **1983** | **8** | **D** |

High quality, elegant wines, especially from Médoc

| **1982** | **10** | **K** |

Magnificent and ripe from all areas

| **1981** | **7** | **D** |

Good wines in 1982's shadow, diluted by rain at harvest

Older fine vintages: 1978, 1970, 1975 (in Pomerol especially), 1966, 1961

RED BURGUNDY

The most difficult of wines to generalize about: the myriad growers and *négociants* make markedly different wines, and weather can cause big local variations. Comments are based on Côte d'Or *Premiers Crus*. Chalonnais wines follow the same pattern but do not keep so long. Village and appellation Bourgogne wines rarely mature beyond 4–5 years.

| **1994** | **6** | **K** |

Fair to good, but variable as growers battled with patchy weather

| **1993** | **7** | **K** |

Variable owing to weather problems: some fine wines

| **1992** | **7** | **K** |

Good but not for long keeping

1991	6	K

Weather problems

1990	10	L 8+

Third great year in a row: fine, rich but balanced wines

1989	9	L 8+

A hot year: good, perhaps great, wines

1988	9	K

Solid, rich wines, especially in the Côte de Nuits

1987	7	D

Good if light, despite September rain

1986	6	D

Variable due to rot but many good wines

1985	8	D

Good, ripe, balanced wines, some very fine

1984	4	–

A poor, cold year

1983	8	D

Hail and rot in places spoilt high hopes

1982	6	(D)

Large crop of sometimes dilute wines

WHITE BURGUNDY

Côte de Beaune wines, at *Premier Cru* level, form the basis of these ratings. Chablis vintages are broadly comparable, but see also notes at the foot of the chart. Chalonnais and Mâconnais wines: follow the chart, but enjoy them young: few wines except the best Chalonnais and some Pouilly-Fuissé will keep beyond 5–7 years.

1994	7	K

Better than '93, and than '94 reds

1993	6	K

Less good than the reds

1992	8	L 5+

Fine, typical wines, worth ageing

1991	7	D

Lighter, more balanced wines than 1990

1990	8	K

The third in a run of fine vintages: rich, full wines

1989	9	D

A hot year; fine, full, complex wines, but not for keeping

1988	8	D

A large crop, with some wines too light, but on the whole a good vintage

1987	5	(D)

Vintage-time rain dashed hopes

1986	7	D

More acidity and balance than 1985

1985	8	D

Rich, fat wines which sometimes lack balance

1984	4	(D)

A cool year; light wines

1983	8	D

Hot year making rich, powerful wines, some unbalanced

CHABLIS

1993 and 1994 were better than in the Côte de Beaune, but not exceptional.
1992: large crop of full, fat wines.
1991: hard-hit by frost, small crop; top wines can be good.
1990: very good for top wines, others soft.
1989: very good but fat: drink soon.
1988: balanced and typical: drink soon.
Older vintages of Premiers and Grands Crus: 1986, 1985 and 1983 were all good.

CHAMPAGNE

For most champagnes the vintage is irrelevant: makers blend wines of different vintages for consistency. Vintage-labelled wines are produced by the top champagne houses only in very good years. Not every house will "declare" every vintage. Vintage champagne from a *grande marque* house needs a decade in bottle to reach its best. Recent vintage years have been the trio of 1988, '89 and '90 (best of the three), with 1990 perhaps the best; 1986, '85, '83, '82, '79, '76.

ALSACE

Most everyday Alsace wines can be drunk at 1–4 years old; *Vendange Tardive* and *Sélection de Grains Nobles* wines can have a longer life.

In 1994, rain spoilt a potentially superb vintage, but good wines were still made.

1993 was a smaller crop, better than 1992; but Rieslings and late-harvest wines were patchy.

1992 saw a large crop of soft enjoyable wines.

1990, '89, '86 and '85 were superb.

LOIRE

The dry wines of Pouilly and Sancerre, from Sauvignon Blanc, are at their best under 5 years old, with rare exceptions.

Sweet whites of Anjou and Touraine from Chenin Blanc can, in the rare great years (1990, '89, '88 – though '94 had some good ones), last for decades.

Red wines for ageing are made only in warm years: 1990 was the last real one, but some good reds in 1993.

RHÔNE

North and South Rhône conditions can vary. Wines for keeping are the longer-lived, Syrah-based wines of the northern areas– Côte Rôtie, Hermitage – and wines such as Châteauneuf and Gigondas in the south.

1994 was good in the south.

1991, '92 and '93 moderate to poor everywhere.

1990, '89 and '88 all great.

Straight Côtes du Rhône is for drinking young, though some Côtes du Rhône-Villages wines gain from age.

Rhône whites, with rare exceptions such as Hermitage, are best at 2–4 years old.

GERMANY

Vintages here differ not just in quality but in style: traditionally, the best years are warm ones – those yielding lots of sweet (Auslese and above) wine. Cooler years, such as 1991 and 1984, with good Kabinett wines, are not to be despised. Spätlese and above wines in great vintages can keep for decades, and even Kabinett wines can, in the right years, improve for 8–10 years. Rheingau wines are perhaps the longest-lived, though well-balanced Mosels can last well too.

Great sweet wines were made in 1990, '89 and '88. 1993 was good in Baden and Pfalz, and 1994 is very promising.

The more southerly regions, such as the Pfalz and Baden, make wines which mature faster.

No-one is quite sure how modern German reds will age: do not keep them too long.

ITALY

Tuscany: the best recent vintages are 1990, 1988 and 1985.

Simpler Chianti does not need more than 2–4 years' ageing. Chianti Classico and Rufino are at their best at 4–8 years old. Brunello di Montalcino and Vino Nobile di Montepulciano, plus the growing legion of "super" *vini da tavola*, are at their best at 10+ years old.

Piedmont: Barolo and Barbaresco reds demand bottle-age, though the more modern style of winemaking favoured by some producers means faster-maturing wines. Old-fashioned Barolo from good vintages may take 10 years to become approachable, and will last in bottle for 20 years. Barbaresco starts to become accessible in 4–5 years.

Few Italian whites are designed to age; the exceptions are modern-style Chardonnays.

CALIFORNIA

The enormous size of the California vineyards, and their great variation in conditions, grapes and winemakers' intentions, make useful vintage judgements hard to come by. Most California wines are enjoyable young, though a limited number of top reds, especially Cabernet Sauvignon and Meritage, and Chardonnay whites, are designed for bottle-ageing. Prestige Chardonnays can gain from 5 years or more in bottle.

Good recent vintages: 1994, 1991, 1990.

AUSTRALIA

The great variety of Australia's regions and wines make generalizations impossible. Contrary to myth, conditions can and do vary: drought, floods, bush fires and heat waves add to the confusion.

In general terms, Australian red wines such as Cabernet Sauvignon, Pinot Noir and Shiraz are ready sooner than their northern hemisphere equivalents.

White wines for ageing include Rieslings and Semillons which can last 20 years; Chardonnays are mostly made to drink young. However wines from the same grape, and area, will differ in their ageing potential according to the maker's methods and intentions.

Mass-produced wines here are far less subject to vintage variation than more expensive ones, and are made to be drunk as soon as they are released for sale. Some vintage wines are aged by their makers and only released when ready: back labels will say so. Remember that harvest in Australia is in February–April, so all wines are six months older than northern hemisphere wines with the same vintage date on the label.

Good recent vintages are:

1992, which was cool and unsuccessful in the Hunter; better in South Australia. Some good solid reds were made.

1991 saw a small crop, from which came some good reds which could improve further

1990 had some good reds, mostly now past their best

NEW ZEALAND

Very new vineyard areas, and a variable climate, make vintage reports on New Zealand hard to compile.

1995 saw a large vintage after several small ones. Rain at harvest-time affected some of the cooler regions, such as Marlborough, but overall quality is good.

1994 was a very good vintage, especially for Marlborough area whites.